My Travel Adventures
and Secret Recipes

Culinary Adventures with Secret Recipes

CHEF WOLFGANG HANAU

MY TRAVEL ADVENTURES AND SECRET RECIPES
CULINARY ADVENTURES WITH SECRET RECIPES

iUniverse books may be ordered through booksellers or by contacting:

iUniverse
1663 Liberty Drive
Bloomington, IN 47403
www.iuniverse.com
1-800-Authors (1-800-288-4677)

ISBN: 978-1-4917-8093-0 (sc)
ISBN: 978-1-4917-8095-4 (hc)
ISBN: 978-1-4917-8094-7 (e)

Library of Congress Control Number: 2015920837

Print information available on the last page.

iUniverse rev. date: 03/04/2016

Cooking with my secret recipe book is an adventure in fine dining. Following the recipes in this book, you can cook in your own kitchen the same kinds of wonderful meals many of my friends have enjoyed in their homes.

Continue reading about the exciting adventures I experienced in my travels to many countries, embracing legendary foods.

PRAISE FOR THE BOOK AND AUTHOR

To all international foodies,

Wolfgang Hanau is the quintessential international chef, baker, cook, etc.

I have known him for twenty years, and his extraordinary rise to culinary excellence is on par with only a few professionals who can turn out a myriad of foods suitable for a worldly market. His recipes surely reflect on his talent and allow you, the reader, to enjoy a panoply of tastes.

I was CEO of Dean & De Luca, a truly international food palace. One of my great takeaways was my constant contact with an exceptional cadre of food geniuses from all parts of the world.

Wolfgang is one of those people.

Let's eat.

Thomas J. Thornton Jr.
Palm Beach, Florida

———————

In late August of 2002, I met Wolfgang Hanau in New Orleans, where he served with Copeland's Investments as a culinary vice president. While I was going through my initial hiring process, Mr. Hanau proved to be a very knowledgeable, instructive, and helpful interviewer. His love for the industry was apparent every day I worked for him. His employees could always approach him for guidance and business advice. Because of his efforts, I have witnessed tremendous growth with the Al Copeland company.

There were many successful projects completed as a result of Wolfgang Hanau's tenacious pursuit of the company's goals and his working with and communicating well with the executive staff. This enabled the regular staff to understand and follow all procedures given to them to be executed.

After leaving the company, I stayed in touch with Mr. Hanau as a friend as well as professionally. His deep religious beliefs that guided him through all his successes have been an inspiration to me.

It is with deep pleasure and much enthusiasm, and without any reservations, that I give my wholehearted recommendation for any and all of his future endeavors.

Sincerely,

Johannes Brugger
Executive Chef and Culinary Consultant
Los Angeles, California

It is with great pleasure that I write about my experience with Chef Wolfgang Hanau and his book *My Travel Adventures and Secret Recipes*.

I have always wanted to learn how to cook but never did anything about it, mainly because my wife, Judith, is such an excellent cook. That all changed when I met Wolfgang.

He told me about his world travel, adventures, and recipes. He was so kind as to show me his manuscript, and I was hooked.

Wolfgang agreed to teach me how to prepare and serve quality food using the very best ingredients and, naturally, his expert skill. We prepared a wonderful filet and cod dinner and on another occasion the best shrimp chowder that I have ever tasted.

Wolfgang's patience, expertise, and teaching methods are outstanding. He makes you an active participant, and I feel that I have already acquired skills that I never thought possible.

I look forward to many such experiences and cannot wait to see his book when it is published.

John S. Brauner
Amateur Chef
Mount Joy, Pennsylvania, and Delray Beach, Florida

CONTENTS

PREFACE

Comments by Publisher's Editor

"This is a unique publication in that it combines an autobiography and cookbook in one text. Because of the close social and historical ties between food and culture, I believe this book will be of great interest to readers who are food enthusiasts, as many such people are always looking to gain perspective on the world they live in via culinary experiences. This book brings life and food together in one tidy package."

As an introductory note, I invite you to join me on camelback rides in the Sahara desert or cruising on luxury ocean liners, meeting celebrities at culinary destinations that offer sun, fun, and welcome escapes from the ordinary.

My Travel Adventures and Secret Recipes reveals the incomparable pleasures of fine foods and travel adventures in many flawless ways unknown to many lovers of fine food and to those in search of new culinary destinations.

This book contains a very selective group of ethnic, international, and local recipes, hundreds of which are from the pages of Chef

Wolfgang Hanau's secret recipe book, collected over more than fifteen years, never published before.

It's an exceptional, well-rounded batch of recipes with a terrific range of dishes, made possible only through Chef Wolfgang Hanau's extensive travels while working as a chef at some of the greatest resorts and hotels: Switzerland's famous Schinznach Bad, Kurhaus, and Park Hotel, where the begum and Aga Khan were regular guests; the glamorous Park Hotel Reuteler in Gstaad, where many of Hollywood's famous movie stars enjoyed the ultimate in winter sports while surrounded by the beauty of the Swiss Alps; the Dorchester Hotel in London; and the Michelin five-star hotel the Plaza Athenee, in Paris, which provided the ultimate in hotel living for Aristotle Onassis, Maria Callas, and the superrich from Europe's royal and industrial aristocracy.

Chef Wolfgang Hanau also worked at equally famous resorts and deluxe hotels in the Caribbean and USA known for their five-star cuisine.

INTRODUCTION

With the aid of this book, written by an expert in fine dining, it is easy to cook in your own kitchen the same tasty meals Europeans and Americans love to bring to their families' tables.

After all, the book's author was born, raised, and educated in Eastern Europe, home to the ancestors of many of America's families, where he learned to love good cooking from his mother's and grandmother's kitchens.

With French flair, Bavarian specialties from Munich's Oktoberfest, Switzerland's renowned international cuisine, and service to the royal family at the Dorchester in London, Chef Wolfgang Hanau learned to create exquisite meals, each day practicing cooking from great menus in restaurants of world-famous chefs: Chef Christian Luis Diat at the Plaza Athenee in Paris, Chef Paul Becaud in Gstaad, and Executive Chef Eugene Kaufeler at London's Dorchester Hotel.

Chef Wolfgang Hanau tells you of his expertise in cooking for friends and relatives in grand style, including meals that are simply, easily, and economically prepared.

Wolfgang's ancestral home

Oma's Family

Wolfgang's brother and sisters

CHAPTER 1

Growing Up in East Prussia and Bavaria

WHEN I WAS A CHILD, the leaves that fell and tumbled through the wind brought thoughts of happiness into my life. As all living things still do. Leaves are alive. They breathe and bring peace, love, harmony and happiness to the mind—for us to be transformed by the renewing of the mind.

There I was, as a boy, running through the fields of wheat and barley and rye in East Prussia. Mama was always watching out for us, constantly concerned about our happiness and health, both physically and spiritually.

Mama would follow me carefully with her eyes as I ran into the bright sunshine, blue skies, and golden fields of grain in this rich and blessed country in northern East Prussia, near the big city of Tilsit, on the Memel River. Mama loved sitting beside the fields of grass with wildflowers abound at her side, painting farmhouses and the wildflowers. Mama had studied painting and classical music, and as we walked together, she taught me the song "The Happy Wanderer." I have beautiful memories of my mother and the summer leaves falling upon us in East Prussia. All those that were alive then are

1

gone now. My hands reached down to catch a big white leaf that fell on me, blown down by the first cold winter storm. But God decided that it was too early for me to come home. I still had not met Jesus, and life had not fully touched me. Yet I knew, Mama had told me, that Jesus Christ had been near me from the earliest years of my life. How marvelous it was to think back of the many times in my life when I did not know Jesus Christ, yet He always kept His eyes on me. Was I a big problem? Only God and Jesus Christ can answer that question.

The wonderful thing about a fallen leaf is that it is like the story of Jesus Christ being with me and never leaving me out of sight. Jesus Christ wants us, loves us, and died to forgive us so He can bring us to true home. And our Father will look at us and smile, and He will praise His only begotten son, Jesus Christ, for having saved us. He has saved us so many times over so many years. I have been alive for many years, and still a sinner. I love God, Jesus Christ, and the Holy Spirit so much that I fail to find the words to express this love. Do we ever doubt God? I am a sinner, and Satan treats all of us alike. He puts doubts into my mind every day so that I feel compelled to cry out for help in all of my angst. God is the creator, and His promise to us is that He will never give us a burden too heavy to carry. And so He reaches out for me with Jesus Christ at my side. In my mind, God holds my left hand near my heart, and Jesus Christ walks on my right side so I can lean on Him. Just to touch Jesus Christ, to touch His garment, His hands, His feet, and His hair will bring relief. Satan lost his power over my mind, my body, and my heart instantaneously. Jesus Christ has set me free from all attachments to people, places, and things of the past and present.

Remember that God wants us to be blessed with riches—the children of a rich Father. Mama told me that Jesus is not going to give up on us. Remember that we can read in Nehemiah 9:17, "But you are God, ready to pardon, gracious and merciful, slow to anger, abundant in kindness and you do not forsake us ever."

There are many leaves on our tree, such as the pungent, onyx-colored leaves of the willow tree at the school yard which eventually will turn to a bright and then a darker green. Eyes cannot follow the transformation. Our hands cannot feel its changes from color to color, and often we are not able to smell the leaves. Yet they are there.

When I was nine years old, Mama helped develop my musical gifts. We went to speak to Frau Valpahl in her chic and smart apartment at one of the high-rent, fashionable districts of Tilsit. As a little boy growing up in a country village with fewer than one hundred people living there, I found the big city fascinating. "Hohe Strasse" was the center and meeting place of the rich and influential citizens of Tilsit and East Prussia. It was hardly the place to go shopping on a teacher's salary.

The leaves would fall, and then they would be picked up by men in clean blue coats handling long shovels and brooms. Horses and carriages passed by carrying well-dressed people to their places of business and entertainment. Ladies wearing beautiful hats with ostrich feathers were driven to elegant cafés lining the sidewalks. The other big boulevard in Tilsit was the "Deutsche Strasse," a great political backdrop worthy of any movie director's attention. Schools—wonderful schools with highly polished bricks and marble slabs imported from Italy and fancy iron gates bearing flowers painted in gold or bronze colors—greeted grown-ups and schoolchildren. Mama had graduated as a student here at the lyceum, a school for rich, well-dressed girls destined to be well educated. I was enrolled as a student at one of the schools—Humanistische Gymnasium.

Summer—with the tantalizing heavy aroma of red, purple, and

pink roses lining the streets in the morning—was the time of the year I liked best. My mind and heart were filled with the wonders of the world I knew, that they were the creation of God, our Father in heaven. Forever engraved in my mind and thoughts were the creations of the beautiful world we lived in and everything in it.

As I look out of the window dreaming, in a world of phantasies I can see the purple leaves of olive trees of countries yet for me to see and to discover.

At Home in East Prussia

Collecting the leaves from rosebushes in our rose garden at the schoolhouse, I was reminded of the full impact God's creations have made ever since I was a little boy walking from the old brick schoolhouse in Balzershoefen to the small, timid railroad station in Lesgewangen.

The street was empty, and it was early in the morning when I left our house, the schoolhouse where we lived. The train, as always, would stop for three or four minutes for six children and the occasional farmer and his wife, dressed in their Sunday best to go to the big city. There was one more stop between our little station and Tilsit. Ragnit was the seat of the county and provincial government, with the state government offices in Koenigsberg.

Why did I count the leaves of the roses I had gathered on my way to school? In my mind, I saw the wonders of God and Jesus Christ in every leaf and on every cobblestone; even the ice cream vendors were surrounded by a holy shine.

My favorite thing during my years in school were the unforeseen imaginations of people. I remember Frau Dr. Bremen, our math teacher, a mysterious and loving human being. Never mind that math was not the most important subject at the gymnasium. Frau Dr. Bremen seemed to have the aura and appearance of a saint. Looking through the wondrous eyes of a nine- or ten-year-old who lived his first year away from home in a big city, I saw my math teacher as being surrounded with the pure white light of Christ. An aura of gold and white lines and arrows shaped a circle around her face and head. My keen sense of what was real told me the magic of God's creations. God created His masterwork right among us, before our eyes.

Sitting under the my personal tree of life, the old willow tree on the meadow near our schoolhouse, I could see the ironsmith's house and workshop. Hot irons were hammered during the day to fit the hooves of our farmers' horses. No more today. It is sad that only the mystery of memories of this small village in Prussia exists.

I looked forward to sitting under the willow tree when I came home.

The leaves would fall in summer and they were fewer than in the fall. The leaves of this tree were long and slender. The tree grew lots of golden lime blossoms. The bees flew into its mysteriously outstretched arms. Bees are not concerned about leaves. The slender, gracious green leaves God sent to me were to remind me not only of His eternal grace that He promised to bring to us but also of everything that is so beautiful underneath the sky. The sky, I remember today, did not give us a single day of rain for many weeks now. Maybe the rain came when I was asleep.

My books and my everyday toys included a big red ball with blue polka dots; my teddy bear, with most of his fur gone and more bald spots than I dared to count; marbles made of clay and glass; and a jump rope with red wooden handles, which belonged to my two sisters, Rose and Jutta, and which the other boys of my age always wanted to use.

How strange that I could remember the faces of so many leaves.

Jesus Christ was always standing next to me. He showed me and reminded me of the days ahead in my life when life would interact with temptations and desires beyond my reach and not always easy to resist. It is wonderful and marvelous to know and remember today that amid everything in life, wherever I was, Jesus Christ was with me. God's leaves from His tree promised His presence. Anyway, my eyes saw God's face and the face of Jesus Christ and the Holy Spirit's power shining upon me through the branches and nests of blossoms of this great old tree.

But summer went, and fall arrived suddenly. My favorite spot was still underneath the old willow tree. Gigantic partly leaved and partly bald sticks were there where the leaves used to be. The ironsmith was still hammering. The horses were still brought to be shoed by Mr. Brenker, the ironclad man with a black-and-blue leather apron.

Mr. Brenker had two sons, Emil and Guenter. When they were old enough to be drafted and serve in the army, Mr. and Mrs. Brenker often discussed with Mama the need to sell their business. The two sons were soon gone, and so was the pounding of red-hot iron horseshoes. It seemed to me a sad and sullen village.

God looked down onto our village and told us of changes in all our lives that were in His plans. But I was confident that whatever God's plans for us were, we would be well served. My walks to the railroad took much, much longer in fall, and my feet moved slower, and I felt my shoes which seemed to be very heavy.

Would Jesus Christ walk with me every morning to school even if I didn't know where my next year in school would be?

I made some good friends in class at the gymnasium. Mama invited my friends to spend their harvest vacation with us in the fall for one or two months in our little village and with us in our home and old schoolhouse. Bruno was my best friend from home. He lived next to us in one of the Neubachers' houses. Bruno's father was working for the Neubachers on the farm, and his mother was doing their laundry. What was washed would hang to dry in the cool, crisp, and windy autumn air on long wires, flowing in the wind. And we were glad and enjoyed the wind. It not only would dry our shirts and pants, but it would also blow away the clouds that covered the disappearing sun. As the wind moved the trees and branches, I thought the trees were making the wind. Oh yes! I was convinced that without the trees there could be no wind. Mama spent the better part of an afternoon explaining to me the winds and the purpose of trees and branches.

Bruno's parents could not afford to buy new shoes and clothes for him to go with me to the gymnasium. In their family the music the children played was the soft music of mouth organs. We all played the mouth organ in front of our house before we went to sleep.

The sounds of music would disappear and could not be heard anymore once we were away from our house. At night the only lights came from the two small windows of Bruno's modest white-patched home. The house was given to them to live in once they started working for the farmer and was theirs as long as they worked for the Neubachers, who owned the house.

Our schoolhouse, where we lived because Mama and Papa were the teachers, was the center of the village and the meeting place for the farmers and their families to be seen. Sounds of classical music and laughter and celebrations could be heard there on many Sundays but also on other occasions, when birthdays and holidays were celebrated with music, rich foods, and drinks. It was a blessed life we enjoyed. I liked the smell of coffee and cigars and the smell of freshly baked cakes and breads, which abundantly filled the air and which could even be smelled on the street that passed by our rose garden.

Our house could be entered from the courtyard, leading to a heavy large door and a vestibule inside of our home which served our family as the changing room at winter time when lots of snow was outside and we all needed heavy boots, winter coats, scarfs, gloves, and hats to protect and keep us warm and which were neatly stowed there. From the entrance hallway a few steps away was the kitchen with a huge stove for cooking with firewood and charcoals. The dining room was next to the kitchen and so was the children's playroom with all of our toys and study desks. Every day our rooms were inspected by Mama and Papa. They also came there to speak to us or help us, when we needed help with our homework. Papa's library was also on the first floor with the long wall holding a large collection of books behind glass doors and his enormous, hand-carved desk nearby to show his study. Then there was the big round table which he frequently used when meeting with students and their parents or other teachers.

All of our bedrooms and baths were on the second floor.

No two days seemed to be alike. It was a happy childhood filled with fun and great expectations about what the next day would bring. But could our childhood remain so happy forever?

As the season changed, my friend the old willow tree in the front of the school yard, began to fall asleep. I knew that God would never allow the tree to die, so it had to be asleep. The trunk of the tree was rather chubby halfway up, with a deep split right down its center. In winter the tree became a cozy hiding place for wild rabbits, many of which visited our village. Mama told me they ate the cabbage she had left for them in our *Hintergarten* so the rabbits would always find their favorite food here. The tale in the village had it that one night a big bolt of lightning had struck the old tree. But nobody in the village knew the age of the tree or when the lightning had struck. The tree had always been there and always split in the center.

My friends from school came to visit with me, and so did Manfred, my best friend. Manfred was fun to be with because he was mischievous. He happily agreed to come along with us. He came with Bruno and me to explore places in our village and do things we had never done before. We would go out to catch frogs together and venture out on the ice in winter. One day he agreed to come along with us.

I don't remember if Mama knew of our plans and where we were going, and I am even less sure that Mama would have approved of our plan to walk into the shallow, dark, overgrown waters of the big pond where ducks and geese were washed. We were not there to wash the birds but to catch wild frogs. The cold dimples of dark, mucky waters appeared to be full of frogs, which we could hear croaking at night as soon as the sun had set. Some of the little frogs paddled to the surface.

In spite of Mama's warnings, but to prove my total independence, I walked barefoot. Before I knew it, I stepped on a broken bottle and began to bleed. I could see blood pouring from my feet—a lot of blood, it seemed.

Mama was the doctor in our village, not just for our family but also for the whole village. There was no other doctor for many kilometers. She was also Mama to me, and that was the scary part of it. Keeping that in mind, my homecoming was not the happiest. I was very well aware of any consequences.

First Mama fixed the problem. She was good with stitching up the cuts, but it hurt even when I looked away. Then came the unavoidable spanking for not following her orders. Manfred and Bruno seemed very sad to be standing by, not being able to help me in spite of their efforts, since each was willing to take one-third of the blame. But the greatest misery of all was being scolded in front of my friends.

Mama was not only the doctor in our village but she was known to make the most awesome freshly baked apple pancakes.

Mama's *Apfel Flinsen* (pancakes) were always a great treat for everybody in our family: Rose, Jutta, Joergi, and me. Mama's big bowl of freshly grated apples from our garden were more than enough to serve all of us. And Mama made sure that there were always some extra "Flinsen" for our friends from the village when they came by. Who could resist? Word would always get out quickly.

MAMA'S RECIPE FOR APPLE PANCAKES ("FLINSEN")—APFEL PFANNKUCHEN

Yield: one 10" or 12" or 16" pancake

INGREDIENTS:

4 large eggs
½ cup unbleached all-purpose sifted flour
½ teaspoon salt
1 cup and 2 tablespoons cinnamon sugar
½ cup milk
12 ounces soft butter
1 large Fuji apple, peeled, thinly sliced, or grated
more cinnamon sugar (approximately 2 tablespoons) to taste*
1 cup powdered sugar to be sprinkled after baked and cooled off

DIRECTIONS:

1. Beat eggs. Sift flour, salt, and cinnamon sugar together in large bowl. Add eggs to dry ingredients alternately with milk. Mix to make a smooth batter.
2. Spread butter over bottom and sides of cold cast-iron skillet. Pour in batter and place in a hot (400 degrees F) oven. Bake 20–25 minutes,

in preheated 400-degree oven, reducing heat to 350 degrees F for the last 5 minutes. Add thinly sliced apples and 2 tablespoons cinnamon sugar. Pancake should puff up at the sides and be crisp and brown.

3. Sprinkle with sifted powdered sugar and briefly place underneath salamander or broiler until lightly caramelized.
4. To serve, place skillet on large platter with side of chilled chunky applesauce and 1 cup extra cinnamon sugar.

To make cinnamon sugar add to one cup sugar 1 tsp cinnamon, stir to blend.

It was the early part of spring in April of 1945. It was meant to be the end for my sleepy friend, the old willow tree at the school yard and for me and for all of us who lived in the village, as we would have to part from each other. The Russian planes would fly very low now over our village every night to drop off a few wax-and-black-painted bombs. First we found it to be odd and such fun to admire these huge egg-like creations, which we believed were toys for us to admire. But soon we found that the huge wooden bombs were actually purposely dropped off. Hiding in them were ammunition, food, clothes, and other things for the Russian prisoners, who were working on the farms and who would come in the mornings to collect whatever had been sent to them. With no more German police and soldiers in our village, nobody thought of stopping them.

Real bombs were sent over Tilsit, where Oma lived until she decided to come and stay with us where it was much safer. Oma had her own ways of cooking, and her warm German potato salad and soups were legendary. She made pea soup and chicken soup with fresh vegetables and her own homemade noodles and potato soup over crisp toasted rye croutons Then there were her fruit soups, which she could make very day when the time was right from fruit fresh from our trees and bushes in the garden or from Mama's fruit, preserved in glass jars.

But when Joergi was born and Oma was not with us, it fell upon me to do the cooking for Mama and Rose and Jutta. And did I enjoy it! It may have been the influence of our French heritage that made me try to cook with sauces and eggs and fresh duck breast for breakfast, and to bake from Mama's old recipe books and taste the excitement of new foods we had never tried before.

OMA'S WARM GERMAN POTATO SALAD

Yield: 6 servings

INGREDIENTS:
4 pounds white or golden potatoes (best for peeling), preferably small
2 medium white onions, peeled and diced
16 ounces vegetable or meat broth, hot, preferably homemade
2 tablespoons parsley, chopped
2 tablespoons marjoram, chopped or any other fresh herb
2 tablespoons chives, chopped
6 tablespoons vegetable oil
1 teaspoon German-style mustard
salt, white pepper, sweet Hungarian paprika, sugar, and German-type liquid seasoning (e.g., Maggi or Knorr Aromat—available in specialty Kosher or German delis) to taste
a few splashes of apple cider vinegar

GARNISH:
2 hard-boiled eggs, sliced
1 cup diced tomatoes
½ cup chopped chives
Optional: 12 ounces crumbled crisp bacon or chopped Black Forest ham

DIRECTIONS:

Note: For mixing all salad ingredients, please use wooden spoon.

1. Wash potatoes and boil to al dente. Peel and slice thinly while still hot.
2. While potatoes are boiling, peel and dice onions. Dice tomatoes, slice eggs, and chop chives.
3. After potatoes are peeled and sliced, place with diced onions in a bowl. Pour hot broth over potatoes and onions. Add flavors and seasonings to taste, together with mustard and vinegar. Cover bowl with tight-fitting lid and towel and let stand 20 minutes.
4. Add garnish before serving.

I would many years later create identical dishes with added touches of Americana. Soon after I began cooking, my appetizers, soups, and sandwiches became the standard fare in our house. Later on, with Mama's help as the great cook she was, we also prepared new luncheons at midday for dinner. Lunch at the big round table in our dining room was always the big meal at our house.

I remember I really didn't like spinach. My sister Rose's favorite dish was a pudding made of cream and eggs and semolina and served with fresh raspberries and a fresh raspberry sauce. Jutta fell in love with Mama's tapioca pudding, which she made with fresh, dark cherries from the cherry tree behind the stables and occasionally was topped with heaps of freshly whipped *Schlagsahne* (whipped cream).

I will never forget the day that I hid my plate of spinach in the enormously big green-tile oven. Mama left the dining table for a few minutes during lunch. It seemed like a perfect opportunity for me to hide my plate of spinach while treating the oven to a great lunch, I thought. Mama did not appreciate my thoughts and naturally wondered what had happened while she was away for a few minutes. The rather obvious giggling of Rose and Jutta and their staring at the oven gave it all away, however. The plate of greens was recovered and served to me again, with a little spanking to top it off.

Today I am in love with some wonderful creations based on spinach and a multitude of other greens, which I have come to enjoy and cook with and which have brought much admiration and fame to my healthy vegetarian secret recipes.

A lady from Ohio fell in love with my dandelion pie to such a degree that she felt compelled to write, telling me that it had become one of her family's regular Thanksgiving dishes. The recipe, as you find it within these pages, was the grand-prize winner at a chefs' competition in the Midwest. By the way, today I cannot think of a more beautiful and sensuous dish than this one, which uses thinly sliced, chilled, dark red smoked goose breast nestled between poached and sautéed baby spinach greens with tiny red potatoes and fresh brussels sprouts in a warm dill-and-spinach butter sauce.

While I can easily remember and trace my life back to Rucken, East Prussia, my most vivid memories during the Second World War are always connected to Mama and Papa. Papa was a strict person and was difficult for me to love and get to know. Papa believed in strict obedience and demanded it as far back as I can remember even when he was my teacher at school. There is an image in my mind of us walking together into the forest, which extended right to the front door of the schoolhouse in Rucken where I was born. Papa reminds me of what I conceive of today as the typical strict German schoolmaster.

Papa kept a nice, highly polished wooden cane with him, and he liked to point at things by lifting the cane. The forest, I remember, was mysterious, with an aura of scariness, yet it was beautiful. One can hardly find such a forest today.

There is an old Prussian folksong Mama loved singing, "Land der dunklen Waelder und der tiefen Sees," which translates to "Land of Dark Forests and Deep Seas." It's a beautiful song with deep, touching melodies. Papa would take me walking with him quite often. I was too young to go to school. When Jutta was born in 1938, I was barely four years old.

"Papa and Wolfi went for a *Spaziergang*," Mama would tell Rose, who was seven at the time. "And the Scheusslers are coming for coffee and cake." Mama took a great deal of pride in cooking and baking. One can hardly imagine today making the selection of cakes she would prepare for any occasion like this. The Scheusslers—with Mr. Scheussler being head of forestry and in charge of the northeastern Prussia state-owned forests, which bordered on Lithuania to the north and Poland and Russia to the west—were no strangers at our home. Mr. Scheussler would have so much fun playing with me. Sitting on his knees, I enjoyed him rocking me and eventually letting me fall down to the floor between his polished black boots. Every time he came to visit, Mama told me, he would ask me my name and where we lived. My answer was always the same: "I am Wokka Hanuk, born in Rucken F., Kreis Friedrichwsalde." I was always rewarded with a special gift.

Mr. Scheussler's forest-green suits were pressed immaculately. He was my godfather, and of course I wanted to be a forester. What would be more natural for me than wanting to become a forester like Mr. Scheussler when I grew up? "Wolfi," he would say without fail, "tell us your name." How well I knew what was coming and what he expected me to say. After an initial refusal, to get that extra rocking, I would say, "Wokka Hanuck of Rucken F., Friedrichswalde." A round of applause would follow, which was the moment everybody had waited for so we could be seated at the coffee table.

Mama's spread of delectable desserts would include such beautiful things as raspberry and streusel kuchen, *apfel* torte, *Schwarzwailder Kirsch* torte, *Mandelhoernchen*, *Bienenstich*,

Napfkuchen, Gugelhopf, chocolate kuchen, and variously shaped cookies and sweet Danish rolls. Silverware, our best, was at the table with Mama's beautiful damask tabletops and napkins to steal the show. The table linens were wedding presents from her beloved grandmother. Sitting on the table were many aged photos showing her wearing the high fashions of that time, brought to her by her husband, a very wealthy farm and city property owner who had traveled to every country in Europe and was known to be a high-stakes gambler in Baden and Monte Carlo.

The coffee, brewed in three sleek silver cans with fancy handles, was served with cream from a heavy crystal pitcher and sugar cubes in silver jackets. All of the pieces had a brilliant shine and were polished. The Schlagsahne was served from chilled crystal bowls framed by a gold-handled container.

Besides the Scheusslers, there were the Blunks. Mr. Blunk held the position of principal teacher at Papa's school. There were always two teachers. Then there were the Prinkles. Mr. Prinkle held a teacher's position at a neighboring school. He looked jolly good and was always very friendly and very kind to us, a good friend to everyone. His big belly fit his white pants perfectly. The balding Mr. Prinkle wore rimless glasses on his big smiling face. Also at the table was Tante Lusche, Mama's only sister, Uncle George, and the children. The conversation was casual, and the room was filled with laughter and happy talk.

"Ernst," Mr. Prinkle inquired, "what are your plans now that you want to move on to your own school?" Everybody knew of Papa's plan and that he had asked the State of East Prussia for his own, larger school now that Mama was expecting Jutta and there would be five of us. "Well, with Uncle George here we must bid him farewell first before we can move." Uncle George, as everybody in the room knew, was our bicycling uncle. He was beloved by everybody, but we were happy to send him on his way again. Uncle George lived near Koenigsberg in central East Prussia but would take his well-kept bicycle on the road every summer. No prior announcements were sent to his relatives, and he never made his plans known to the families he would visit. This often created some unforeseen surprises. So we all knew Uncle George would arrive to stay with us and would be in need of a temporary home until he decided to continue his travels. Eventually he would be sent off with a large bag, which he had brought along, stuffed with sandwiches, fruit, and other goodies, along with bottles of juice and lemonade. He also brought an envelope with traveling money, just in case. He did not tell anybody where or when he was going.

Uncle George wore quite a spectacular outfit, consisting of a combination of a naval officer's uniform, high cavalry leather boots, and leather gloves to match. The boots were heavy, and the navy uniform was made of linen. In the backpack he carried a complete bicycle repair kit, just in case. Uncle George was known to always be in good humor, and that is why everybody couldn't help but enjoy his company. He also was filled with witty little stories he had collected during his travels.

Without anyone asking the question, Uncle George answered it: "George wants to stay a few days longer." Silence and then laughter ensued as we proceeded to leave the coffee table.

A loud "Who did this?" was followed by bearlike laughter from Uncle George a few minutes later. Rose and I had taken a few minutes before coffee was served to attach a big bunch of balloons to his navy hat, which he had taken off and which was now hanging from a bunch of balloons tangled in the upper branches of a big fir tree outside our house. Everybody denied knowing who would play such a joke on Uncle George while Papa, not too happy about the incident, prepared to climb the tree. Rose and I giggled, feeling swell that Papa and Mama now had a better chance of preparing Uncle George's traveling pantry sooner rather than later. And Papa would be ready to leave sooner rather than later for his new school and teaching job in Balzershoefen. Needless to say, we were called into Papa's library to be talked to after dinner.

Cakes and pastries, as usual, were the hot topic of discussion between the ladies. "Herta, can you give me this recipe and what directions should I follow when making the chocolate torte *mit Schlag*?" Mrs. Prinkle inquired. Mama accepted these compliments, indulged in all the good conversation, and enjoyed that everybody had such a good time. "Just one more piece, Herta," I overheard Tante Lusche saying. Even with her slender, manicured figure, she could not resist the temptation to try just one more. Mama was all about sharing and enjoyed providing and serving. This is what Mama was known for by everybody in the village. Everybody was in love with Mama, and she loved everybody. Mama was a good woman who loved and was loved.

Tante Lusche was the younger of Oma Kaemereit's two daughters. Beautiful, slim, very photogenic, and dressed in the latest high fashions, she had been featured in several fashion magazines. "Tres chique," one of the fashion writers had written below her picture. She was a high-fashion model and much in demand in Berlin at the time. Mama worked as an educator and teacher, educating the children of Graf von Schwerin and Holstein's family at the fabulous Franz Liszt Villa, near the Tiergarten district. The Von Schwerins were related to Franz Liszt, the Hungarian pianist and composer. Mama shared her room, her food, and her income with her sister. Tante Lusche, while very much in demand and busy as a fashion model, had never been able to support herself. Her partying and fun-loving life left little to be saved. Her appearance was elegant. She was well liked in the high-fashion world of luxury and opulence during the prewar days when Berlin was the cultural center not only of Europe but also of the world. She worked as a photo model for famous magazines and could be seen in pictures with politicians and the industrial giants of the Ruhr and Saar. She could be seen dancing at parties and attending the opera, balls, and many fashionable events attended by the likes of Marlene Dietrich and Richard Tauber.

The last of the imperial German empires and of the Weimar Republic, under iron chancellor Bismarck, had reached their zenith. And, Tante Lusche's life had also reached its zenith. "Luschchen," Mama said to her, "are you going to be here tonight to watch the [von Schwerins'] children?" Mama had been invited to attend the Berlin premiere of one of Richard Strauss's new operas, *Der Rosenkavalier*. The Von Schwerins had invited Mama to be their guest.

Joachim Zieten von Schwerin, the ten-year-old son of the von Schwerins, who had overheard Mama's conversation with her sister, threw a tantrum. Totally unexpected and out of control, he started screaming in a loud voice. He was rolling on the floor accusing Mama of being a teacher he no longer wanted at his house or educating him or his two sisters if she insisted on going to the opera instead of spending the evening with him. Mama, not knowing how to calm his temper, reached out to spank his derriere, which in turn brought only forth more of Joachim's uncontrollable temper. Drawn by the unheard of screaming of his son, Graf von Schwerin entered the room. Joachim, to Mama's total surprise, immediately brought his temper under control. When the Graf asked what had happened, Joachim stood up in front of his father and declared, "Papa, this was private between me and Fraeulein Herta." Graf von Schwerin withdrew from the room without any further questions. The situation had resolved itself. The scene would become one of Mama's most vivid and remembered stories of her time in Berlin.

When Joachim, twenty-three, had become a most celebrated general field marshal in Kaiser Wilhelm's army, she lovingly recalled this incident of having spanked him.

The von Schwerins loved Mama since she had been brought up with an excellent background in visual arts, music, and education. They were known to be tremendously wealthy, owning property and valuable objects. Because of grants and wealth inherited from generation to generation, they had been educated in Berlin, Paris, and Moscow and could trace this wealth back to the Thirty Years' War in the 1700s. Mama had become part of the circle of the well-educated aristocracy of Europe, while Tante Lusche was part of the partying world of Berlin, mixing with the younger influential set of officers, young doctors, brilliant attorneys, and students.

Tante Lusche became pregnant while still very young. While she did not try to hide her pregnancy from Mama, Mama helped her to avoid becoming a scandal by inviting her to live with our family. Later Edda, a beautiful little girl, was born. Tante Lusche was able to temporarily hide from the fashionable world of Berlin, where she would later return. Oma Kaemereit cared for Edda as if she were her own daughter. Whenever Oma visited us, Edda always traveled with her, and nobody thought anything of it. We loved Edda and loved and cared for her in our own way. In our mind, she was just another sister to us, another member of our family.

When Tante Lusche returned to Berlin, Mama decided to go ahead with her career educating children in private as a governess. Mama moved to Dessau, and she taught the family of Dessau's director of the Dresdner Staatsopera House. She loved it there.

Tante Lusche gave birth to another daughter, who was adopted after birth by an American family living in New York. The father of the adopted little girl lived in New York and was a financial manager on Wall Street. He didn't stay in touch with Tante Lusche, who never heard more about the whereabouts of her second daughter. Later—much later, in the 1960s, when I lived in New York City—Tante Lusche asked me if I would inquire about a person she had lost touch with in America. But she wasn't prepared to give me a name, and nothing came of it.

Mama's career seemed to go off into different directions. The opera house director in Dessau asked her to audition for a career in singing. The opera house's general manager promised to further her career, provided she was willing to marry him. Mama was not; she was already committed to Papa. Knowing that he would also stay faithful to her, Mama stayed two years longer in Dessau before she returned home to Tilsit. She then started work as an accountant and sales expeditor for an international moving company.

In Tilsit, where she was well known, she was confident that she would earn well. Her friends from her lyceum days were married or held influential positions in Tilsit or across the Koenigin Luise Bridge, which crossed the Memel River into Lithuania. The bridge was named in memory of Koenigin Louise, who had traveled from Tilsit with Napoleon, across the river Memel to Russia, where he was eventually bitterly defeated in Moscow. On her way back from Russia with Napoleon, she stayed at a small winter cottage near the bridge in Tilsit, which can still be seen. Her love letter to Napoleon Bonaparte, engraved with her diamond ring, sits in one of the windows.

Mama also exceeded in sports, running short distances for competition, fun, and pure enjoyment, always looking forward to meeting people. She was asked by a young career lieutenant, heir to a fortune in properties and hotels, to marry him. Again she refused, thinking of her promise to Papa. Papa at the time was studying at the university in Konigsberg to earn a master's degree in education. He graduated with honors and was sent to various smaller schools in East Prussia as an intern. Not too long after that he was sent to Rucken. Mama and Papa were married before he accepted that position.

The year was 1934, the year I was born. Many events and new things happened to our family very quickly. There was our move to Balzershoefen; this was a sleepy little village dominated by the borders of Poland and Russia to the west. One of the families that lived in the village were the Tummescheids. Ilse and Arno Tummescheid's family lived a different and distant life apart from the rest of the village. Soon after our arrival, Mama and Ilse Tummescheid became good friends, developing a special relationship with common interests. They were both educated in Tilsit. A typical afternoon for Mama and us was to spend an afternoon at the Tummescheid estate. With more than one hundred rooms to choose from, we would often spend time in Ilse's drawing room, which was equipped as an art center with every possible craft and art to be practiced or studied. Under the able eyes of her personal art instructor, the conversation was varied and interesting. How well I also remember the children's playrooms, which occupied the larger part of an entire floor.

Henner, the oldest of their three children and the apparent heir to the estate, played the role of an arrogant landowner at an early age, imitating his father's talk and manners. We were three or four years apart. "Wolfi, tell me about your day in school," he asked. The Tummescheid children were the only children in the village who had their own tutors. Rather than answer the question, I preferred to draw his attention to another subject: "Henner, you have so many wonderful toys here," or "Are you ready to go riding?" I wanted to avoid talking about school. I was aware of Papa's negative outlook on the Tummescheids' life. They had decided to ignore that they were a part of our community. Papa made very few or no efforts to get to know them. Besides, Papa was known for his strict ways and for punishing those who were disobedient and arrogant. Henner, very much like his father, was arrogant and inconsiderate of others' needs and wants. He even behaved like this with his parents. Being so young, I liked the feeling of abundance and luxury I saw at the Tummescheids' home, which was unlike any other house in the village. Holger, Tummescheid's other son, was two or three years younger than I was, but he quickly became the perfect playmate for my younger sister Jutta, who was born in Balzershoefen. Holger adored Jutta, since his own little sister, Anette, was too small to play with him, and Henner, three years older, was too demanding and unconcerned about Holger and the rest of the family.

Anette, a pretty baby girl only a few months old, had a crown of beautiful curly dark hair, and her brilliant green eyes reminded one of a phantasm of the ocean. She was adored by everyone who saw her for the first time. Arno, Ilse's husband, was a major general in the army reserve. He trained Trakehner horses—chubby horses with strong legs that could run at great speed in short-distance races. Arno was known as Mr. Trakehner, and he was widely recognized as the authority on Trakehner racehorses.

Mr. Tummescheid owned a stable of twelve Trakehner racehorses. Mama painted several of his horses. Arno did not object when Mama needed the horses for a special session. In a certain way, it was appropriate for him. He would walk up and down the feeder aisles at the stables, watching as the paintings progressed. He was always elegantly dressed in a high-buttoned light-gray-and-blue uniform with silver spurs on his riding boots and a monocle on his left eye. It all added to an appearance of aristocracy, which he enjoyed showing. He wanted to be the outsider. For years the Tummescheids owned the only automobile in the village of Balzershoefen.

· I remember the time when Mrs. Tummescheid, accompanied by her children, invited us for a car ride to Tilsit, which turned out to be a wild ride. While we were riding in the car, we noticed the floor was loose and ready to fall down. At that time, there were no known mechanics between Balzershoefen and other cities and the city of Tilsit. When I was older, Mama told me that the Tummescheids were actually near broke and probably could not have afforded the repair of the car or anything else in need of repair at the estate. Yet they lived the lives of the super rich. Anna, their elderly housekeeper, rarely if ever got paid, Mama was told. But to this loyal old soul, the Tummescheids could not do wrong. She would not complain but kept her thoughts to herself. Mama got to know Anna well and was a friend to her. When Mama talked to Ilse about it, Anna was promptly paid.

Then there was the Tummescheids' children's tutor, Britta, a pretty young woman who came to the Tummescheids from the city through an ad in the *Memelwacht*, a large newspaper from Tilsit.

"Britta, it seems to me that your fiancé should have gone home first to see his parents before visiting with you," Mama told Britta. Britta didn't respond to Mama's criticism of her soldier bridegroom coming right from the warfront to stay with her before seeing his parents. Neither did she attempt to justify his visit to her. His recent leave of absence from war without first seeing his parents seemed to be the important thing for Britta. But she did blush. Even at age eleven, I thought Britta was extremely attractive and beautiful, and I secretly wished that I were old enough to have her as my bride.

Britta stayed at our house, which both served as our home and was a one-classroom village school. At the time, while Papa was away, it was completely in Mama's hands. Mama had become the teacher when Papa volunteered to join the army. But before Papa was actually called to action in the war against Russia, he was called to serve at a training camp in Allenstein, Masuren. Mama decided that we should visit him. I don't know if Papa knew that we were coming or if this was to be a surprise. The train ride from Tilsit to this southern lake part of Prussia seemed a never-ending journey through vast cornfields, forests, towns, and railroad stations without a single stop. Once in Allenstein, we could not do anything but wait for Papa to pick us up. All of us were tired and hungry, and we were promised a special treat when we visited Papa.

After what seemed to be hours of waiting, Papa was finally there like I had never seen him before. He appeared in uniform with highly polished boots and a black belt to match. I thought that he looked really sharp. I was impressed. I never knew how Mama felt. We visited Papa's apartment, which had been assigned to him by the army. And there was his landlady who washed and cleaned his laundry and the apartment. She did whatever Papa needed to have done to make his stay more enjoyable. Mama didn't like the arrangement too much. During our stay over the weekend, I remember the city's big park and playgrounds with whipping seats, swings, and all sorts of other trinkets to amuse us. Then, when we left on Sunday night, Papa promised to see us soon at home.

THE ALLENSTEIN BBQ RECIPE

Yield: 4 entrees

INGREDIENTS:

1 large eggplant
salt
2 eggs
¼ cup chopped marjoram or other fresh herb to taste
salt and pepper to taste
½ cup light cream

2 cups whole-wheat flour, sifted

2 cups whole-wheat bread crumbs

1 cup Tilsit cheese, shredded

1 pound red potatoes

1 pound pumpkin meat, peeled and seeded, cut to match size of
potatoes

½ cup barbecue sauce, your favorite brand

½ cup vegetable oil

8 ounces sweet butter

GARNISH:

3 medium onions, peeled and thinly sliced

chopped marjoram to taste

salt and pepper to taste

DIRECTIONS:

1. Cut eggplant vertically into ½" slices (you should end up with about 12 slices.) Lightly sprinkle eggplant with salt on both sides and blot dry after fifteen minutes with paper towels. Set aside.

2. Make egg wash in a large oval bowl, about the diameter of the eggplant, eggs, marjoram seasoning, salt and pepper, and light cream.

3. In one bowl place whole-wheat flour, and in another bowl place whole-wheat bread crumbs, mixed together with Tilsit cheese.

4. Dip the eggplant slices into the whole-wheat flour, then into the egg wash, and finally into the breadcrumb-and-cheese mixture.

5. Sauté the eggplant slices in a large skillet over medium-high heat in a mixture of butter and vegetable oil until both sides are lightly browned.

6. Meanwhile, boil potatoes and pumpkin meat together in lightly salted water until done, about fifteen minutes. Drain and mash.

7. Place the mashed pumpkin and potatoes in the center of a large platter, topped with sautéed eggplant slices. Top with a dash of BBQ sauce and top all with crunchy roasted onions, made as follows:

8. Toss onions in vegetable oil with salt, pepper, and chopped marjoram. Place in one layer in 495 degree F hot oven on a large baking sheet. Sprinkle with more salt, pepper, and seasoning and close the oven

door. Turn the onions from time to time. Take completely out of the oven once crispy and lightly browned for 10 minutes. Sprinkle over eggplants and the mash.

Back home Mama was teaching school. It was a very hot summer. The wheat and the corn were ready to be harvested, along with the potatoes right after that.

Across from the Tummescheids' estate, the Maurischats and their two sons, Peter and Arno Jr., all worked the fields. Occasionally we were asked to help harvest bundles of corn, loaded onto huge and high horse-drawn wagons. They owned the most up-to-date and modern equipment of any farm nearby. We played and had lots of fun, collecting the leftover grains and falling on the clean-swept floors in the stables. In winter they would arrange for fun-filled sleigh rides for all the village children. With two or four horses, the sleighs were nicely prepared with furs and heavy, warm blankets, and they stopped quite often for a few snowball fights.

On one such Sunday afternoon in December 1944, we stopped at our house at the school. We split into two groups while throwing snowballs at each other, using the fence of our rose garden as the dividing line separating the two teams. Nobody knew that Peter was playing unfairly, putting pieces of ice into the snowballs, until one of them hit me, splitting my upper lip. I started to bleed heavily. Mama came to the rescue. "Wolfi, come here into the house," she called. I was hurting badly and gladly followed her into the kitchen, where a big pot of hot water was always on the stove. She added wood and coals to the fire so the water would soon be steaming hot.

Mama had learned a lot from Dr. Siloff, who was the only doctor available to the village and willing to come and make house calls when the need was there. Dr. Siloff lived twenty kilometers away in Rautenberg, too far away for us to call for help that day, So there was no question Mama had to be the doctor. She washed my lip with steaming hot water, disinfected the cuts, and put a big bandage on it. I could not go outside again. Peter's parents no longer allowed him to throw snowballs.

Our kitchen had a huge wood-and-charcoal-fired stove with open flame and iron rings to shield the heat. Whenever it was urgent to get boiling water quickly, we would remove some of, if not all of, the rings on the stove, and the fire would reach the pots directly. But the pots got very dirty from the smoke and fire.

Christmas was just around the corner. "Who wants to come along to pick up Oma from Lesgewangen at the railroad station?"

The station was a small cabin that could hold a dozen people at the most, with a ticket window at the end, three benches along the walls, and one more bench outside. That day there would be nobody outside, since it was too cold and snowing. The pond in the village was frozen solid, and my hands and feet felt just as cold as the ice and snow on the road. Mama made sure we always wore two pairs of gloves, a long scarf, long underwear, a face cover, and warm undershirts, which she and Oma would knit from our Angora rabbits' fur, when it was this cold. Oma and Edda would spend all their Christmas and New Year's Eves at our house. When they arrived, preparations were well underway as we all made our Christmas gifts.

We made letter openers and holders; napkin rings; hairpins for Oma, Mama, Rose, and Edda Wide; red hair ribbons for Jutta; and rattles filled with dried peas and pebbles for Joergi. We drew pictures and gave each other our favorite collections of *Lack Bilder*, with pictures of flowers, animals, and exotic fruit, written with foreign words we had collected all year long. There was so much we would do, and there was so much fun and excitement in the air while we were making gifts for each other. Our little brother, Joergi, was just about two years old, and everybody wanted to spoil and play with him. We usually split our candies, which were wrapped in pretty Christmas paper, with Joergi, which was not exactly what Mama had in mind. Joergi just loved all of the attention and the candies, and before long he began chewing them. We also wrote poems for Mama and Papa. This year Papa was missing from our family, and nobody knew what had happened to him in Russia after they wrote to us and told us that Papa was a "missing person." I remember that Mama spent a day and night alone in her bedroom, praying and contemplating life without our Papa. That night her hair turned to a silvery white.

Fun and secrecy surrounded every room and all floors in our house. This was so much part of our family and remains one of the fondest of my memories. Papa's picture, in his soldier uniform, was always beside our dinner table with a lit candle next to it during the day.

On Christmas Eve we all had a hot bath and went to bed in the afternoon, still trying to rehearse Christmas poems we had to recite later in front of everybody, while our presents, which were wrapped with loving care, waited for us underneath the tree. The whole house smelled mysteriously wonderful from Mama's and Oma's baking of Pfefferkuchen and almond cookies glazed with white and red and green sugar crystals. Lots and lots of other delicious cookies and candies were also in the making; these were not only our reminder that St. Nicholas had been at our house but also gifts of love from Christmas angels who visited us at this time of the year.

For Christmas Eve dinner there were the thin, long, crackling *Frankfurter Wuerstchen*, platters of cold meats, smoked fish and goose breast, smoked goose legs, liver pate, and warm potato salad. All of this was some of my most favorite food, which I will always remember. Freshly baked rolls and stollen were still warm, and so was the glühwein and hot lingonberry juice on the buffet, served from large carafes.

We opened our Christmas presents on Christmas Eve.

On Christmas Day Mama roasted the goose. One or two geese were brought to the table with potato dumplings, potato pancakes, red cabbage, and apple strudel with Schlagsahne for dessert. Dumplings and potato pancakes came from peeled, grated potatoes grown in our garden, which were stored in large bins filled with sand in the cellar when it got too cold. Crunchy fried croutons, fried in Goose *Schmaltz* with *Grieben*, were stuffed inside the dumplings, and baked apples were served with the roasted geese. These memories always come to my mind when Christmas is near. I still love the fat goose legs roasted or smoked, which came in pairs of two sown together and were smoked in the smoker in the upper loft. The meat, dark red in color, was sliced very thin to preserve all the flavor. The air was filled with the aromas of the geese and freshly baked breads.

My childhood centered so much around the wonderful world of food. Mama made stollen and *Napfkuchen, Bayerische Topf Nudeln,* Dresdner cakes and *Plunder* and puff pastry windmills filled with chocolate, apples, and nuts. The aromas of red cabbage and goose gravy filled the air and surrounded us and the dishes we enjoyed so much every year. Mama made *Waldmeister* pudding and semolina with raspberry sauce, as well as Jutta's favorite dessert to this day: raspberry tapioca pudding with vanilla sauce.

We spent Christmas at home in 1942, with Papa having been missing since New Year's Eve of 1941. We were told of the Russian army approaching Prussia, steadily coming closer and closing in on East Prussia and Germany. Mama listened every night to the

BBC news in Germany. She had a much clearer picture of what was happening than the rest of those living in the village.

It was against the law to listen to the BBC or any foreign newscasts, and Mama would ask us to leave the room when she turned on the radio.

All the time there was much going on: secret meetings at the Neubachers', the Resescheidts' and Maurischats', and at our house. Nobody else could be invited. Mr. Resescheidt, the mayor of the village, admitted to Mama that his loyalty was not with the Reich and Hitler, and he promised Mama to help if and when she decided to leave.

"Come to us with your children," he told Mama. Apparently he had his own plans to leave as the Russians came closer.

During these last weeks that we were together, we had the feeling that we were brothers and sisters, bound together by an invisible force, with the same destination and destiny. We all tried to escape the unbelievable occurrence of being conquered and invaded by the Russians and tried not to believe the stories of massacres told by refugees from Eastern Europe who had come and had left. We heard of stories of Russian Cossacks with swords in their horses' saddles. Many of the Russian soldiers, as it turned out, were uncontrolled and furious in their search for and obsession with wristwatches, which they would wear up and down their arms. They dismantled light switches, which they shipped home to Russia, expecting to have electric light once they mounted the switches on their walls at home.

A few Russian prisoners of war who had stayed at the Neubachers' home came to help Mama and work in our gardens. They were good, warm, and friendly men, compassionate human beings who told us about their families back home and how much they missed them. They were very handy in carving toys out of firewood they found in our courtyard. They used hot iron rods to decorate the toys with flowers, butterflies, and the faces of the people they loved back home, and even of us children. These were works of art and craftsmanship.

How wonderfully people get along in peace, loving one another, not threatened, not fighting or killing or commanded by wicked criminals or by evil dictatorships.

To our delight, the Russian prisoners in the village often dropped by our house unannounced to cook or bring us prepared food from Russia. We were amazed that with so much on their own minds they would want to take time to be with us and help us, their "enemies." We were told by a young Russian lieutenant that on many nights a small Russian spy plane would land in the fields behind our cow pastures to bring supplies and civilian clothes to their imprisoned, captured comrades. Among the weapons and other war-related items, they slipped in food and a few cooked meals from their families back home. At night when the few remaining German guards had fallen asleep, the Russian prisoners would leave their haystacks in the stables—where they slept with the cows, horses, chickens, and goats—and make contact with a plane to receive supplies. It all worked out perfectly for them, and with our blessing, it remained undiscovered until we had to leave. Only then were we able to deeply appreciate the human side of Russians who actually were not different from us.

"The mayor of Tilsit, a close family friend, is on the telephone, Frau Hanau." One of the Neubachers' maids had been told by Frau Neubacher to run quickly and ask Mama to come to the phone. Mama rushed away to hear what it was all about. In less than ten minutes, she returned with a message for Oma and for us. "Let us get packed. We must leave in less than an hour for the railroad station." Our initial reaction was that there was no way we could, in spite of all the talk for weeks and months, get ready to leave our home so quickly. However, we had packed our own little suitcases weeks before, and it was no longer a matter of deciding which toys or other few favorite things we wanted to take along. We were always told we would soon be back home again, but we also understood that the much-talked-about emergency time had arrived.

For the last time, I watched Mama taking her own little brown suitcase, the one with the elegant purple lining inside. She took one more look at what she had so carefully set aside. There were Papa's letters he had sent from Russia, bound into two folders together with our savings book, life insurance policy, a few precious pieces of Mama's jewelry, and, just in case, some money. It proved later that Papa's letters, written with nonerasable ink pens, were the only papers that meant much to us; these were some of the few things to survive the war, together with our memories. Lifelong savings, insurance policies, and savings accounts would not be honored by any German authority or bank except in East Prussia, which was to be no longer.

A Red Cross train stopped in Lesgewangen within an hour after we had arrived. Mama's name was on a Red Cross officer's list, and so was Oma's and our names. We were given a bench where we sat next to wounded soldiers. And so it was that we were allowed to board the train in less than three minutes. Oma was with us. Edda had left several weeks before to live with Tante Lusche and her new family in Bavaria. This was where Mama was going to take us. The train was filled with some of the few leaving the eastern front of war, going south or west to German hospitals. They were all men like Papa, fighting a war to protect families like us, much like the soldiers of every nation who fought this war for their families.

When we left home, Mama had changed the bed linens, all the lights were switched off, and the doors were locked. The house was prepared to welcome us back when this terrible war was over. There was no doubt in our mind that our sudden departure would become a sudden return home. Little did we realize that it was our country that had committed atrocities and crimes on humankind that would haunt the country and world for years to come, and that East Prussia would be split by two nations: Russia and Poland.

Weeks before we left, the people in the village had been asked to do a "secret digging." In our house we hid silverware, precious gold, old jewelry Mama had inherited, and crystal, much of it gifts from Mama and Papa's wedding. Mama wrapped original oil paintings in oilcloth to provide protection from digging animals or bad weather. It was all buried underneath a huge truckload of charcoal for the kitchen and stoves for the big schoolhouse and our living rooms.

Since then I have often thought about what had been so beautiful but also about what had been frighteningly awful and had brought death and devastation. At times it is still vividly in front of me. I knew also that the war had brought big, hefty gains to those who were committed to greed, hate, and anger and to the ensuing horrors of war, which brought hunger and devastation to the untold millions of people of the world. How often do I also sit now and remember to listen to the silent world of innocence and the happy laughter and music and voices of children that come to my mind.

With the spirit of peace, love, and understanding, I am glad to bring the "happy" food of this beautiful world to you. I invite you to look at my recipes and try all or some of the many dishes I have provided recipes for. All of the recipes were created in loving memory of the times when I traveled the lands and oceans and worked in the many kitchens of many countries. I created simple and sometimes not-so-simple dishes. Plates such as East Prussia's colorful Christmas plates, or *Leipziger Allerlei*, are filled with the fun of great expectations for you to discover and of me writing about them.

I have created foods that come from the Russians, the Bavarians, the French, the Italians, and the Jamaicans, as well as foods from Greece and the Americas. It's a true renaissance of food, with roots anchored in faraway countries you may read about and discover in the stories of *The Arabian Nights*. I have included foods from the past empires of Persia, India, and the Chinese dynasties; food from islands with tropical palms, such as Hawaii, the Philippines, and the Canary Islands, and from the palatial kitchens of the kings of Thailand; foods from the island of Capri and the Adriatic and Mediterranean Seas; foods inspired by Axel Munthe and his chefs, who created the Herculean kitchen of his Roman home with modern Swedish accents. What a wonderful gift it has been in my life to create with God's blessings and work with what was given to me. Cook this food and serve it in earthen bowls or on gold-plated trays and take it to those in your family whom you love; serve it on special occasions to celebrate. You will find my recipes are created with thoughts of love, togetherness, and wonder. Starting with nothing but my wish to try what was new to me allowed me to create without prejudice and recollect what should be or can be. So go ahead; put on your apron and get to know the secrets of this chef's recipe book, revealed for the first time here for you to discover. You will find the dishes surprisingly easy to understand and prepare.

We continued on the train ride to Tante Lusche's new home in Hummendorf in Bavaria. I soon had the feeling that she really did not expect us to come at all. To all of us it appeared, and it certainly seemed to me, that she remained distant and without a warm welcome when she showed us to a small room on the upper loft floor, under the roof. There was just enough room for a regular bed, two half-sized beds, and a crib. Only after Mama spoke up to her and Uncle Ludwig did she give Oma her own bedroom next to ours. We had a stove in our room but not much else. But then again, Tante Lusche may have wondered why we would be in need of more room for furniture, considering the few things we had brought with us.

We played with our cousins Lenz and Buts. Buts is an abbreviation meaning "chubby," and she was a little chubby. I loved Buts. She was friendly and happy to share her hiding places and little treasures with me. After a week's stay playing in their huge, beautiful garden with lots and lots of blooming flowers and with fruit trees of many varieties, we were eventually told by our uncle that it was too dangerous for us to be in the garden because of the possibility of hidden ammunition that could explode. But with no German or foreign troops there, it seemed to be a far-fetched possibility to me.

At the time, Bavaria was far removed from the war, unlike what we had experienced in East Prussia. Occasionally we were invited to eat with the family in the dining room at the big, long table. Uncle Ludwig, as head of the family, sat at the head of the table. He was offered the food that came from the kitchen first, and he was served first. Uncle Ludwig was a great eater. He would take the biggest piece of meat for himself before it was passed on to anybody else— and lastly to us. I never, until then, knew it to be the custom for the head of the family to eat first and have the best of everything.

On several occasions, Uncle Ludwig told Mama that it had been Tante Lusche's decision to assign us the modest living quarters in this big house with limited privileges in the large kitchen, not allowing Mama to use the laundry room at all. We soon learned, however, that what seemed a puzzle at the time was in God's divine order.

Our time in Hummendorf passed rather quickly and soon

would be forgotten. Mama was offered one of two available teacher's positions in the village, and one of the amenities was an apartment with two bedrooms—one of two apartments in a building next to the school.

Mr. Grasso had been a German prisoner of war in America and had just returned home. "No one is more efficient and creative at discovering opportunities in the grimmest of times than the Americans," Mr. Grasso told us. For a short time, he was a daily visitor to our family. Mr. Grasso promised to show Mama "how to do business in America."

"Mr. Grasso may be coming tonight," Mama would mention to us almost each day. We chuckled, knowing that he wanted to pick up some things from us to barter with the Americans—mostly fresh food. In return he always brought things that were impossible for us to get, like chocolates, Life Savers, chewing gum, chicken noodle soup in large cans, real coffee, cookies, and sometimes American-made clothes for us, or shoes, which were otherwise impossible to get.

Mama started to prepare dinner, and we were busy cleaning our rooms because we had just moved into our new home. Rose and Jutta were assigned to do the tidying up in the new apartment, and I was helping Mama in the kitchen. Joergi was too young to know what the apartment needed or what Mama wanted it to look like. He met a few children in the neighborhood, and they played outside.

On one of the evenings, Mr. Grasso came to visit, he brought Eric Brandstaedter along. He was his new friend, who said that he had been a major in the German army. He had escaped from a prisoner-of-war camp in Russia. He had also been imprisoned in Hungary by the Russians and then escaped again. Now that he was in Bavaria, he decided that he wanted to live here in Hummendorf, where there were no Russian soldiers. He made us feel very uneasy, not like Mr. Grasso. We could not put it into words, but we all disliked Eric, and we told Mama as much. Eric was just not the person we could like. He always found ways to criticize whatever we did. When both men had left for the evening, we talked to Mama. She insisted that we should give Eric time to adjust to his new life. She had made up her mind and had her own opinion and was not about to agree with us children. At this time, she could not sense that anything was wrong.

We had moved from the schoolhouse with two hundred steps up a hill, to a small apartment with two rooms and a kitchen at the house of a blacksmith at the other end of the village. While living at the schoolhouse, Mama had started her own business of homemade, hand-painted Bavarian wooden crafts. Mr. Gaebelein, the carpenter who had lived only one house from the schoolhouse, had always been in a position to supply Mama with what she needed: napkin holders, bookshelves, jewelry boxes, plain boards to be painted with prayers, and other souvenir crafts the American soldiers wanted to send home to their families in America. The Americans preferred to pay with cigarettes, tobacco, and candies, and Mr. Grasso had no problems exchanging those for food or cash on the black market in Bamberg.

For quite a long time it was good for Mama to be able to support us this way. And whenever Mama was in need of cash, she could also walk into a local gift store in Kronach, only five kilometers away. Shop owners waited for her to sell her crafts on consignment, which were soon bought by American soldiers. When we had lived in Hummendorf, Mama had become quite a celebrity. She was loved and appreciated by locals and refugees from Czechoslovakia and Hungary, giving them work and steady income from her flourishing business. Mr. Gaebelein had a hard time keeping up with her demand for more products. Eric found work with this carpenter as a helper and began to make himself at home at our apartment, many times sleeping over. He would come every night for dinner. We disliked him more and more. Then Mama talked about getting married again. I guess he tried to make friends with me when he offered to help me with math, biology, or geography. "No mathematical problems," he would say. "That I cannot solve." He complained to Mama that I was unfriendly.

Eric started to talk of buying a large, beautiful home for us and a car and new clothes for all of us. Following this announcement, Mama told us one Monday that she had arranged for me and Rose to go to private schools away from home. Away from her Jutta, and Joergi. She found a school for Rose in Bamberg at a Catholic order of English nuns and a similar school with room and board for me in Regensburg at the Alumneum.

Within a month we left for our schools, both of us feeling sad and heavy hearted, fully aware that it was not Mama's decision alone, but that Eric had persuaded her to send us away. Now Mama would be left with Jutta and Joergi, the two youngest. With Eric Brandstaedter's wish a reality, Eric was set to establish his presence in our family.

And so it came about, a week or so later, that Mama and Eric were married. After his denazification, Eric had a job with the state justice department. Mama had decided to shut down her business in Hummendorf and move to a village close to Wuerzburg, where Eric had bought a small, partially finished building from a farmer who was in bankruptcy. It was an unfinished building of stacked concrete blocks that was never finished and would keep the same uninviting look.

Mama and Eric were married in secret and without any of us present. Eric took Mama to a little pub for a glass of wine for their celebration. "Herta," he said, using his name for her, "I have arranged for us to celebrate at a village vintage pub." Mama mentioned that one glass of wine was brought to their table and no dinner was served. So much for the celebration. Jutta and Joergi were not invited, and my sister Rose and I were away in school.

Within a few weeks of the wedding, Mama's, Jutta's, and Joergi's lives turned into a living nightmare. Eric would not speak to them except with unkind words. He did not like Mama's cooking, he did not like the way Mama made the bed, and he did not like to listen to music. No music was allowed in the house. To ensure there was no music, he demolished the radio, breaking it with his bare fists. A little later, Mama realized that she had fallen for the lies of an evil and wicked person. Her life, along with Jutta's and Joergi's, had entered a frightening chapter. Within a year, Mama had become a frightened and fearful person.

Rose and I finished and graduated from our schools. Rose began an apprenticeship in an agricultural school at a dairy farm near Munich. I started my apprenticeship as chef and baker in a shop in Starnberg, near Munich, living at Mr. Popp's house and business. Jutta and Joergi still lived with Mama and their stepfather under the most awful and unfortunate of circumstances. On Sundays they were told to collect rocks and stones, which Eric put on top of piles of dirt in order to finish construction of the house.

My apprenticeship in Starnberg turned out to be a lot of fun. I loved both Mr. and Mrs. Popp, and they loved me as they loved their own children. Their many gifts and kindnesses to me often brought tears to my eyes. Eric provided no allowance for clothes for either Jutta or Joergi. Mama secretly painted again, hiding her work. She started to paint for farmers and businesses in the neighborhood. With the money she earned, she bought clothes for Jutta and Joergi. Jutta was not allowed to go to her school's homecoming, and Joergi had a fistfight with a bad ending. This was life at home.

CHAPTER 2

Travels as a Chef

Switzerland, Schinznach Bad, Zurich, Gstaad, London, and Paris

THE YEARS OF MY APPRENTICESHIP and my time at the culinary school in Munich were very successful and good for me. The dean of the school appointed me to be the leader of all circular grade elements. Having mastered all my exams with the highest grades at the end of my two-year apprenticeship and schooling, I had earned the diploma from the city of Munich as the city's number-one public school student. I knew I was ready to go into the world.

Mr. Popp was unhappy when I told him that I wanted to leave. But then the day came when I had to tell him of an offer I had received to work in Cologne as a graduate in culinary arts.

"Wolfgang, we want you to stay here, and I don't think that you are ready so soon after graduation—joining another new environment with new people, working with new recipes and with different workmanship," said Mr. Popp, giving me advice. I knew he cared. He blushed underneath his thinning hair, as he had done on many occasions before when he had to make announcements or decisions that affected him in any way. I noticed that small pearls of worry and doubt were on his forehead. He not only liked me, but I was to him like a son leaving home. "I have signed an agreement, and I must leave," was all I was able to say.

But not too soon I found out that his predictions were right. I was soon sorry I had not allowed myself more of the happy times at his house, at his business, and with his family to gain more knowledge and wisdom and experience before moving on.

With happy memories of my friendship with Michael, and with memories of my secret love for Judy, who worked as an apprentice in sales, I would fondly recall the good times I had in Starnberg.

But here I was, having arrived in Cologne! I had arrived at the huge domed railroad station across from the historic wartime monuments, which were now in rubble along with destroyed buildings and the remains of the magnificent old Gothic cathedral, one of Europe's most beautiful churches. I had to find my way to the location where I was to work and where I would meet the owner of the business who had signed the work agreement I carried in my pocket.

To my surprise, the house number I was looking for was not painted on the front of the building. There was a ruined building near the sidewalk; a number was painted on the front of the sidewalk, and an arrow pointed to a staircase leading to an opening beneath the street.

I was greeted by the owner's son, who brought me to a room that appeared to be a bomb shelter left behind from the attacks. The room underneath the street had two bunk beds, a bench in unfinished wood, two chairs, and a dresser for my shirts, socks, and underwear. I had just begun to settle down and start unpacking when another person arrived. The man seemed upset. Not saying a word, he took a look at the quarters and did not bother to wait for the owner. He did not even bother to unpack his small suitcase, which was on the floor next to him. Without saying a word, he turned himself around and left as quickly as I had once seen a man leave the scene of an accident.

Meanwhile, I finished unpacking and arranging what little I had as well. My things included Mr. Popp's gifts and books, his farewell present, and Mama's pictures, which she had sent me with her love and prayers. Regardless of the modesty of my quarters, I wanted to try to make a go of it. The business owner arrived and introduced himself. He asked me to start work at midnight. The workshop was next to my room, connected with a sad-looking door.

It had not been a good night for me! I was not able to sleep or to rest. I had so much on my mind. Working in this environment was not friendly. The day's production sheet had a list of items that were unknown to me. The night seemed to last forever and ever and did not come to an end. I was happy when it all came to a halt. They must have felt the same way as I did. I received a day's pay, and without much to say I was on my way, off to my next adventure. With my maroon cardboard suitcase in one hand and a train ticket in the other, I returned to the railroad station. Hardly feeling like eating anything, I departed on the next train to Düsseldorf, a one-hour ride from Cologne, up the Rhine River.

Not knowing anybody in Düsseldorf, but being aware that it was the metropolis of high fashion, elegant cafés and shops, I strolled down the "Koe," the major artery of the city and easily one of the most beautiful, wide boulevards of any city in Europe. I looked into different restaurants, cafés, and pastry shops. On that first afternoon, I walked into a pastry shop where I was made welcome by warm, friendly people who invited me to get acquainted. Mr. Koch, the business owner, who not long ago had escaped from East

Germany, was a kind and warm person. I had not met his likes since leaving the Popp family in Starnberg. He was willing to offer me work. His pastries looked beautiful. They were first class. His business was ready and prepared for the next day. We left time at night to do leisurely things, enjoying a few hours together doing whatever we wanted to do.

To be working again was a true relief for me, but by now I was pretty much broke, with very little money left. To ask Mama for help would be very difficult for me to do while she was taking care of Joergi and Jutta without any help. Having this on my mind, I accepted Mr. Koch's invitation to stay with him, and I was immediately accepted as a family member. At night we often enjoyed playing soccer in the park. His twin boys and beautiful wife, Barbara, came along. Before they were married in East Berlin, Barbara had been a fashion liaison for high-fashion models as part of the East German communist government. She coordinated fashion shows and traveled to other communist countries in Eastern Europe. When I arrived with her husband and met her for the first time, she was dressed elegantly in Western fashions, which suited her. She lived in Düsseldorf, which was one of the centers of Western nouveau fashions. I told her that I was certain she would soon be approached to play a part in this city's fashion world. I liked both Erwin Koch and his wife, Barbara. It was so easy to get to know them before we got ready to leave and continue the next day's work at the pastry shop. Our days together passed easily and quickly.

While Erwin helped me get on my feet and find a place I could call home, I remained restless.

The largest, most successful bakery and café in Dusseldorf was Keulertz. Mr. Keulertz, I must mention, came to visit Mr. Koch's neat little pastry shop. Mr. Keulertz pulled me aside briefly to speak about future plans for his own thriving business and how I could fit into his plans for expansion. He provided a place for me to stay, and he suggested that I should start in his Danish specialty department.

Mr. Keulertz was of heavy, chubby stature, and he wore rimless gold glasses. He carried a walking stick with him; it was a beautiful mahogany stick topped with large, silver carved deer and flying eagles. Mr. Keulertz asked me to move into the company's dormitory with ten other members of his staff. It had been very difficult for me to leave Erwin and Barbara and their twin boys, since I felt like family.

Mr. Keulertz's family was not involved in the everyday business. On the few occasions I met Mrs. Keulertz, a tall, tired-looking skinny woman who rarely smiled, I was happy that she was not a person I had to deal with. She looked scary to me, and some of the staff were also afraid of her. She possessed a sharp tongue and was unwilling to forgive and forget if she was aware of a wrong made by anybody who was working for the company. Unfortunately for everyone working for Mr. Keulertz, he had developed a severe infection in his eyes, and there was talk that he might lose his eyesight. His wife decided to come and spend most of her time at the business. Mr. Sterz was my department head. Mr. Sterz, who was a soft-spoken, kind, and friendly man from Munich, asked me not be upset with Mrs. Keulertz's manner, her rough talk, her cynicism, and her often unjustified criticism. But I saw no need to live in an unfriendly environment and decided to leave. Life could be unbearable.

Summer was at its height in Düsseldorf, and around the Rhine, trees were blooming. On my day off one Sunday, I walked into a lively, beautiful restaurant on the banks of the Rhine in Benrath, just outside of Düsseldorf. The Rheinterrassen was a very busy restaurant where I wanted to apply for a chef or pastry position. I asked to meet the executive chef—a tall, handsome man who made me feel more than welcome. He showed me the kitchen and pastry shop.

The general manager, a woman in her forties, was busy but spent some time talking to me. Karl-Heinz, head of the pastry and dessert department, treated me like a son. He asked if I would like to meet a young woman, a friend of his in her twenties who worked at the restaurant and lived by herself. Her name was Lisbeth, and she took a liking to me. I was very shy—too shy to make any advances. I had the feeling that Karl-Heinz, in spite of being married to his beautiful wife, Anna, made up for my shyness. On several occasions I would surprise him by embracing Lisbeth in, of all places, a walk-in cooler.

But every summer comes to an end, and so did this summer at Benrath, giving way to autumn. And with the flowers no longer in full bloom, the elegant Rheinterrassen restaurants would soon close their doors for business until summer came again. Tourists visiting from foreign countries, as well as visitors from the countryside around Düsseldorf no longer strolled the parkways embroidered with colorful beds of roses, dahlias, gladiolas, and the beautiful range of colors from the many trees in fall.

It was the time for wine grapes to be harvested on the Rhine. Karl-Heinz and Lisbeth, it seemed to me, were harvesting their own wine of intimacies, perhaps unknown to his wife. I had thought about Lisbeth. And he asked me to be closer to him and his wife. There had been numerous times that I was invited to spend an evening at his house with him; his wife, Anna; and Lisbeth. How naive for me to guess the reason for me to be invited. Shyness prevented me from participating and accepting his invitation again.

The winter season in Switzerland was just about to begin. I was very serious about working in foreign countries. I thought of all that could be ahead for me. I thought about adventures and experiencing other ways of life and customs. What other country could have enticed me, a young restless and ambitious chef ready to meet fame, more than Switzerland?

And opportunities appeared to be in abundance! One of my first contacts in Switzerland was Chef Paul Becod of Gstaad and Schinznach Bad. We received forty Swiss francs a month for working as chefs, which could hardly justify the word "salary." But the excitement of working in Switzerland and the experiences I gained would be instrumental in shaping the rest of my career as a recognized well-traveled chef.

Schinznach Bad, a small and quiet little village of one hundred or so people, was nestled right on the banks of the Aare River between Basel and Lucerne. I was surprised to find a whole slew of other German chefs and very few chefs from Switzerland, but some chefs from Italy. The Italians almost always held the lower-paying jobs.

In Italy at that time, young chefs were not required to serve an apprenticeship, which put these young men at a disadvantage compared to other Europeans. Not that we were better paid at forty Swiss francs a month with free room and board, working six days, averaging well above ten hours a day, with no overtime and no bonus or other rewards at the end of the season.

I had become fast friends with many of the chefs at the spa, particularly with Dieter Schwindt. Dieter and I became the best of friends, sharing our most intimate, personal thoughts and ideas of what we hoped to achieve and wanted to be, and wishing that our paths in this life would cross again. Even our not-so-Kosher adventures of getting out of bed in the middle of the night when everybody else was asleep and climbing the vineyard hills up to the old Habsburg Castle were great times.

The old Habsburg was a relic, left over from the time the Habsburgs of Austria ruled Switzerland. This was the time of William Tell, the Swiss folk hero and sharpshooter from Lucerne who led his freedom fighters against the Austrians and won independence for the mountainous Swiss regions of central Europe. While digging deep into the rubble at the old castle, we found treasures and relics, worthless to others, left perhaps by tourists. But we had fun unearthing broken glassware and earthen pottery, leather belts, hats, worthless jewelry, and what turned out to be of great value to us: bundles of love letters dating back to who knows when, written in old German no longer taught in Swiss schools.

"How exciting, Wolfgang!" Dieter asked me to shine a light onto these old scriptures. There was only the light of the moon, shining bright and friendly down at us, and the mood of the night encompassed the ruins of the castle. The fog over the vineyards, the familiar earthy smell of pine trees, and the unusual silence perfectly matched our own feelings of solitude and friendship at the time.

There was even a letter in English, and Dieter said, "Listen, Wolfgang, you could always ask Carla to translate the meanings of love and devotion to you." My mind was heavy, and my feelings were confused about what I thought of my secret love for Carla. In Schinznach she was the personal governess of a wealthy woman from England. Staying as a guest at the spa, I would meet Carla every day during my lunch break. Carla would push her mistress's wheelchair to the spa's hot sulfur springs, famous throughout the world for being the hottest thermal springs, healing many ailments, and attracting the rich and famous to come and stay and be healed miraculously. Hot sulfur spring water is what nature and the spa gave so generously and freely for the taking to those who came to drink it. The water could be smelled from far away, and it was not a pleasant smell. To visit the old wooden tubs at the spa and to bathe and feel rejuvenated, one had to pay lots of good Swiss francs. The Swiss are known to be blessed with a good sense for making money and for being good businessmen.

I was nothing but stunned when I saw Carla for the first time. She seemed to me one of God's most beautiful, dainty creations.

I usually left the spa's kitchen after lunch to change and play tennis at the hotel's tennis club courts. After the games we were allowed to go swimming in the Aare River behind the *Kurhaus* park, with its tall trees and manicured flower beds. We always met to play doubles on the courts, with Chef Becod and his girlfriend Hermine on one side, and Dieter and me playing on the other.

The chef, French by birth but a Swiss citizen now, looked to me like the personification of a short little barrel of beer. Speaking just a few words with a Swiss German dialect, not at all resembling the German language as I knew it, he was a very strict and demanding executive chef. He was also demanding in private as a person. He was the president of the UH Swiss Chefs' Association. He worked like a computer. He was very strict with waiters and all service personnel, who had to line up at an open window to the kitchen in single file to receive their orders. The chef himself expedited the orders and stayed at the window to control the food, which was not given to the servers without a coupon signed by the German maître d'hôtel.

The food was always very tasty, rustic, and not presented the way one could see dishes served in fancy gourmet magazines. The meals could also have been ordered and prescribed by one of the spa's doctors or dieticians. Hermine, in a separate little neat kitchen, would prepare all the specially ordered meals. I thought that Hermine should have been on a special weight-reducing diet, since she did not feel very well. While approximately a whole head taller than Chef Becod, she was the best friend he could have wished for, taking care of his needs and trying, most often in vain, to control what he ate. She was intelligent, well read, and in her late thirties, and she took an immediate liking to me like an older sister would. Hermine was Swiss German, but she spoke fluent French, as most Swiss do. Her special friendship with Dieter and me were among the many advantages we were afforded at the spa. Playing on the hotel's tennis courts and taking advantage of the spa's hot tubs without charge when patients didn't show were some of our privileges.

In Schinznach, everybody worked long hours to receive one of the certifications for having worked as a chef at one of the top five-star resorts and spas in Switzerland. We stayed at the hotel's dormitory, an old, vacated wing of the hotel that was no longer used for its world-class clientele. We would walk at six in the morning through the sleepy park to the main kitchen and have breakfast together at a long table, with Chef Becod sitting at the head of the table and Hermine at his right side. Hermine would arrive first, and the chef a half hour later, saying a very tired "Bon Jour tout le monde." We all enjoyed a very healthy, plentiful, and wholesome Swiss breakfast with café au lait, fresh rolls and croissants, homemade jams, and sweet butter, which were delivered to the kitchens fresh every morning from a nearby farm. The food served to the hotel's guests was the same as what was served to us, the chef's crew. Guido Meyer, the head pastry chef and baker, would bring platters of breakfast and afternoon cakes and pastries, the same food that was served in the mornings and afternoons in the park and on the terraces of the Kurhaus. Like all food from the kitchens, these items were delicious and could be compared with the very best in the world, which Mr. Meyer, in the winter season, served at luxury hotels in Davos or St. Moritz.

After breakfast, all the chefs would depart to their assigned kitchen, with Dieter working as the garde-manger with Mr. Meyer, while I worked at the pastry and bake shop downstairs. The bake shop was in the basement with steps leading up to the main kitchen. Cautious rays of sunshine shone through a few storm gutters, while we were able to watch guests going to and coming from the hotel or the spa. There was just enough light for us to not feel that we were being locked underground, away from all that was happening outside.

Lunch was served to both hotel and spa guests on the partially covered terraces in the fantastic settings of the park and forest.

Because we were usually not too busy for lunch, we prepared more of the well-known exotic creations of the foods one would find in big-city five-star hotels of France, Italy, or England, or at famous spas, like Baden and Wiesbaden, in Germany or Monte Carlo, France. For the pastry chefs it meant creating tall, frozen ice cream drinks and *coups au glace* with fresh-cut fruit or berries from the hotel's own gardens and farms. The head gardener, a tall and humble Italian Swiss farmer from the Lake Lugano region of the Tessino province, religiously saw to it that we were supplied with whatever the season offered, brought to us fresh on the very first day it would come to the markets. He was wonderful to talk to, as he was extremely educated and knowledgeable in farming and about the growth of vegetables, fruit, and all that grew in gardens and fields. He wore a green coat, pants, and jacket underneath a long overcoat, his feet hiding in high black boots. We were supplied with produce from all the regions of Switzerland, which were as varied as the times of the year, and with what was offered to us, from as far north as Scandinavia to south of the Alps. There were fresh limes and all types of citrus fruit, pineapples, apples, cherries, early- and late-season tomatoes, artichokes, avocados, and multicolored fresh herbs with some mentioned only in kitchen dictionaries.

At the chef's table we were served lunch at two in the afternoon, mostly from cold platters with meat, seafood, salads, and ice creams with fruit and petits fours from the patisserie. Then it was off to tennis. The afternoons always passed too quickly. The Aare, here still a small river, bypassed our magnificent park. After swimming we would rest on the large, hard river rocks or on the narrow, sandy small beach before returning to the dormitory to change into chefs' uniforms.

Dinner was served early, starting at six in the evening. We were very busy with hotel and spa guests alike. People came from the nearby cities of Zurich, Basel, and Luzern to enjoy world-class food and listen to the spa's visiting orchestras, opera and ballet companies, and live jazz bands from every corner of the Americas. The resort, offering breakfast and dinner to all guests, was booked solid throughout the seasons, with many guests staying all summer long for consecutive years.

Some of the most famous and rich, the Aga Khan and begum, and the English and Danish royal families and their staffs, came here to visit the hot springs, known to many to heal rheumatic fevers and many illnesses. Nature offered them the opportunity to enjoy their fortunes of wealth. They did not have to take care of their own needs or those of their families and friends at this spa in Switzerland, which provided everything they could wish for.

I personally lived in the hope that my passionate admiration and secret love for Clara would be healed. For years, summer after summer, working and living in Schinznach Bad, Clara was here while I worked. But I was always too shy to ask to meet her until it finally happened when I did not expect it; on the last day at Schinznach Bad.

While it's true that unrequited love hurts, I was praying to be fulfilled in my desire for love to be my companion throughout my life. For love is beautiful and perfect when anchored deep into your mind. It is beautiful to remember and cannot leave us ever. Nobody except Dieter knew how I felt.

Dieter invited me to visit him and his family in Westfalia. Dieter's family was influential and prominent in educational circles throughout the state of Westfalia. His father and mother were considered intellectual rocks in the community where they lived. His father was a teacher and engineer, while his mother was a doctor. Both of Dieter's brothers were studying law at the university in Remscheid.

In one of the years between the seasons in Switzerland, I worked for Hungenbachs in Remscheid. I missed Dieter. He was visiting and working in other countries, spending most of his time in the south of Switzerland or the western regions of Italy in Toscany.

The long summers in Schinznach lasted from early spring to late fall, and yet they seemed to be so short. Every season seemed to come to a close too soon. The hotel's general manager, Mr. Schaerer, reserved the season's last Sunday for a much-applauded carnival and costume ball for employees of the resort. The hotel guests served employees from an elegantly arranged, most luxurious and sumptuous buffet prepared by all of the chefs. All of them gave it their best. There were salmons smoked with native birch wood and other fresh seafood from the lakes of Switzerland and from the rivers and the oceans of northern waters and the Mediterranean. There were heavy prime ribs, roasted and grilled, and whole roasted baby lambs and sheep of the Alpine region, waiting and ready to be carved. There were wild young piglets and wild deer, as well as a scrumptious display of fresh fruits and vegetables from the hotel's gardens, with red, white, green, and purple sauces. The music was Swiss country music from the French, German, and Italian regions. Mr. Schaerer played piano beautifully during most of the evening. I and the others were given the opportunity to play the piano, show the art of yodeling, or do magic tricks. The masterpiece I was able to contribute to the glamorous buffet was a tall white clock tower, as tall as I was, made of snow-white sugar with bridges and tunnels leading from one level to others, filled with dark Swiss chocolate truffles and sprinkled with crystallized violets. The tower, much admired, served as a spectacular centerpiece of the buffet.

CHEF WOLFGANG HANAU

December 7, 2011

Wolfgang Hanau
1010 North Olive Avenue
West Palm Beach, FL 33401

Dear Wolfgang:

Thank you for entering the Lindt Fall Recipe Contest! We received such fantastic entries from all around the nation but your Palm Beach Chocolate Praline Cheesecake recipe certainly caught our attention (and our taste buds) and placed 1st!

We hope that you enjoy your new KitchenAid Stand Mixer (which will be sent by KitchenAid directly), as well as your year's supply of Lindt Chocolate!

Happy holidays and again, thank you!

Sincerely,

Lindt & Sprüngli (USA) Inc.

Included in this shipment:
GRAND PRIZE: One (1) grand prize winner will receive a year's supply of Lindt Chocolate to be awarded in the form of twelve (12) 5.1 Lindor truffle bags, twelve (12) Lindt Excellence bars, one (1) bulk box of five hundred and fifty (550) Milk Lindor truffles, one (1) box of Lindor truffles, one (1) box of Swiss 4.9 oz Tradition de Lux, one (1) box of Petits Desserts Collection, **a KitchenAid ® 7-Quart Bowl-Lift Residential Stand Mixer** *(sent from KitchenAid under separate cover)* and one (1) Lindt Chocolate Passion Recipe Book.

LINDT & SPRÜNGLI (USA) INC.   ONE FINE CHOCOLATE PLACE   STRATHAM, NH 03885-2592 USA
TELEPHONE (603) 778-8100   TELEFAX (603) 778-3102   INTERNET: www.lindt.com

*Lindt Fall Recipe Contest: Grand Prize Winner

November 23, 2011 - Posted In: Entertaining, Promotions - Posted By: Lindt

The grand prize winning recipe for the Lindt Fall Recipe Contest is the *Palm Beach Chocolate Praline Cheesecake* by *Chef Wolfgang Hanau from West Palm Beach, Florida*. Wolfgang created this cheesecake in honor of a dear friend **Maida Heater**, and now it has become his signature dessert. Made with Lindt Excellence 70% Cocoa Nut Crunch and Lindt Grandeur Dark Hazelnut Chocolate bar, it is simply delicious! Congratulations Wolfgang!

Ingredients:

For the crust:

- 1 3.5 oz bar LINDT Excellence 70 % Cocoanut crunch bar, ground or very finely chopped
- 1 cup chocolate graham cracker crumbs
- 4 Tbsp melted sweet butter

For the Filling:

- Three 8-oz packages (24 ounces) cream cheese
- 1 ¼ cups dark brown sugar, firmly packed
- 1 ½ tsp vanilla extract
- 3 large eggs
- 1 cup LINDT Grandeur (5.3 oz) dark hazelnut chocolate bar finely chopped

For the Chocolate Praline Sauce:

- ¼ cup dark brown sugar, firmly packed
- 4 Tbsp sweet butter
- ½ cup LINDT chocolate fudge sauce
- 1 cup LINDT grandeur (5.3 oz) dark hazelnut chocolate bar, chopped

Directions:

The crust:

1. Combine all ingredients and press into the bottom pf a 9-inch spring form pan.

The filling:

1. Combine the cream cheese with the grown sugar and vanilla. Add eggs, beating until smooth.
2. Stir in LINDT finely chopped hazelnut chocolate bar.
3. Pour into crust and bake in a preheated 300 degrees F hot oven for 90 minutes (until barely set) Cake will continue to set as it cools.
4. Cool on rack without removing mold. Cake may be prepared up to 48 hours in advance, if covered and refrigerated.

The Chocolate Praline Sauce:

1. Heat brown sugar and butter, stirring until smooth.
2. Whisk in LINDT chocolate fudge sauce. Bring to a boil.
3. While whisking, boil for 5 minutes until sugar begins barely to caramelize.
4. Add chopped LINDT hazelnut chocolate bar.
5. Cool to, lukewarm Serve cake slices with ladle of sauce.

Makes one 9-inch cake – 12-16 slices

- Recipe printed in **"Secret Recipes and Travels , by Chef Wolfgang Hanau" published by iUniverse**

This was a wondrous farewell to the place where we had lived and had loved and would continue to love with all of our hearts and souls as long as we will remember. I would have come back again to work and live there, but I knew that it was the law to work for no more than four consecutive years in Switzerland. But I also wanted to see the rest of the world. Yes, I soon would enjoy and cherish the next stage of my life. It was to be fifteen years later before I would come back to visit the resort, bathe at the spa, and enjoy the hotel with its world-class food and musical extravagancies, when Jeannie, Lisa, Ryan, and I spent one week at the hotel reliving all I had seen there.

Before I left Schinznach, Chef Becod had made arrangements for me to work at Café Du Nord on Zurich's infamous Bahnhofstrasse, the boulevard where shoppers of the world meet. Bodo, who had worked with me as a chef in Schinznach, visited me in Zurich with Knut from Düsseldorf. We had plans to rent a sailboat to go boating and to swim in Lake Zurich, Switzerland's largest lake.

What a day it was! We had a very difficult time just getting out of the harbor. In fact, we had to be towed. None of us were experienced or knew how to maneuver this big, beautiful boat. We agreed to take turns steering and felt that it had to be with the wind at our back, which would give us the best opportunity to sail. Yet, while nobody dared mention it, we saw many other boats happily passing by in the same wind. How weird! Or was it?

When we jumped off the boat into the lake to swim, the water was ice cold. No wonder, because it was melted snow from the glaciers behind us. Back in the boat, we discovered to our great surprise and dismay that we had drifted away quite a distance from the city and the harbor. We attempted to turn the boat back in vain. What were we going to do since it would soon be dark? And we were starving. With loud voices we called for help, hoping that some friendly mountain mate would hear and help us. Help came in the shape of an experienced Swiss boatman, who steered us to a safe harbor. Safe at last! I will always remember this day on the lake.

Winter is big business in Gstaad, in the Bernese Oberland mountains of the Wispillen, Eggli, and Wasserngraat. Each and every one of these downhill mountains possesses magnificent major skiing slopes. They require elaborate and skilled skiing expertise.

Here in Gstaad, it was skiing instead of tennis in the afternoons for us. With Mama always trying to help me and thinking of me, she had saved enough from her painting money to buy me ski boots, a blue sweater, pants, a sun hat, gloves, and ski caps. What a Mama I have!

My first attempts ever to ski were at Wisspillen, the easier slopes of the three. For me, it was the perfect experience, and I returned there for the rest of all of the seasons I worked in Gstaad. "Gstaad, you know, is not for beginners," Hermine had warned me, sending me off with her good wishes and prayers. There were, unfortunately, no doubles to be played while skiing! Neither did she or Chef Becod ever go skiing. But she knew how to give me advice about what to do. What a smart, intelligent, and well-read woman she was! I could trust her to tell me the truth. "Wolfi, from time to time you need a little downer," she would tell me, having known me now for several seasons. Well, it was true. If things were going too smoothly for me, I could feel myself being overwhelmingly lifted up into heavens of happiness, where I no longer counted my blessings. Very simply, Hermine would take the time to point out to me the difficulties we all will face one day when things just won't go well or be easy. Her advice would give me time to think in between flights of happiness and defeat.

The skiing was always good, and the chalets we shared at the Grand Hotel Park were the very same ones reserved for some of the world's great names in entertainment and show business. Audrey

Hepburn, Frank Sinatra, Douglas Fairbanks Jr., Liberace, and many more were regulars.

But the highest point of the season was reserved for the Montgomery Cup in long-distance ski jumping, with the retired field marshall presenting the winners' trophies. Every year the world's leading ski jumpers would come to Gstaad to compete and win trophies and big money. The event counted toward world ranking among long-distance jumpers.

Chef Wolfgang Hanau with Sir Montgomery (Monty) of Alamaia

Again it fell upon Chef Becod and his chefs to create another fabulously famous international celebration with tables of food and wines we had become known for. The farewell dinner for this important event, under the baton and direction of Chef Becod and prepared at the kitchens of the Grand Hotel Park in Gstaad, was served at the elegantly furnished and marvelously decorated ballroom. It was also served at all of the hotel's restaurants, which were closed to the public that day.

The music, performed by the Swiss National Symphony at the ballroom under the direction of Herbert von Karajan with Yehudi Menuhin as the featured soloist, was combined with the great jazz band of Xavier Cugat from Spain. The many pictures taken at the event, together with all the chefs, Sir Monty, and the Swiss Olympic national ski team, have preserved one of my most treasured memories. I am able to remember these pictures in my mind after so many years. The insight, supernatural wisdom, and knowledge of our minds allow us to remember and are the basis of our love of the past and present.

David Harding, the banquet assistant manager at the Dorchester Hotel in London, was a regular guest in Gstaad, staying at the Palace Hotel. I first met David while skiing at Wisspillen. On my way down the slopes, I noticed a person who was totally covered in snow falling, then getting up, then falling again and getting up, possibly in great pain. To the rescue I went! "Hello, I am Wolfgang. Let me help you," I said.

"By golly, yes, thank you. Let me introduce myself to you," he said, as he proceeded to reach for his business card. Before I knew what he was up to, there it was, elegantly inscribed in gold letters with the name of London's Dorchester Hotel on Park Lane, on an oversize textured, embossed card.

My own skiing was not great, and so we tumbled down to the bottom of the mountain, holding on to each other, until we reached the ski station. The ski lift from there goes to the top of Wisspillen. Looking at my watch, I saw that I should have been at the kitchen ten minutes before. "David, I should have been back at work," I said. The dinner for chefs was served at 5:00 p.m. sharp, with no exceptions. I wondered out loud how could I make it in time.

"Wolfgang, please have dinner with me later, if you will. After work. I will reserve a table at the Palace Hotel. After dinner we can listen to Maurice Chevalier at the nightclub." It all sounded tempting and wonderful. And I really wanted to talk to David about working at the Dorchester Hotel after finishing the upcoming summer season in Schinznach. I had verbally promised Chef Becod that I would return for one more summer to Schinznach.

"Very well then, we will meet at the Palace at eleven p.m.," I said. David reached out to shake my hand, and I quickly departed. He seemed to be in good shape now that he could take a horse-drawn sleigh up the mountain to the Palace Hotel.

My own destination was my very own chalet at the Park Hotel Reuteler, one of Gstaad's great resorts with an unbelievably great reputation for its food. The chalet where I stayed was warm and furnished in the style of a typical Swiss chalet with fireplace and all. I quickly changed into my chef's uniform and walked toward the kitchen, having no eyes for anything but the kitchen. As I was well aware, I had missed dinner, and I had missed it by quite some time. Both Hermine and the chef looked surprised to see me back at work. I obviously had been missed. Giving my brief story of what happened, having helped David get back onto his feet, I was offered a special dinner from the guests' dinner menu. I politely declined, thinking of my late dinner yet to come at the Palace. No, I didn't mention it to anybody.

The evening went smoothly until I learned that I was the designated chef that night, serving late snacks from the grill at Harry Schraemli's bar, with Harry Schraemli playing the keyboards; there would never be enough room for all who wanted to come and listen to him and hear his artistry. Harry Schraemli was known as Switzerland's foremost nightclub pianist. No wonder so many Americans from California's west coast came here to listen to him. He would play tunes from Broadway, Glenn Miller, from Tony Dorsett to Ken Stanton and the Rodgers & Hammerstein era. No wonder the atmosphere downstairs at the club was sizzling with excitement and thrillingly invigorating when I arrived. To the envy of other hotels in Gstaad that hired large, expensive bands to entertain their guests at night, Harry Schraemli had an exclusive engagement at the Park Hotel for years. We drew so many guests to our nightclub and bar that after midnight the bar was no longer able to handle additional business and, without fail, would not admit additional customers.

It was not before one o'clock in the morning when I arrived at the Palace Hotel. David, as promised, had made reservations under his name for two at the nightclub, where Maurice Chevalier was the attraction. David was dressed elegantly with an English-style dark purple tuxedo, a ruffled white dress shirt, and an oversize bow tie, which was ever so popular then. My own wardrobe was less spectacular. I wore black pants with a thin satin stripe, a black tuxedo jacket, a white shirt, and a smaller-sized continental black bowtie.

David would greet me with a broad smile and a warm, friendly handshake. He had ordered a pair of aged French cognacs in large snifters and a small carafe of water. It was too late for dinner. Spicy little finger foods were served and placed at the table.

To a roaring wave of applause, Maurice Chevalier arrived at the club, said hello to a few people, and proceeded to the small stage set for him. Many French tourists stayed at the Palace. Maurice dedicated the evening to his film *Gigi*.

On another occasion, visiting the Palace Hotel's swimming pool, I overheard Swiss waiters talking about the French and German visitors and how they were known to be stingy with their tips, but giving credit to American guests for their generosity.

Following the conversation, I knew the thing for waiters to do in Gstaad was to work at the Grand Hotel Park, with the majority of guests being American. Guests at the hotel would fly in with jeeps, which were equipped to climb mountain roads better than any European car, sparing no expense to ride the waves of American luxury between hotels in Gstaad and St. Moritz. That was the thing to do. Hors d'oeuvres and appetizer buffets with French escargots in Picard, *petit Monsieur* sandwiches, and whatever else chefs could offer for a price (which was of no concern to the super rich). There were freshly shucked oysters from Louisiana and oysters Rockefeller prepared at Antoine's in New Orleans. Clams casino here were served in a variety of shapes, with exotic dips and sauces. Cappuccino could be purchased from an espresso bar at one in the morning. Delicately flavored champagnes and flavorful martinis were the go-to at the hotels.

David and I partied as good friends do till early in the morning, with promises to take on the Wispillen mountain again the next day.

The possibility of working at one of the world's premier hotels, the Dorchester, was very exciting, and it would be a dream come true for me. David immediately started to arrange an employment agreement with Mr. Williams, the staff manager at the Dorchester Hotel. As soon as I had finished working the summer season in Schinznach, I was on my way. I took a train from Zurich to Calais. Then I traveled by ferry boat from Calais to Dover, and from there it was just a few scant hours until I arrived at London's Victoria Station. The first person to greet and embrace me with a hearty welcome was, of course, David. Dressed, as ever, in dapper light pants and a gray flannel jacket, with a long, flying white handkerchief hanging from his pocket and a red carnation in the buttonhole, David was the consummate well-dressed English gentleman in summer.

We were driven in the hotel's avant-garde limousine to the

Dorchester. At the Dorchester, David had arranged for me to meet with Mr. Williams and Eugene Kaufeler, the famous Swiss executive chef who reigned over some two hundred chefs in the kitchens at the hotel. Kaufeler was famous in the culinary world as executive chef for the hotel, at Europe's largest kitchen, where he catered to dignitaries and royalty. Two hundred chefs from all corners of the world were willing and able to perform in their areas of culinary expertise, working together in perfect harmony under Monsieur Kaufeler and the six executive sous chefs' eyes. The kitchen was enormous and immaculately cleaned by a staff of more than one hundred people from Poland.

The pastry department was headed by Chef Louis. He was of Italian-Swiss heritage and known for his creations in spun sugar: hand-blown lifelike balloons, decorated woven baskets, and numerous other artifacts. Baskets with floral and fruit arrangements were from Chef Louis and were decorated with rainbow-colored ribbons. Many of his works on display in the hotel lobby were offerings to spur-of-the moment parties that demanded the finest, most artful edible centerpieces on their tables. The Dorchester Hotel was the favorite place for entertainment for the Duke of Edinburgh. He came to the Dorchester not only to attend banquets but also to dine royally at the Pavilion restaurant.

David took special care to ensure that I met celebrities, dignitaries, politicians, and Hollywood stars, as well as the rich sheiks of Arabian oil fortunes, who regularly stayed at the Dorchester, their favorite luxury home away from home.

The Dorchester Hotel was known for its lavish floorshows put on by the Toppers, London's answer to Radio City Hall's Rockettes. The Dorchester Restaurant was the place to be entertained with avant-garde food pastries and the Toppers. The display of petits fours, *mignardines*, and other small pastries was sensational.

My primary responsibility was to direct and supervise the production of banquet foods, with an emphasis on lavish displays of fancy desserts presented at the restaurant from rolling carts and served from gold-plated sterling trays.

The silver room, as it was known at the Dorchester, was managed by a Polish general known to everybody as John. John was an intellectual scholar of classical music and history. He had studied before the war in Berlin and Vienna before he was called to join the Polish army. Eventually he fled to England. Then he was called back to Poland to serve his country, which was at war with Germany. He spoke fluent German and several other languages, as well as English. Whenever we had an opportunity, we engaged in interesting conversations, with classical music and European history as the main topics and of special interest to us. We concluded that the world and Europe would never be as it was before 1945. John would supply our department and all the chefs with his highly polished, mirrorlike platters, trays, and dishes of sterling silver, as well as precious gold-plated chafing dishes.

The average daily number of banquets at the Dorchester amounted to two hundred special affairs, which made it the world leader in number of banquets served. This made it the world's leading money-making hotel. The chef's special banquet manager, Frank, would deliver all menus and announcements for banquets to each department head. Frank received his information from Mr. Colombo, head of banquets and catering, or from David, who was his assistant. My close relationship with executives and managers at the Dorchester, including Mr. Ronus, the managing director, quickly brought respect, admiration, and, in some cases, envy.

I soon became acquainted with some other leading chefs, such as Gunter, born in Giengen, near Stuttgart, who was an extremely talented chef who worked at the likes of the Palace Hotel in St.

Moritz. We regularly exchanged some fine, innovative culinary delicacies. Then there was Leo, a Swiss chef from Zurich. Having lived and worked in Zurich, we had much to talk about. Klaus Irrgang, a tall, blond good-looking chap from Berlin, became a close personal friend.

All of my friends and I shared a common interest, which was classical music. We tried to get tickets to any of London's seven major world-class symphony orchestras. There was, of course, London's famous Royal Festival Hall and Albert Hall, as well as other smaller concert halls. The Festival Hall, with its unique and close seating to the orchestra, offered tickets at bargain prices; they went on sale two months ahead of each concert. Since this fitted our budget fine, it was obvious that we had to be aware of all concerts at the Festival Hall. All available tickets for the special seats were sold on the day they went on sale.

On my days off I enjoyed strolling along the river Thames to the Royal Festival Hall, if for nothing else but to get the latest published list of concerts months in advance. Guenther and I had at any time a dozen or so concert tickets in our wallets. We enjoyed not only the concerts but also the ambiance at the Festival Hall.

On the day David brought me to meet with Mrs. Gibbons in Fulham, near Putney Bridge, the fog was very thick—almost frighteningly heavy to those seeing it for the first time. Mrs. Gibbons was a friend of David's mother. Living at Mrs. Gibbons's house, I was blessed to get to know one of the kindest and most caring people I would ever know. She had not heard the name Wolfgang before we met, so she called me Wolfe, which was fine. Mrs. Gibbons's one-story brick house looked like many others on Doneraile Street. It is not rare in London to find that all homes in the same neighborhood look alike. Mrs. Gibbons's favorite saying was "One egg looks like another."

"Wolfe, you are welcome to help yourself to any food in the kitchen," she would say. I did help myself quite often, after working in her garden or coming home late from work. Coming home many times in the afternoon, Mrs. Gibbons would invite me to sit down with her for tea and canapés, which she lovingly prepared with different crackers and biscuits, little tidbits of watercress, and thinly sliced cucumbers, with sardines or with ham and eggs. I would prepare delicate little German snacks, mainly with different types of sausages, which Mrs. Gibbons thought was food to be eaten only when food was rationed, as it had been in England during the war. There were just the two of us living in her home. Mrs. Gibbons started the fireplace in my room when it was cold and I stayed late to work at the hotel. Then I would continue to feed the fire on some unfriendly winter evenings. Mind you, it gets quite cold and nasty in London. This is the time when London's infamous fog angrily engulfs the metropolis. Busses will stop in the midst of traveling. Taxis drop off passengers wherever they are, and everybody looks for the nearest Tube station for the underground. The 30 and 70 bus lines would take me from Fulham to Hyde Park Corner, or from Marble Arch to the Dorchester. On Sundays I enjoyed walking through Hyde Park in the morning, listening to the speakers, a part of the uniqueness of London on Sunday.

At sunset, with the sun still shining behind a cloudy, foggy sky, the colors appeared to be more red than the brilliant orange I remembered from home. Looking from a window of one of the Dorchester's banquet halls, I looked at fancily dressed men, who looked very elegant even during the week. All of this was new to me. Men wore gray jackets, a red carnation in the buttonhole, with striped pants and silk ties in silver. When it got dark in the evening and came time for dinner, a more formal tuxedo or plain, elegant, hand-tailored suit would be more appropriate to wear. Ladies usually wore hats and gloves and preferred to arrive in long stretch limousines, rather than taxi cabs.

The sun was not a clear sun. It was always behind a veil of light gray and often hidden by low, dark clouds. This is the way the sun shines upon London Bridge.

David would pick me up on many of his afternoon breaks to see a movie with him on Leicestershire Square. Or we would go to the Strand or other places in the West End that were close to the Dorchester. As soon as we settled down into our seats at a theater or cinema, David would fall asleep. Because he had to return in the evening to manage and be the host at functions, he would be ready and dressed for the occasion in the afternoon when we met. When banquets were scheduled to be late and longer-lasting than planned, he was given a room at the Dorchester to stay overnight. If it wasn't too late, he would travel back to his mother's house in Ealing, near the airport.

On many occasions he would pick me up at night to visit one or several of the numerous private clubs in the West End where he was a member. The nightlife in London was mostly in and around clubs, and it was not uncommon to be a member of a dozen or more private clubs.

In spite of all the long hours David worked, his private life was very active. David usually dated very attractive, beautiful, intelligent, and well-educated women. I met Monique, a French fashion magazine editor living in London, who confided in me how much she enjoyed dating David. She described him as "A true gentleman who never expected after a date spending the remainder of the night with her." I was blessed with meeting many beautiful and simultaneously interesting people in London.

Ulrike, who worked as an au pair in an elegant apartment on Park Lane, was from Berlin. She took care of the teenage children of one of the most socially prominent couples in London, the Dr. Gordon Moons. Their apartment was close to the Dorchester Hotel, also overlooking Hyde Park. The rent they paid was astronomically high. Ulrike, surrounded by luxury, was extremely demanding. Unfortunately, my wages of ten pounds per week did not give me the means to compete with Dr. Moon's circle of friends, who pursued Ulrike to date and entertain her.

But I also had the privilege of making the acquaintance of a warm and friendly girl named Anette, the child and daughter of the banquet director at the Claridges Hotel. I met Anette when David introduced me to her father. She was not as tall and slender as a model, yet she had a charming way of making up for it by always dressing very worldly, up to date and very French. Anette was very pretty. Her face was framed by dark, curly hair, and her skin had a deep suntan from the sun in the south of France, where she grew up. She frequently went back to Nice, in the French Riviera, where she was born and grew up.

David also introduced me and escorted me to social gatherings of the Anglo Norwegian Society. The chairwoman of the organization was Ruth, an elderly English lady who lived in Coventry on an estate where she lived year-round. On quite a few Sundays, the Anglo-Norwegians would spend a day on a bus to visit historic mansions and estates of the national registry. Most of the association's members came from Norway. Being born in Germany, I noticed at first a slight hesitancy and a somewhat reserved welcome by the Norwegians to accept me into their own closed society. However, this would soon be a thing of the past, because I would become very active in many of their dinner affairs and banquets.

The great banquet for the Norwegian Society was planned for the week before Christmas. I remember this so vividly since it was the occasion of a traditional Scandinavian Christmas celebration at London's famous Tate Gallery. Thanks to David and Ruth, I was chosen to bring the flaming bird into the dining hall and, while carving, read from Charles Dickens's *A Christmas Carol*. A very festive affair it was!

After the carving of the turkey, there was traditional English plum pudding served, flaming and drenched in brandy sauce. Little did I know before coming to England that plum pudding, with the suet pastry crust lining the tall pudding crocks, was actually made one year before Christmas.

Christmas Day and Boxing Day I spent with the Gibbons family. The first year I was in London, the celebration was on Doneraile Street at Mrs. Gibbons's house. The following year the party was at her son Harry's. Harry was a CPA. The year after that we would all go to her daughter Sheila's. They were three loving families celebrating together. I was accepted in their families and welcomed warmly. How little did we, back home, know the happy and close-knit life of families in England! I enjoyed that time of the year in London, which was quite different from the holidays we spent in Germany.

On Christmas Day the three families traveled together to Westminster Abbey to listen to the choral music of Handel's *Messiah*, celebrating the birth of our beloved Savior, the baby Jesus Christ. The *Messiah* is probably best known and performed more often in England than in other countries, as Handel had lived and composed most of his music there. After listening to the offering, we would go visit Mrs. Gibbons but spend the rest of the day with Harry and Sheila. The windows in many homes in London's neighborhoods were left open, with Handel's masterful music sounding loud and clear in many otherwise quiet neighborhoods.

It was almost embarrassingly clear that Janet, Harry's daughter, had a crush on me, and to confirm this, her younger sister, Sheila, told me about it. After Christmas I invited Janet for dinner. Enough said. Living at Mrs. Gibbons's, Janet's grandmother's, home, I did not feel too comfortable dating Janet.

David also invited me to spend Christmas with him at his mother's house. He invited a whole slew of his bachelor friends who were not able to spend the holidays with their families. I asked David to invite my friend Klaus instead of me, which he did. Klaus seemed quite embarrassed the day after he had spent Christmas with David. It was the kind of Christmas party he wanted to forget.

David, other Norwegians, and I were invited to spend the remainder of the holy days at Ruth's countryside estate. Nobody who was there with us will forget a particular incident with Ruth's cats. I for sure will remember her guest bathroom! Everybody knew of her love for cats, but nobody mentioned to me that her cats were everywhere. Cats loved Ruth and her rustic home. Ruth had a collection of cats of all breeds and colors that she had found. She also had bought several purebred Siamese cats. They all shared her home, and some, as I found out, lived in her bathroom. First I noticed that the curtains, hiding book shelves and storage bins, began to move like magic. I sat down, and what a scare! From behind of all of the curtains, cats of every size and shape escaped from their hiding places to head toward me—seeking attention, I assume. I had no choice but to be very friendly. To scream was out of the question.

Every year in January, London's well-known Hotelympia would go on the stage at Hammersmith Palais—not too far from Fulham, but the exhibition halls were quite a distance from the Dorchester. This was a one-week yearly event for all of England's famous hotels and restaurants to showcase chefs and culinary masterpieces. For this occasion, Mr. Kaufeler, our executive chef, invited me to appear with him at a BBC radio show with overseas visitors and culinary celebrities.

Master Chef Eugene Kaufeler, a Swiss national living in London, is a highly respected master of culinary arts. He asked me to work with him and to become his executive administrative assistant, arranging his schedules of visiting major culinary arts festivities and events throughout the world that he thought might be of importance. I was not ready to assume such a commitment. I did not intend to live and work in England for an indefinite period of time. I consequently declined to accept this most generous and complimentary offer, which could possibly have elevated me immediately into a respected and more-recognized and better-paid position. But my goal at the time was to see much more of the world.

Instead I discovered for the first time my ability to write and put my feelings and emotions on paper, which was a whole new world for me. I also began to paint. I spent many nights sitting in front of a burning fireplace in my small room at Mrs. Gibbons's, writing and painting, which soon became my favorite Sunday activities. I never took it further. Most poetry and novels I wrote paid homage and respect to all basic human elements. My first ever realization of seeing the many street people living without homes in London was that we were all brothers and sisters in Christ.

My work at the Dorchester, meanwhile, had become routine with not much to look forward to anymore. And if it had not been for David showing me glamorous and exciting ways to live, which London is so famous for, my days would have been filled with boredom and not knowing what it is that makes London the most fascinating city in the world to live in.

I remembered the late prime minister D'Israeli saying "Those who are tired of London are tired of life. London offers everything that life can offer."

One night I accepted an invitation by one of David's illustrious friends to an evening at Covent Garden. It was during one of the intermissions during Verdi's *Nabucco* that Barry, David's friend, talked to me of his fun playing squash at the Royal Automobile Club. Being aware of the exclusiveness of the club, I tried hard not to accept his invitation to meet him there, but to no avail. Instead, he seemed to sense why I was hesitant, and he quickly offered to send a complete RAC outfit plus rackets and balls to the hotel. Again I politely declined the outfit, but I promised to meet him at the club later in the week for tea. "Don't you enjoy racquetball?" Yes, I did, and I wanted to see the club, possibly the most exclusive men's-only sporting club in London, if not the world.

We played several games, had a shower, and I followed him to his flat in Kensington, close to Buckingham Palace. Kensington is part of London's West End, where many of the royal family's relatives and court-appointed staff live year-round, with a full view of Buckingham Palace. By elevator we went straight to Barry's penthouse flat on the top floor. I immediately noticed that the door we entered was concealed from the inside. Without anyone lifting a hand, the entrance and the remaining doors no longer could be seen. While not an expert on invisible doors, I still tried to understand the mystery of what had just happened. Barry escorted me to an elaborately decorated dining alcove with several tables, of which one was generously laden with exotic foods, both hot and cold. He had a bar stocked with Dorchester-type chilled champagne, wine, hard liquor, and cordials. "Help yourself, Wolfgang," Barry said, pointing to many of the exotic delicacies.

Magically, large photos of men in the nude appeared on the table from nowhere. Without much of an introduction, Barry began to speak of the adventures in erotica he had enjoyed in Scandinavia. At the same time he also elaborated on a few of his intimate affairs with some well-known and beautiful women in England. They were attracted to him, he said, because of his financial and social connections stemming from the appraisals he had carried out for the queen's properties. He also said he invested large amounts of money for the royal court. I had heard enough to scare me and make me feel uncomfortable, so I wanted to leave. He surely must have felt my discomfort and thought that his expectation of what he hoped would follow later that night at his penthouse was no longer realistic. He clapped his hands, and doors magically opened. With a polite and cordial handshake, I left Kensington Palace looking for a taxi home to Fulham. It was two in the morning.

Back at Hammersmith Palais, Chef Kaufeler asked me and three other chefs from the Dorchester kitchens to represent England and the Dorchester Hotel in competition with other countries and institutions. We would be allowed to prepare and exhibit whatever we chose. My entries were in four categories: desserts, petits fours and mignardins, chocolate showpieces, and dinner side dishes. For a period of two weeks we worked at the hotel kitchen during the day, and many times well into the night. Our goal was set: winning medals for England as well as the grand prize for a single hotel operation among the eighteen competing countries.

My work was well rewarded with the exhibition's silver medal, the second-highest ranking of all prizes in the renowned culinary world exhibition in London.

I quickly became a central part of scheduled interviews and other culinary events, all of which I enjoyed immensely. I felt gratitude for the creative talent God had given me, which I had probably inherited from Mama, an artist in creative painting, poetry, and music.

During the last day of celebrating this successful culinary event, the chefs were introduced to a number of culinary masters from England and around the world.

As a result of my achievement at the culinary competition, I was invited by George Marin, general manager of the Hotel Plaza Athenee in Paris, for an interview that lasted the better part of an afternoon. The wonderful and very exciting outcome of our meeting was an invitation to join the culinary staff at the most famous of all hotels in Paris, the French Metropolis. The invitation and offer was such an enormous event in my life that I was left speechless. I was only too aware of the glitzy haute cuisine at the Plaza Athenee and the unspoken but well-known and secret desire of most of my fellow chefs to work with the most renowned chef of our time, Monsieur Christian Louis Diat. I gratefully accepted Mr. Marin's invitation, and we agreed that it was to be in two months' time, May 1, that I would start my assignment of working with the twenty or so chefs at the Plaza Athenee and its most famous Le Relais restaurant on Avenue Montaigne, next to the Theater des Champs Elysees and across the street from Christian Dior's fashion boutique.

BEARNAISE SAUCE

Yield: 4 servings

INGREDIENTS:
3 egg yolks
¼ cup water
3 tablespoons white wine or chicken broth
2 tablespoons tarragon vinegar
2 teaspoons minced shallot
2½ teaspoons minced fresh tarragon, divided
8 whole peppercorns, crushed
½ cup cold butter

DIRECTIONS:
1. In a small heavy saucepan, whisk egg yolks and water. Cook and stir over low heat or simmering water until mixture bubbles around edges and reaches 160 degrees, about 20 minutes.

2. Meanwhile, in a small saucepan, combine wine or broth, vinegar, shallot, 1½ teaspoons tarragon, and peppercorns. Bring to a boil. Reduce heat; simmer, uncovered, for 10 minutes or until reduced to 2 tablespoons. Strain and set liquid aside.

3. Cut cold butter into eight pieces; add to egg-yolk mixture one piece at a time, stirring after each addition until melted. Stir reserved liquid and remaining tarragon into prepared sauce. Serve immediately.

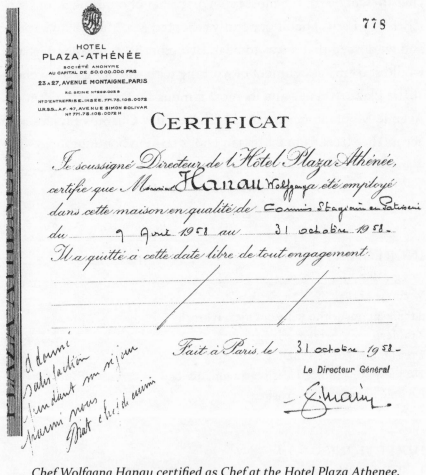

Chef Wolfgang Hanau certified as Chef at the Hotel Plaza Athenee, Paris, by Chef De Cuisine Diat and General Manager George Marin

As an added, wonderful surprise, I was told that Gunter, my friend, had taken the opportunity to ask Mr. Marin for an interview with the intention of joining me in working at the Plaza Athenee. I was so happy to hear that Gunter was given the opportunity to start at the sauté station at the hotel Plaza Athenee. Even though we would be in different departments of the kitchens, we would still be able to spend much of our time together, not only at work but discovering Paris, this beautiful city on the Seine, and the French countryside.

Knowing each other well, as friends who shared an interest in the same beautiful things, such as fine cooking, entertainment, concerts, and museums, we both were equally looking forward to this newest adventure. Where else but in the traveling world of chefs was this possible? Gunter was scheduled to depart one month later to Paris, as he had a lease that was too costly to break. I had no such agreement with Mrs. Gibbons.

Time drew closer to say good-bye to London and to toast, with a freshly brewed pot of British tea, the easy way of life in Britain, which I had adapted to quickly. The farewell was sweetened with another step in the direction I wanted to go and with the new ways I was ready to explore. It was still only the beginning of my chosen career in the culinary field. Little did I know then that all my expectations and more would become a reality. All of what I expected in my life was happening. It is so hard for me to remember which of the many months I lived in Paris I enjoyed most. While London for me will always remain the world's most interesting city, Paris certainly takes the place as the world's most beautiful, elegant, exciting, and well-planned metropolis.

Paris, with its wide avenues, the sparkles of the Champs-Élysées and L'Arc de Triomphe; the Avenue l'Opera; Avenue George Cinque; Avenue Montaigne; the Plaza Athenee; the high-fashion boutiques of Dior, Balmain, and Jacques Fath; the Theatre des Champs-Élysées, the Seine River and Place Alm a Marceau, and the commanding Tour d'Eiffel, were all meant to be the exclamation mark for all of the excitement and beauty of Paris. I could go on and on.

After I arrived in Paris, my first stop was the Plaza Athenee. This is where I had planned to meet with Monsieur Marin, the general manager and my sponsor. He was not at the hotel, and I dared to ask to meet with the executive chef, Christian Louis Diat, instead. I might as well have asked to meet with the king of France! Monsieur Diat was king and Napoleon all wrapped into one.

Chef Diat quite obviously believed that not too much culinary art or talent could be imported from across the English Channel. He was brought up to believe that food from the Britons was of no character, had no taste, and was not created with imagination. As for me, I had seen beautiful creations and some of the finest prepared food I would ever taste while in London. But then again, I had to wonder if the Dorchester, with its many European chefs representing many nations, really did represent the English way of cooking. To me it did.

"Ca va, jeune chef?" he inquired, when I was introduced to him by the restaurant's general manager. The chef had, as may have been expected, quite an elaborate office right in the center of the kitchen. The kitchen itself was sectioned off into three basic parts. The one closest to the restaurant saw the saucier and his sauté station, with two or three chefs attending to prepare orders most of the time. Next to it was the rotisserie, roasting and grilling meats and seafood. The *entremetier,* or vegetable cooking station, and the seafood department, with selections from oceans, rivers, and lakes from all over the world, was located very close to the chef's office behind crystal-clear glass dividers. Here is where the most famous of all dishes at the Plaza Athenee were prepared. Such dishes, including lobster soufflé Plaza Athenee, for many years were tasted and tried by food critics of the world and found to be worthy of their fame and high price. I was eager to learn the secret recipe for the lobster soufflé. The cold seafood served from the kitchen was directed by Madame Cologne. She was the undisputed queen of oysters, shellfish, and all of the restaurant's cold food platter selections, freshly squeezed juices, seasonally arranged fruit baskets, and de rigueur salads. The chef's preferred place was around the cool air-conditioned kitchen, as it was for all the chefs. The third department, with a kitchen all of its own, is where I worked and earned rewards and recognition. It was the *patisserie*, under the capable management of Monsieur Vivant, who had just recently left a chef's position at the Toque Blanche in New York City. He spoke English very well, with a distinguished French accent that, to me, sounded charming.

I met a pastry chef from Germany at the Plaza Athenee who worked with me, plus several chefs from France, a chef from Spain, and another chef from England. Everything we prepared was made with the utmost care and expertise that one could expect from one of the world's leading hospitality institutions.

I soon learned that we had to earn our right to work at the Plaza Athenee from week to week. Each and every week we were evaluated, based on our performance. Chef Diat would post on the kitchen blackboard the particular station where each of the chefs would be working the following week. If a chef's name was missing from the board, it meant he no longer was allowed to work in the chef's kitchen. It was as simple as that. Nobody, but nobody, would enter his sanctuary unless an appointment in advance was granted by Chef Diat. And this applied to everybody. Evan Monsieur Marin, the general manager of the hotel, had to call for appointments to see the chef.

Other famous visitors to the Plaza Athenee included Maria Callas, the Duke of Windsor, and Henry Krupp of Bohlen Halbach. Many celebrities and dignitaries staying at the Plaza Athenee attempted to make appointments to speak to Chef Diat. Many celebrated guests staying at the Plaza made their home at the hotel for an entire winter or summer season, occupying an entire floor, which included accommodations for their servants. Thus, an audience with Chef Diat, who was appointed by French president Charles De Gaulle to be a member of the Legion d'Honeur, was surely the greatest honor for a French citizen. We soon would learn to understand, respect, and adhere to the strictest of all protocols. The one interruption he permitted was in the garde-manger kitchen every day sharp at 10:00 a.m., when all chefs in the kitchen met with Chef Diat for an aperitif. All that was said was a short "À santé," after which each chef would return to his or her work station.

A private conversation with the chef was not on anybody's mind. I learned after I had left Paris to live and work in America that, to my dismay, Chef Diat had been suffering with a grave illness for most of his life. This certainly explained much of his disposition and eating habits, which mostly centered around petits carrots from Vichy, petite Belgian endives, and freshly picked baby salad greens topped with a few drops of cold-pressed extra-virgin olive oil and, occasionally, a few crumbs of soft, ripened fat-free goat cheese. Even though I had chosen French as a third language in Regensburg, the first few days and weeks in Paris were nightmarishly difficult for me. Many nights after I had finished work and returned to my room, I would stay awake, rehearsing French vocabulary, trying to remember words and how to ask for things and how to lead a conversation in fluent French.

On the day of my arrival, I was determined to find a room or small studio not too far from the hotel. With a modest weekly salary of forty French francs, I could hardly afford or think of living in the neighborhood of Avenue Montaigne, near the Plaza Athenee, which also was near the French president's *Palais* on the corner of Champs-Élysées and Avenue Montaigne. Single rooms didn't exist, and those that did were reserved for servants of the presidential palace or the staff of foreign ambassadors. Apartments or studios, if available, would cost a multiple of my monthly salary.

My first night in the City of Lights was at the foot of the Eiffel Tower. Place Alma Marceau, the closest Metro station near the Plaza Athenee, was just a two-minute walk away from the hotel, and this is where I spent the first night. In one hand I carried my little brown suitcase, which held all my belongings. In my other hand I had a paper sack with a sandwich, lovingly prepared by Mrs. Gibbons, a razor, toothbrush, and soap still wrapped in waffled green paper Mama had given to me. It still had the price tag of a shop in Wurzburg. I went down the steps to the subterranean street. A freshly baked baguette and an apple would be my first dinner à *la Français.*

The night seemed to be long, and I could hardly wait for the morning light. Oh boy, was I waiting for daylight to come. By no means had I been the only overnight tenant at the Metro, a Parisian landmark called by Parisians "Metro Eiffel," just because it was the Metro station for the Eiffel Tower with armies of tourists coming through there all day and night. I found a place to shave and wash my face, and I was on my way back to see Mr. Marin for help in finding a room or any affordable accommodation in which to put my belongings. I didn't need much.

It was back to see Monsieur Marin, the sophisticated French gentleman I had met and talked to on that one decisive afternoon in London. Wearing rimless glasses, he was in his early fifties with a thin mustache and wore a soft, perfectly ironed striped dark suit.

He was the picture of a perfectly dressed hotel general manager. It appeared that he had expected me. He stretched out his well-manicured hand to welcome me. Monsieur Marin was very kind and concerned, asking if he could help me find my way around. This he could do indeed! In as few words as possible, but in fluent French, I was able to explain that I had been unable to find a room and that I had spent the night at the Metro station near the hotel. He was quick to respond that it had always been the most difficult thing for him to do. Having said this, he started making a few phone calls to friends, while I was asked to sit down at the comfortable upholstered chaise lounge in his office.

Fortunately, it did not take him more than a few minutes to look at me with a big smile, and all my fears and concerns were gone. God was on my side and watched over me. With a few strokes, he scribbled an address onto one of his business cards, which he handed to me. It read "48 Bis Avenue Mozart, pres de Bois de Boulogne, La Muette Metro." To be sure, he had been successful in finding what I needed. The person to see was Madame Vielfaure, wife of one of his friends, a stockbroker on the Paris Bourse, he explained. With perfect directions in my hand, I was on my way. Two Metro stations from the hotel was Avenue Mozart. And close to the station I quickly located 48 Bis. I felt like a true Parisian. The building was an older sophisticated apartment house showing great character with its stone-carved walls and a wonderful antique front door, carved in dark oak and decorated with polished brass rings that served as doorbells.

Madame Vielfaure was a young, vivacious French woman in her early thirties who dressed in seductive, elegant French haute couture. She wore a long, thin lavender-and-blue lounge gown, which turned my thoughts to some imaginary French high-fashion showrooms. Her attractive figure filled almost the entirety of the doorway to this beautiful, richly appointed French apartment. Deep red carpets intertwined with paintings of laughing women on balconies overlooking the Bois de Boulogne. The sparkling light of a crystal chandelier shone dimly above the Louis XIV furniture, including a long table laden with fresh fruit and flowers from the countryside. The entire layout was just too overwhelming to me, a young chef ready to go to work and learn the secrets of French cuisine.

"Jeune homme." She must have addressed me several times before I could grasp everything I saw. Stretching out her well-manicured hand to welcome me, she invited me to come in. "Please enter," she continued in English, with a very charming Parisian accent. "I have heard all about you from George Marin, my dear friend," she said.

The more I looked at the luxurious surroundings, the more I wanted to live there, but I was not sure if I could afford to live in such a place. After a few words of casual conversation, my doubts were all but gone as I was shown up to the fourth floor by elevator. There I was escorted to a tiny little room—a mansard, as it was called. This was a reward I was ready to accept as I started my new life. Even after so many years, it isn't difficult for me to describe the entire layout of the mansard room underneath the roof. It contained a narrow, short bed covered with two blankets and a pillow, and a commode for shirts and the other few things I brought with me. There was also a one-door wardrobe with a few wire coat hangers left over from a visit to the dry cleaners, and a door leading to the common hallway. A window, part of the shingled roof, leaning dangerously to one side, gave an astounding view of the city right above my bed. The view from the glass window was a very treasured view, as it turned out. From my room I could see rooms in neighboring buildings. I was to learn the many secret adventures of those who were not aware or did not care to live according to old customs of living incognito. The window would open upward, as I discovered by pushing it.

Rent for the room was certainly within my budget at five francs a month. Good timing was essential in order to shave or take a bath in the sink or go to the bathroom! My room, along with five other rooms of similar proportions, opened onto the fourth floor, which had the only available sink and bathroom available for all of the floor's tenants. There were handrails attached to the sides of the latrine to hold on to when in need. It turned out that it was never a problem to either find room at the sink or to attend to one's other necessities when in need.

To arrive on time at the Plaza Athenee, I left one hour before my scheduled work. On the first day, I met all the chefs in the basement of the hotel, where we had to change from our clothes to chefs' uniforms. And from there we went straight to the kitchen.

Monsieur Vivian introduced me to all the chefs working in the pastry department. He decided everybody's job responsibilities and functions. Recipes were posted, and my first hands-on job was to prepare the ultimate ice cream and sorbets for our demanding hotel guests. Needless to say, all leftover frozen *glaces* were melted first thing in the morning to become part of a new batch of frozen desserts. This was to avoid small frozen crystal solids, which would add an unacceptable crunch to an otherwise smooth and perfect glace.

The aperitif hour at ten in the morning could not be missed. It brought Monsieur Diat out of his hidden chef's office into the kitchen with a very Parisian "À santé" to all of us present. Next came the preparation of lunch for the chefs' table, with the executive chef not joining. The sous chef, Marcel, took his place at the head of the table. He was the instigator of much talk about

French-German controversies, his favorite conversation, without regard or acknowledgment of the presence of three German chefs. The food for the chefs was excellent and the same as they served to hotel guests. Among those staying at the Plaza Athenee were Maria Callas, Aristotle Onassis, and the super-rich war baron Alfred von Krupp and Halbach. Each of them occupied an entire floor at the hotel, including chambers for their servant chefs, maids, and butlers. My first day was short. I was very busy concentrating on preparing every item with the utmost quality and appearance. Monsieur Diat, *Le Chef*, would personally see each and every dish leaving the kitchen. There were no returns ever. We were serving true perfection.

My first day went by uneventfully, and I had a chance to speak to a few of my newly made friends from work. Gilbert, the youngest member of our team, invited me to join him for a game of tennis. At the end of the day, I had a good feeling of what life for me was going to be like here in beautiful Paris. After the tennis game we visited a small outdoor café on Place Alma Marceau. With a glass of wine, we enthusiastically showered all bypassing young women with admiration and ahhs and ohs with words spoken in hope of a rendezvous. The flower shop at the Plaza Athenee was located just off the lobby, and we were permitted to use the flower shop's walk-in refrigerator if additional space for refrigeration was needed in the kitchen.

Yvette, the flower girl, served flowers and bouquets of flowers with a flair of elegance and Parisian charm. Yvette liked me, and I liked Yvette, and she confided in me that she liked to date foreign men. With my basic French, I was able to tell her that I thought she was as lovely as the most beautiful of the flowers in her shop. I wanted to perfect my knowledge of French and registered with the Alliance Francaise. Yvette offered to drive me to school, or we would take the Metro or bus. We enjoyed being together as much as we were able to and always talked about our dreams and ambitions. We were both young—in our early twenties—and unattached, and we found pleasure and happiness in holding hands, looking into each other's eyes, and watching people passing by. At the alliance, many students from Germany and other countries spent their vacation here or worked in Paris as au pairs to learn French.

Maria, a young blonde girl from Westfalia, her curly hair tied into two short pigtails, was seated next to me. She was beautiful. Maria reminded me of a picture of a rather shy blonde curly haired, grown-up schoolgirl. She looked a lot like my sister Rose. She was fluent in French, with no German accent. We quickly became friends and met many times after classes, when Yvette was not able to wait for me. We loved each other's company and promised to explore Paris together. Both of us were in Paris for the first time.

How much I loved Paris, and how much I enjoyed life! Romance and the opportunity to meet someone like Maria was changing my life. Meanwhile, I enjoyed my work and working with everybody at the hotel. Maria's father, the owner of a chain of regional department stores, was obviously concerned. My own concern was to stay in close touch with my work, school, and with Maria. My wish was to be her close friend and boyfriend. She seemed to be willing to make room in her life for me. Never before had I met a girl and friend so close to me. We spent many of our Sundays together, as we then both were free and not working. One Sunday we went to Fountainebleau Park with Guenter, from London, who was now working here with me at the Plaza Athenee.

On one Sunday Guenter and I assembled a real French country picnic lunch for Maria, Guenter, and me. We went to the gardens of Versailles to lie down in the soft cut grass, looking at flowers and butterflies and counting the hours, which passed quickly. On another Sunday we went to Saint Chartres.

The word was out at the Plaza Athenee that Hilton Hotels would open its first hotel in Europe in Berlin.

Back in Switzerland, in Schinznach Bad, I had a bad infection in my right hand from cutting fresh fruit and meat and working with pastry flour. I traveled to Düsseldorf to a specialist who wanted to help me heal the wound. He told me that I might never be able to keep away infections if I didn't stop working in food preparation. But this would mean giving up my baking and cooking profession, which I liked and did so well.

I heard again that the Hilton Hotel in Berlin was hiring people who spoke other languages besides German. I decided to travel to Berlin for an interview. And now that Maria had left to go home to Germany, my incentives to stay longer in Paris were gone. On my way to Berlin, I wanted to visit Maria in Muenster.

The first part of my trip from Paris to Berlin took me by train to Frankfurt. The journey was rather boring traveling by myself. My thoughts were with Maria and with a new job in Berlin, since this was my future, I thought.

On arriving in Frankfurt, I was able to make arrangements to rent a VW Bug to drive to Muenster, where I planned to meet with Maria, who was expecting me.

CHAPTER 3

More Travels

Berlin, Cruise Boats, Lisbon, El Vigo,
Spain, Las Palmas, Tenerife, Canary
Islands, Madeira, Morocco, Casablanca,
Bournemouth, Wuerzburg, Bad Gastein,
Naples, Capri, Sorrento, Senegalia,
Venice, Merano, Vienna, New York City

THE WEATHER ON THIS EARLY September day in Frankfurt was cold, foggy, and wet. I drove on the Autobahn, where one can meet travelers in a hurry. The traffic was fast, and the constant blinking on and off of headlamps from cars behind me made it anything but easy to stay on the right side and not swirl sideways off the road. I was able to see thick forests and the occasional riverbed on my right side, with heavy traffic to my left. The wheels of the small car suddenly spun out before I was able to get my car under control. I ended up upside down. I had driven way off to the right side of the road. My car tumbled several times, turning from the roof to the wheels and back onto the roof with the wheels upside down again. The Beetle ended up stuck between two large trees. The spot where I had landed was heavily wooded. I tried to cautiously move. I then tried to open the doors. The car did not move, and I was able to crawl out of the VW.

It was no more than two to three minutes later that a nice young couple bent over me and the car. After a few words of introduction, my rescuers, who were from Muenster and knew Maria and her parents, offered to drive me to my hotel, which I had booked from Paris. The police arrived in the meantime, and I left the car in their care. They promised to take care of all the paperwork and return the Bug to the rental agency in Frankfurt.

I thanked God that I was not hurt. I had not suffered the slightest of injuries and felt no pain. I was blessed. I waited until the morning before I called Maria. She was very concerned. She brought her own car to the hotel, and her father had given her the names and addresses of some of Westfalia's most renowned restaurants, assuming that this was where I would feel immediately at home. With Maria being so close again, it brought to my mind thoughts of wanting her to be with me for a long time to come.

The bishop of the city of Muenster was her father's brother, her uncle. It was he who had threatened, she told me, to disallow her any future welcome into the Catholic Church if she did not end her romance with a Lutheran. It was intolerable and unthinkable for her to date somebody of the Lutheran faith.

I wondered what it was that he knew that I didn't know. In particular I would remember this bishop when, at a later date, I experienced the same treatment in the United States.

Nobody in the world could have described the city of Berlin better to me than Mama. When Mama told me of her exciting and beautiful life in Berlin before the war, her description was that of an elegant, lively city, the cultural hub of Europe.

The Ku-Dam, perhaps Europe's most sophisticated boulevard, with its many cafés, cabarets, and nightclubs had been frequented by Marlene Dietrich and her admirers. It was crowded with the crème de la crème of high society, open until the wee hours of the morning. Simply put, the city had what it took to be Europe's number one.

Mrs. Weber's high-ceilinged mansion was at Eisenacherstrrasse 1, one of the few beautiful remaining pre–World War II apartment buildings, frequented by young high-ranking officers stationed in Berlin before the war. It was near the zoo and the new Hilton Hotel, just across from the ruins of the famous bombed and totally destroyed Kaiser Wilhelm Gedächtniskirche, with one of its towers still lying in ruins. Mrs. Weber, a lady in her early sixties, lived in a building that once was a symbol of prewar Berlin with all of its glamour. She was clearly distinguished in appearance and in her expressions, but she was also a very friendly, helpful lady. She was quite different in appearance from the adorable, down-to-earth Mrs. Gibbons in London and the elegant, fashionable Madame Vielfaure in Paris.

Frau Weber had been in the beauty-product wholesale business until the end of the war, when the Russians dropped tens of thousands of bombs and destroyed what little was left of the city. So much of what was once treasured was lost in a few nights. This apartment building on Eisenacherstrasse—with its high ceilings and beautiful old tapestries, golden frills, and gold-framed pictures in the corridors—had never fallen to the bombardment or even been partially destroyed; this was amazing, considering all of the dreadful things that had happened. But the eastern part of Germany was still tightly closed at its borders. My life took a turn when the new modern shiny city bar at the Hilton Hotel opened with its American ballroom. The rooftop restaurant quickly became the place to be seen for the nouveaux riche of East and West Berlin. I started to work in various positions. The hotel, unfortunately, under its all-American management had been in constant turmoil since it opened.

One of the assistant managers, Mr. Irgang, newly brought aboard from America, was grossly overpaid compared to his European counterparts. He was always in search of making more money in any way possible. He was a man with no portfolio and was not able to communicate except in English with an American accent. He was considered by many to be useless. He was always in search of making deals—not for the hotel, but for himself. He was ready to make an extra buck from the taxis, the florist, or car rentals as commission for his referrals. The hotel manager, Mr. Olard, an old pro who better fitted the European picture of a hotel manager, was fired when he did not introduce Conrad Hilton to the staff when he arrived for the opening of the hotel. Instead, Mr. Strand was appointed general manager of the hotel. I met him years later when he was manager at the Waldorf Astoria in New York City. The food served at the Hilton Hotel's restaurants was, without exception, unimaginative, inferior American fare. When the hotel opened, the chefs were Swiss. But even for American palates, the selection of foods was at best mediocre and unacceptable.

Who was responsible? That was a difficult question. The unprecedented departure of the original group of Swiss chefs shortly after the opening may have been the answer.

Many of the employees, who had been hired before the opening of the hotel and who had gone through extensive criminal and personal background checks, were gone within a month. Some of them were fired for expressing their disappointment with the new American management, an administration without flair and know-how.

I met Hella at the rooftop restaurant. She had been there with her parents a few times before I met her. She was always dressed with a French flair, which the French describe as *tres chic*. Hella reminded me of my dates in Paris, showing a French charm and *savoir de vivre* not too often seen in Germany. She had long blonde hair, neatly tied into a knot of uneven proportions, giving her a certain sophisticated personality and appearance. Hella caught my eye, and she answered, smiling at me. We spent beautiful, long evenings together, sometimes enjoying wonderful food in some of Berlin's romantic restaurants or at beer and wine gardens. At other times we sat underneath a tree and just talked.

Her parents had bought tickets for us to attend the Opera Ball, a social highlight of the season. Berlin's foremost social gala was held each year at the German state opera house, the Deutsche Staatsoper. The opera house was formidably illuminated for that occasion days in advance.

Hella arrived in a see-it-to-believe-it light green silk pantsuit, drawing a lot of attention. I wore a black tailcoat and white gloves. As we entered the glamorous opera lobby, many photos were taken. The names of those arriving at the gala affair and the names of parents were formally announced by a page boy who was dressed in a velvet Wagnerian costume. The seats on all floors of the opera house were exchanged for more comfortable seats than regular everyday chairs. Our seats were underneath hanging baskets of tropical flowers brought in for the night from Italy. Buffet tables elegantly dressed in damask table linens with heavy silverware and crystal candelabras were loaded with expensive foods from countries that were printed on the opera's program for the evening.

Tickets had been sold out at high prices for this illustrious soiree in one of the world's greatest cities. It was hard to believe that a few hundred yards away, American, French, and Russian troops were facing each other in preparedness for what might be ahead. We danced on the opera stage. Hella had introduced me to her younger sister and to several of her parents' friends. I could not help but think how wonderful it was to be alive, to be free and uncommitted to any place in the world. I was again overwhelmed, and I thanked God that I lived the life He had chosen for me, to love and live to the fullest with His blessings. At two in the morning, we were picked up by her father's chauffeur, and I was dropped off at the Eisenacherstrasse address of Mrs. Weber. Hella and I promised to thank her parents for this beautiful evening and to meet the next day, Sunday, since I did not work.

Ever since I started in culinary arts, I'd had my mind set to enjoy my profession the world over and travel as a chef to see and live in as many countries and continents as I possibly could fit into my life. I didn't feel an urgency to rest or be bound by borders or be anchored to places with ties of any kind. While I had made no contacts with countries outside of Europe, I had applied for work with shipping and cruise lines. The first answer I received to my inquiries came while I was still in Berlin. The company operated a group of cruise liners with home ports in Pireaus, Greece; Bremerhaven, Germany; and Southampton, England. Not having traveled on large boats before, I wondered if I would adjust to traveling at sea. Not thinking through any of the consequences, I simply was in favor of taking many opportunities to travel and experience my dreams. How well my dreams, reality, and imagination would merge, and there was still more to be discovered. Would traveling be a permanent part of my life?

For the interview, I was invited to travel to the cruise line's German office, in Bremerhaven. The building was an old prewar partially bombed building on the waterfront, near the harbor. I arrived in time to meet Mr. Henry, a fair-skinned, tall, blond German seagoing man in his early forties. It was not long before we were relaxed and comfortably speaking to each other. We would develop a genuine friendship based on trust over the next three years.

"Wolfgang, I am in need of a very trustworthy personal assistant, someone who is loyal and knowledgeable who will travel with me aboard this ship, working as my trusted associate and friend, following my directions and requests to help in any capacity where my presence is required," he said. He wanted me to represent him and the cruise line when needed. At this time the *Athens*, a 25,000-ton cruise boat cruised the Mediterranean, the Black Sea, and Africa, with stops in the Canary Islands, returning on to Southampton. The *Athens* also embarked to the Americas and Canada in the summer months. I was asked to help lay out floor plans, assign seating plans, and help passengers feel at home as soon as they came aboard the ship.

Chef Wolfgang Hanau, 2ⁿᵈ from right, Director of Food and Beverage at the luxury Cruise Liner Athens

I told Mr. Henry that I had applied for a position as steward in the dining rooms and restaurants. I wondered what had happened to make him change his mind when we met? I quickly realized that a great, unexpected opportunity had occurred—much more than I had wanted! I would be his personal assistant! Furthermore, I thought that once I was aboard the ship, I would probably be able to achieve greater experience and a better position than what I had wanted. I had heard stewards made a ton of money on cruises, many of them able to buy their own restaurants or hotels, becoming wealthier than even the captain.

"When do we sail?" I inquired.

"How is your English, Wolfgang?" he replied.

I continued my conversation in English only to learn that Mr. Henry's high school English was no match for what I had practiced for years in London, having received a bachelor's degree as an interpreter from Cambridge University. For the rest of the afternoon, Mr. Henry took me aboard my soon-to-be seagoing home for the following years.

The *Athens* was actually the smallest of a group of six cruise ships all owned by a Greek financial wizard. This proved to be a life-changing event for me. Quite obviously, a luxury liner, the boat, was for first-class passengers only. The lower decks, which were all the decks below main, remained closed during the cruise. On North Atlantic trips in the summer, all the decks, I was told, would be occupied. I was shown a very spacious kitchen, the two restaurants, many more bars, and the cabins on the upper decks. I would have private accommodation in a first-class cabin. There was no doubt that Mr. Henry had decided to put his best foot forward for my unique position working as his personal assistant and as number two in complete charge of the kitchens and all public facilities.

"Well, let's see, I would like you to be here with me in two days before we ship out" were the words I heard him say. "This gives you plenty of time to set up table assignments for the upcoming cruise, which is the number-one priority for both you and me. Here is how it works: Passengers can be assigned to dine at one of two different seatings in each of the restaurants. Most experienced English-speaking cruise passengers prefer a small table, for privacy. We therefore will keep the majority of preassigned seat tickets for the second seating for the smaller tables, which have been preassigned and are unknown to anybody but you and me. The tickets for the small tables will appear as if they had already been assigned."

Since the majority of passengers had cruised before, they invited the chief or me to visit them in their cabin as soon as they had completed their cabin check, not having received a seating assignment yet. When either Mr. Henry or I paid a visit to a cabin, we were able to produce the favorable tickets for the small table, which they had expected, and we were handsomely rewarded with great praise. We left it to everybody's guess how we were able to make it possible. That was the reality aboard the ship. Not realizing how rewarding my work would be, I had set my mind on working as a table steward on a part-time basis during one meal at dinnertime only. We would see! Having had the grand tour, and having met Captain Zacharia, the ship's captain, I found myself walking a bit tipsy halfway down the stairs from the bridge deck to the upper and main decks onto the gangway, until I was back on solid ground. With a small wave splashing my feet as a farewell, I was on my way back to Berlin, saying good-bye for now to the boat and my new chief.

I gave my notice and said good-bye to the Hilton Hotel after just about six months of working there. My mind was already aboard the *Athens* and with Mr. Henry. I decided to leave Berlin for Wuerzburg the next day, where I planned to rest for three to four days with

Mama, Rose, and Erich, who had just moved into their own new apartment on the outskirts of the city.

The time spent in Würzburg was a little hectic, with Mama making sure that I had enough underwear and socks, very important to all mamas and their traveling boys. "Just in case," Mama packed overstuffed sandwiches into my suitcase, but I didn't even notice them. Rose and Erich were so sweet as to offer their living room to me as my temporary bedroom, and Britta, their three-year-old baby daughter immediately became my favorite playmate and friend. We played in the nearby park or underneath clotheslines or any other imaginable spot in the neighborhood. Time flew by. No matter what happened now, I was going to work on the *Athens*. It was a sure thing.

The first time I handed out table cards, I was immediately able to make new friends with the passengers. Most passengers seated at the first dining time were friendly and easy to please. The passengers seated at the second dining were more demanding. The seating tickets were in either Mr. Rodenberg's or my pocket. I was aware that we would have to work the cabins after all passengers had arrived. I had to quickly understand this process. I also learned how the daily mileage at sea worked. The captain alone would be informed of the mileage traveled each day before passengers knew the mileage, and this was how the captain made good friends.

By the time we set sail on my first day at sea, I was very tired and ready to fall asleep. Ship life made me tired and ready for the next day's adventure.

We left Bremerhaven on our first cruise—to the Canary Islands. Our first stop was Lisbon, Portugal, a beautiful city to watch when approaching the harbor with tourists from the world over coming to buy antique silverware, silver serving trays, silver jewelry, and silver coffee and tea sets. One can find lots of such things in Lisbon priced as great bargains. After riding the "Flight of Angels," a taxi took me to the Christ in the Harbor statue. Many cruise ships, including our own, had made this sight the most popular attraction in Lisbon. From there it was on to Estoril, now home to toppled former monarchs of Europe. The soft hills above us showcased many elaborate estates sitting next to each other. Forgotten of what was many years ago only with memories of past glory. Then there were Lisbon's beautiful restaurants and private clubs that enjoyed regular visits from aristocrats. I was not able to resist a visit and sample some of the Portuguese foods. While most of the seafood was fried, the taste can be described as continental, cooked with a good dose of wine or alcohol. There was no food or meal I tasted that I thought to be a real knockout.

Crossing the Bay of Biscayne in rough waters for the first time, I experienced what it was like to be on a boat without stabilizers. We were physically thrown from one corner of the boat to the other, and my only desire was to go on deck, which was awash with slippery salt water. My only rescue was a few thick, heavy ropes to hold on to. Nevertheless, I was getting dreadfully sick, vomiting and turning a pale yellow in my face. I vowed to get off the ship as soon as possible at the next harbor. Mr. Henry watched me. I was struggling to stay on my feet, with only one desire on my mind—to make it back to my cabin and lie down. It would help me, I was sure. No such luck; Mr. Henry had locked my cabin. Coming out of his hideaway with a wry smile, he grabbed me. "No way, Wolfgang! You are not allowed to lie down. You'll get over this as soon as you get rid of all that is scary and the bad feeling and taste have come out of you. You will never get seasick again!" He was right, of course. I stayed on deck for a few more hours, and when it was time for me to go to bed at my regular time, I already felt much improved and almost fine. The following day we were still in the Bay of Biscayne, still on the boat, and my passport was in the captain's office. Thinking about the day before made me want to conquer the sea and this ship and not give up.

The stop after Lisbon was El Vigo, off the west coast of Spain. What a jewel on the bay. As it was dressed in dark clouds when we arrived, we were not able to see this small Spanish seacoast village in bright sunlight until a few hours later. El Vigo is a small, sleepy Spanish seacoast town with streets lined with cobblestones and washed-out lime trees. The roofs of most of these Spanish homes were overgrown with moss and covered with antiquated tiles, some broken and in need of repair. At night in my cabin I gave thanks to God for all I had seen and all that was yet to come.

Seeing the glory of past Roman settlements and the beauty of this small town before us, our steps took us ashore for a short time to walk through the village's narrow street, bathed now in sunshine. The oldest buildings at the very end of the street were home to the mayor, the police, and city hall. A post office was next to these official places and also signaled the beginning of a fishermen's paradise. Fishing boats stretched alongside the water all the way into the center of town. We were not able to spend more than two hours there. I imagined that the life of the people here must have been the same for a hundred years or more, the inhabitants living in peace and blessed with love for the rest of the world to see.

Our ship had become the town's sensation for the day, and children of all ages, shy and timid at first, came to life, taking a look at us and the boat. They eventually followed us to the gangway, asking for gifts and money. An accordion player joined the crowd, followed by a group of teenage girls who danced to his tunes, which were filled with happiness and enjoyed by everybody. We applauded their efforts and offered our tokens of appreciation.

When we were back aboard again, lunch was served. All the meals for the crew were cooked by our Greek crew members. The ship's crew did not participate in the passengers' meal menus. The Greek food was spiced with seasonings of the Mediterranean, such as thyme, oregano, basil, and marjoram.

Steaming ahead, we left for the island of Las Palmas, one of two of the Spanish-owned Canary Islands, which I was looking forward to seeing. I was also curious to see if life away from the Spanish homeland was like life we had seen in El Vigo. It was crowded with tall structures near the harbor, and I sorely missed the old Spanish architecture. Many European tourists lived here now, away from home. I read in the ship's newsletters that more Germans made their homes in Las Palmas than in Bremen. Indeed, I saw local newspapers printed in both Spanish and German. The British were here in smaller numbers, shying away from the expensive life on the island. But I met several Swiss families there. It can always be assumed that where the Germans and Swiss were on one day, the Americans would follow on the next.

On this first day in Las Palmas, I was scheduled to remain aboard on duty. My interest and attention were fully captivated by an incident I reluctantly observed. A young man was carried away by a group of older men. It appeared that he was trying to resist. I called one of the ship's officers to notify the police. When the police came, the same scenario was repeated several more times. I later learned that it was a custom for relatives of the boy's father to come and "rescue" the youngster from temptation. Today was Good Friday, a holy day. This old Catalonian custom, accompanied by loud, spiritual songs and music with trumpets and cymbals, preceded a long procession of women and children dressed in black. They were followed by men in colorful torero costumes that were red and gold, the colors of the Spanish flag. A large, heavy cross was carried by the men and women in the crowd to show the painful crucifixion of our Lord. Young women and children, not able to carry the heavy cross, fell on their knees while others took their place, helping to carry the burden. The procession took several hours and went on until darkness. The ship's crew and passengers were not supposed to embark or disembark until midnight. The crowd of mourners following the cross dispersed. We departed later than planned and should have been on our way to Tenerife a long time prior. A Spanish buffet of tapas and island food was served when we departed.

We arrived in Tenerife at noon the following day. It was Easter Sunday, and the sun was warm. Groups of schoolchildren singing Spanish folk songs awaited our ship on the docks. Sweet young voices sang and danced flamenco. A group of girls in their twenties also danced flamenco in colorful Spanish costumes. The governor and mayor of the Spanish province officially welcomed us to the larger of the two Spanish islands in the Canaries. It was all prepared as a welcome for us: dancing, music, island foods served from straw baskets, and wine from the Canaries. It was a paradise in the middle of the ocean. Happiness radiated from the faces of these beautiful people. It was Easter, and the arrival of our boat was exciting news. There were citizens of Spain and Germany and other European areas to welcome us.

I met Graf von Bollings, head of the legal department of a vast European industrial empire, who had moved to Tenerife, his second home now. He introduced us to his granddaughter, who was on vacation from Ulm, a city on the Danube known to many travelers for its magnificent single-tower Gothic cathedral. Any surrounding homes of natives living here year-round were modest in comparison to the home of the German industrialist. His plush Spanish-design home was surrounded with splendid flower gardens. His granddaughter, Kathen, offered to show us the island. Her grandfather had been voted the honorable mayor of Tenerife.

He invited me as his guest to enjoy a traditional Spanish Easter dinner at this home, and I gratefully accepted. His Spanish villa was magnificent in architecture and design. It was located on a hill with a fantastic panoramic view of the entrance to the harbor and of the harbor itself. He could see a thousandfold enlargement of life on the island with a telescope mounted on the high point of his property, leading to the balcony of his private quarters. One view showed sailors on our boat, on guard. The immediate impact it had on me was to make me change my plans and my lifestyle; I wanted to live on this island.

Madeira, Portugal's sole Canary Island, was on our schedule for the following two days. Many nautical miles before we arrived at the port of Funchal, the capital of Madeira, the shoreline of this shiny, bright island reflected a silver coating the likes of which I had never seen before. Did my eyes deceive me? Was this not utopia? Mountains with evergreen trees seemed to be dressed with the blues of the sky. Remembering pictures I had seen before, I was looking forward to seeing and experiencing this painting by nature in its great splendor. This epic picture was there right in front of me. The usual cloudy skies we had seen across islands we had visited before were not there. Soon we were surrounded by small rowboats and motorboats there to greet us. The port of Funchal was crowded with natives waiting for our cruise boat to arrive, as there was very little other work for them. Real life was suspended to welcome our boat. Small native boats were loaded with Madeira-embroidered linens that they tried to sell or barter for cigarettes. They sold beautiful hand-embroidered tablecloths, towels, linens, dresses, and even wedding gowns bearing flowers or canary birds. The asking price was reasonable compared to prices on the mainland. Some of their crafted linens were unfinished and sold for even less. For a carton of American cigarettes, they offered a large tablecloth and twelve matching napkins. Bottles of Madeira wine, offered by local stores, we were warned, could be of inferior quality. Real Madeira wine would best be purchased in the city. Very popular with tourists were summer sleigh rides under the hot sun from the top of a mountain to the harbor. This never failed to attract the attention of tourists. Snow for the sleigh rides in the summer was provided by fine sand from local beaches.

The sleigh ride was as smooth as it could be compared to the mountains at home in Bavaria. I was amazed and impressed to see and hear wild canaries making their homes here. With their brightly colored feathers, they appeared to be used to tourists. Some came to sit on our shoulders with the softest little feathers, but they were hard to touch or catch. The little birds made an incredible squeaky noise. The air in Madeira hurt my eyes. It was filled with tiny saltlike particles, which was annoying. I wondered if other tourists experienced the same thing. I remembered having a similar experience at the hot sulfur spa in Schinznach Bad, Switzerland. I remember that the manager there, Herr Schaerer, had previously worked at Reid's Hotel in Funchal. I planned to see the hotel, curious about how it would compare to the Swiss hotel where I had worked for several seasons. Reid's Hotel, which was off the coast of West Africa, was called "the Grand Old Dame" of all island hotels. The hotel was a true treasure to behold. I will always remember my first impression of the immaculately trimmed green lawns dotted with light purple and snow-white bouquets of flowers looking down from the hotel's balconies at its arriving guests. The entrance looked like another beautiful large portal of flowers. The projected elegance of the hotel belied all of the poverty just a few hundred yards down from the mountain. One could not see locals walking through the bronzed iron gates bearing the hotel's name painted in gold letters.

Long, soft-colored carpets connected the gates to the entrance of the hotel.

Casablanca was our first stop on the African continent. Cruises took us there during spring and in summer. Every possible national shipping line makes at least one stop in Casablanca. The huge port was surrounded with cargo containers and refineries. Many ships had started from here to travel all over the world. Casablanca was the final stop on our winter and spring cruise before we returned to Southampton. The port in Casablanca was always an adventure, blending the old African traditions with the new. Even cruise passengers were looking forward to going shopping here in the native stores for handwoven carpets, camel saddles, and other unique paraphernalia. Others wanted to go gambling in the largest, most elaborately furnished casino on the African continent and see the classic bar from the movie *Casablanca*, starring Humphrey Bogart and Ingrid Bergman, still named Rick's American Bar. The ship's crew also could not wait to get there for their last shopping spree before going home. My schedule allowed me to accept an invitation by a duke's family from the midlands, friends of Sir Winston. I was shown pictures of the famous Blenheim Palace and other national treasures of England where Sir Winston was born. The duke each winter booked three cruises for his family. He loved our ship and knew many of the crew. This was to be the final one this spring. I enjoyed speaking to members of his family, and we became acquainted—so much so that he invited me as his personal guest to stay at his grand estate.

It was a warm, but not hot, day in Casablanca, with the air getting really hot after the month of April. The duke took me along with his family for a rickshaw ride through the original old town of Casablanca, which I remembered from the movie. It was a rough ride over cobblestones—a very rough ride.

A member of the royal family of Morocco, being a business partner with the owners of our shipping line, took pleasure in inviting the officers of our ship to his palatial home on the coast of Morocco, just more than one hundred miles northwest of Casablanca. This proved to be a story out of the book of *One Thousand and One Nights*. The palace, built of imported snow-white marble from Italy, could not have been more beautiful in anyone's imagination. Illuminated at night, Bedouins sang native Arabian songs of eternal life and the everlasting peace of all people on earth. We were able to hear their beautiful voices loud and clear, sounding strange to our ears.

When we arrived, the palatial gates opened seemingly magically and we were immediately stopped there by Moroccan guards. Following an Arabian horseman riding ahead of us, we were whisked into the silver moonlight. We were asked to leave our cars behind. Few words were spoken. We were offered to choose between a horseback or camel ride to the palace. Mr. Henry, who was also an invited guest, chose the camel ride, and so did I. The camel ride to the palace was slow, and we arrived there in an hour. To our surprise, the enclosed ménage of our first welcome was delivered by a beautiful young veiled woman who bade us welcome, speaking perfect English without an accent. We were expected and welcomed by hostesses in flawless Arabian veils and in native dresses, with their bare feet in silver sandals. They escorted us to the dinner table and began serving. Seated on an elaborate flower-blossom-loaded table was the Arabian-dressed hostess, who had been our escort and was our company for the evening. The young hostess at my side was from Nice, France. She told me her story, which sounded like a fairy tale of being invited for dinner to the Ritz Hotel by an Arabian prince while vacationing on the French Riviera. Little did she expect that she would accept an invitation to live as his guest at the palace with all of the privileges extended to his own family, together with her mother and baby, who were waiting for her in France.

Chef Wolfgang Hanau's Elephant ride with a load of Arabian carpets in Casa Blanca

A cavalry of Arabian horsemen riding Arabian horses helped us get to a building occupied by the prince. Our first view was that of a most elegant, richly furnished Moroccan dining hall. At the far corner an American jazz band played Glenn Miller and other music to dance to. On the center of the dining table was an ice carving of an Arabian horse that had been carved into a block of ice. The meal was French, with a few dishes prepared by a German chef at the palace. His father and he both loved everything German, and he told me that he owned a fleet of thirteen custom-built Mercedes-Benz cars.

I had been invited to the celebration of my lifetime in those years when I traveled the world. We were brought back to our boat, the mighty cruise liner *Athens*. Never had I seen before, nor have I seen since, the display of wealth I saw in Arabian countries. Neither have I seen any greater poverty. Many of those living in the city of Casablanca slept overnight in manmade holes underneath the sand of the Sahara desert.

But there was also "Swiss Town" in a different part of Casablanca. This part of Casa Blanca had evergreen lawns and homes built in the style and architecture of Switzerland. The streets in Swiss Town were lined with European-run shops and restaurants managed by European chefs and businessmen.

The large contingent of the European and American populations in Casablanca could afford to pay for luxuries imported from the Continent. Prices charged for merchandise here were equal to those prices charged in Basel or Zurich. My own walks in the morning would take me to the Casablanca carpet market. Handwoven Moroccan, Tunisian, Algerian, and genuine Persian carpets, camel saddles, jewelry, and leather goods made from camel leather interwoven with camel hair were on display and for sale. The bargaining expected by merchants in Arabian countries is fierce. While we were en route to Marrakesh, we experienced the severest of all African earthquakes in Agadir. Because of the terrible consequences of this earthquake, most of the roads to and from Marrakesh, Morocco's capital, and into the interior of the country, were destroyed. Nevertheless, we were permitted to travel into the deserts of the Sahara. Bedouins and caravans of camels laden with spices and incense stopped just ahead of us in what was seemingly the home village of the wandering tribe. We walked past tents with displays of exotic herbs and spices. The perfume of their displays reminded me of phantasies in fairy tales and travels into the magic of Arabian wonderlands. Street vendors with magical goods and displays of strangely cooked foods were for sale, but nobody we asked knew the origins of the goods. The streets were seemingly endless, and nobody knew where they began or ended.

Our day's trip ended in Fedalah. This rather splendid seaside resort was built and owned by local principals, who were our hosts. The resort was built solely for the pleasure of invited European friends and business partners. The absolute luxury was recognized throughout all appointments. Starting at the palace, all accommodations culminated in luxury spa apartments and elegant restaurants serving an abundance of exotic foods and wines, which was overwhelming. A nearby airport, a private airfield, had been especially built for guests from overseas and Europe. The major principal used his private airplanes to travel frequently to Paris, Geneva, Munich, and Rome, I was informed. On that day, as several private planes landed, nobody seemed to take notice of the new arrivals that were in a class of their own. Monarchs of foreign countries and tycoons from European and American banks met here to play for pleasure.

As the fishing season for sardines and the season for locally grown mandarins, figs, and dates came to an end, so did our own cruise come to an end in Casablanca. My last visit into the city took me to the casino. I was the only player of roulette on one table, with perhaps fifty tables open. I was rewarded with a hefty win, my biggest ever at any casino. I walked back to the ship. We were scheduled to set sail the next morning, back to England, to Southampton or Bournemouth. Mrs. Gates, widow of the late Mr. Gates of Bournemouth had invited me to visit her at their home in the south of England while our ship was in dry dock for at least a week. She mentioned to me the names of the city's most famous spas. Bournemouth, England, is known as the city of culture, music, galleries, and some excellent restaurants. My stay was particularly enhanced by the popular recognition of Mrs. Gates as one of our company's most valued passengers. Mrs. Gates took every first-class cruise offered year-round. Her driver picked us up at the harbor. Her house was large yet simple, beautifully furnished with the finest imported pieces of antique furniture. Her gardens were trimmed in the English manner and tradition. Her trees and shrubs were shaped like flowers and animals, camels and horses, wild beasts and peacocks. The lawns were neatly trimmed and groomed to accommodate all of the summer flowers of England—gladiolas, tulips, and roses—which were in full bloom. Every crew member on the *Athens* knew Mrs. Gates as our most valuable customer. Everybody knew her by name. Everybody loved her.

Mrs. Gates was known to stewards as a good tipper. A car accident years ago had left her without the use of either one of her legs. She was wheelchair bound. Her friendliness and true Christian nature made her very lovable. She loved herself and others alike, smiling at people she never had met. She was in love with our world and with her inner self. Her outer appearance was never of any consequence. She reflected and brought to this world peace, love, happiness, and harmony. Anguish, hatred, vengeance, and discontent were unknown to her. Meeting Mrs. Gates for the first time, one was taken by her true beauty. She was able to show what it meant to be here on Earth and to love one another. I was one of the few aboard the ship to spend some special time with her, getting to know her closely.

A call from Mama came while I stayed with Mrs. Gates. I had waited for this call since leaving Berlin almost two years before. The message was an invitation to visit the American consulate in Frankfurt, for my visa was now available for me to be able to immigrate to the United States. I had to be ready to go and immigrate within a month. I was overjoyed. Thomas F. Robinson, brother of the chairman of Coca-Cola of Rhode Island, was my sponsor. I had met him on one of his trips to Cobh, Ireland, both as he crossed the Atlantic from Boston and then again on his way back. We became friends, having in common not only classical music and culinary arts but also the art of communication. He then promised to arrange for me to be able to immigrate to the United States.

Mama had made her own plans to travel together for a month while I was waiting for my visa. She planned for me to travel with her to Venice and Rome, with stops in Bad Gastein and Vienna. Mama had made arrangements in advance for both of our train tickets and for everything else we could possibly need. What wonderful memories I would be able to take with me. At long last we would take our long-planned trip together, just Mama and me. Mama took her painting utensils, and I took my Hohner harmonica. We promised to travel light. Each of us carried a small suitcase that could easily be taken onto the train and everywhere else when we wanted to rest. We had no agenda or plans other than to be with each other this last month. We planned to stay in private homes whenever possible to avoid high-priced hotels. The only exception would be Vienna at the Hotel Sacher, when we stayed at pensions in Rome and Venice and at a sun- and flower-filled villa on the island of Capri. We went to Naples and Herculaneum and came back from Capri to Sorrento and its beautiful orange groves lining the streets along the seaside.

In Naples we had to try true southern Italian cooking. Laced with the earthy flavors of olive oil, the cooking complemented the narrow streets, crowded with happy, laughing children singing Neapolitan folk songs. I remembered the voice of my favorite Italian tenor, Guiseppe de Stefano, who grew up in Naples. What a blessing to live here under the everlasting sun, with oceans and the history of early Christians and the Apostle Paul writing letters from prison that would shape the world and our lives. Several restaurants served fresh seafood on top of pasta, pizza with fresh mozzarella, and all the good things from this part of the peninsula.

We visited an old, rustic southern Italian seafood trattoria to try endless dishes and enjoy their oyster dishes, which are well known to Neapolitan cooking. The most delicious shellfish dish was served with white truffles, mushrooms, and red strings of fresh saffron served over a very thin homemade spaghetti-type pasta, with a tomato sauce made from local fresh tomatoes and lots of garlic.

But a boat we had booked to Capri would leave at six in the morning, and we had to hurry to get some sleep. On our way to the hotel, we were joined by Carlos, a Neapolitan troubadour who serenaded Mama with songs and spoke of Naples and the beauty of the island of Capri, where he lived. His curiosity to learn of our plans for the following day was well rewarded when he learned what our plans were for the next few days.

The boat trip to Capri was uneventful, with natives of the island going home loaded with goods they had bought in Naples. And there were more tourists taking the trip to Capri.

The sun in Capri was shining brightly, and it felt to us to be wonderfully warm. Carlos had waited for us in Naples at the foot of the boat, and as soon as we stepped aboard, he joined us. He would follow us during the rest of our stay as our self-appointed local guide and musically gifted companion. We liked the hotel villa he had recommended, which offered us two wonderful views from our rooms overlooking the Adriatic Sea and beautifully appointed flowering Mediterranean gardens.

One day we walked to Anacapri, visiting Axel Munte's villa

on our way across the island. It was completely refurbished in the Emperor Augustus style of ancient Rome.

Mama brought along a few small excavation tools, and we tried to find small treasures underneath old, historic ruins; this was permitted by law in some places on the island. Digging carefully so as not to break any of the treasures we hoped to take home, we were blessed with a handful of broken pottery pieces.

We also walked a street named "Via Krupp" after Baron Von Krupp, whose family owned an old Roman-Etruscan-built estate near the southern shores of Anacapri.

The Blue Grotta, to our big disappointment, was not bathed in a blue light at all and did not live up to what we had expected from the photos we had seen in travel brochures.

After the days of long walks in the sun and digging for treasures, we took the boat back to picturesque Sorrento.

As dusk was setting, we were still in Sorrento with no idea where to go but to catch a train up north. The next train, a local train, was scheduled to leave at night to our next stop, Senegalia, where we decided to sleep overnight. We left the station and walked into a small, quiet, and cute village. It looked as if the village were in the process of growing, with new homes being built all over. Our eyes were focused, looking for rooms to rent or possibly just for overnight accommodations. What we found was a darling little house, smack on the ocean, with a hand-painted sign in one of the windows.

My little handheld dictionary did the expected job for us. We were made welcome and shown to two connecting rooms with a shared bathroom on the upper of two floors. Giovanni and his two teenage sons were quick to offer to get our luggage, which was not much, from the train station. And after a thoroughly cleansing shower, both Mama and I were totally ready to accept an invitation for home-cooked Italian foods in one of the local trattorias. But to our surprise, we had hardly reached the bottom of the staircase when Stella, Giovanni's wife, took both of us on one of her arms to escort us to an absolutely charmingly laid-out dining room.

The long table and eight chairs were bleached white from the salty ocean air and sunlight. The table was set with an enormous selection of Italian antipasti, salads, and pasta with seafood, beef, veal, and pork. The desserts included a foamy variety of sabayoni and fruit tarts. I can honestly say that I had never seen a display of so many Italian delicacies, and my mouth was watering as I could hardly wait to sit down. We prayed and listened to the soft guitar music played by Carlos, one of the sons of the family, and the high tenor voice of his brother. It could not have been more romantic or "Italian." The candles were lit and placed on the table and in the windows. Wine was poured from large straw-covered bottles and carafes, and we were ready to give thanks again with our hands folded and heads bowed. In the air was the definite smell of freshly baked breads. Mama and I decided to take a long walk along the water after dinner and we were looked at curiously by neighbors sitting on the steps of their homes or just being together with a glass of wine, enjoying the cool breeze and fresh air of the sea.

When we returned to our Senegalia home on the sea, I was able to make arrangements with Giovanni to go fishing with him in the morning. Giovanni was a fisherman. This is how he made his living. He assured me that we would catch "rubies of the sea," and I was ready to learn what it was that he called rubies. Mama decided to get her painting materials ready and walk to the ocean to paint our home. Time after time we laughed when we thought of our plans, wishing to go to Sicily.

We also kept in touch with Rose and asked her to open any big envelope addressed to me from the American consulate. She told me that my visa for the United States was waiting to be picked up this month. It was now time for us to go home and have the beauty and stillness of Senegalia and going on our way north with a stop in Florence. The city was known for its many silver, gold, and jewelry shops on the Ponte Vecchio. We looked forward to seeing the works of master painters Michelangelo, Da Vinci, and others on view in churches or publicly displayed.

In just two days we were ready to go on. We wanted to stop in Bolzano and take a train to Merano. We knew the Bavarian Alps, but the Italian Dolomite Alps were very special. We knew that the wines grown here were rich, with bouquets of wildflowers and fruits. They were different from our crisp, clean wines. Their color, similar to that of the country wines of southern France, sparkled with a red velvet shade. Their aromas were very fragrant and sweet. We also remembered that our ancestors, before immigrating to East Prussia, came from the Tirol region of Austria. Many of the people here spoke German by choice. The locals went out of their way to make us feel very welcome.

Merano is a neat, modern, beautiful alpine mountain resort. There are beautiful promenades bordering the mountain slopes. Meadows were filled with the smell of small fringed yellow mountain flowers, and many of the leafy, full-bodied older trees showed an orange-brown color on their bark, as deep in color as the Tyrolean wines. We spent a few days here before returning again to Vienna with a stopover in Bad Gastein, which we had enjoyed so much on our way to Italy weeks earlier. We enjoyed hearty Austrian food: *Kaiserschmarrn*, Wiener schnitzel, and roasted veal. Austrian wines may be the most underrated wines in the world. We enjoyed the wines greatly, their texture like honey. We took a ride into the countryside. Mama almost bought an old mountain farmhouse near where our ancestral home was located. She loved this part of the world. But walking through the house, we felt it must have been abandoned for many years. It was probably too costly to restore it to its original state, especially because it was very close to Vienna. Vienna is one of the most cosmopolitan cities of Europe, with lots of things to do and with very busy streets. My painter friend, Franz Bueb, the officially appointed painter of the Viennese Opera House and the Lipizzaner horses, made his home here. The Vienna woods and the Danube River were a romantic sight and will not be forgotten. Our visit included the *Heurigen Wein Stuben*, spread out in beautiful gardens with the background of many of the operettas and waltzes of Johann Strauss.

Once we had arrived again at the old Sacher Hotel, we made a stop at the Sacher Café and pastry shop. What a treat! The day of departure from Vienna came too soon and ended our vacation. We were looking out the windows on our trip home, stopping first in Munich then going on to Würzburg, where Rose, Erich, and Britta awaited us.

On our first morning in Wurzburg the day was sunny and quite warm. Mama had rented a one-bedroom apartment on top of Dressel's butcher shop. In the meantime we waited for Mama's apartment to be completely redone. This would be in the center of Wurzburg, near the archbishop's residence. Mama and I went out to eat every day in different restaurants, and we walked a lot. We remembered some who had passed away. Mama enjoyed speaking of her past as a young woman and of our time together when I was a child.

Mama and I walked alongside the Main River on many evenings, looking into windows of art galleries, many of them showing Mama's paintings. "Wolfi," she said, holding my hand very strongly, "you must know that God has blessed me in a special way to be alive and to know what to do and work in my life. If you wish to confirm what

I told you, inhale the beautiful aroma of good spirits that are with us, who are walking with us." She had told me before of her experience with good spirits surrounding her with the fragrant dust of aromas from heaven. We would visit one of the many small, intimate wine cafés near the monastery and the river. I always kept in mind that our time together would be short and precious, with moments of love and appreciation for each other and God.

Mama told me of her visit to the Julius Spital Hospital, where she met one of the fascinating and great writers of the postwar era, Frau Dr. Arndt, who was called to be a member of Dr. Adfenauer's first postwar cabinet in West Germany. These wonderful conversations and Mama's spiritual experiences will stand out forever in my memory of her.

We returned to Rose and Erich and her pretty little three-year-old girl, Britta. This is where I read the good news of the letter she had received in my absence. Two of the passengers I had met at TSS New York had arranged to sponsor me to come to the United States. I went to visit Mama's travel agency to book a cabin on the QE2, leaving from Southampton to New York. With my savings from working on the boat and in Berlin, and with a generous gift from Mama, I was able to pay for the ticket. This was all I had. My vision of going to America had always been centered on doing things the way the early immigrants of that great country had done to make a go of it. Mr. Robinson, the chairman of the Coca-Cola Company, had told me that he came as a nonpaying passenger to America from Ireland, jumping the boat and delivering papers and messages, and that is how he had started his life in America.

I remember God told me that not until 2015 would I understand God's words in Isaiah 64:4: "God acts on behalf of those who wait for him."

It is difficult to understand how to mature, since we also believe that God is telling us to go ahead and do things now. "God helps those who help themselves." Mama was blessed with supernatural wisdom, and she encouraged me to wait until God was ready to open the right door for me. It really was not for me to understand God's will. Not knowing the way God wanted me to walk, I remembered the time of our rescue from the approaching Russians before the war came to an end.

I decided I wanted to start my new life in New York, and New York it was! Thomas F. Robinson, the postmaster of Pawtucket in Rhode Island, would meet me and welcome me to New York and America.

Mr. Robinson and his family came in a huge station wagon to pick me up. He had never told me a thing about his family. I had no idea that he had seven children! They all fit into the wagon and showed painted signs reading, "Wolfgang, Welcome to America." Mr. Thomas's face was filled with an expression of kindness, and his eyes seemed to be laughing—an impression I will always remember when I think of him. "We have come to take you home, Wolfgang. We all are very anxious and excited to see you getting started," he said. "My brother is the one for you to see." And he emphasized the fact that as the chairman of Coca-Cola, he would be able to open the door for me to any hotel in New York. I was only vaguely aware at the time of the importance of Coca-Cola in the world, since Coca-Cola was not sold in Germany at this time. I also did not understand the importance of being chairman of the United Fund. I had just arrived in America where "everything is possible." My immediate concern was where to stay with my very limited cash of $120.00 and seeking a job. "Mr. Thomas, where should I stay overnight?" The $120.00 I had would have to pay for food and transportation and anything else. But, I knew that I was a strong walker. Of course, taxis did not come to my mind.

Off we drove to the YMCA on Thirty-Fourth Street, just off Fifth Avenue, near the New York City library, which was a landmark I wanted to remember. My primary job was to find work. I knew that God was with me. I know now that it was always my ability to make it on my own. I had faith in God that He would always provide for me and answer all my prayers. I went to quite a few hotels, knocking on doors, and I was always sent to the next place because I did not belong to a union. One of the hotels I tried was the #1 Fifth Avenue Hotel, near Washington Square. Walking through the sparsely furnished hotel lobby to the reception desk, all I noticed were the scattered little old ladies sitting on worn-out sofas with designs of autumn leaves on them. For some reason I felt very good, thinking that this would be the starting place for me in America. A bellman referred me to the hotel owner's offices on Park Avenue, where I first met with Morton Wolf, his brother, the other owner of the hotel. He made it very clear to me that he was concerned about my personal background in Germany. I must have given them the answers they wanted to hear, as I was offered a job as a maître d', taking the place of a man who had left for vacation for one month.

I then searched and found a modest hotel room close to the hotel in the Village on Eighth Street, at a place called the Marlboro Hotel. I met my first friend in New York at work, Evan, a piano student at the Julliard School of Music. He played at the piano bar every night where I worked. He particularly enjoyed playing the tunes from *The Sound of Music*; I think that he played that music to please me and remind me of my home in the mountains of Bavaria and Austria. The bar was considered very successful. There was always a full house. The drinking was heavy, and many cases of empty bottles had to be exchanged from the storeroom each day. Evan was a tall, rather shy young man in his early twenties. He invited me to visit him at his furnished room in upper Manhattan on a Sunday afternoon. There I listened to him playing the piano while a record player added the music of an orchestra to accompany his music for a piano concerto. I enjoyed his company and the music.

I worked every evening at the #1 Bar, and I wanted to understand how to get around New York City and what bus or subway I should use to get from place to place. I also needed to find a place to eat, with a modest budget of two dollars per day. Every day for a couple of days I sent a picture card to Mama, which I knew she would enjoy. She wrote back telling me that everybody expected me to be a millionaire soon. After four weeks, my job came to an end as soon as the maître d' returned from his vacation, which I had expected. I was offered a job as the restaurant manager at the Volnay Hotel, on the Upper East Side of Manhattan. The general manager of the hotel was Mr. Lewiston. He was a soft-spoken man and very quiet. I liked Mr. Lewiston from the very first time I met him. A few years before we met, he had a heart attack. He had to be very careful going up the stairs, and he was not to get stressed or excited. He did not speak too much, and I liked that too. I was curious to find out how he would communicate with the two owners. Unlike him, they liked to speak.

I gave up my room at the Marlboro Hotel downtown since traveling took too long and was too expensive. Mr. Lewiston showed me an ad from the *New York Times* for a furnished room at 142 East Seventy-First Street, not too far from the Volnay. I tried to get an appointment with Mrs. Euros, the owner. Her full married name was Eurostophis, a Bulgarian name she had adopted after marrying Anthony. The building was an old brown-brick twelve-story structure, home to wealthy New York singles and couples, and the rent was very high. Everywhere I went in New York, I was able to meet famous and interesting people, who were always very nice to me. Movie stars like Audrey Hepburn lived across the street on Seventy-First Street. I was happy to move out of the Marlboro in the Village because somebody had climbed up the outside ladder, come through the window, and stole my treasured camera I had brought with me from Germany, a Voigtlander. The hotel manager did not care; nor did he do anything about it. He said that it was my fault for not closing the window.

Mrs. Euros looked elegant and sophisticated and well educated. She was also an interior decorator and had published a book under the name Marjorie. She had obviously been brought up in a well-mannered way. Her father had served as an admiral at sea. She went to school in Washington, DC, before she was married. She had inherited a small fortune, but very little was left when I moved into her apartment. My room used to be the servants' quarters, but there were no servants when I arrived. Her husband was a native of Bulgaria and, according to her, was a freeloader who did nothing. He had gone through every bit of her inheritance in the few years they had lived together. They had been married five years when I met her. Mrs. Euros had no income, savings, or investments. It appeared that all the money she had was the rent I paid for the room. We enjoyed each other's company and our conversations at night after work. I thought that she and Mama could have been really good friends. They both had similar backgrounds in arts and a solid intellectual education. She told me that she had finally decided to go to Reno for a divorce from Anthony. She left without telling him about it and asked me to take charge of the apartment. Anthony had left after she departed, but he came by a couple of times to collect a few things he had forgotten. After only three weeks in Reno, Margo was back in New York, and she was very happy that the burden of her ex was no longer on her back. He was no longer her responsibility.

Anthony, in the meantime, was living the high life who knows how. He invited me to come to his Rockefeller office. It consisted of a suite of three offices with his name prominently displayed at the entrance in gold letters. I wondered out loud if it must have come as a shock to him when Margo decided to go to Reno for the divorce. He no longer would be able to afford flying to Europe with a Cadillac and chauffeur. That had been his lifestyle for five years. Who knows how he had managed to move into a new apartment on Fifth Avenue at Eighty-Sixth Street. Margo did not know, because her only bank account at Chase was empty. She did, however, go to help him get organized on Fifth Avenue. Under the circumstances, I am convinced he would have been better off living in Europe, perhaps. Margo told me that he identified himself as an industrialist with huge holdings in oil futures from Libya. None of this, of course, was true.

Time went by quickly, and I was fully occupied in my new position at the Park Lane Hotel. I remember when Margo invited me for dinner one night at the Mayfair and the King Kong Bar. Neither of us, for sure, was able to afford it, but she insisted on inviting me, being too proud to show the outside world that she no longer could afford to live the lifestyle of her past. The surroundings at the Mayfair Hotel were elegant, attracting people dressed to the nines, but so was Margo. She wore a black silk dress that fell loosely from her broad shoulders, and she was partially covered by an old, slightly worn, thin mink stole.

Not too long ago I had changed my job from the Volnay, where the old ladies came for a tuna sandwich roll and iced tea, to the Park Lane Hotel on Park Avenue. I was made very welcome at the Park Lane Hotel, where Mr. Gerald Parker was the general manager, and I enjoyed speaking to Margo about my recent change for the better.

The Park Lane Hotel, which was later renamed the TWA Building, was opposite the Waldorf Astoria and, facing east, opposite the Barclay Hotel, where Mr. Robinson, of the Coca Cola company, maintained his offices.

Lady Astor, Sir Winston Churchill, and Hollywood actors like Errol Flynn liked to stay at the old-fashioned but well-kept luxurious suites at the Park Lane, entertaining at the Tapestry Room for lunch, brunch, or dinner. Just after working with Fred Stamm, the executive steward, Mr. Parker asked me to manage the Tapestry Room. Mr. Parker showed great faith in my work, receiving many compliments from managers. His associate, John Weber, the banquet director, became a special friend and colleague of mine, and so did the German chef George Eisenberg, who had been at the Park Lane for more than twenty years.

An incident I will never forget got the chef in trouble with the union because of the pastry chef coming from the islands. He did next to nothing to deserve the title of a pastry chef, since the Park Lane bought pastries from the Roosevelt Hotel, which was also part of NYC Central Railroad Hotels. He was, however the shop chairman of the local union at the Park Lane Hotel. Taking his union position too much to heart, he told George Eisenberg, the executive chef, not to participate in the service of banquets. Mr. Eisenberg had many attributes, but patience was not one of them. He made this very clear to the pastry man with a kick step into his ———, which caused the entire kitchen crew to laugh at the union boss. The union complained to Mr. Parker, who had to hold his hand above the chef to prevent him from being fired.

Managing the Tapestry Room at the Park Lane was a privilege that had to be earned, and it was a compliment, as I had been working less than one year in New York City. The Park Lane was considered a deluxe hotel at the level of the Waldorf Astoria, the Plaza, and the Pierre Hotel. Two of the regular customers in the Tapestry Room were Mr. Roemer and Mr. Dillard, president and chairman, respectively, of the Princess Hotel in Bermuda.

Koehl, Landis and Landan, inc.

Advertising

May 1st, 1959

PARK LANE
Newspaper ad - 50 lines

```
            L U N C H E O N
            on Park Avenue

       A handsome way to entertain
       business associates, when
       you pause for a mid-day re-
       past in the quiet elegance
       of the Tapestry Room.  Park
       Avenue sunshine filters through
       Vienna Shades, and adds cheer
       to the rich Burgundy decor and
       soft glow of crystal chandel-
       iers.  Excellent cuisine is
       enhanced by punctilious service.
       Smart for cocktails and dinner,
       too.

          TAPESTRY ROOM

       P A R K    L A N E
       Park Ave., 48th to 49th Sts.
       PLaza 5-4100
```

*NY Times referral to the Park Lane Tapestry Room
managed by Chef Wolfgang Hanau*

CHAPTER 4

Recipes

Recipes in this chapter are not only from countries mentioned in chapters 1, 2, and 3 of this book but also from parts of the world I visited later in my travels, which will be covered in my next book, *My Travel Adventures and Secret Recipes, Book 2.*

RECIPES

APPETIZERS-STARTERS-SOUPS

BREADS

BURGERS

CHICKEN-DUCKLING

DESSERTS
CAKES–CUPCAKES–TORTAS

CHEESECAKES

EGGS–PANCAKES–FRITTATAS–CREPES–WAFFLES

FISH–SEAFOOD–OYSTERS–SHELLFISH

GRAIN

HERBS

ICE CREAMS

LETTUCE

MEAT

PASTA-NOODLES

PEPPERS

POTATOES

RICE

RAINFOREST ACAI BERRY COOKIES

Yield: 24 cookies

1½ cup stone-ground whole-wheat flour

1 teaspoon baking powder

1 teaspoon baking soda

1 cup chopped macadamia nuts, toasted

½ cup freeze-dried acai berries (available in health food stores, including Whole Foods markets)

1 cup date sugar, divided

½ cup smooth, unsweetened apple sauce

¼ cup canola or palm oil

1 tablespoon grated orange zest

3 tablespoons acai berry juice

DIRECTIONS:

1. Whisk flour, baking powder, and baking soda in a large bowl.
2. Whisk ¾ cup sugar, applesauce, oil, orange zest, and juice in a medium bowl until smooth. Make a well in center of dry ingredients and pour in all wet ingredients. Mix until well blended. Cover with plastic wrap and chill for 30 minutes.
3. Preheat oven to 350 degrees. Line a baking sheet with parchment paper or a nonstick baking mat.
4. Put remaining sugar into a small flat-bottomed dish or pan. Roll the dough with floured hands (it will be very wet) into 1½" balls, then roll in sugar to coat. Place 2 inches apart on the prepared baking pan.
5. Bake cookies until lightly browned, 12–15 minutes. Cool on the pan for a minute and then transfer to a wire rack to cool completely.

AMSTEL LIGHT PORTOBELLO GORGONZOLA BURGER

Yield: 4 servings

1 bottle Amstel Light, flat
4 (4") portobello caps
¼ teaspoon salt
¼ teaspoon black pepper
2 tablespoons minced garlic, divided
1 tablespoon chopped Italian parsley
2 teaspoons light olive oil
¾ cup (2 ounces) crumbled gorgonzola cheese
3 tablespoons reduced-fat mayonnaise
4 (2-ounce) whole-wheat kaiser rolls or ciabatta rolls, lightly toasted
2 cups trimmed arugula
½ cup bottled roasted peppers, sliced

DIRECTIONS:

1. In a bowl accommodating 4 portobello caps, combine 1 bottle flat Amsteel Light, salt, pepper, half the garlic, and chopped parsley. Mix well. Marinate portobellos for up to 1 hour.

2. Dry portobellos on paper towels. Season again to your taste with salt, pepper.

3. Heat olive oil in large nonstick skillet over medium-high heat. Sauté 4 minutes or until tender, turning once. Add remaining garlic to pan, sauté 30 seconds. Remove from heat.

4. Combine cheese and mayonnaise, stirring well. Spread about 2 tablespoons mayonnaise mixture over bottom half of each roll. Top each serving with ½ cup arugula and 2 tablespoons peppers. Place 1 mushroom on each serving and top with halves of rolls.

GOLDEN APPLE CHEDDAR PANCAKES

Yield: 2 servings

2 tablespoons unsalted butter

1 large sweet apple (I prefer Gala or Golden Delicious), peeled and
 cored and cut into ¼" wedges

½ cup whole or skim milk

½ cup unbleached all-purpose flour

4 eggs, lightly whipped

½ cup golden mild or medium sharp cheddar, cut into ¼-inch cubes

¼ cup ricotta cheese

3 tablespoons sugar

½ teaspoon vanilla extract

¼ teaspoon salt

½ cup chopped walnuts

½ cup golden raisins

powdered sugar for dusting

FOR CINNAMON-SUGAR RICOTTA CHEESE

Stir together ½ cup ricotta and 2¼ tablespoons cinnamon sugar (2
 tablespoons sugar blended with ¼ teaspoon cinnamon)

DIRECTIONS:

1. Position rack in middle of oven and preheat to 450 degrees F.
2. Melt butter in a medium (9" or 10") skillet over medium heat, then
   transfer 1 tablespoon to a blender.
3. Add apple wedges to the skillet and cook, turning once, until they
   start to soften (approximately 3 minutes).
4. Arrange wedges around edge of skillet.
5. Meanwhile, mix milk, flour, eggs, sugar, vanilla, and salt with butter
   in blender. Blend until batter is smooth. Add cheddar and ricotta. Stir
   and pour over apples. Sprinkle with walnuts and raisins.
6. Transfer skillet to oven. Bake for fifteen minutes or until pancake is
   puffed and golden. Dust with powdered sugar, cut into wedges, and
   serve immediately with bowl of cinnamon-sugar ricotta.

APPLE JAM–FILLED COOKIES

Yield: 16 cookie bars

3 cups plus 2 tablespoons whole-wheat flour, divided
1 teaspoon sea salt
1¼ cups (2½ sticks) butter, chilled and cubed
1 large egg, beaten
5 tablespoons water
1 tablespoon apple cider vinegar
6 cups sliced, cored, and peeled apples
½ cup apple juice.
1½ cups light brown sugar
½ teaspoon cinnamon
2 tablespoons whole-wheat flour
4 tablespoons tapioca
2 tablespoons soy milk

DIRECTIONS:

1. In a mixing bowl combine 3 cups of flour with salt. With fork, crumble butter into flour mixture. Set aside.
2. In a second bowl combine egg, water, and vinegar. Pour into flour-crumb mixture and stir until just combined. Shape the bowl into 2 balls.
3. Preheat oven to 425 degrees F.
4. On a clean, floured surface, roll out half the dough to fit a 10" × 15" baking sheet, leaving a ½" border on the sides. Place dough on baking sheet. Set aside.
5. In a medium bowl, combine apples, sugar, cinnamon, 2 tablespoons flour, and tapioca. Bring to a boil, stirring occasionally until apples are soft. Allow to cool. Arrange over dough on baking sheet in an even layer.
6. Roll out remaining dough and cover apple jam. Brush top of dough with milk. Bake 10 minutes. Lower heat to 375 degrees F and bake an additional 25 minutes. Cool completely, and trim outer ½" of crust from all sides. (Use trimmings as crumbs for ice cream desserts.) Cut remaining dough into 16 jam-filled cookies. Sprinkle with powdered sugar and place underneath broiler for sugar to caramelize.

APPLE PIE AND CHERRY WALNUT COBBLER

Yield: 2-4 dessert servings

1 tablespoon shortening

4 cups store-bought ready-made apple pie filling

¾ cup sugar

1 tablespoon cornstarch, sifted

1 teaspoon cinnamon

2 cups frozen sour cherries, defrosted and drained

1 teaspoon lemon juice

½ teaspoon almond extract

1 can refrigerated buttermilk biscuits

2 eggs

2 tablespoons water

1½ cups (8 ounces) walnut pieces

4 tablespoons 10x powdered sugar

DIRECTIONS:

1. Heat oven to 400 degrees F. Grease an 8" × 8" baking dish with 1 tablespoon. shortening; set aside.

2. Empty apple pie filling into a large bowl and mix with sugar, cornstarch, and cinnamon. Heat in a 2-quart saucepan over medium-high heat. Add cherries. Cook until thickened (approximately 3 minutes). Remove from heat. Stir in lemon juice and almond extract. Pour filling into baking dish and set aside.

3. Place biscuits evenly over filling. Make egg wash by blending eggs with water or milk. Brush biscuits with egg wash and sprinkle with walnuts and with dusting of powdered sugar. Bake the cobbler for 15 minutes in preheated oven until golden and bubbling.

APRICOT-GLAZED MUSHROOMS
OVER MIXED BABY GREENS

Yield: 6 servings

1 pound mixed mushrooms: chanterelle, baby portabella, cremini,
   shiitake
½ cup extra-virgin olive oil, divided
sea salt and freshly ground black pepper to taste
1 thinly sliced medium red onion
3 cloves fresh garlic, crushed and chopped
3 tablespoons balsamic vinegar
¼ cup apricot jam
12 cups baby mesclun greens: arugula, frisée, watercress, red oak,
   Boston Bibb
1 cup coarsely shredded fresh buffalo mozzarella cheese

DIRECTIONS:

1. With the oven rack in the center of the oven, preheat oven to 425
   degrees F.
2. In a large salad bowl, mix mushrooms with 3 tablespoons oil, salt
   and pepper, sliced red onions, and chopped crushed garlic. Roast on
   a lightly oiled sheet pan, occasionally turning the mushrooms until
   golden brown and tender, about 15–20 minutes. Remove from oven
   to cool.
3. In a medium bowl, whisk vinegar, apricot jam, and remaining oil.
   Season to taste with sea salt and pepper.
4. Place mushrooms, greens, and fresh mozzarella in a salad bowl and
   toss gently to mix. Add just enough dressing to lightly coat the salad,
   and serve.

THICK ASIAN BARBECUE SMOKED PORK CHOPS

Yield: 8 (1½"-thick) pork chops

1 cup Asian barbecue sauce, plus extra for brushing
½ cup Japanese steak sauce, plus extra for dipping
8 (1½"-thick) pork chops

DIRECTIONS:

1. Mix the barbecue sauce and Japanese steak sauce together in a shallow glass pan.
2. Add the pork chops and marinate for up to 3 hours at room temperature or refrigerate overnight. Discard the marinade.
3. Smoke over a low hickory-wood fire (at 225 degrees F) until meat easily pulls away from the bone (about 2 hours). If combining wood and charcoal, reduce the cooking time to 1½ hours.
4. Turn the pork chops on the grill three or four times, brushing thoroughly with the barbecue sauce.
5. Serve immediately with Japanese steak sauce on the side for additional dipping.

ASIAN SZECHUAN BARBECUE RIB SANDWICH

Yield: 12 servings

3 tablespoons San-J sauce, Szechuan
3 cups San-J sauce, Asian BBQ
12 ribs, precooked, boneless, 4-ounce each rib
3 baguettes French bread, as needed, split into 6" sections

DIRECTIONS:

1. Mix San-J Szechuan or your favorite sauce or San-J Asian BBQ sauce in a 2-quart sauce pan and bring to a boil for 10 minutes. Remove from heat and use as a base for ribs.
2. Marinate ribs in BBQ sauce of your favorite brand. Heat through.
3. Assemble sandwiches and serve with extra San-J Szechuan sauce.

AUTHENTIC ITALIAN MEAT SAUCE
with Fresh Porcini di Ciociaria

Yield: 6 servings, with pasta

6 ounces fresh porcini mushrooms, sliced

6 ounces fresh porcini mushrooms, or 1 ounce dried porcini mushrooms steeped for 15 minutes in 1 cup warm water and squeezed to remove excess water

1 small onion, chopped

3 tablespoons olive oil

2 tablespoons butter

1 celery stalk, chopped

1 small carrot, chopped

1 pound lean ground meat (part beef, part pork, depending on your favorite meat sauce)

sea salt to taste

1 cup white wine

½ cup milk

¼ teaspoon nutmeg

1 can Italian tomatoes, chopped, including juice

DIRECTIONS:

1. In a 5-quart casserole, sauté onions over medium heat, using all the oil and butter.

2. When onion becomes translucent, add celery and carrot, and cook for about 2 minutes. Add beef quickly bit by bit; salt to taste. Cook until meat just slightly browns. Turn up the heat, add wine, and, stirring slowly, cook for 3 minutes, or until most of the wine is evaporated.

3. Chop mushrooms coarsely. Stir mushrooms (fresh and sliced or dried and chopped) into the meat sauce.

4. Reduce the heat slightly, add milk and nutmeg, and, stirring slowly, cook for 3 minutes or until most of the milk has evaporated. Add tomatoes and stir briskly. When the sauce bubbles, reduce the heat to low, adjust seasoning, and cook about 3–4 hours. If necessary, add more water to achieve desired consistency.

WHY THIS RECIPE MEANS A LOT TO ME

Mama and I met Virgil Nerli in Rome on our visit to Italy. As we were traveling by train from Milano to Rome, Virgil, sitting across from us, was fascinated with our translation of Italian restaurant menus into English. While we conversed in mixed Italian and English, the subject, of course, was food: Italian food and regional specialties.

Virgil's family lived in the town of Ciociaria, located in the district of Latium, a short distance by train southeast of Rome. La Ciociaria, like all of Latium, is the land of sheep's milk ricotta, Pecorino Romano, and Strozzapreti di Porcini, the latter of which is made with gorgeous, fragrant porcini mushrooms.

Virgil insisted on inviting us to visit and stay with his family, and before long, another hour's trip from Rome, we arrived in the charming little town of La Ciociaria.

Any visit to Latium during porcini season (spring and early summer, exactly the time we were there) must include a visit to Rome's pine forests to gather porcini mushrooms.

While we sampled many wonderful porcini dishes, our favorite was the Nerlis' homemade pasta with the above authentic Italian meat sauce with fresh porcini di ciociaria.

AVOCADO AND SWEET CHILI BLUE CRABS

Yield: 4 servings

FOR CRAB-GINGER PASTE
6 each shallots, thinly sliced
4 each garlic cloves, crushed
1 (2") galanga (very pungent type of ginger), thinly sliced
7 ounces Thai crab paste (crab kapi)
1 teaspoon sambal belecan

FOR SRIRACHA MIXTURE
4 tablespoons sriracha
1 tablespoon mirin
1 tablespoon nam pla (fish sauce)
2 tablespoons honey
2 tablespoons dark soy sauce
3 tablespoons tomato puree
3 tablespoons ketchup
2 teaspoons sesame oil
1 teaspoon tomato paste

YOU ALSO NEED
8 large blue crabs, 4–6 ounces each, 2 pounds total
2 tablespoons peanut oil
1 egg, beaten
4 Mexican hass avocados, peeled, pitted, and sliced thinly
jasmine rice cakes, fried, as needed
dill, chopped, as needed

DIRECTIONS:
1. Combine first four ingredients for the crab ginger paste in a blender or food processor, and then add sambal belecan. Pulse.
2. In a mixing bowl combine sriracha, mirin, fish sauce, and honey. Whisk in dark soy sauce, tomato puree, ketchup, sesame oil, and tomato paste and reserve the sriracha mixture.

3. Bring a large pot with 4 quarts of water and 2 teaspoons salt to a boil. Rinse crabs (they must be alive) under running cold water. Cook crabs in boiling water 5 minutes. Transfer to a cooling rack. Pull bottom from each crab. With a sharp knife, cut a crack into each of the claws.

4. Heat peanut oil in a sauté pan over medium heat, Add reserved crab ginger paste and gently heat until aromatic, about 3 minutes. Add reserved sriracha mixture and bring to a boil. Remove pan from heat for 10 seconds and slowly drizzle well-beaten egg into pan, whisking constantly to smoothly incorporate, being sure not to scramble egg. Mixture should thicken to the consistency of a light sauce.

5. Transfer crabs to paper towels to drain and then add to chili-tomato mixture. Toss crabs to gently coat.

6. Place two crabs on each of four serving platters and top with thinly sliced avocados. Pour enough steaming hot chili sauce to generously coat avocados and crabs in each bowl. Sprinkle each bowl with dill and serve with fried jasmine rice cakes.

AVOCADO-RICOTTA FRITTATA
with Smoked Salmon or Prosciutto

Yield: 4 servings

Blending ricotta into the eggs gives the frittata a puffy, soufflé-like appearance. Thinly sliced prosciutto or smoked salmon and perfectly ripened hass avocado lend a New Orleans–type avant-garde flavor.

2 tablespoons extra-virgin olive oil

1 small bunch scallions (greens and whites thinly sliced)

2 cups baby arugula leaves

4 large eggs

¼ cup ricotta cheese

1 ounce prosciutto or smoked salmon (your choice), very thinly sliced and diced

2 medium hass avocados, peeled and diced to ¼"

salt and freshly ground pepper to taste

½ cup shredded emmentaler cheese

2 tablespoons minced fresh Italian parsley or basil leaves

DIRECTIONS:

1. Preheat broiler. In a 10" ovenproof skillet over medium heat, heat 1 tablespoon of olive oil and sauté scallions and arugula leaves until soft (about 1 minute).
2. In a medium bowl, beat the eggs until blended. Mix in the ricotta and prosciutto or smoked salmon. Mix in the arugula mixture, avocados, salt, and pepper.
3. In the same skillet over medium heat, heat the remaining 1 tablespoon olive oil and pour in the eggs. Reduce the heat to low and cook, lifting from underneath, until the eggs are set. Sprinkle with cheese and place under the broiler for a light brown color. Serve warm or at room temperature, garnished with parsley or basil leaves.

AVOCADOS SHARING THE HEALTH

Yield: 4servings

4 hass Mexican avocados, peeled, pitted, and sliced
1 cup quinoa
2 cups water
½ teaspoon fine-grain sea salt
1 can garbanzo beans, or dried equivalent
½ cup cilantro, chopped
½ red onion, chopped

FOR TAHINI DRESSING
1 garlic clove, smashed and chopped
¼ cup tahini
zest of 1 lemon
scant ¼ cup fresh lemon juice
2 tablespoons extra-virgin olive oil
2 tablespoons hot water
scant ½ teaspoon fine-grain sea salt

FOR GARNISH
8 sprigs fresh cilantro
8 lemon wedges
4 tablespoons diced red onions

DIRECTIONS:
1. Rinse the quinoa in a fine-mesh strainer. In a medium saucepan, heat the quinoa and water until boiling. Reduce heat and simmer until water is absorbed and quinoa fluffs up (about 15 minutes). Quinoa is done when you can see the curlicue in every grain, and it is tender with a bit of pop to each bite. Drain any extra water and set aside.
2. While the quinoa is cooking, make the dressing. Whisk together the garlic, tahini, lemon zest and juice, and olive oil. Add the hot water to thin a bit, and then the salt.

3. Toss the cooked quinoa, beans, cilantro, red onion, and half the dressing. Add more dressing if you like, and season with more salt to taste.
4. On four chilled salad platters place 1 red lettuce leaf, 1 layer of quinoa salad, and 1 layer of sliced avocado, and repeat, ending with 1 layer of sliced avocado. Sprinkle with additional tahini dressing and cilantro.
5. Serve with sides of lemon, chopped red onions, and fresh cilantro.

BABY BEEF, CHILI, AND ENGLISH CHEESE BURGER

Yield: 4 servings

2 small dried chipotle chiles, stemmed and seeded and chopped

1 cup premium mayonnaise

4 (3-ounce) ground beef patties

4 ounces blue cheese, crumbled (preferably English stilton)

4 slices mild cheddar cheese

4 buns of your choice, split and toasted

4 lettuce leaves, crushed

4 slices vine-ripened tomatoes

DIRECTIONS:

1. Prepare chipotle chili mayonnaise: In a small bowl, combine chopped chipotle peppers and premium mayonnaise. Stir until blended.

2. Grill or broil baby beef patties on both sides until 160 degrees F or desired temperature of at least 140 degree F.

3. When hamburgers have cooked through, top with 1 ounce stilton. Place 1 slice cheddar on each burger and melt under broiler or salamander.

4. Briefly place burger, bun bottom, and top of bun under broiler or salamander to toast.

5. Spread 1 tablespoon chili mayonnaise on cut side of bun top. cover bottom part of bun with lettuce and tomato slice. Place burger on bun, cover with top bun, and serve immediately.

BACALA DEL MARE SKILLET
With Raisins, Onions, Tomatoes, and Pine Nuts
Yield: 4–6 servings

If you purchase a whole side of bacala, first cut it into pieces that will fit into a large pan for cooking. Cover the bacala with abundant water and soak for a minimum of 24 hours, in a cool place like a basement or, if necessary, in a refrigerator. Change the water 3 or 4 times. After 24 hours, taste a bit of the fish for saltiness. If it is still very salty, change the water and soak for 24 hours longer, again changing the water three or four times. Bacala is ready, generally, when it has nearly doubled in bulk. Just trim off the skin and cut into portions for this recipe.

½ cup extra-virgin olive oil, divided
2 pounds prepared CFE bacala, cut into 4–6 portions
flour for dredging
2 large onions, peeled and chopped
8 garlic cloves, peeled and chopped
8 sprigs fresh thyme
3 large red tomatoes, peeled, seeded, and chopped; or 1 (28-ounce) can
    plum tomatoes
½ cup dark raisins, soaked in hot water until plump, and drained
¾ cup toasted pine nuts
2 dashes balsamic vinegar
salt and freshly ground pepper to taste
2 handfuls fresh Italian parsley, chopped

DIRECTIONS:
1. In a large skillet, heat ¼ cup of the olive oil. Dredge bacala in flour, shake off the excess, and place in the skillet. Cook over moderate heat, turning once, until the fillets have a light golden crust. Transfer to a plate and set aside.
2. Heat the remaining ¼ cup olive oil in the same skillet, and sauté the onions until they are soft. Add the garlic and sauté briefly over low heat until it gives off its characteristic aroma. Add the thyme sprigs,

tomatoes, and raisins. If using canned tomatoes, crush them with your fingers as you add them to the pan. Cook until the tomatoes release their aroma and liquid (about 10 minutes). Add the pine nuts, balsamic vinegar, and salt and pepper, and reduce the heat to medium low.

3. Gently place bacala fillets in the pan, adding any accumulated juices from the bacala. Spoon some of the sauce over the bacala, and sprinkle with half of the chopped parsley. Cover and cook at a gentle simmer until bacala begins to flake, about 6–8 minutes. Transfer bacala to a platter.

4. Add remaining parsley to the sauce and reduce the sauce over high heat for about 2 minutes. Spoon the sauce over the bacala and serve.

BACON-WRAPPED MAPLE-LEAF CHICKEN WINGS

Yield: 6–8 servings

Maple syrup adds a touch of sweetness to this creamy horseradish sauce.

2½ pounds chicken wings (about 12 wings)

12 strips bacon

¾ cup maple syrup

½ cup creamy horseradish sauce

1 small onion, diced

2 tablespoons Dijon mustard

2 teaspoons worcestershire sauce

12 celery sticks

DIRECTIONS:

1. Cut off wing tips and discard; cut wings in half at joint.
2. Wrap chicken wing with bacon strips and fasten with toothpick to prevent bacon from falling off.
3. Combine syrup, horseradish sauce, onion, and Dijon mustard in a small bowl; reserve ¾ cup marinade and refrigerate. Pour remaining marinade into a large zip-top freezer bag; add chicken and seal. Refrigerate 8 hours, turning bag occasionally.
4. Remove chicken from marinade; discard marinade. Place chicken, skin side up, on a lightly greased rack in a broiler pan. Broil 3 inches from heat for 8 minutes or until bacon and chicken are browned.
5. Place wings in a 3-quart slow cooker. Cover and cook on low for 4 hours. Serve with reserved ¾ cup marinade and celery sticks.

Note: Spicy! The spiciness of this appetizer varies depending on the brand of horseradish sauce used.

FARM-FRESH EGGS WITH YOGURT
Arugula, Orange, Berries, and Baby Carrots

Yield: 4 servings

¾ pound arugula

2 tablespoons olive oil

salt

4 eggs

¾ cup Greek-style yogurt

1 garlic clove, crushed

1 bunch baby carrots (about 12)

1 tablespoon olive oil

1 bunch scallions, chopped

juice of 1 orange

½ cup fresh blueberries or raspberries or sliced strawberries

DIRECTIONS:

1. Preheat oven to 300 degrees F. Place the arugula and olive oil in a large pan, add some salt, and sauté on medium heat until arugula wilts and most of the moisture has evaporated (about 5 minutes).

2. Transfer to a ovenproof dish and make four deep indentations in the arugula. Carefully break an egg into each hollow. Place in the oven to cook for 10 minutes or until the whites are set.

3. Mix the yogurt with the garlic and a pinch of salt. Stir well and set aside.

4. Steam carrots over boiling water in a covered pan for about 20 minutes, until tender. Rinse in cold water and drain well.

5. While carrots cook, heat olive oil in skillet. Add scallions and sauté on low heat for 5 minutes. Add orange juice and berries and heat gently for a few minutes. Combine with carrots and divide orange-berries-carrots mixture onto four individual warm platters.

6. Top each fresh carrot-berry serving with one of the baked eggs over arugula and serve with garlicky yogurt.

BAKED LOUISIANA SWEET POTATOES
with Dried Fruits and Walnuts
Yield: 6 servings

6 medium Louisiana sweet potatoes, scrubbed clean and dried

1 cup walnut pieces

½ cup raisins or dried cranberries

¼ cup unsweetened shredded coconut (optional)

2 tablespoons maple syrup

1 teaspoon freshly grated lemon zest

¼ teaspoon ground cinnamon

¼ teaspoon ground nutmeg

½ cup apricot preserves

1½ cups apple cider

1 tablespoon butter

½ teaspoon vanilla extract

DIRECTIONS:

1. Preheat oven to 375 degrees F. Lightly coat a shallow 8" × 12" (or similar) baking dish with cooking spray.
2. Core sweet potatoes all the way through with an apple corer, making a 1"-wide hole. Peel the upper third of each sweet potato. Using a sharp paring knife, score the flesh about ¼" deep around the circumference, more or less where the peeled and unpeeled areas meet. With the paring knife angled down, cut a shallow crater around the top of the hole to help hold preserves. Set aside while you make the filling.
3. Place walnuts, raisins (or dried cranberries), and coconut (if using) in a food processor. Chop the mixture fairly well, but not too fine; you want it to remain somewhat textured. Add syrup, lemon zest, cinnamon, and nutmeg; pulse several times to combine.
4. Place the sweet potatoes in the prepared baking dish and gently press ¼ cup filling into each cavity. Spoon a generous tablespoon of preserves onto the crater of each sweet potato.

5. Combine cider and butter in a small saucepan; heat over low heat until the butter has melted. Remove from the heat and stir in vanilla. Pour the liquid over and around the apples.

6. Cover the sweet potatoes loosely with tented foil and bake on the center rack for 30 minutes. Remove foil and baste sweet potatoes well. Continue to bake, uncovered, for 20–35 minutes more (depending on the size of the sweet potatoes), basting every 10 minutes, until the sweet potatoes are tender throughout. The best way to test them is with a thin bamboo skewer; the slightest bit of resistance near the center is okay, because they'll finish cooking as they cool. Let the sweet potatoes cool right in the pan, basting periodically. Serve warm, at room temperature, or cold, with some of the pan juices spooned over each.

BAKED MARYLAND SOFTSHELL CRABS

Yield: 8 servings (2 softshell crabs per serving)

16 softshell crabs
16 ounces shredded fat-free or low-fat cheddar cheese
4 egg whites, beaten
2 teaspoons chopped marjoram
2 teaspoons garlic powder
2 cups fresh, salt-free bread crumbs
2 tablespoons minced garlic chives
16 ounces Glenn Muir salt-free, no-sugar-added organic tomato sauce
16 sprigs Italian parsley

DIRECTIONS:

1. Clean crabs as needed. Place crabs in running cold water to rinse thoroughly. Dry crabs and gently lift up the apron on each crab and stuff the inside of each crab with 1 ounce shredded fat-free or low-fat cheddar cheese. Dip each crab into egg white and season with marjoram and garlic powder.

2. Place seasoned crabs onto bread crumbs and cover tops of crabs with bread crumbs. Lay crabs side-by-side in a greased baking dish and sprinkle evenly with garlic chives. Pour tomato sauce over all. Bake at 350 degrees F for 40 minutes. Serve with two crabs per plate, each crab topped with a sprig of parsley and with salad on the side.

BANGKOK WATERFALL GREENS BURGER
with Mango Salsa

Yield: 6 burgers

FOR THE SALSA
2 small mangoes
2 tablespoons coarsely chopped fresh cilantro
1 tablespoon lime juice

FOR THE BURGERS
2 pounds ground beef sirloin steak
⅔ cup fish sauce (nam pla)
½ cup lime juice
4 tablespoons chopped scallions
4 tablespoons chopped cilantro
½ cup mint leaves, chopped
3 tablespoons ground roasted sticky rice
2 tablespoons toasted sesame seeds
1 teaspoon ground chili pepper
sesame oil and sea salt as needed to taste

FOR THE WATERFALL GREENS
1½ tablespoons toasted sesame oil
3 cups shredded napa cabbage
1 cup shredded carrots
¾ cup sliced scallions
¾ cup lightly salted peanuts, coarsely chopped
2 tablespoons lime juice
1 tablespoon soy sauce
¼ teaspoon ground black pepper
½ cup coarsely chopped fresh mint
6 burrito-size (large) flour tortillas
½ cup purchased peanut sauce

DIRECTIONS:

1. In a small bowl, stir together the mango, cilantro, and lime. Cover and refrigerate until ready to serve.

2. Combine beef and remaining ingredients, divide into six equal portions, cover with plastic, and refrigerate to a temperature of at least 40 degree F. To grill, build a medium-hot fire in a gas or charcoal grill. Brush burgers with sesame oil and season to taste with sea salt. Cook, turning once, for 8–10 minutes for medium rare.

3. Add sesame oil to shredded cabbage and stir in all remaining ingredients except peanut sauce. Place in refrigerator to a temperature of at least 40 degree F.

4. Spread the center of the tortillas with 1 tablespoon peanut sauce. Top with waterfall greens and the burgers. Fold in two ends of the tortillas, then roll up. Place on the outside of the grill, seam-side down. Heat for about 1½ minutes. Serve with mango salsa.

BARBECUED CHORIZO BURGER ON A STICK

Yield: 12 servings

1¼ cups cider vinegar
¾ cup ketchup
¾ cup chopped red onion (1 large)
¾ cup dried tart cherries
⅓ cup honey
2 dried ancho chile peppers, stemmed, seeded, and finely diced
2 cloves garlic, slivered
¾ teaspoon ground coriander
⅛ teaspoon ground cloves
12 Johnsonville chorizo patties
salt and black pepper to taste

DIRECTIONS:

1. In a large saucepan combine vinegar, ketchup, onion, dried cherries, honey, chile peppers, garlic, coriander, and cloves. Bring to boiling; reduce heat. Simmer, uncovered, about 20 minutes or until dried cherries and chile pepper are softened and mixture is slightly thickened. Cool slightly. Transfer mixture to a blender or food processor. Cover and blend until nearly smooth; set aside.

2. Sprinkle chorizo patties with salt and pepper as desired. Insert a wooden skewer into short side of each patty.

3. For a charcoal grill, grill patties on the rack of an uncovered grill directly over medium coals for 7–9 minutes or until patties are slightly pink in center and juices run clear (160 degrees F), turning once halfway through grilling. (For a gas grill, preheat grill and reduce heat to medium. Place patties on grill rack over heat. Cover and grill as directed.) Brush sauce over patties during the last 5 minutes of grilling. If desired, reheat and serve additional sauce on the side.

4. Serve with fries, and cabbage slaw between toasted sliced kaiser rolls.

Note: To prevent wooden skewers from burning while grilling chops, soak them in water for 30 minutes before inserting into patties.

BASIL, FRESH MOZZARELLA, AND TOMATO PANINI

Yield: 2 sandwiches

FOR BASIL CREAM
1 cup cream cheese
½ cup mayonnaise
½ cup fresh, all green basil; leaves, loosely packed

FOR SANDWICH
basil cream, as needed (see above)
Boston Bibb lettuce, as needed
2 (9" square) pieces of focaccia (sliced horizontally and lightly toasted)
¼ cup balsamic vinegar
1 tablespoon lemon juice
6 (½") slices fresh mozzarella
6 thick slices vine-ripened tomatoes (5 × 5 size)
6 thin slices prosciutto (about ½ ounce)
12 really fresh large green basil leaves

DIRECTIONS:
1. Blend basil cream ingredients together; refrigerate.
2. Lightly toast focaccia squares in preheated oven at 395 degrees F.
3. Spread each half with basil cream. Top with Boston Bibb lettuce.
4. Mix balsamic vinegar and lemon juice. Dress fresh mozzarella and tomato slices in mixture. Place on top of Boston Bibb. Alternating between tomatoes and fresh mozzarella, add 3 slices of each to each sandwich and garnish with 6 basil leaves.
5. Cut squares into halves and serve with basil sprig on the side.

FORBIDDEN FRUIT BABY BACK RIBS

Yield: 6 Servings

FOR THE SPICE RUB

2 tablespoons smoked paprika

2½ teaspoons dried basil

2½ teaspoons dried thyme

1½ teaspoons garlic salt

1½ teaspoons dry mustard powder

1½ teaspoons freshly ground black pepper

FOR THE BARBECUE SAUCE*

4 cups ketchup (a 40-ounce bottle yields 4 cups)

2 cups apple juice concentrate

1½ tablespoons red chili powder (ground chiles)

½ tablespoon ground allspice

½ teaspoon ground cumin

2½ tablespoons worcestershire sauce

½ teaspoons hot pepper sauce

1 (750 milliliter) bottle Zinfandel

½ teaspoon freshly ground black pepper

FOR THE RIBS

3 racks baby back pork ribs (each 2¼–2½ pounds)

2 lemons, cut in half

YOU ALSO NEED

1½ cups wood chips, preferably hickory, soaked for 1 hour in cold water, covered and drained.

DIRECTIONS:

1. Mix all spice rub ingredients in a small bowl to blend.
2. Whisk all barbecue sauce ingredients together in a large bowl. Keep covered in the refrigerator until needed. Makes 6 cups.

3. Remove the thin, papery skin from the back of each rack of ribs by pulling it off in a sheet with your fingers, using a corner of a kitchen towel to gain a secure grip, or using a pair of pliers.

4. Rub cut lemon over front and back of ribs, squeezing as much as possible to release all the juice. Set aside for 5 minutes. Rub ribs liberally with spice rub and let sit, covered, for 15–20 minutes.

5. Set up the grill for indirect grilling and place a large drip pan in the center. Place all the wood chips in the smoker box; place pans on flame. Preheat grill to high: 500 degrees F. When smoke appears, reduce the heat to medium: 325–350 degrees F.

6. Place ribs, bone side down, on center of cooking grate over drip pan. Making sure they are *not* over a direct flame. If a three-burner gas grill, is being used, light burners on right and left, leaving center flame off. If using a two-burner gas grill, light burner on side opposite drip pan.

7. Cover grill. Turn and reposition ribs every 30 minutes, brushing with the barbecue sauce. Each time re-cover the grill. Continue to cook about 1½ hours. The ribs are done when the meat is very tender and has shrunk back from the ends of the bones. Always maintain temperatures at or near 325–350 degrees F, adjusting the vents if needed. 15 minutes before serving, brush again with barbecue sauce. Remove ribs from grill and let rest 10 minutes before cutting into individual 2- to 3-rib portions. Warm remaining sauce and serve on the side if desired.

* Not only is this sauce delicious, but it needs no cooking! This recipe yields more sauce than you will need for 6 servings, but it keeps about 6 months in the refrigerator. (It's great on chicken too.)

LOUISIANA BARBECUE SHRIMP

Yield: 4 servings

I consider this my family's best recipe. (I lived In New Orleans until 2005, when Hurricane Katrina approached.)

FOR SHRIMP
24 colossal (U-10) Gulf shrimp, peeled and deveined (keep heads and shells for base)
1 cup heavy cream
2 sticks butter
2 tablespoons freshly ground black pepper
hot French bread

FOR SHRIMP BASE
2 tablespoons olive oil
1 cup shrimp peelings (heads, shells)
1 cup clam juice
1 cup worcestershire sauce
1½ tablespoons Creole seasoning
1 whole clove garlic
2 tablespoons lemon juice

DIRECTIONS:
1. Combine all shrimp ingredients in a sauté pan set over high heat and boil until shrimp are fully cooked and pink. Remove shrimp to a serving dish. Continue to reduce sauce until it is thick enough to coat the back of a spoon and is the color of melted milk chocolate.
2. Sauté shrimp peelings in olive oil until bright red. Add remaining ingredients and simmer. Reduce by half and strain through a china cap. Discard solids.
3. Divide shrimp among four bowls and ladle sauce atop.
4. Serve with hot French bread.

BEARNAISE SAUCE

Yield: 4 servings

Bearnaise sauce is closely related to hollandaise sauce but features wine and tarragon.

3 egg yolks
¼ cup water
3 tablespoons white wine or chicken broth
2 tablespoons tarragon vinegar
2 teaspoons minced shallot
2½ teaspoons minced fresh tarragon, divided
8 whole peppercorns, crushed
½ cup cold butter

DIRECTIONS:

1. In a small heavy saucepan, whisk the egg yolks and water. Cook and stir over low heat or simmering water until mixture bubbles around edges and reaches 160 degrees (about 20 minutes).
2. Meanwhile, in a small saucepan, combine the wine or broth, vinegar, shallot, 1½ teaspoons tarragon, and peppercorns. Bring to a boil. Reduce heat and simmer, uncovered, for 10 minutes or until reduced to 2 tablespoons. Strain and set liquid aside.
3. Cut cold butter into eight pieces; add to egg-yolk mixture one piece at a time, stirring after each addition until melted. Stir reserved liquid and remaining tarragon into prepared sauce. Serve immediately.

BELGIAN ENDIVES
with Fruited Brown Rice
Yield: 4 servings

4 medium heads Belgian endive, cut in half horizontally
4 outer leaves removed from each head of endive
2 cups plain nonfat yogurt

FOR FRUITED BROWN RICE
½ cup brown rice
¼ cup water
¼ teaspoon salt (optional)
¼ cup dried currants
½ cup dried nonsulfured apricots, chopped
¼ cup slivered or coarsely chopped almonds, toasted
½ teaspoon ground cinnamon

FOR GARNISH
4 teaspoons chopped cilantro leaves as a garnish.

DIRECTIONS:
1. Pick over rice, discarding any broken grains or field debris. Place rice in a colander or sieve and wash under running water; drain.
2. Place rice, water, and salt (if used) in a 1-quart saucepan over medium heat. Bring to a full boil, reduce temperature to medium low, and cook, covered, until grains are tender and separated and liquid is absorbed (about 30–35 minutes). Let rest, covered, for 10 minutes before serving.
3. When rice has finished cooking, stir in currants and apricots, almonds and cinnamon.
4. Place 1 head of endive into each of four small bowls (preferably oval bowls), and surround the endive half with four of the outer leaves. Ladle fruited brown rice on top and add a dollop of yogurt and chopped cilantro leaves. Serve remaining yogurt on the side.

BELLA SUN LUCI MEDITERRANEAN SWORDFISH SKEWERS
with Sun-Dried Tomato Pesto Risotto

Yield: 4 servings

4 cups hot Bella Sun Luci Sun-Dried Tomato Risotto, prepared according to manufacturer's directions

FOR SUN-DRIED TOMATO PESTO
1 (8.5-ounce) jar sun-dried tomatoes
extra-virgin olive oil from the sun-dried tomatoes jar, and more if needed
2 sprigs thyme, leaves only (optional)

FOR MEDITERRANEAN SWORDFISH SKEWERS
1 pound swordfish, tuna, or salmon, cubed to ¾"
1 medium red onion, cut into 1" pieces
¼ cup Bella Sun Luci olive oil
1 teaspoon ground ginger
1 teaspoon paprika, or pinch cayenne pepper
¼ cup chopped fresh mint
2 tablespoons lemon juice
salt and freshly ground pepper to taste

DIRECTIONS:
1. Light a fire in a charcoal grill. Alternately arrange fish and onion pieces on skewers. Brush with Bella Sun Luci olive oil. Combine ginger, paprika, and cayenne pepper. Sprinkle skewers with spice mixture. Grill over medium-hot coals 6–8 minutes, turning and brushing with Bella Sun Luci olive oil as necessary. Remove fish and onions from skewers. When ready to serve, sprinkle with mint and lemon juice. Season with salt and pepper to taste.

Variation: 1 teaspoon each of ground cumin and turmeric or 2 teaspoons curry powder may be used in place of ginger and paprika.

2. Empty entire jar of sun-dried tomatoes and its oil into the bowl of a food processor fitted with a steel blade. Add the thyme, if desired. Process into a smooth puree, adding additional Bella Sun Luci olive oil, 1 tablespoon at a time, to achieve the proper texture.

3. To make a pretty presentation, mold a cup of the sun-dried tomato pesto risotto into a teacup and invert onto a serving plate. Repeat for the remaining three servings. Remove fish and onions from skewers and serve next to the risotto, then sprinkle with mint and lemon juice.

Note: To prevent wooden skewers from burning, soak them in water for 30 minutes prior to use.

BERRY FARMER'S GIANT MACAROONS

1 (14-ounce) can nonfat sweetened condensed milk
1 teaspoon almond extract
2 cups sliced almonds
2 cups coconut flakes, preferably unsweetened
1 cup giant blueberries
½ cup chopped shelled pistachios
2 large egg whites
¼ teaspoon salt

FOR GARNISH (OPTIONAL)
¾ cup bittersweet or semisweet chocolate chips
¼ cup chopped shelled pistachios

DIRECTIONS:
1. Position racks in upper and lower thirds of oven; preheat to 325 degrees F. Line two large baking sheets with parchment paper or silicone baking mats.
2. Whisk condensed milk and almond extract in a large bowl until combined. Pulse almonds in a food processor (about 10 quick pulses) until broken into small pieces. Stir the almonds, coconut, blueberries, and ½ cup pistachios into the condensed-milk mixture.
3. Beat egg whites and salt in a medium bowl with an electric mixer on medium high speed until soft peaks form (about 1 minute). Fold half of the egg whites into the coconut mixture. Add the remaining egg whites, gently folding into the mixture until just combined. Drop 1 teaspoon of dough onto a prepared baking sheet and top with another teaspoon of dough, making a double-tall giant macaroon. Repeat with the remaining batter, spacing the macaroons 1" apart.
4. Bake the macaroons, switching the pans from back to front and top to bottom halfway through, until the coconut is lightly golden, 18–22 minutes (sweetened coconut will brown faster than unsweetened). Let cool on the pans on a wire rack until cool to the touch, 30 minutes.

5. Optional garnish: Place ½ cup chocolate chips in a microwave-safe bowl and melt in the microwave on medium in 30-second bursts, stirring after each burst to ensure even melting, until completely melted. (Alternatively, melt the chocolate in a double boiler over hot water, stirring constantly.) Stir the remaining ¼ cup chips into the melted chocolate until smooth. Drizzle or spoon the melted chocolate over the top of each cooled macaroon; sprinkle with pistachios. Let the chocolate dry completely before storing or packing.

BISTRO CHICKEN PARMIGIANA

Yield: 4 servings

1 cup olive oil
4 boneless, skinless chicken thighs (about 4 ounces each), pounded ¼"
    thick
Kosher salt and freshly ground black pepper to taste
½ cup flour
3 eggs, lightly beaten
1 cup seasoned Italian bread crumbs
2 cups your favorite marinara sauce
1 cup shredded mozzarella
½ cup grated parmigiana cheese
½ cup chopped fresh basil leaves

DIRECTIONS:

1. Heat oil in a 12" skillet until an instant-read thermometer reads 325 degrees.
2. Working in batches, season chicken with salt and pepper and dredge in flour, shaking off excess. Dip in eggs and coat in bread crumbs.
3. Fry breaded chicken in oil, flipping once, until golden and cooked through, 5–7 minutes. Transfer chicken to paper towels to drain; season with salt and pepper.
4. Heat oven broiler to high. Spread ½ cup sauce evenly in a 9" × 13" baking dish. Arrange chicken over sauce, overlapping slightly. Top with remaining sauce and sprinkle with mixture of mozzarella and parmigiana cheese. Broil until cheese is melted and browned, 2–4 minutes. Sprinkle with basil leaves.

BISTRO GULF SHRIMP
with Crispy Goat Cheese–Topped Potatoes
and a Creamy Tratoria Alfredo Sauce

½ cup chicken broth
1 package frozen diced potatoes with onion, any brand
¾ cup sun-dried tomatoes in olive oil, finely diced, divided
16 ounces fresh pink Gulf shrimp, steamed, peeled, and deveined
2 yellow bell peppers, roasted, seeded, and julienned
½ cup sun-dried tomatoes in olive oil, drained and julienned
1 bunch fresh cilantro, washed, dried, and chopped, divided
16 ounces crumbled goat cheese, divided
2 cups prepared Alfredo sauce (store-bought)

DIRECTIONS:

1. Heat oven to 400 degrees F. Place chicken broth and Simply Potatoes diced potatoes with onion, blended with ¼ cup diced sun-dried tomatoes, in bottom of 2-quart baking dish.
2. Add steamed, peeled, and deveined pink Gulf shrimp, spread evenly over potatoes in baking dish. Sprinkle with roasted julienned bell peppers and ½ cup sun-dried tomatoes. Sprinkle with 4 tablespoons chopped fresh cilantro
3. Sprinkle with 8 ounces crumbled goat cheese and evenly ladle Alfredo sauce over everything.
4. Bake 15–30 minutes or until edges are bubbly. Sprinkle with remaining goat cheese; bake 1–2 minutes or until cheese begins to melt.

BITTER CHOCOLATE CUPCAKES

Yield: 12 cupcakes

FOR CUPCAKES

3 ounces grated English stilton cheese (to be sprinkled in the bottoms
　　of cupcake cups)

1 ounce unsweetened baking chocolate or 90% cocoa

½ cup hot English stout beer

1 cup granulated sugar

¾ cup plus 1 tablespoon unbleached all-purpose flour

½ cup unsweetened natural cocoa powder

generous ½ teaspoon baking soda

¼ teaspoon baking powder

scant ½ teaspoon salt

1 large egg

¼ cup canola oil

½ cup buttermilk

¼ teaspoon pure vanilla extract

FOR FROSTING

2 cups powdered sugar

1 tablespoon unsweetened natural cocoa powder

⅓ cup malted milk powder

9 tablespoons (1 stick plus 1 tablespoon) unsalted butter, at room
　　temperature

2 tablespoons boiling stout beer

DIRECTIONS:

1. Preheat oven to 300 degrees F. Line twelve cups of a muffin tin with
   paper liners. Sprinkle bottoms of cups with equal amounts of grated
   stilton cheese.

2. Place the chocolate in a medium bowl with the hot stout beer. Let
   stand, stirring occasionally, until the chocolate is melted and the
   mixture is smooth and opaque.

3. In another medium bowl, combine the sugar, flour, cocoa powder, baking soda, baking powder, and salt, and whisk to combine well.

4. In a large bowl, beat the egg with an electric mixer until it is pale yellow in color, about a minute or two. Slowly add the oil, buttermilk, and vanilla extract, beating to combine well. Slowly add the melted-chocolate mixture and beat to thoroughly combine. Add the dry ingredients and beat on medium speed until the batter is just combined. Using a rubber spatula, scrape the sides of the bowl and briefly fold the batter to be certain that all of the dry ingredients are incorporated.

5. Divide the batter evenly among the twelve prepared muffin cups. Bake for 20–25 minutes, or until a toothpick inserted in the center of a cupcake comes out clean. Cool the cupcakes for 15 minutes in the pan, then gently transfer them to a rack to cool completely. They are *very* delicate and tender, so take care.

6. When the cupcakes are cool, make the frosting. In the bowl of a food processor, combine the powdered sugar, cocoa, and malted milk powder and process to mix well. Add the butter and process to blend. Stop the motor and scrape down the sides of the bowl with a rubber spatula. Then, with the motor running, add the stout beer. Process briefly, until the frosting is smooth. Frost the cupcakes in loose swirls and serve.

BLACK PEPPER NASOYA TOFU
with Dried Mango
Yield: 6 servings

1 package Nasoya extra firm tofu, cut into 18 pieces (sliced into 3 pieces lengthwise and 6 times across)

3 large mangoes, peeled and seeded and cut into 6 slices

14 tablespoons grape-seed oil

6 scallions, thinly sliced

3 tablespoons minced fresh ginger

3 tablespoons minced garlic

1½ tablespoons crushed black peppercorns

½ cup sweet soy sauce

2½ tablespoons soy sauce

4 tablespoons granulated sugar

3 tablespoons fresh lime juice

1½ tablespoons fermented black beans, rinsed, squeezed dry, and chopped

½ tablespoon sea salt

FOR GARNISH:

1 small jicama, peeled and cut into fine dice

1½ cups thinly sliced baby pea shoots

DIRECTIONS:

1. Heat a convection oven or regular oven to 295 degrees F. Place a wire rack on top of a baking sheet, lined with parchment or aluminum foil. Place tofu pieces on wire rack; cook until roasted to a light amber color. Remove from oven, cool, place aside, and cover until ready to serve.

2. Keeping the oven hot, repeat the same procedure as with the tofu but with mango slices. Cook mangoes until chewy; remove from oven and reserve.

3. Heat 2 tablespoons grape-seed oil in a skillet set over medium heat; add scallions, ginger, and garlic. Cook, stirring, 1 minute. Add peppercorns; cook until fragrant.

4. Add soy sauces, sugar, juice, black beans, and salt. Bring to a boil; reduce heat to medium high and simmer 2 minutes. Remove from heat, place in a blender, and blend until smooth. Set aside.

5. For each serving, heat 2 tablespoons oil in a small wok or heavy skillet. Set over high heat. Add 3 tofu pieces; cook until crisped and pour off any extra oil. Add 2 tablespoons black pepper sauce and 1 tablespoon water. Toss to coat the tofu. Add 2 mango slices; cook until warm. Remove from heat; spoon tofu and mango in center of service plate; scatter with jicama and garnish with pea shoots.

INDIVIDUAL BLUEBERRY POT PIE
with Sour Cream
Yield: 6 individual pot pies

1½ cups all-purpose flour
¼ cup light brown sugar
1½ teaspoons baking powder
¼ teaspoon ground cinnamon
⅛ teaspoon ground nutmeg
⅛ teaspoon salt
½ cup butter, cut into pieces
½ cup sour cream, divided
21 ounces Lucky Leaf Premium blueberry pie filling

FOR TOPPING
½ cup sour cream
¼ cup heavy cream
¼ teaspoon cinnamon
1 teaspoon sugar

DIRECTIONS:
1. Spoon flour lightly into measuring cup. Combine flour and next five ingredients in a food processor. Pulse until combined. Add butter and pulse six times or until mixture resembles coarse meal. With processor on, add 3 tablespoons sour cream, processing just until combined. Press mixture gently into a 4" circle on plastic wrap, and cover in a refrigerator for 20 minutes.
2. Preheat oven to 400 degrees F.
3. Divide remaining sour cream among six ramekins, reserving 3 teaspoons for topping.
4. Unwrap chilled dough and divide into six equal portions. Make into balls and pat balls on floured surface into a rough disk that will cover tops of ramekins (about 4"). Top blueberry pie filling with dough circles inside tops of ramekins (not crimped as with conventional pies). Brush top of each crust with remaining sour cream.

5. Place ramekins on a baking sheet and place in 400-degree F oven. Bake for 20 minutes or until crust is golden brown and fruit is bubbling. Serve warm or at room temperature with topping of mixture of whipped sour cream, heavy cream, cinnamon, and sugar.

BOSTON GREEN MUSSELS
and Biscuits in a Chowder
Yield: 4 servings

1 cup julienned parsnips
1 cup thinly sliced red onion
2 garlic cloves, minced
2 teaspoons olive oil or canola oil
24 green New England mussels, scrubbed clean
4 cups clam broth
¼ cup dry white wine
1 tablespoon marjoram
1 cup (8 ounces) fat-free plain yogurt
1 cup fresh or frozen peas
¼ teaspoon each curry powder, salt, pepper, ground cumin, and ground
  ginger

FOR THE BISCUITS
1 cup all-purpose flour
1 teaspoon baking powder
¼ teaspoon baking soda
¼ teaspoon salt
4½ teaspoons cold butter or stick margarine
½ cup fat-free plain yogurt
1½ teaspoons dried parsley flakes

DIRECTIONS:
1. In a large nonstick skillet, sauté parsnips, onion, and garlic in oil
    until tender. Add mussels cook and stir for 5 minutes for the mussels
    to open. Discard any mussels that stay closed. Combine broth and
    wine and marjoram; add to the skillet. Bring to a boil and stir for 2
    minutes. Reduce heat; stir in yogurt, peas, and seasonings. Transfer
    to a shallow 2+-quart baking dish coated with nonstick cooking
    spray; keep warm.

2. Combine flour, baking powder, baking soda, and salt in a bowl. Cut in butter until crumbly. Stir in yogurt and parsley. Drop eight mounds over warm mussels mixture. Bake, uncovered, at 350 degrees F for 25–35 minutes or until biscuits are golden brown and chowder bubbles around the edges.

OPEN-FACED BREAKFAST CREPES

with Smoked Trout and Chilled Horseradish Crème Fraîche

Yield: 4 servings

FOR CREPE BATTER

2 cups flour

2 scant cups milk

⅔ cup water

2 eggs and 1 extra yolk

1 teaspoon curry powder

pinch salt

1 tablespoon canola oil

dash soda water

YOU WILL ALSO NEED

4 smoked trout fillets, lightly cooked

3 hard-boiled eggs, chopped

⅔ cup fish stock (consommé or broth)

⅔ cup white wine

juice of 1 lemon

6 tablespoons sweet butter

1 large onion, chopped

1½ cups chopped mushrooms

3 tablespoons flour

1½ cups light cream (half-and-half)

½ cup finely chopped parsley

½ tsp each finely ground white pepper and sea salt

¼ cup grated swiss cheese

FOR HORSERADISH CRÈME FRAÎCHE

1 cup crème fraiche, chilled

1 tablespoon grated fresh horseradish

DIRECTIONS:

1. Preheat oven to 200 degrees.

2. Whisk together all the crepe ingredients except the soda water. Leave batter to rest and add a dash of soda water after 30 minutes.

3. Make 8–12 thin crepes in a crepe pan (6"–8") and stack between layers of kitchen towels.

4. Sauté onions and mushrooms in butter until soft. Add flour, cook 1 minute, and make into a sauce, adding stock, wine, lemon juice, and cream. Stir in parsley, pepper and salt.

5. Spread 2–3 crepes on each of four hot dinner plates and add 1 trout fillet on top of each crepe. Top trout fillets with chopped eggs and equal amounts of seafood mushroom sauce. Lightly fold ¼ of each crepe over sauce and sprinkle with grated swiss cheese.

6. Briefly place underneath broiler to melt the cheese. Remove plates from oven.

7. Blend crème fraîche with grated horseradish, keep chilled, and serve chilled horseradish crème fraîche with hot smoked trout crêpes.

BRIE AND APPLE SKILLET BREAKFAST

Yield: 6 servings

FOR CORN BREAD

2 cups self-rising buttermilk cornmeal mix
½ teaspoon salt
freshly ground black pepper to taste
3 large eggs, lightly beaten
½ cup buttermilk
1 tablespoon butter, melted
3 tablespoons honey
2 apples, peeled, sliced or grated and cored
1 apple, diced to ¼"
1 apple, thinly sliced
1 small red onion, diced to ¼"
½ cup diced (¼") tomatoes
1 clove garlic, minced
1 small chili pepper, seeded and minced
16 ounces ripe Brie cheese, sliced

FOR TOPPING

4 tablespoons honey
1 apple, thinly sliced
4 large eggs, slightly whipped
1 tablespoon extra-virgin olive oil
8 ounces ripe Brie cheese, sliced
1 tablespoon fresh tarragon, chopped
6 sprigs tarragon (for garnish)

DIRECTIONS:

1. Preheat oven to 425 degrees F. Place a 9"–10½" cast-iron skillet in the oven to heat.
2. Whisk cornmeal mix with salt and pepper.
3. Whisk the eggs, buttermilk, butter, and honey in a medium bowl and add the egg mixture to the dry ingredients. Mix with a rubber spatula. Gently stir in diced apples, onion, tomato, garlic, and chili pepper.

4. Remove the hot skillet from the oven and coat with cooking spray. Pour in half the batter, spreading evenly. Top with sliced Brie and add remaining batter.
5. Bake corn bread until golden brown, for about 20–25 minutes. When corn bread is ready, a knife inserted in the center will come out clean.
6. Drizzle honey over the corn bread, and top with sliced apples. Make soft scrambled eggs with olive oil and evenly spread scrambled eggs over the apples. Add sliced Brie cheese and place underneath broiler for the cheese to warm to the melting point. Sprinkle corn bread with chopped tarragon, and garnish each serving with a sprig of tarragon.

BROILED JAPANESE ALASKAN HALIBUT
with Peanut Butter Coconut Curry Sauce
Yield: 4 servings

Halibut's mild flavor allows the bold flavors of the peanut butter, coconut, and curry to shine. Serve this dish with rice, which will absorb the thin sauce.

1 teaspoon dark sesame oil, divided
2 teaspoons minced, peeled fresh ginger
2 garlic cloves, minced
1 cup finely chopped red bell pepper
1 cup chopped scallions
1 teaspoon curry powder
½ cup peanut butter
2 teaspoons red curry paste
½ teaspoon ground cumin
4 teaspoons low-sodium soy sauce
1 tablespoon brown sugar
½ teaspoon salt, divided
1 (14-ounce) can light coconut milk
2 tablespoons chopped fresh cilantro
4 (6-ounce) halibut fillets
cooking spray
3 cups hot cooked basmati rice
4 lime wedges

DIRECTIONS:
1. Preheat broiler.
2. Heat ½ teaspoon oil in a large nonstick skillet over medium heat. Add ginger and garlic; cook 1 minute. Add pepper and onions; cook 1 minute. Stir in curry powder, peanut butter, curry paste, and cumin; cook 1 minute. Add soy sauce, sugar, ¼ teaspoon salt, and coconut milk; bring to a simmer, but do not boil. Remove from heat; stir in cilantro.

3. Brush fish with ½ teaspoon oil; sprinkle with ¼ teaspoon salt. Place fish on a baking sheet coated with cooking spray. Broil 7 minutes or until fish flakes easily when tested with a fork. Serve fish with sauce, rice, and lime wedges.

BROWN RICE TORTILLA ESPAÑOLA

Yield: 4–8 servings

This classic Spanish dish can be served for breakfast, cut into cubes for tapas, or presented as a summer lunch with a bowl of gazpacho. A quick note: Add the brown-rice mixture while it's hot enough to start cooking the eggs but not so hot as to puff them.

¾ cup Spanish olive oil
6 ounces brown rice, cooked al dente
3 ounces serrano ham or prosciutto, thinly sliced and diced
⅓ cup canned piquillo peppers or pimientos, finely chopped
1 tablespoon thyme leaves
1 medium yellow onion, peeled, halved, and thinly sliced
6 eggs, lightly beaten
sea salt and freshly ground black pepper to taste

DIRECTIONS:

1. Heat oil over medium-high heat in a 10" sauté pan. Reduce heat to medium and add mixture of cooked brown rice, diced serrano ham, peppers or pimientos, thyme, and onions and season with salt and pepper. Cook, lifting and turning the frittata until rice is still soft but not brown, about 10–12 minutes.
2. Beat eggs in a large bowl until pale yellow.
3. Transfer sautéed frittata-rice mixture with a slotted spoon to beaten eggs. Scoop rice mixture without stirring and add to skillet lightly sprayed with olive oil, until bottom begins to brown (about 4 minutes).
4. Transfer to broiler pan and brown until set and golden on top. Cut into wedges to serve.

BUTTERNUT SQUASH AND TOFU GRILLED MUFFINS

Yield: 8 servings

2 (16-ounce) packages of water-packed firm tofu, drained
4 Bays multigrain English muffins, lightly toasted with a light brushing
    of peanut oil
1 cup fresh lime juice
1 cup honey
½ cup lemongrass, peeled and thinly sliced
4 tablespoons low-sodium soy sauce
½ teaspoon freshly ground black pepper
4 garlic cloves, peeled and minced
1½ teaspoons chili paste with garlic
2 tablespoons peanut oil
8 leaves baby iceberg lettuce
1 cup cilantro leaves
4 tablespoons dry-roasted peanuts
1 cup small mint leaves
1 cup fresh basil leaves
1 large butternut squash, peeled, seeded, and julienned

DIRECTIONS:

1. Cut 2 packages tofu into eight equal slices.
2. Place tofu slices between several heavy-duty paper towels. Place a cutting board on top, and let the paper towels draw the moisture away for 20–30 minutes. (The tofu is ready when a slice is easily bendable without tearing.) Place tofu in a single layer on a cookie sheet.
3. Combine lime juice, honey, lemongrass, soy sauce, pepper, garlic, and chili paste in small saucepan, and bring to a boil. Cook one minute, stirring well to dissolve honey.
4. Pour mixture evenly over the tofu, cover with plastic wrap, and let rest for one hour.
5. Prepare your barbecue grill or oven broiler.
6. Remove tofu from the marinade, and coat lightly with peanut oil, reserving the marinade.

7. Place tofu on hot grill, and cook until each side is golden brown, about 3 minutes per side. Or place 6–8 inches underneath broiler.

8. Place one baby iceberg lettuce leaf on each toasted muffin half, and place one slice of grilled tofu on each baby iceberg leaf. Sprinkle with cilantro, peanuts, mint, basil, and julienned butternut squash. Serve with the reserved marinade.

CAJUN OYSTER BROCHETTE
with Hot Diced-Tomato Habanero Rémoulade
Yield: 6 servings

FOR OYSTERS
1 pint Louisiana shucked oysters

12 pieces apple wood–smoked bacon

1 cup Cajun flour (1 cup all-purpose flour and 3 tablespoons Cajun spice)

butter to sauté, as needed

lemon wedges and tarragon sprigs, for garnish

FOR HOT DICED-TOMATO HABANERO RÉMOULADE SAUCE
½ cup mayonnaise

1 (10-ounce) can Ro*Tel hot diced tomatoes with habaneros

1 teaspoon Dijon mustard

1 cup Cajun flour (homemade [see above] or store-bought)

1 tablespoon capers

juice of 1 lemon

pinch (1 teaspoon) fresh tarragon, chopped

DIRECTIONS:
1. Combine all rémoulade sauce ingredients, and gently mix with a large wooden spoon. Add tarragon last.
2. Lightly drain oysters, and then dredge in Cajun flour. Set aside.
3. Cut bacon into equal lengths, about 3" long, and wrap 1 piece around each oyster. Skewer 4–5 oysters on each skewer, and sauté in skillet over medium high heat 3 minutes on each side.
4. Drizzle about 4 ounces (8 tablespoons) rémoulade sauce on each plate, top with oysters brochettes, and garnish with lemon wedges and tarragon sprig.

CAJUN SPICED CEREAL MIX

Yield: 30 halves

15 jalapeño peppers

3½ cups shredded Italian-style or Mexican-style cheese mix, store-bought, divided

3½ cups hand-crushed* Wheat Chex, divided

8 ounces cream cheese, softened

1 teaspoon Cajun seasoning

3 eggs

2 tablespoons milk

1 cup shredded cheese for topping

DIRECTIONS:

1. Preheat oven to 450 degrees F or convection oven to 375 degrees F.
2. Cut peppers in half, and remove seeds and membranes.
3. Stir together 2 cups shredded cheese, 2 cups hand-crushed Wheat Chex, 8 ounces softened cream cheese, and 1 teaspoon Cajun seasoning in a large mixing bowl.
4. Spoon cheese mixture into pepper halves.
5. Lightly beat together eggs and milk in a deep and shallow container, and coat stuffed peppers in egg mixture.
6. In a separate bowl mix together 1½ cups Chex and 1½ cups cheese.
7. Dip egg-coated peppers in Chex-and-cheese mixture, making sure the mixture stays on the egg-coated peppers, pressing, if necessary, with your fingers to make the crumb mixture stick.
8. Move pepper halves onto a lightly greased baking sheet, putting them close together so they touch each other. Top generously with additional cheese.

* Hand-crush Chex so pieces will remain in coarse chunks rather than being finely crushed.

CALLE OCHO GRILLED CHICKEN
AND FRESH MANGO SKEWERS

Yield: 12 servings

Strolling along Calle Ocho on Sunday afternoons has become our family's favorite excursion into this Caribbean-flavored part of Miami. To taste one of the wonderfully prepared specialties of the islands is, of course, the highlight of our adventure on Sunday. And of all the beautiful, tasty dishes, our favorite ones are the grilled chicken mango skewers, charcoal broiled by any of the vendors, often prepared street-side.

1 cup diced (¼") yellow aji peppers
1 pound boneless, skinless chicken breast
2 medium fresh mangoes, peeled and seeded
2 tablespoons extra-virgin olive oil
3 cobs fresh corn (or 2 cups canned or defrosted frozen corn kernels)
3 scallions, diced to ¼"
1 tablespoon butter
1 tablespoon sesame seeds, (preferred toasted)
2 tablespoons diced (¼") scallions
sea salt and freshly ground pepper to taste

DIRECTIONS:
1. Cut chicken breasts and mangoes into 1" cubes. Skewer about 4 pieces each of chicken and mango cubes, alternately, on each of 12 skewers. Lightly brush skewers with extra-virgin olive oil.
2. Place the corn cobs with 2 cups hot water in a sauté pan and cook over medium heat until the corn kernels are soft.
3. In a separate sauté pan, heat the butter with the scallions and add the drained corn kernels or cobs. Add a dash of sea salt. Sauté lightly.
4. Grill the chicken-and-mango skewers. Place about ½ cup corn in center of the plate. Place grilled chicken-and-mango skewers across the corn. Sprinkle with sesame seeds and chopped scallions.

Note: To prevent wooden skewers from burning, soak them in water for 30 minutes prior to use.

CANDIED CHOCOLATE ALMOND CRANBERRY CLUSTERS

Yield: about 25 clusters

FOR THE CANDIED ALMONDS

¼ cup water
½ cup cane sugar
½ tablespoon ground cinnamon
1 cup peeled, blanched almonds

YOU WILL ALSO NEED

18 ounces semisweet chocolate
1 cup Craisins (dried cranberries)
1 cup candied almonds (above)

DIRECTIONS:

1. To make the candied almonds, combine the water, sugar, and cinnamon in a saucepan over medium heat. Bring to a boil and add the almonds. Cook and stir the mixture until the liquid evaporates and leaves a syrupy coating on the almonds. Pour the almonds on a baking sheet lined with wax paper. Separate almonds using a fork. Allow to cool about 15 minutes.

2. Melt the chocolate in a double boiler. Remove from heat and cool slightly. Stir in dried cranberries and sugar-candied almonds. Drop by tablespoons onto a cookie sheet. Let harden at room temperature or chill in refrigerator.

CANTON-GRILLED TOFU WITH GREENS

Yield: 6 servings

Look for Asian greens (tatsoi, mizuna, and/or pea shoots) packaged as a salad mix. They're slightly more bitter than many spring greens and will stand up well to this aromatic, vinegary dressing.

FOR DRESSING

1 small carrot, peeled and coarsely chopped
½ cup prepared carrot juice
2 tablespoons white or yellow miso
2 tablespoons rice vinegar
2 tablespoons sesame oil
1 tablespoon coarsely chopped candied ginger
½ teaspoon minced garlic
1 table spoon Domaine de Canton ginger liqueur

FOR TOFU AND GREENS

28 ounces water-packed firm tofu, drained and rinsed
½ cup Domaine de Canton ginger liqueur
2 tablespoons honey
2 tablespoons peanut oil, and more for grilling tofu
2 tablespoons reduced-sodium soy sauce
½ tablespoon fish sauce
1 tablespoon sweet chili sauce
2 teaspoons minced garlic
10 ounces mixed Asian greens or baby spinach
additional Domaine de Canton ginger liqueur to drizzle on top of
    grilled tofu just before serving

DIRECTIONS:

1. Puree carrot, carrot juice, miso, vinegar, oil, candied ginger, garlic, and ginger liqueur in a blender or food processor until smooth.
2. Slice each tofu block crosswise into five slices; pat dry with paper towels.

3. Combine Domaine de Canton honey, oil, soy sauce, fish sauce, sweet chili sauce, and garlic in a small bowl. Spread half the marinade in a large baking dish, and top with the tofu slices. Spread the remaining marinade over the tofu, covering completely.
4. Preheat grill to medium high. Oil grill rack with peanut oil. Grill tofu until heated through, 2–3 minutes per side. To serve, toss greens with the dressing. Divide among six plates and top with the tofu.

Notes: The color of miso (fermented soybean paste) depends on how long it's aged. In general, the lighter the color, the milder the flavor. It will keep in the refrigerator for more than a year.

Fish sauce, a savory, salty sauce used in Chinese cooking, is made from fermented fish, beans, garlic, and rice wine. It can be found in the Asian food section of large supermarkets or at Asian markets. Use it in stir-fries and marinades with beef, chicken, or tofu.

Tip: To oil a grill rack, oil a folded paper towel, hold it with tongs, and rub it over the rack. (Do not use cooking spray on a hot grill.)

CANTON MARKET CHICKEN SOUP

Yield: 8 servings

What is so obliging about this hearty chicken soup is that you can add any vegetables that suit your fancy: napa or savoy cabbage, mushrooms, chinese broccoli, broccolini, onions, leeks, mustard or turnip greens, celery, or whatever tickles your bonnet. Just be sure that you don't overcook the vegetables. Spice it up with Asian-style chili sauce, such as sriracha, and/or serve the soup over noodles to make it a more-substantial main dish.

½ ounce (about ½ cup) dried shiitake or mixed dried mushrooms
3 cups boiling water
1 tablespoon peanut oil or canola oil
2 cups diced onion
3 cloves garlic, thinly sliced
6 (⅛"-thick) slices peeled fresh ginger
6 cups reduced-sodium chicken broth
¼ cup reduced-sodium soy sauce
1 teaspoon green cardamom
1 whole star anise
⅛ teaspoon cayenne pepper
2 pounds boneless, skinless chicken thighs, trimmed and cut into 1" pieces
1 fennel bulb, cored and cut into 1" pieces
8 scallions, whites cut into 2" pieces and greens chopped, divided
1 pound napa cabbage, preferably baby napa, white stems sliced lengthwise and greens chopped, divided
2 cups (4 ounces) mung bean sprouts (see note)
½ cup chopped fresh cilantro
2 teaspoons toasted sesame oil
¼ cup Asian-style chili sauce (such as sriracha)
¼ cup Domaine de Canton ginger liqueur

DIRECTIONS:

1. Place mushrooms in a heatproof measuring cup, and cover with boiling water. Soak for at least 30 minutes, up to several hours. Remove the mushrooms from the water, remove and discard stems (if any), and cut into ⅛" slices; set aside. Strain the soaking liquid, and reserve.

2. Heat oil in a large soup pot or dutch oven over medium heat. Add onion, garlic, and ginger, and cook, stirring, for 5 minutes. Pour in the reserved mushroom liquid, broth, soy sauce, cardamom, star anise, and pepper. Bring to a boil. Reduce to a simmer and stir in chicken. Simmer for 20 minutes.

3. Stir in fennel, scallion whites, and the reserved mushrooms, and cook for 5 minutes. Add napa cabbage stems, return to a simmer, and cook for 3 minutes more. Add greens and bean sprouts; cook until the greens are just wilted (about 2 minutes more).

4. Discard the cardamom and star anise. Ladle the soup into bowls. Garnish each bowl with scallion greens, cilantro, a ¼-teaspoon drizzle of sesame oil, and Asian chili sauce. Add Domaine de Canton ginger liqueur, and allow to float, not stirring into the soup. You may serve Domaine de Canton ginger liqueur on the side as an aperitif.

CANTON SALISBURY STEAKS
with Sautéed Watercress
Yield: 4 servings

16 ounces ground 90% fat-free sirloin of beef or lamb
½ cup finely diced red bell pepper
½ cup chopped scallions
2 tablespoons plain panko bread crumbs
2 tablespoons Domaine de Canton ginger liqueur
2 tablespoons dry sherry, divided
1 tablespoon minced fresh ginger
2½ teaspoons peanut oil, divided
8 cups (2 bunches or 2 [4-ounce] bags) trimmed watercress
¼ cup Domaine de Canton ginger liqueur

DIRECTIONS:
1. Place rack in upper third of oven; preheat broiler. Coat a broiler pan and rack with cooking spray.
2. Gently mix beef or lamb, bell pepper, scallions, panko, Domaine de Canton ginger liqueur, 1 tablespoon sherry, and ginger in a medium bowl until just combined. Form the mixture into 4 oblong patties, and place on the prepared broiler-pan rack. Brush the tops of the patties with 1 teaspoon oil. Broil, flipping once, until cooked through, about 4 minutes per side.
3. Meanwhile, heat the remaining oil in a large skillet over high heat. Add watercress, and cook, stirring often until just wilted (1–3 minutes). Divide the watercress between four plates. Return the pan to medium-high heat. Add Domaine de Canton ginger liqueur and the remaining 1 tablespoon sherry. Cook, stirring, until smooth, bubbling, and slightly reduced (about 1 minute). Top the watercress with the salisbury steaks, and drizzle with the pan sauce.

Note: Sherry is a type of fortified wine originally from southern Spain. Don't use the "cooking sherry" sold in many supermarkets; it can be surprisingly high in sodium. Instead, purchase dry sherry that's sold with other fortified wines in a wine or liquor store.

CARAMELIZED BANANAS FOSTER BREAD

Yield: 8 servings

FOR BANANAS FOSTER

2 medium firm bananas, peeled

1 tablespoon butter

6 tablespoons light brown sugar

¼ cup freshly squeezed orange juice

⅛ teaspoon cinnamon

2 cups low-fat vanilla ice cream or frozen yogurt (optional, as side)

YOU WILL ALSO NEED

1 cup all-purpose flour

½ cup whole-wheat flour

½ cup cornmeal

2 teaspoons baking powder

½ teaspoon salt

fresh ground pepper to taste

3 large eggs, lightly beaten

½ cup buttermilk

1 tablespoon butter, melted

1 tablespoon honey

2 cups coarsely mashed caramelized bananas Foster (see above)

cooking spray

DIRECTIONS:

1. Cut bananas in half lengthwise. Melt butter in a nonstick skillet over medium-high heat. Add brown sugar, and lay the banana slices on top, cut side up. Cook undisturbed for 20 seconds, then add rum (or orange juice) and cinnamon. Cook for 10 seconds, then turn bananas carefully and cook for 45–60 seconds more, basting with the pan sauce. Set aside momentarily.

2. Preheat oven to 425 degrees F. Place a 9" iron skillet (or similar ovenproof skillet) in the oven to heat.

3. Whisk all-purpose flour, whole-wheat flour, cornmeal, baking powder, salt, and pepper in a large mixing bowl.
4. Whisk eggs, buttermilk, butter, and honey in a medium bowl, and add the egg mixture to the dry ingredients. Preferably mix with a rubber spatula. Stir in the coarsely mashed bananas Foster.
5. Remove the hot skillet from the oven and coat it with cooking spray. Pour in the batter, spreading evenly. Bake the bread until golden brown and a toothpick inserted into the center comes out clean (20–25 minutes).
6. Serve with low-fat vanilla ice cream or frozen yogurt.

CARIBBEAN BARBECUE SEA BASS
and Spicy Tropical Risotto
Yield: 4 servings

FOR RISOTTO
1½ cups arborio rice
6 tablespoons sweet butter
3 tablespoons olive oil
1 medium onion, chopped
4½ cups chicken or vegetable broth
1 cup Dole canned pineapple orange banana juice
½ teaspoon minced fresh ginger
¼ teaspoon saffron
1 tablespoon jamaican jerk seasoning
½ teaspoon cayenne
Kosher salt and fresh ground black pepper to taste

FOR BARBECUE SAUCE
½ cup Dole canned pineapple orange banana juice
¼ cup soy sauce
3 tablespoons olive oil
1 tablespoon jamaican jerk seasoning

FOR BARBECUE SEA BASS AND PINEAPPLE
4 (6-ounce) sea bass fillets
8 Dole pineapple slices

DIRECTIONS:
1. In a heavy-sided saucepan, melt 3 tablespoons butter and the olive oil together, stirring well. Then add onion and cook for 1 minute. Add the arborio rice and cook for another minute, stirring well.
2. Meanwhile, warm the broth and Dole pineapple orange banana juice together and bring to a slow simmer. Add ½ cup of the broth-and-juice mixture to the rice mixture, constantly stirring. As this liquid is absorbed, add another ½ cup. Continue to cook and add warm

broth-and-juice mixture in this manner for 20 minutes. When most of the broth has been added to the rice, finish the risotto with the remaining butter and stir rapidly to incorporate. Check the seasoning and add salt and pepper if necessary.

3. Mix all barbecue sauce ingredients thoroughly. The sauce can be stored in a glass jar for two weeks.

4. Heat grill for 10 minutes. Brush the sea bass fillets and pineapples generously with the sauce, and grill for about 1½ minutes on each side. Serve sea bass fillets and pineapples with the spicy tropical risotto.

CARIBBEAN GOURMET ROAST CHICKEN
with Plantains
Yield: 4 servings

½ cup chopped scallions (green part only)
1 medium poblano or Anaheim seeded pepper, chopped
2 tablespoons olive oil
1 tablespoon balsamic vinegar
1 tablespoon chopped fresh thyme
1 tablespoon sea salt
1 tablespoon ground black pepper
1 tablespoon honey
1 tablespoon ground allspice
4 (6-ounce) boneless, skinless chicken breasts
4 split ripe plantains or bananas
1 mango, peeled, seeded, and sliced

DIRECTIONS:

1. Mix first nine ingredients with a wooden spoon in a glass bowl until well combined. Place chicken in same large glass or ceramic bowl. Rub marinade mixture all over chicken breasts. Marinate from 1 hour to overnight. Strain marinade, separating solid parts from the liquids.

2. Preheat oven to 375 degrees F. Place chicken breasts with liquids of strained marinade on lightly greased rack set in large roasting pan. Add 1 cup water to pan to prevent pan drippings from scorching. Roast chicken 15 minutes. Turn chicken over and roast 15 more minutes. Turn chicken over again and add sliced plantains (or bananas) and mango to rack. Broil chicken, plantains, and mango slices for 1–2 minutes until chicken breasts are mahogany brown and an instant-read meat thermometer registers 160 degrees F when inserted into innermost part of chicken breasts.

3. Transfer chicken and tropical fruit slices to platter. Top with reserved solid green parts of marinade. Tent with foil and let stand 10 minutes. Place in freezer bag in freezer until ready to be served.

4. Remove from freezer 30 minutes to 1 hour before reheating at 375 degrees F in preheated oven. Place chicken breasts, fruit, and marinade greens on rack in roasting pan, uncovered. Remove from oven when heated through. Enjoy this exotic freshly cooked dinner at your leisure.

CARIBBEAN LOBSTER SOFRITO PIZZA

Yield: 1 (12") pizza (8 slices)

FOR THE SOFRITO
20 annatto seeds
⅓ cup olive oil
3 bacon slices, diced
20 garlic cloves, minced
1 red onion, chopped
1 yellow onion, chopped
20 small red peppers, seeded and diced
5 plum tomatoes, chopped
1 tablespoon ground coriander, toasted
1 jalapeño, seeded and finely diced
8 cups chicken broth or water
salt and pepper to taste
½ bunch oregano, chopped

FOR THE PIZZA
1 (12") gourmet pizza crust
1 teaspoon chopped garlic
1 cup Caribbean lobster (crayfish) meat (meat from a 1-pound lobster),
   diced, raw
3–4 ounces sofrito
1 cup crumbled queso blanco
½ yellow pepper, seeded and diced
½ Anaheim or poblano pepper, seeded and diced
1 scallion, sliced across into rings
8 lime wedges

DIRECTIONS:
1. Heat annatto seeds in olive oil over medium-high heat. Add bacon,
    garlic, and onions. Cook 5 minutes. Stir in red peppers, tomatoes,
    coriander, and jalapeño. Add broth and salt and pepper to taste.
    Simmer 30 minutes. Add oregano; simmer 15 minutes more. Strain

mixture, reserving liquid. Puree mixture to a coarse texture. Add liquid if needed.

2. Heat remaining olive oil in a nonstick skillet. Add garlic; cook until lightly toasted. Add raw lobster meat and cook until tender; set aside to cool. (If lobster meat is cooked, just heat and set aside to cool.)

3. Preheat oven to 450 degrees F.

4. Line a vented pizza pan with parchment paper trimmed so that edges don't hang over the sides and do not touch oven walls. Spread sofrito on dough, leaving a ½" border. Top with cheese, lobster, peppers, and scallions. Reduce oven temperature to 425 degrees F and bake for 10 minutes, rotating often, until golden brown and crispy. Serve immediately with lime wedges.

CARIBBEAN MIONETTO BOWL

Yield: 10 servings

3½ ounces Grand Marnier
3½ ounces dark Caribbean rum
4 bottles Mionetto Prosecco Brut
1 ounce sugar
6 carambolas
4 lemons

DIRECTIONS:

1. Cut carambolas and lemons into thin slices and then into quarters. Add all the fruit pieces into a large crystal or heavy cut-glass fruit bowl. Sprinkle with sugar and Grand Marnier and pour the rum over it. Allow to marinate for up to 2 hours. Just before service, fill the bowl with 4 bottles of Mionetto Prosecco Brut. Serve in champagne flutes with swizzle sticks.

CARIBBEAN PLANTAIN SOUP

Yield: 6 servings

3 green (unripe) plantains
1 tablespoon pineapple or apple vinegar
2 tomatoes, seeded and chopped
2 bell peppers, seeded and chopped
2 scallions, chopped
½ tablespoon achiote paste
2 tablespoons olive oil
4 cups vegetable broth, or as needed
salt and pepper to taste
24 ounces coarsely chopped or ground pork

DIRECTIONS:

1. Cut plantains in half, leaving skin on, and boil in water to cover until tender. Drain, cool, peel, and mash to a paste. Place in slow cooker.
2. Place the vinegar, tomatoes, bell peppers, scallions, and achiote in a blender and puree.
3. Heat oil in large pot. Add tomato and vegetable puree. Cook, stirring frequently, 10 minutes. Place together with plantains in slow cooker for 2 hours.
4. Add salt and pepper.

Serving suggestion: add 1 tablespoon crumbled goat cheese to each serving.

CAYENNE AND DRIED CHERRY DEVILED EGGS
with White Albacore Tuna and Almonds
Yield: 14 (4-ounce) servings

14 hard-boiled eggs
½ cup mayonnaise
½ cup sour cream
1½ teaspoons Dijon mustard
1 teaspoon fresh lemon juice
¼ teaspoon cayenne pepper
1 cup chopped scallions
24 ounces white albacore tuna, flaked
1 cup chopped dried cherries
1 cup sliced almonds, lightly toasted and crumbled, divided
¼ cup chopped cilantro leaves

DIRECTIONS:

1. Cut eggs in half lengthwise. Remove yolks to medium bowl. Reserve 24 white halves. Finely chop remaining 4 white halves.
2. Mash yolks with fork. Add mayonnaise, sour cream, mustard, lemon juice, and cayenne pepper, and mix well.
3. Add chopped egg whites and chopped scallions, and gently fold in white albacore tuna flakes, chopped cherries, and half the toasted, sliced, and crumbled almonds. Mix well.
4. Spoon 1 heaping tablespoon yolk mixture into reserved egg-white halves. Sprinkle with mixture of remaining toasted sliced almonds and cilantro leaves.
5. Refrigerate, covered, to blend flavors.

BLUE CHEESE CEREAL SLAW

Yield: 6 servings

12 cups angel-hair coleslaw mix
24 cherry tomatoes, halved
1½ cups coleslaw salad dressing
3 cups crumbled blue cheese or gorgonzola
3 cups Wheat Chex
1 cup bacon bits

DIRECTIONS:

1. Preheat oven to 375 degrees F.
2. In a large bowl combine blue cheese crumbs, Chex, and bacon bits. Spoon onto an aluminum-foil-lined baking sheet and place into preheated oven.
3. Turn blue-cheese-Chex mixture from time to time until crumbs are crispy and lightly browned.
4. In another large bowl, combine coleslaw mix, tomatoes, and salad dressing. Cover and refrigerate until ready to serve. Just before serving, sprinkle with crunchy Chex and blue cheese crumbs.

CEREAL HOT WINGS

Yield: 8 servings

3 cups Wheat Chex, crushed
1½ teaspoons salt
½ teaspoon black pepper
2 pounds chicken drumettes
vegetable oil

FOR SAUCE
½ cup (1 stick) butter
½ cup V8 juice
¼ cup ketchup
⅓ cup hot pepper sauce, or to taste

DIRECTIONS:
1. Combine crushed Wheat Chex, salt, and pepper in a shallow bowl. Coat the wings with the Chex mixture.
2. Heat 2–3 inches oil in a fryer or heavy pot to 365 degrees F. Fry the wings, a few at a time, until golden brown on all sides and cooked through, about 10–15 minutes. Drain on paper towels.
3. Combine all sauce ingredients in a small saucepan. Bring to a boil. Dip cooked wings in the sauce. Serve with blue cheese dressing and fresh celery and carrot sticks.

EXTRA-SHARP CHEDDAR BERRY NAPOLEONS

Yield: 24 servings

1 (10-ounce) package frozen sweetened raspberries

1 tablespoon port wine

1 tablespoon raspberry liqueur

1 (16 ounce) package frozen phyllo dough, thawed

1 cup butter, melted

2 cups fresh raspberries

2 cups fresh blueberries

2 cups fresh sliced strawberries

3–4 tablespoons orange liqueur

¼ cup heavy whipping cream

1½ cups Black Diamond extra-sharp cheddar cheese spread

DIRECTIONS:

1. Place the raspberries, wine, and raspberry liqueur in a blender; cover and process until pureed. Strain the raspberry mixture, reserving juice. Discard seeds. Set aside.

2. Layer 2 sheets of phyllo dough on a baking sheet. Brush with butter. Keep remaining phyllo covered with plastic wrap and a damp towel to prevent it from drying out. Repeat layers four times. Cut stack in half lengthwise, then cut widthwise, forming twelve rectangles. Repeat with remaining dough on three additional baking sheets. Bake at 375 degrees F for 6–8 minutes or until golden brown. Cool on pans on wire racks.

3. In a large bowl, combine berries, orange liqueur, and 2 tablespoons raspberry juice. Toss to coat. Cover and refrigerate for 30 minutes.

4. Meanwhile, in a mixing bowl, beat cream until it begins to thicken. Add extra-sharp cheddar cheese spread and, with a paddle attachment, combine cream and cheddar spread to a consistent creamy texture.

5. Drizzle 1 tablespoon remaining raspberry sauce over each serving plate. Place 1 phyllo rectangle over sauce. Layer each with ¼ cup berries and 2 tablespoons cheddar whipped cream. Top with remaining phyllo.

WISCONSIN CHERRY SIRLOIN BURGER

Yield: 5 servings

Tart dried Wisconsin cherries lend pizzazz to these grilled sirloin burgers.

1 egg, slightly beaten
½ cup ready-to-eat cherry granola (store-bought)
¼ cup sliced scallions
2 tablespoons chopped almonds, toasted
½ teaspoon dried oregano leaves
½ teaspoon Italian-style seasoned salt
¼ teaspoon pepper
1 pound uncooked lean ground sirloin of beef
½ cup dried Wisconsin Montmorency cherries
¼ cup red tart cherry jelly, melted
5 hamburger buns, split
5 lettuce leaves

DIRECTIONS:

1. In large bowl, stir together egg, ready-to-eat cherry granola, scallions, almonds, oregano, Italian-style seasoned salt, and pepper. Add ground sirloin of beef and dried Wisconsin Montmorency cherries; mix well. Shape mixture into five ¾"-thick patties. (Patties will be soft.)

2. Grill patties over medium coals for 12–14 minutes or until juices run clear, turning once halfway through grilling.* Brush with jelly during the last 5 minutes of grilling time. Serve on buns with lettuce leaves.

*Patties may also be cooked in contact grill. Preheat contact grill for 5 minutes. Cook patties in grill for 6–9 minutes or until juices run clear (160 degrees F). Drizzle with jelly mixture after cooking. Serve as directed above.

CHEWY BACON ALMOND BARS

18 ounces almond paste (not marzipan; see note)
18 ounces Sugardale bacon bits, divided
¼ cup superfine sugar
½ teaspoons salt
4 tablespoons amaretto liqueur
1 cup powdered sugar

DIRECTIONS:

1. Preheat oven to 375 degrees F. Combine the almond paste and 9 ounces Sugardale bacon bits plus sugar, and salt in a large mixing bowl and, using your hands, knead together until mixture is just incorporated. Add the liqueur and gently work it into the paste to form a smooth dough.

2. Sift the powdered sugar into a mixing bowl. Using a ½-ounce metal scoop, scoop out individual portions of the dough and place each in the bowl of mixture of 9 ounces remaining bacon bits and powdered sugar. Coat each ball completely with mixture of powdered sugar and bacon bits and place on a parchment-lined baking sheet, leaving a 1" space between each macaroon. Pinch together the sides of each macaroon with your fingers and thumb, and make a finger-indented well in the center; each macaroon should look somewhat like a little volcano. Let the macaroons sit out for 20 minutes to dry out. Bake until golden brown, about 10–12 minutes. Remove from oven and let cool completely. Serve immediately or store in an airtight container.

Note: Almond paste is similar to marzipan but contains less sugar and no fillers. (Some versions of almond paste do contain cream or eggs; to make this recipe vegan, ensure that your almond paste contains no eggs or dairy.) Marzipan will not work for this recipe.

CHICAGO STOCKYARD STEAK BURGER
with Chipotle Butter, Belgian Endive, and Heirloom Tomato Slices
Yield: 6 burgers

2 pounds ground sirloin
¼ cup pinot noir

FOR CHIPOTLE BUTTER
¼ pound butter, softened
1 teaspoon garlic salt
1 tablespoon finely chopped shallots
½ teaspoon ground white pepper
2 teaspoons snipped fresh marjoram
1 tablespoon olive oil
1½ teaspoons fresh lime juice
1 teaspoon paprika
3 teaspoons finely chopped chipotle pepper in adobo sauce
6 sun-dried tomatoes in olive oil, drained and finely chopped
2 teaspoons toasted ground cumin

YOU WILL ALSO NEED
vegetable oil spray
6 large kaiser rolls, seeded
6 slices mild cheddar cheese
⅔ cup light mayonnaise or ⅔ cup grape-seed-oil Vegenaise* blended
  with 2 tablespoons chipotle butter
3 heads Belgian endive, halved lengthwise
6 large ¼"-thick heirloom tomato slices
6 thin slices red onions
1 sprig marjoram and 2 Kosher dill pickle slices (optional, as garnish)

DIRECTIONS:
1. In a grill with a cover, prepare a medium-hot fire for direct-heat
   cooking.
2. In a small bowl, stir together butter and remaining ten ingredients.
   Set aside ½ cup.

3. In a medium-sized bowl, gently combine the sirloin, pinot noir, and all but ½ cup of the chipotle butter. Divide the sirloin-steak mixture into six equal portions and shape into 4" round patties.

4. Spray the grill rack with vegetable oil. Brush the patties from both sides with chipotle butter, then place the patties on the grill. Cook, turning once, until done as preferred (4–5 minutes on each side for medium rare). During the last few minutes of cooking, top each patty with a slice of cheddar cheese. During the last minute of cooking, open the rolls and toast them, facedown, on the outer edges of the grill.

5. In a small bowl, combine mayonnaise and chipotle butter. Spread the mixture on the cut sides of the toasted rolls. On the bottom half of each roll, layer half of each Belgian endive, burger, tomato slice, onion slice, and other roll half. Add the 2 slices Kosher dill pickles and a sprig of marjoram to each burger as optional garnish, if desired.

* Available in natural-foods markets.

CHICKEN BREAST FILLETS VERDE-BLANCO
with Fresh Buffalo Mozzarella, Arugula,
and a Fine Herb Pine Nut Crust

Yield: 3 servings

3 (8-ounce) boneless, skinless chicken breast fillets, pounded thin (to
⅓") with finely diced herbs (mix of 1 tablespoon each chives, Italian
parsley, marjoram, tarragon)

salt and freshly ground pepper to taste

12 large hydroponically grown arugula leaves, folded in half

9 large basil leaves

12 fresh ripe blackberries

3 thin 1-ounce slices fresh buffalo mozzarella cheese

3 size-100 scoops Breakstone's sour cream

12 tablespoons toasted pine nuts

unbleached, sifted all-purpose flour, as needed, to coat chicken fillets

2 eggs' worth of egg wash with fine herbs (see above) and salt and
freshly ground pepper to taste.

½ cup fine bread crumbs, blended with 1 cup toasted, coarsely ground
pine nuts

1 tablespoon fine herbs (see above) and ½ tablespoons Spanish paprika

3 tablespoons extra-virgin olive oil

3 tablespoons sweet butter

1 teaspoon crushed fresh garlic

1 tablespoon fresh lemon juice

FOR GARNISH

12 each snow peas, ends trimmed and blanched

12 each blackberries

6 sprigs fresh basil

3 teaspoon honey

DIRECTIONS:

1. Pound chicken breast fillets with fine herbs, salt, and pepper. Lay
    flat on a work table and layer the stuffing ingredients in this order:

4 folded arugula leaves, topped with 3 basil leaves, 3 blackberries, 1 slice buffalo mozzarella, and 1 scoop sour cream with toasted pine nuts. Roll each chicken breast fillet to enclose the stuffing. Tie with thin thread, dust with flour, dip in seasoned egg wash, and roll each serving in a well-seasoned mixture of pine nuts, fine herbs, and bread crumbs. Sauté each fillet for 2–3 minutes in an 8"–10" sauté pan in mixture of extra-virgin olive oil and sweet butter. Turn once for color, and add a touch of garlic and lemon juice and 3 teaspoons honey to the skillet. Turn again to ensure doneness. Finish cooking just before serving, in a preheated 400-degree F oven for 3–4 minutes or until hot and ready to serve.

OYSTER AND VEGETABLE CHOWDER

Yield: 6 servings

2 (8-ounce) cans Chicken-of-the-Sea whole oysters, with juice

1 (11-ounce) bag steamed fresh vegetables (fresh frozen baby broccoli
    blend; I used Birds Eye)

1 quart clear, fat-free, reduced-sodium chicken broth; clear seafood
    stock; or oyster liquor

1½ pounds russet potatoes, half of them cooked and then mashed, half
    uncooked but cut in small dice

1 medium onion, small dice

2 stalks celery, small dice

2 bell peppers (1 green, 1 red), cut into small dice

3 minced garlic cloves

¼ cup flour

3 bay leaves

1 cup soy milk

1 cup light sour cream

Kosher salt and finely ground white pepper to taste

1 tablespoon Cajun-blend seasoning chopped with 3 sprigs fresh basil

1 bunch scallions, thinly sliced

2 tablespoons olive oil (optional, offered as an add-on)

DIRECTIONS:

1. In a saucepan, steam vegetables in their pouch in simmering water for
   5–6 minutes or until they are almost tender. Set aside.
2. In another saucepan, bring broth to a boil.
3. Mix diced potatoes, onions, celery, peppers, and garlic in medium
   bowl. Dust mixture with flour. And add all to broth.
4. Reduce heat to simmer and cook for 2 minutes.
5. In a medium bowl, blend mashed potatoes with soy milk and sour
   cream with a wire whisk. Add to chowder.

6. Bring chowder to a boil again before adding Chicken-of-the-Sea whole oysters and juice; add Cajun seasoning with basil, and season to taste with salt and pepper. (I personally don't see a reason to add additional salt.) To serve, sprinkle each serving with sliced scallions and offer olive oil as an add-on.

CHICKEN POT PIE

Yield: 6 entrees

This chicken pot pie is studded with peas, mushrooms, carrots, and onions and topped with tender whole-wheat biscuits with extra-virgin olive oil. The savory sauce gets a rich taste from reduced-fat sour cream, but with less fat and fewer calories than regular sour cream would provide. And it ends up just as delicious and comforting as you expect.

FOR FILLING

¼ cup plus 2 tablespoons extra-virgin olive oil
1 cup frozen pearl onions, thawed
1 cup peeled baby carrots
2 tablespoons extra-virgin olive oil
10 ounces cremini mushrooms, halved
2½ cups reduced-sodium chicken broth, divided
¼ cup cornstarch
2½ cups diced cooked chicken or turkey
1 cup frozen peas, thawed
¼ cup reduced-fat sour cream
¼ teaspoon salt
freshly ground pepper to taste

FOR BISCUIT TOPPING

¾ cup whole-wheat pastry flour (see note)
¾ cup all-purpose flour
2 teaspoons sugar
1¼ teaspoons baking powder
½ teaspoon baking soda
½ teaspoon salt
1 teaspoon dried thyme
2½ tablespoons extra-virgin olive oil, divided
1 cup nonfat buttermilk

DIRECTIONS:

1. Heat ¼ cup extra-virgin olive oil in a large skillet or dutch oven over medium-high heat. Add onions and carrots. Cook, stirring, until golden brown and tender (about 7 minutes). Transfer to a bowl.

2. Heat the remaining 2 tablespoons extra-virgin olive oil in the pan over medium-high heat. Add mushrooms and cook, stirring often, until mushrooms have browned and their liquid has evaporated (5–7 minutes). Return the onions and carrots to the pan. Add 2 cups broth and bring to a boil; reduce heat to a simmer. Mix cornstarch with the remaining ½ cup broth; add to the pan and cook, stirring, until the sauce thickens. Stir in chicken (or turkey), peas, sour cream, salt, and pepper. Transfer the filling to a 2-quart baking dish.

3. Preheat oven to 400 degrees F. Whisk whole-wheat flour, all-purpose flour, sugar, baking powder, baking soda, salt, and thyme in a large bowl. Using your fingertips or 2 knives, add 1½ tablespoons extra-virgin olive oil to the dry ingredients and mix until crumbly. Add buttermilk and remaining extra-virgin olive oil. Stir until just combined. Drop the dough onto the filling in six even portions. Set the baking dish on a baking sheet.

4. Bake the pot pie until the topping is golden and the filling is bubbling (30–35 minutes). Let cool for 10 minutes before serving.

Note: Whole wheat pastry flour is milled from soft wheat. It contains less gluten than regular whole-wheat flour and helps ensure a tender result in delicate baked goods while providing the nutritional benefits of whole grains. It is available in large supermarkets and in natural-foods stores. Extra-virgin olive oil makes the crust extra flaky and reduces the number of calories. No other ingredient can complement the bouquet of vegetables as well as extra-virgin olive oil.

ASIAN CHILI OF SEA CLAMS
with Toasted Sesame Udon Noodles

Yield: 4 servings

cooking spray

2 cups diced onions

½ cup julienned carrots

½ cup water chestnuts, sliced

½ cup chopped scallions

½ cup dried wood ear mushrooms, chopped

½ cup bamboo shoots, julienned

2 tablespoons chile garlic paste

1¼ pounds IQF chopped sea clams

3 tablespoons brown sugar

½ teaspoon ground black pepper

¼ teaspoon salt

2 (15-ounce) cans pinto beans, drained and rinsed

2 (14.5-ounce) cans diced tomatoes

1 (14-ounce) can sea clam juice

2 chipotle chiles, canned in adobo sauce, minced

FOR GARNISH

½ cup light sour cream

chopped scallions

toasted sesame seeds (see below)

FOR NOODLES

1 (7 ounces) package udon noodles

½ chopped pepper each: red, green, yellow

4 scallions, minced

½ cup green peas

2 tablespoons sesame seeds, toasted in a dry skillet

DIRECTIONS:

1. Heat dutch oven over medium-high heat. Coat pan with cooking spray. Add onion and next seven ingredients (through chopped

sea clams), sauté for 8 minutes, or until sea clams are browned and vegetables are tender. Add sugar and next six ingredients (through chipotle chiles) to pan, stirring to blend

2. Bring a large pot of water to a boil. Add udon noodles and cook until tender, about 3 minutes. Drain and place in a serving bowl.

3. In a microwave-safe bowl, combine the green, red, and yellow peppers with scallions and peas. Heat in the microwave until warm, but still crisp. Add to the noodles in the bowl, and pour the chili over udon noodles in each of the serving bowls.

CHILLED PAPAYA CARAMELIZED ONION SOUP
with Shrimp

Yield: 6 servings

3 cups sliced sweet onions (12 ounces)
1 tablespoon extra-virgin olive oil
1½ cups papaya pulp
1½ cups fat-free, no-salt-added vegetable broth
½ cup coconut milk
1 tablespoon chopped fresh tarragon leaves
½ teaspoon pepper
fat free sour cream or soy cream, as needed (optional)
fresh tarragon sprigs, as needed
2 ounces small cooked, shelled shrimp

DIRECTIONS:

1. Sauté onions gently in oil in a nonstick skillet until tender and sweet (about 15 minutes). Set aside ½ cup onions for garnish.
2. Place remaining onions in electric blender along with papaya, broth, coconut milk, chopped fresh tarragon, and pepper. Process until pureed. Chill. Serve in chilled glasses or wide-rimmed bowls with a dollop of soy cream or fat-free sour cream in center of each. Curl reserved onions over the sour cream (or soy cream) and garnish each with fresh tarragon and small kabob of shrimp.

LA DOLCE VITA RICH AND SWEET
ORGANIC CHOCOLATE BARS

Yield: 20 bars

FOR CHOCOLATE-BAR MIXTURE

1 cup unbleached all-purpose flour
1 cup sugar
½ cup (1 stick) Organic Valley European-style cultured butter, softened
⅓ cup organic Green and Black's baking cocoa
½ cup Organic Valley organic whole milk
¼ cup Organic Valley organic sour cream
1 Organic Valley organic whole egg
½ teaspoon baking powder
¼ teaspoon salt

FOR GLAZE

½ cup powdered sugar
¼ cup Organic Valley European-style cultured butter, softened
2 tablespoons organic Green and Black's baking cocoa
3 tablespoons Organic Valley organic whole milk
½ teaspoon vanilla
½ cup chopped pecans

DIRECTIONS:

1. Heat oven to 350 degrees F. In large mixer bowl, combine all chocolate-bar-mixture ingredients and beat at medium speed, scraping bowl often, until smooth (2–3 minutes).

2. Pour into 13" × 9" baking pan. Bake for 20–25 minutes or until cake begins to pull away from sides of pan.

3. In a small mixer bowl combine all glaze ingredients except pecans. Beat at medium speed, scraping bowl often, until well mixed (1–2 minutes). (Glaze will look grainy until spread over chocolate bars.) Stir in pecans and spread over hot bars. Cover and refrigerate or freeze immediately until ready to serve. When you are ready to serve, cut into 20 bars and serve. The bars do not need to be thawed before serving

CHOCOLATE-COVERED ALMOND AND CRANBERRY HOLIDAY COOKIES

Yield: 36 cookies

This cookie dough, with regular oats in the batter, needs to be chilled for several hours or overnight before baking.

¾ cup all-purpose flour (about 3⅓ ounces)
¾ cup whole-wheat flour (about 3½ ounces)
¾ cup regular oats
½ teaspoon baking powder
¼ teaspoon baking soda
¼ teaspoon salt
½ cup dried cranberries
5 tablespoons chocolate-covered almonds, coarsely chopped
   (store-bought)
¾ cup packed brown sugar
5 tablespoons butter, softened
2 tablespoons honey
¾ teaspoon vanilla extract
1 large egg
1 large egg white
cooking spray

DIRECTIONS:

1. Lightly spoon flours into dry measuring cups; level with a knife. Combine flours, oats, baking powder, and the next four ingredients (through chocolate-covered almonds) in a large bowl.
2. Combine sugar and butter in a large bowl; beat with a mixer at medium speed until light and fluffy. Add honey, vanilla, egg, and egg white; beat well. Add flour mixture to sugar mixture; beat at low speed until well blended. Cover and refrigerate 8 hours or overnight.
3. Preheat oven to 350 degrees F. Scoop cookie dough in 1-tablespoon-size portions onto lightly greased baking sheet pans and bake for 15 minutes or until lightly browned, turning the sheet pan once.

CHOCOLATE HAZELNUT TORTE

Yield: 24 servings

FOR TORTE
1 pound 3 ounces eggs
10 ounces sugar
9 ounces cake flour
1 teaspoon baking powder
⅓ cup cocoa powder
4 ounces finely ground toasted hazelnuts

FOR CHOCOLATE ALMOND CREAM FILLING
1½ quarts heavy cream
30 ounces bittersweet chocolate, chopped
7 ounces coarsely ground toasted hazelnuts

FOR GARNISH
16 ounces shaved bittersweet chocolate, 75% cocoa
16 ounces toasted hazelnuts, crushed

DIRECTIONS:
1. Beat eggs and sugar together, then warm them over simmering water to 110 degrees F. Whip the egg mixture to the ribbon stage (about 10–12 minutes). Sift together the flour, baking powder, and cocoa powder, then carefully fold it into the whipped eggs. Fold in the ground hazelnuts. Spread onto a paper-lined full-sheet pan. Bake at 400 degrees F for 8–10 minutes. Cool. Trim the cake and transfer it to a clean sheet pan fitted with a pan extender.
2. Heat the cream, without boiling, over medium heat. Add the chocolate. Cover and let sit for about 10 minutes or until the chocolate melts. Add the ground hazelnuts, then whisk until the mixture is smooth. Cool to room temperature, then chill briefly in the refrigerator. Whip the filling until lightened; spread it evenly over the chocolate cake. Cover and refrigerate or freeze.
3. Garnish sides and top of torte with shaved chocolate and toasted hazelnuts.

CHOCOLATE MALT CUPCAKES

Yield: 12 cupcakes

FOR CUPCAKES
1 ounce good-quality semisweet chocolate, finely chopped
½ cup hot brewed coffee
1 cup granulated sugar
¾ cup plus 1 tablespoon unbleached all-purpose flour
½ cup unsweetened cocoa powder (not Dutch process)
generous ½ teaspoons baking soda
¼ teaspoon baking powder
scant ½ teaspoon salt
1 large egg
¼ cup canola oil
½ cup buttermilk
¼ teaspoon pure vanilla extract

FOR FROSTING
2 cups powdered sugar
1 tablespoon unsweetened cocoa powder (not Dutch process)
⅓ cup malted milk powder, such as Carnation or Horlicks
9 tablespoons (1 stick plus 1 tablespoon) unsalted butter, at room
    temperature
2 tablespoons boiling water

DIRECTIONS:
1. Preheat oven to 300 degrees F. Line twelve cups of a muffin tin with paper liners.
2. Place the chocolate in a medium bowl with hot coffee. Let stand, stirring occasionally, until chocolate is melted and mixture is smooth and opaque.
3. In another medium bowl, combine sugar, flour, cocoa powder, baking soda, baking powder, and salt, and whisk to combine well.
4. In a large bowl, beat egg with an electric mixer until it is pale yellow in color, (about 1–2 minutes). Slowly add the oil, buttermilk, and vanilla

extract, beating to combine well. Slowly add the melted-chocolate mixture, and beat to thoroughly combine. Add the dry ingredients and beat on medium speed until the batter is just combined. Using a rubber spatula, scrape the sides of the bowl and briefly fold the batter to be certain all of the dry ingredients are incorporated.

5. Divide the batter evenly among the twelve prepared muffin cups. Bake for 20–25 minutes, or until a toothpick inserted in the center of a cupcake comes out clean. Cool the cupcakes for 15 minutes in the pan, then gently transfer them to a rack to cool completely. They are very delicate and tender, so take care.

6. When cupcakes are cool, make frosting. In the bowl of a food processor, combine powdered sugar, cocoa, and malted milk powder, and process to mix well. Add butter and process to blend. Stop the motor, and scrape down the sides of the bowl with a rubber spatula. Then, with the motor running, add the water. Process briefly, until the frosting is smooth. Frost the cupcakes in loose swirls and serve.

CHOCOLATE PRALINE, PUMPKIN, AND PEAR PIE

Yield: 3 Pies, 8 slices each

FOR PIE SHELLS

4 cups cornflakes crumbs

2 cups all-purpose flour

1½ cups unsalted butter, cold

½ cup vegetable shortening, cold

4 ounces ice water

1 cup chopped glazed pecans (from 5-ounce bag)

3 tablespoons chopped crystallized ginger

FOR FILLING

6 eggs

½ cups sugar

3 teaspoons cinnamon, ground

2 cups heavy cream

1 can (15 ounces) pumpkin (not pumpkin-pie mix)

9 fresh or canned pear halves (peeled and cored) pureed

FOR CHOCOLATE PRALINE TOPPING

½ c dark brown sugar, packed

8 tablespoons sweet butter

1 cups chocolate-fudge sauce (I like Lindt best)

2 cups premium dark-chocolate bars with nuts or almonds, chopped

FOR GARNISH

12 dark chocolate truffles, cut in half

DIRECTIONS:

1. Preheat oven to 325 degrees F.

2. In a food processor or blender, blend first four ingredients until mix resembles a coarse meal. Add water until dough forms. Refrigerate 15 minutes. Roll out dough and use to line three 9" pie plates. Place pie plates on baking sheet. Bake in 325-degree preheated oven 8–10 minutes until lightly browned—*not until fully browned*. Divide

chopped glazed pecans and crystallized ginger evenly among the three shells.

3. In the meantime, mix filling ingredients until well blended. Pour into partially baked crusts. Return pies to baking sheet and place in oven. Increase heat to 350 degrees F. Bake 45–50 minutes or until knife inserted into center of pie comes out clean. Cool on cooling rack for 1 hour before serving.

4. Heat brown sugar and butter, stirring until smooth. Whisk in chocolate-fudge sauce. Bring to a boil. While whisking, boil until sugar just begins to caramelize (about 5 minutes). Add chopped dark chocolate with nut bars. Cool to lukewarm.

5. Serve pie slices with ladle of sauce, topping each slice with ½ dark chocolate truffle.

CRISPY ITALIAN CHRISTMAS BERRY CHOCOLATE MERINGUE TORTA

Yield: 6 servings

FOR MERINGUE
4 large egg whites
7 ounces caster (light brown) sugar
4 ounces bittersweet chocolate (70% cocoa), plain, finely chopped

FOR FILLING AND DECORATION
8 ounces heavy whipping cream (40%)
10 ounces excellent quality dark bittersweet chocolate (70% cocoa), finely chopped
1 pound mixed berries (raspberries, blackberries, cranberries, blueberries)

FOR CARAMEL SHAPES
4 ounces caster (light brown) sugar
2 ounces water

DIRECTIONS:
1. Preheat oven to 225 degrees F. Line two baking sheets with baking parchment and draw 3" circles, using a pastry cutter as a template.
2. Whisk egg whites until they form stiff peaks. Whisk in the sugar a teaspoon at a time to begin with and then in a steady stream as the egg whites thicken. When all the sugar has been added, fold in the chopped chocolate.
3. Spread the meringue over the drawn circles and bake for 2 hours or until dry and crisp. Allow to cool in the turned-off oven, then carefully remove from the parchment.
4. To fill and decorate, place cream and bittersweet chocolate in a bowl over a pan of hot water and leave until chocolate has melted. Set aside until thick enough to spread, stirring occasionally.
5. Heat sugar to dissolve in a heavy pan with 2 ounces water. When sugar has dissolved, boil rapidly until golden brown. Dip base of the

pan in cold water. Using a teaspoon, drizzle the caramel over a sheet of parchment in desired Christmas-themed shapes (e.g., angels, trees, etc.). Leave to cool and set.

6. Sandwich meringues together in threes with the bittersweet chocolate cream and fruit. Decorate with caramel Christmas ornaments just before serving.

CHUNKY MILK-CHOCOLATE-CHIP LOAF CAKE

Yield: 12 generous slices

1 cup firmly packed light brown sugar

½ cup Organic Valley European-style cultured butter, softened

1 large Organic Valley egg

1 cup Organic Valley sour cream

1 teaspoon vanilla extract

1½ cups unbleached all-purpose flour

1 teaspoon baking soda

1 teaspoon baking powder

2½ cups Black & Green's organic milk chocolate chunks, divided

1½ cups walnuts, halves and pieces, divided

½ cup Black & Green's organic baking cocoa

DIRECTIONS:

1. Preheat oven to 350 degrees F

2. In a large mixing bowl, cream the sugar and butter together. Add the egg, sour cream, and vanilla, beating well after each addition.

3. In a separate bowl, combine the flour, baking soda, and baking powder. Gradually add dry ingredients to the creamed mixture and stir to combine.

4. Gently fold into the batter 2 cups Black & Green's milk chocolate chunks and 1 cup walnuts.

5. Spoon the batter into two 9" × 5" × 3" baking pans, greased and dusted with Black & Green's organic baking cocoa.

6. Bake for 50 minutes or until a toothpick inserted in the center of the loaves comes out clean. Let the cakes cool in their pans on a wire rack for 15 minutes.

7. Meanwhile melt the remaining ½ cup milk chocolate chunks in a hot-water bath. Carefully remove the cakes from the pans and drizzle the melted chocolate over the top. Sprinkle with the remaining walnut pieces.

CINCO DE MAYO VEGGIE NACHOS

Yield: 6 servings

1 bag two-colored corn tortilla chips
4 cups Mexican-style salsa (store-bought, your choice)
2 cups Dole stir-fry medley
1 cup diced Dole organic celery (¼" dice)
1 cup diced Dole organic radishes (¼" dice)
2 cups cheese sauce (store-bought, your choice)
2 cups shredded pepper jack cheese
1 cup sliced ripe Kalamata olives
olive oil cooking spray

DIRECTIONS:

1. Spray flattop grill with olive oil spray and grill all vegetables: Dole stir-fry medley, diced Dole celery, and Dole radishes. Turn occasionally with a spatula until vegetables are thoroughly heated through.

2. Meanwhile, heat tortilla chips in oven at 350 degrees F to be crispy and hot on a large ovenproof platter or baking sheet. When hot, toss tortilla chips on platter with grilled vegetables and Mexican-style salsa.

3. Top tortilla chips with cheese sauce and shredded pepper jack cheese. Place platter with tortilla chips on grill with cover. Allow cheese to melt, and sprinkle all with sliced Kalamata olives.

4. Divide into six servings as an appetizer and serve immediately.

CARNIVAL MAPLE-GLAZED CINNAMON BUNS

Yield: 12 buns

You will be amazed when you taste these New Orleans Mardi Gras maple-glazed cinnamon buns. They are so good for a nonyeast roll! I might not even go back to the effort of yeast-type rolls, just because these are so fast and the results are *that* good. And even though I almost always end up tinkering with recipes, there is nothing that I would tinker with here at all. They take forty minutes to make, and I am on the slow side. The texture is really nice and breadlike. They are delicious even without adding butter—and this is coming from someone who always used to make a very rich brioche-style cinnamon bun that took three days to start. This will be my new go-to recipe.

cooking spray for the pan
¾ cup cottage cheese (4% milk fat)
⅓ cup buttermilk
¼ cup Burton's maple syrup
2 ounces (4 tablespoons) unsalted butter, melted
1 teaspoon pure vanilla extract
9 ounces (2 cups) King Arthur unbleached all-purpose flour, plus more
    for rolling
1 tablespoon baking powder
½ teaspoon table salt
¼ teaspoon baking soda

FOR THE FILLING
¾ ounce (1½ tablespoon) unsalted butter, melted
⅓ cup packed light or dark brown sugar
⅓ cup Burton's maple syrup
1½ teaspoons ground cinnamon
½ teaspoon ground allspice
¼ teaspoon ground cloves
1 cup (4 ounces) chopped pecans

FOR THE MAPLE GLAZE

6 tablespoons confectioner's sugar

3 tablespoons Burton's maple syrup

DIRECTIONS:

1. Heat oven to 400 degrees F. Grease the sides and bottom of a 9" or 10" springform pan with cooking spray.

2. In a food processor, combine the cottage cheese, buttermilk, maple syrup, melted butter, and vanilla. Process until smooth (about 10 seconds). Add the flour, baking powder, salt, and baking soda and pulse in short bursts just until the dough clumps together (don't overprocess). The dough will be soft and moist.

3. Scrape the dough out onto a lightly floured surface and knead it with floured hands four or five times until smooth. With a rolling pin, roll the dough into a 12" x 15" rectangle. Brush the dough with the melted butter, leaving a ½" border unbuttered around the edges.

4. In a medium bowl, combine the brown sugar, maple syrup, cinnamon, allspice, and cloves. Sprinkle the mixture over the buttered area of the dough and pat gently into the surface. Sprinkle the nuts over the sugar mixture.

5. Starting at a long edge, roll up the dough jelly-roll style. Pinch the seam to seal, and leave the ends open.

6. With a sharp knife, cut the roll into twelve equal pieces. Set the pieces, cut side up, in the prepared pan; they should fill the pan and touch slightly, but don't worry if there are small gaps.

7. Bake at 350 degrees F until golden brown and firm to the touch, 20–28 minutes. Set the pan on a wire rack to cool for 5 minutes. Run a spatula around the inside edge of the pan and remove the springform ring. Transfer the rolls to a serving plate.

8. In a small bowl, mix the confectioner's sugar with the maple syrup. Drizzle maple glaze over cinnamon buns. Serve warm.

CLASSIC TIRAMISU

Yield: 16 servings

This classic tiramisu gets a boost of flavor from the hazelnut liqueur, but you could omit it and still have a delicious dessert.

FOR SYRUP
½ cup sugar
½ cup water
2 tablespoons instant espresso coffee powder
1 tablespoon amaretto
1 tablespoon hazelnut liqueur

FOR FILLING
2 (8-ounce) cartons mascarpone cheese
¼ cup plus 3 tablespoons plus ⅓ cup sugar
1 teaspoon vanilla
1½ cups whipping cream
3 tablespoons dried egg whites
½ cup water
2 (3-ounce) packages ladyfingers, split
2 tablespoons unsweetened cocoa powder

DIRECTIONS:
1. For syrup: In a small saucepan, combine sugar, water, and coffee powder. Cook over medium heat till boiling. Boil gently, uncovered, for 1 minute. Remove from heat; stir in amaretto and hazelnut liqueur. Cool.
2. For filling: In a medium bowl, stir together mascarpone cheese, ¼ cup sugar, and vanilla.
3. In a chilled medium mixing bowl, combine whipping cream and 3 tablespoons sugar. Beat with chilled beaters of an electric mixer on medium speed till soft peaks form. Fold ½ cup of the beaten whipped cream mixture into the mascarpone mixture to lighten; set both mixtures aside.

4. In another medium mixing bowl, prepare and beat dried egg whites and water to stiff peaks according to package directions, adding the ⅓ cup granulated sugar, 1 tablespoon at a time, while beating.

5. To assemble: Arrange half of the ladyfinger halves in the bottom of a 9" × 9" × 2"baking pan. Brush with half of the syrup mixture. Spread with half of the mascarpone mixture, half of the whipped cream, and half of the egg-white mixture. Sprinkle with half of the cocoa powder. Arrange the remaining ladyfingers on top of layers in pan. Brush with the remaining syrup mixture. Spread with the remaining mascarpone mixture, the remaining whipped cream, and the remaining egg-white mixture. Sprinkle with the remaining cocoa powder. Cover and chill 4–24 hours before serving.

OLD KEY WEST CONCH CHILI

Yield: 6 servings

3 pounds conch meat, chopped

1 pound sausage, sliced

½ cup extra-virgin olive oil

1 medium onion, diced

1 bunch scallions, cut into rings

1 tablespoon garlic powder

1 green Ortega pepper, whole, canned, seeds removed and finely diced

½ ounce sea salt

¼ teaspoon freshly ground black pepper

chili powder blend (2 ounces Jamaican chili powder [or chili powder
from any other Caribbean island–grown chile peppers], ½ ounce
California chili powder, and ½ ounce New Mexican chili powder)

½ ounce cumin

½ teaspoon pequin powder

2 (14-ounce) cans clam or chicken broth

1 (6-ounce) can tomato sauce

¼ teaspoon cayenne pepper

hot sauce to taste (e.g., Tabasco or other Louisiana hot sauce)

DIRECTIONS:

1. Sauté onion and scallions in olive oil in a 3-quart pot. Add garlic
   powder and half of chili powder blend. Add half a can of broth, mix
   well, and set aside. Brown sausage and conch in a skillet, about 1
   pound at a time. Drain and add conch to onion mix. Add remaining
   chili powder and remaining broth. Cook for 30 minutes on low heat.
   Add tomato sauce, cumin, cayenne pepper, and pequin powder. Add
   more broth as needed, and cook until conch meat is tender (about 2–3
   hours). Add a dash of hot sauce if needed for heat.

CONCH FRITTER SALAD

Yield: about 8 salads with 6 fritters each and greens

2 pounds finely chopped conch (ask market to put them through a
   grinder)
1 cup mojo sauce or lime juice
¼ cup olive oil
1 finely chopped green bell pepper
1 finely chopped large onion
4 beaten eggs
2 cups flour
1 teaspoon Cajun or Creole seasoning (2 teaspoons for a spicier version)
6 dashes hot sauce
3 teaspoons baking powder
5 tablespoons melted butter or margarine
vegetable oil for frying
8 cups torn salad greens, as needed
½ cup chopped cilantro
tartar sauce and red cocktail sauce for dipping

DIRECTIONS:
1. Marinate conch in 1 cup mojo sauce or lime juice and olive oil for 30
   minutes and drain.
2. In large bowl, mix marinated conch together with next eight
   ingredients. Fry by tablespoon in 375-degree F hot vegetable oil until
   golden, about 3–5 minutes.
3. Place 1 cup greens on each platter and top with six fritters and a dish
   of red cocktail sauce and white tartar sauce. Garnish with cilantro.
   Serve salads with tartar sauce and red cocktail sauce for dipping.

CRANBERRY ORANGE FITNESS REFRESHER

Yield: about 8 servings

32 ounces natural cranberry juice, chilled
¾ cup freshly squeezed orange juice
⅓ cup organic honey
½ ounce frozen orange juice concentrate, defrosted but chilled
¾ cup organic soy milk

DIRECTIONS:

1. In pitcher combine cranberry juice, orange juice, organic honey, orange juice concentrate, and chilled soy milk.
2. Refrigerate until ready to serve. To serve, pour over ice in highball glasses.

CRANBERRY CRAISINS AND
ENGLISH WALNUT SALAD
with Figs, Serrano Ham, and a Mediterranean
Honey-Balsamic Vinaigrette

Yield: 4 servings

⅔ pound mixed baby greens, such as arugula, frisée, green and red oak
    leaf, Boston Bibb, and hearts of romaine
1 small head radicchio
8 fresh mission figs or other sweet and juicy figs
12 paper-thin slices of serrano ham
1 cup Craisins
½ cup California English walnut halves

FOR HONEY-BALSAMIC VINAIGRETTE
2 teaspoons honey
1 teaspoon Dijon mustard
3 tablespoons balsamic vinegar (8 years of age or older)
½ cup extra-virgin olive oil ("green" preferred)
¼ teaspoon sea salt

YOU WILL ALSO NEED
flowers to garnish (orchid blossoms, if available)

DIRECTIONS:
1. Wash and dry greens and radicchio. Tear into bite-size pieces and chill
    in refrigerator. Make the vinaigrette by combining all ingredients in
    a blender until emulsified and smooth.
2. Rinse figs under cold water and pat dry. Cut each fig in half, removing
    tough stem.
3. Toss greens with enough vinaigrette to coat. Toss walnut halves
    and Craisins with a little vinaigrette to make them shiny. Reserve
    remaining vinaigrette.
4. Place salad greens mixed with radicchio on four chilled plates.
    Arrange 3 slices serrano in center of each plate to form a circular

pattern. Stand 4 fig halves in center of serrano to form yet another circle (with stem ends up and cut sides out). Spoon Craisins and walnut halves over figs. Drizzle reserved dressing over figs and serrano. Place 1 small flower (orchid blossom, if available) on top of figs, if desired.

CRANBERRY ZIN BARBECUE RIBS

Yield: 5 servings

FOR BARBECUE SAUCE
¼ cup olive oil
¼ cup garlic
1 yellow onion, diced
½ cup brown sugar
⅓ cup ketchup
2 canned chipotle peppers
2 tablespoons grainy mustard
¼ cup apple cider vinegar
½ teaspoon cumin
salt and pepper, as needed
¼ cup Old Vine Gnarlyhead Zinfandel
¼ cup whole cranberry sauce

FOR DRY RUB
½ cup dark brown sugar
½ cup paprika
⅓ cup garlic salt
2 tablespoons onion salt
2 tablespoons chili powder
1 tablespoons black pepper
1½ teaspoons dried oregano
1½ teaspoons white pepper
1 teaspoon cumin

YOU WILL ALSO NEED
5 (1-pound) pieces of pork loin backs ribs
½ cup fresh curly parsley, finely chopped

DIRECTIONS:
1. Prepare commercial grade smoker to operate at medium heat for indirect barbecue smoking.

2. Add oil to a medium ovenproof skillet and place over heated grill, directly over heat. Sweat onion and garlic until tender and translucent. Add brown sugar and stir until melted. Add ketchup, chipotles, mustard, and apple cider and stir to combine. Bring to a simmer. Add spices, Zinfandel wine, and whole cranberry sauce. Simmer gently, stirring occasionally, for 20 minutes. Remove from heat and puree using a large-handled immersion blender. Cool and set aside.

3. In a small bowl, blend all dry rub ingredients together. Spread dry rub on both sides of ribs. When ready to smoke, place your grate on the grill so that the holes near the handles are over your charcoal pieces; this allows you to add charcoal as needed. Place your ribs in the center of the grate, away from charcoal pieces. Place your rib pieces anywhere not directly over the coals. To keep ribs moist you can spray them with cranberry juice. Baste ribs with barbecue sauce and turn ribs two or three times. Remove ribs from grill at a minimum temperature of 140 degree F and rest for 5–10 minutes. Sprinkle with chopped parsley to garnish.

CREATIVE SALMON AND MUSHROOM PASTA

Yield: 6 servings

1 pound penne pasta
1 pound fresh or canned salmon,* flaked or cubed
1 teaspoon Jane's Krazy Mixed-Up Salt
½ teaspoon Jane's Krazy Mixed-Up Lemon Pepper
½ cup extra-virgin olive oil
½ cup toasted bread crumbs
1 large red onion, thinly sliced
2 ounces crimini mushrooms, sliced, soaked, and drained
4 large garlic cloves, minced
pinch crushed chili peppers
1 pint chicken stock
¼ cup champagne vinegar
3 tablespoons small capers
½ cup basil leaves, thinly sliced

DIRECTIONS:

1. Cook pasta and reserve. Season fresh salmon with Jane's Krazy Mixed-Up Salt and Jane's Krazy Mixed-Up Lemon Pepper. Sauté lightly in 4 tablespoons olive oil. Remove salmon and reserve. Drizzle pan juices over bread crumbs and reserve in a ceramic or glass bowl. Set aside as topping.

2. Heat 4 tablespoons olive oil and sauté the following for 1 minute over medium heat: onions, mushrooms, garlic, and chili peppers. Add chicken stock and vinegar and reduce mixture by half. Stir in capers and basil. Toss with pasta and salmon and heat briefly. Serve with bread crumbs as topping.

*If using canned salmon, add it in the last step.

CRISP ASIAN NAPOLEON SPEARS
with White Asparagus
Yield: 12 servings

1 egg
1 tablespoon water

FOR PANKO BREAD-CRUMB MIXTURE
1 cup Kikkoman panko bread crumbs
1 ounce sun-dried tomatoes
2½ teaspoons granulated garlic
½ teaspoon salt
⅓ teaspoon black pepper

YOU WILL ALSO NEED
1 (17.3-ounce) package puff pastry sheets (store-bought), thawed
24 canned white asparagus spears
1 cup Kikkoman tonkatsu sauce, divided

DIRECTIONS:
1. Heat oven to 400 degrees F. Beat the egg and water in a small bowl with a fork or whisk.
2. Combine all five panko bread-crumb mixture ingredients in a food processor until well blended. It will be slightly red. Place the mixture into a shallow dish. The mixture can be stored in an airtight container for up to 48 hours, if desired.
3. Unfold 1 pastry sheet on a lightly floured surface. Cut each pastry sheet into six 5" × 3" rectangles. Repeat with the remaining pastry sheets, making twelve in all.
4. Place 2 asparagus spears on a long edge of each pastry rectangle. Brush asparagus spears with Kikkoman tonkatsu sauce. Roll up the pastry around the asparagus spears and press the seams and pinch the ends to seal. Brush the tops of the rolls with the egg mixture. Dip the tops into the panko bread-crumb mixture. Place the rolls, seam-side down, on a baking sheet. Prick the tops of the rolls with a fork.

5. Bake for 15 minutes or until the rolls are golden brown. Remove the rolls from the baking sheet and let cool on a wire rack for 10 minutes.
6. Place remaining sauce in a medium-sized bowl. Serve the sauce with the rolls for dipping.

CRUNCHY FRESH FRUIT AND ARUGULA WRAPS

Yield: 4 wraps

4 fajita-size fat-free flour tortillas

FOR THE SALAD
1 tablespoon honey
1 tablespoon balsamic vinegar or lemon juice
2 peaches or other fresh fruit (e.g., apples, pears, nectarines, plums), cut into wedges
4 cups (about 12 ounces) tightly packed arugula, washed and patted dry
1 shallot, thinly sliced
1 cup toasted California walnuts: halves and pieces
1 bunch purple basil washed, patted dry, and cut into thin strips

FOR THE DRESSING
½ cup plain nonfat yogurt
1 teaspoon fresh lemon juice
1 teaspoon Dijon mustard
2 tablespoons honey
2 tablespoons plus 2 teaspoons balsamic vinegar
½ cup extra-virgin olive oil

YOU WILL ALSO NEED
4 ounces low-fat goat cheese, crumbled

DIRECTIONS:
1. In a bowl, combine honey and vinegar or lemon juice with a fork. Add peaches or other fruit. In a large nonstick saucepan, sear peaches or fruit over medium heat for until caramelized (about 2½ minutes per side). Remove from heat and let cool.
2. Meanwhile, make dressing. Whisk together yogurt, lemon juice, mustard, honey, and vinegar in a medium bowl. Drizzle in oil, whisking constantly. Season with salt and pepper.
3. In a large bowl, toss together fruit, arugula, shallot, walnuts, basil, and ½ cup dressing (you'll have about ⅓ cup extra dressing). Divide

among 4 lightly warmed flour tortillas, and top each with 1 ounce crumbled goat cheese. Roll tortillas in jelly-roll fashion and secure at the seams with one long frilled toothpick on each end before cutting in half.

QUICK HOT-AND-SPICY SZECHUAN GRILLED BEEF

Yield: 4 servings

½ cup fresh cilantro
4 cloves garlic, thinly sliced
3 tablespoons San-J Szechuan sauce
1 teaspoon grated lemon zest
1 teaspoon San-J Sweet & Tangy sauce
1 teaspoon grated fresh ginger root
1 teaspoon brown sugar
1 pound lean beef sirloin, cut into ⅛" strips

FOR DIPPING SAUCE
½ cup grape-seed-oil Vegenaise
2 tablespoons chopped fresh basil leaves
1 tablespoon fresh lime juice
1 teaspoon San-J Sweet & Tangy sauce

YOU WILL ALSO NEED
1 each red, green, and yellow bell peppers; cored, seeded, and cut into
    2½" pieces
peanut, sesame, or canola oil cooking spray

DIRECTIONS:
1. Puree cilantro, garlic, San-J Szechuan sauce, lemon zest, San-J Sweet & Tangy sauce, ginger, and sugar in food processor. Transfer marinade to a resealable plastic bag and add beef. Seal bag, toss, and set aside for 30 minutes.
2. Combine dipping sauce ingredients in a bowl.
3. Add 4 pieces of pepper and 2 beef strips on each skewer, alternating beef and peppers. Coat grill rack with cooking spray and heat grill to high. Cook skewers for 3 minutes, rotating once, until meat is no longer pink.

Note: To prevent wooden skewers from burning, soak them in water for 30 minutes prior to use.

DANISH-STYLE SALMON CAKES
with Rösti and Fresh Dill Sauce
Yield: 3 servings

FOR DANISH-STYLE SALMON CAKES

2 (6- to 7-ounce) cans boneless, skinless wild Alaskan salmon, drained

½ cup finely chopped red onion

2 large eggs plus 1 large egg white, lightly beaten

1 tablespoon whole-grain mustard

3 tablespoons chopped fresh dill (or 3 teaspoons dried), divided

½ teaspoon freshly ground pepper

¼ teaspoon salt

4 cups frozen grated potatoes (about 12 ounces)

2 tablespoons extra-virgin olive oil, divided

FOR DILL SAUCE

1 cup reduced-fat sour cream

1 cup buttermilk

3 tablespoons capers, rinsed and chopped

3 teaspoons lemon juice

DIRECTIONS:

1. Combine salmon, onion, eggs and egg white, mustard, 2 tablespoons fresh dill (or 2 teaspoons dried), pepper, and salt in a large bowl. Add potatoes and stir to combine.

2. Preheat slow cooker to low (200 degrees).

3. Heat 1 tablespoon oil in a large nonstick skillet over medium heat until shimmering. Fill a 1-cup measure two-thirds full with the salmon mixture and firmly pack it down. Unmold into the pan and pat to form a 3" cake. Repeat, making three more cakes. Cover and cook until browned on the bottom (3–5 minutes). Gently turn over and cook, covered, until crispy on the other side (3–5 minutes more). Transfer the cakes to the slow cooker; keep warm on low. Wipe out the skillet and cook four more cakes with the remaining 1 tablespoon

oil and the remaining salmon mixture. Cook until the salmon cakes are tender, lightly browned, and well heated through (5–7 hours).

4. Combine sour cream, buttermilk, capers, lemon juice, and the remaining dill in a small bowl. Pour sauce over salmon cakes for the last 1 hour of cooking. Serve the salmon cakes with the dill sauce.

INDIAN-SPICED DARK-CHOCOLATE PIZZA POCKETS

Yield: 7 pockets

Here Italy meets India and Marco Polo's Far East. Each bite of these rich pizza pockets reveals a surprising and exotic fusion of cardamom, coriander, nutmeg, and cinnamon within a warm, gooey dark chocolate–caramel center.

4 ounces semisweet chocolate (62% cocoa)
4 ounces soft caramel candy
2 large eggs
¼ cup pistachios
½ cup heavy whipping cream
2 tablespoons softened unsalted butter
2 tablespoons sugar
1 teaspoon cinnamon
½ teaspoon ground cardamom
¼ teaspoon ground coriander
¼ teaspoon ground nutmeg
14 ounces pizza dough (fresh, or thawed if purchased frozen)

DIRECTIONS:

1. Chop chocolate and caramels into chip-sized pieces and set aside.
2. Whisk eggs and set aside.
3. In the food processor, combine pistachios, heavy cream, unsalted butter, sugar, cinnamon, cardamom, coriander, and nutmeg. Pulse until it is creamy and able to be spread.
4. Divide pizza dough into seven balls, about 2 ounces each. Using a rolling pin, roll each ball into 7" round disks on rolling mat. Using a spatula, spread 1 tablespoon of the pistachio mixture on each. Leave a 1" border around the pizza dough. In the center of the pizza dough, sprinkle 1 tablespoon chocolate and 1 tablespoon caramels. Using a pastry brush, brush around the border of the pizza dough. Fold the pizza dough in half. Pinch the edges together in an upward motion. The edges should be well sealed all the way around. Place three pizza

pockets on a lightly greased baking sheet. Using a pastry brush, brush the top of each with egg wash. Bake in preheated oven at 450 degrees for 10 minutes. Remove and let cool. Repeat with remaining pockets. Dust the tops with powdered sugar or cocoa powder and serve.

DOUBLE-TREAT PECAN TARTS

Yield: 24 servings

These two-treat pecan tarts satisfy the sweet and the tart tooth with far less guilt than pecan pie.

FOR CRUST
¼ cup whole-wheat pastry flour (see note)
¼ cup packed light brown sugar
½ cup walnuts, coarsely chopped
1 tablespoon cornstarch
2 tablespoons unsalted butter
pinch of salt

FOR FILLING
4 ounces dried cranberries (about ¾ cup)
¼ cup Heinz chili sauce
½ cup Ocean Spray whole cranberry sauce
¼ cup packed light brown sugar
2½ tablespoons unsalted butter
4 tablespoons reduced-fat cream cheese
1¼ teaspoons vanilla extract
½ cup pecans, chopped

YOU WILL ALSO NEED
confectioner's sugar for dusting, or whipped cream for garnish

DIRECTIONS:
1. Preheat oven to 375 degrees F. Coat twenty-four mini muffin cups with cooking spray.
2. To prepare crust, pulse flour, brown sugar, walnuts, cornstarch, butter, and salt in a food processor (a mini food processor works well) until the mixture resembles coarse meal. Divide the crust mixture among the prepared mini muffin cups (about 1¼ teaspoons per cup) and press evenly into the bottoms.

3. To prepare filling, combine cranberries, chili sauce, cranberry sauce, brown sugar, and butter in a small saucepan. Bring to a boil over medium-high heat and cook, stirring frequently, until most of the liquid has cooked away (8–12 minutes). Let cool slightly, then process the cranberry mixture in a blender or food processor until processed into a paste. Add cream cheese and vanilla; blend or process to combine. Transfer to a medium bowl. Stir in pecans. Divide the cranberry-nut filling among muffin cups (1 generous teaspoon each), gently pressing the filling down and smoothing the tops.

4. Bake until the crust is golden brown and the filling is lightly cooked (15–17 minutes). Let cool in the pans for 10 minutes. Loosen the edges of the crust with a small spatula or butter knife and transfer the double-treat tarts to a wire rack to cool. Sprinkle with confectioner's sugar or serve with a dollop of whipped cream, if desired.

Note: Whole wheat pastry flour has less gluten-forming potential than regular whole-wheat flour and helps ensure tender baked goods. Find it in the baking section of the supermarket.

PEKIN DUCK AND VEGETABLE STIR-FRY
with Fragrant Basmati Rice
Yield: 4 servings

FOR FRAGRANT BASMATI RICE

¼ cup olive oil, divided

½ cup yellow onion, small dice

fine sea salt, as needed

2 garlic cloves, minced

2 cups water

½ cup green and red Asian kale, small sliced

½ cup cashews, toasted and coarsely chopped

½ cup water chestnuts, sliced

¼ cup lemongrass, finely chopped

FOR PEKIN DUCK AND VEGETABLE STIR-FRY

2 tablespoons olive oil, divided

1½ pound Maple Leaf Farms gourmet flavor marinated boneless Pekin
    duck breast, trimmed and cut into 1" squares and patted dry.

fine sea salt and freshly ground black pepper to taste

1 each medium zucchini and yellow summer squash, trimmed and cut
    into julienne strips

1 small red onion, peeled and thinly sliced

1 garlic clove, minced

pinch dried red pepper flakes

1 red bell pepper, seeded and cut into thin julienne strips

3 tomatoes, peeled, seeded, cored, and diced; or 1 (28-ounce) can
    tomatoes, drained and diced

1 teaspoon fresh oregano (or ½ teaspoon dried)

2 tablespoons chopped fresh thyme

DIRECTIONS:

1. In a heavy-bottomed pot, heat 2 tablespoons olive oil over medium
    heat. When hot, add onion. Cook until soft, stirring occasionally,
    sprinkle with fine sea salt. Continue to cook until onion is translucent,

about 10 minutes. Add the garlic and cook until aromatic, stirring, for about 2–3 minutes.

2. Add rice to the onion mixture. Lightly toast the rice.

3. Add water and bring to a high simmer. Simmer 5 minutes, then cover and reduce heat to lowest possible temperature. Cook for 5 minutes, then remove pan from heat. Allow to steep until tender, about 10 minutes. Fluff rice with a fork, transfer to mixing bowl, and cover with moist paper towel. Reserve at room temperature.

4. In a saucepan over medium heat, heat the remaining 2 tablespoons olive oil. Add the Asian kale and sauté quickly, keeping stirring to a minimum. Season lightly.

5. Remove Asian kale from pan and cool to room temperature until ready to reheat for service. To reheat for service, place small pot filled with water on the stove and bring to simmer. Reheat rice over steam heat.

6. Heat a heavy large skillet or wok over high heat. Add 1½ tablespoons oil. Season duck with salt and pepper. Add duck and cook slowly over low heat until almost a mahogany-brown color on all sides. Do not cook through. Remove duck from skillet and set aside.

7. Heat remaining oil in skillet over medium-high heat, adding zucchini, yellow squash, onion, garlic, red pepper flakes, and bell peppers. Stir-fry constantly for 3 minutes. Return duck and any juices to pan and stir 3 minutes more. Stir in oregano and thyme. Serve immediately with fragrant basmati rice.

FIG AND ORCHID BLOSSOM GRILLED
BREAST OF DUCK SALAD
with Honey-Balsamic Vinaigrette
Yield: 12 servings

FOR VINAIGRETTE

4 ounces honey

2 ounces Dijon mustard

4 ounces aged balsamic vinegar

2 ounces fine sea salt

4 cloves garlic, finely chopped

20 ounces extra-virgin olive oil

½ bunch each chopped cilantro and Italian parsley

FOR SALAD

2 pounds mixed baby greens, such as arugula, frisée, green and red oak
leaf, Boston Bibb, and hearts of romaine

6 small heads radicchio, leaves torn into bite-size pieces

48 fresh ripe figs

12 Maple Leaf Farms boneless Pekin duck breasts, gourmet flavored,
marinated

1 pound alfalfa or sunflower sprouts

8 ounces jicama, julienned

8 ounces fennel, julienned

8 ounces each green and red bell peppers each, julienned

12 orchid blossoms or scallion flowers

60 cucumber curls

½ cup tomato concasse

6 flour tortillas, 8" diameter

6 corn tortillas, 8" diameter

24 fresh ripe figs cut in half vertically

DIRECTIONS:

1. In a blender or food processor combine all vinaigrette ingredients
   except the herbs and olive oil. Pulse at medium speed before adding

the olive oil in a slow stream. When emulsified, add the chopped parsley and cilantro greens.

2. Making the tortilla shells: Heat frying oil in a 12" sauté skillet to 350 degrees F. Cut tortillas in half and fry in the oil. While frying, using tongs to hold them in place, shape tortillas into half circles and cornets from the tortillas.

3. Remove the skin and any sinew from the duck breasts. Grill to desired temperature to inside temperature of 155 degrees F.

4. To assemble the salad, place flour tortilla shells at the back of the plate. Lightly toss baby greens with the dressing, adding torn radicchio leaves. Place greens in center of chilled salad plates. Arrange cucumber curls and corn tortilla cornets in a circle around the greens; placing the cornet tips upward. Thinly slice duck breasts, placing the slices around the salad greens on the perimeter.

5. Toss the remaining julienned vegetables, sprinkling with vinaigrette. Place atop the cornets. On each plate, place 4 fig halves on top of cornets, stem sides up and cut sides out, forming a circle. Drizzle any remaining vinaigrette and tomato concasse over fig halves and duck. Place an orchid blossom or scallion flower in center of salad to crown the beautiful arrangements.

FEST VIGILIANE SEAFOOD PIZZA (FAMILY RECIPE)

Yield: 1 (12" × 14") pizza

FOR SAUCE
2 tablespoons pure Italian extra-virgin olive oil
1 medium garlic clove
1 cup sliced onion
1 can Pastene San Marzano tomatoes (whole tomatoes)
½ tablespoon salt
½ tablespoon sugar
2 tablespoons oregano
½ teaspoon diced chile or jalapeño pepper

FOR DOUGH (YIELDS DOUGH FOR FOUR PIZZAS)
2 envelopes of active dry yeast
2 teaspoons sugar
2 tablespoons Italian pure extra-virgin olive oil
3 tablespoons Tenderflake lard or Crisco
2–3 cups unbleached all-purpose flour
2 teaspoons sea salt
1 egg
¼ cup milk
¼ cup sparkling water (e.g., Pellegrino)
warm water as needed to achieve soft medium texture

FOR TOPPINGS
4 large shrimp
6 scallops
8 ounces mixed fish (calamari, shrimp, mussels, scallops)
4 pieces crab
4 large porcini mushrooms
12 ounces fresh buffalo mozzarella cheese, sliced; fresh mozzarella,
   sliced; or shredded mozzarella cheese

DIRECTIONS:

1. It is very important that you heat the oil for the sauce and add the onions first and the garlic second and fry them to a light golden brown. Add the whole tomatoes. Blend in the salt, sugar, oregano, and chili. Bring to a boil and let cool.

2. To make the dough, put yeast, sugar, olive oil, lard or Crisco, egg, milk, and sparkling water into a large bowl and let sit for 5 minutes. In another large bowl, place the flour and salt. Add the mixture from the previous bowl. Gently mix with hands or machine and add warm water as needed until soft texture is achieved. Once the mixture is well combined and is smooth, remove from bowl. Knead dough until smooth and springy. Place the dough on an oiled pan, cover with a wet cloth, and let rise until doubled in volume.

3. When ready, spread dough gently so it fits in the oiled pan. Spread with tomato sauce. (Don't overdo it or the pizza may get soggy.) Spread with seafood evenly and top with cheese. Cook at 400 degrees F until lightly browned, and then remove from oven. Slice and serve fresh.

FIRST FAMILY BABY BACK RIBS

Yield: 6 servings

2 bottles Gallo Family Cabernet Sauvignon

¼ cup Kosher salt

⅓ cup sugar

2 tablespoons cracked black peppercorns

2 tablespoons ground fennel

1 tablespoon coriander seeds

2 teaspoons juniper berries, crushed

2 teaspoons dried marjoram

4 bay leaves

1 head garlic, halved horizontally

2 (2-pound) racks of pork baby back ribs

DRESSING

4 teaspoons anchovy paste

2 teaspoons minced garlic

6 tablespoons fresh lemon juice,

½ cup extra-virgin olive oil, plus more for brushing

2 tablespoons chopped parsley

DIRECTIONS:

1. In a large saucepan, bring to a boil 2 cups of the wine together with the next nine ingredients, up to and including the halved garlic head. Make sure the sugar is dissolved.

2. Place ribs in a large roasting pan and cover with the brine. Add the remainder of the 2 bottles wine. Let sit, covered, occasionally basting the ribs, for up to 8 hours, refrigerated.

3. Light grill, brush the grate with olive oil, and smoke ribs for 3 hours at 325 degrees F or until tender, turning occasionally until crisp and browned.

4. In a large bowl, add the anchovy paste, 2 teaspoons minced garlic, fresh lemon juice, ½ cup olive oil, and parsley.
5. Transfer the racks of baby back ribs to a cutting board and cut in between ribs. Brush with the dressing. Serve with Gallo Family Cabernet Sauvignon.

FLORENTINE CHOCOLATE, APRICOT, PINE NUT, AND OATMEAL COOKIES

Yield: 4 dozen cookies

2 cups unbleached all-purpose flour

1 teaspoon baking soda

½ teaspoon sea salt

¾ cup sweet butter, softened

1 cup granulated sugar

1 cup brown sugar

½ cup finely diced canned apricots

1 large egg

1 cup old-fashioned oats

1 cup toasted pine nuts

1 (12-ounce) bag milk chocolate chips (2 cups)

DIRECTIONS:

1. Heat oven to 375 degrees F
2. Line cookie sheets with parchment paper.
3. In medium bowl mix flour, baking soda, and salt; set aside.
4. In large bowl beat butter and sugars with electric mixer on medium speed until creamy. Gradually beat in flour mixture. Stir in oats, nuts, and 1 cup milk chocolate chips. Drop dough onto cookie sheets by rounded tablespoons, about 2" apart. Bake 15 minutes or until lightly browned. Remove from cookie sheets to cool on racks.
5. In small microwavable bowl, microwave remaining 1 cup chocolate chips on high for 1 minute, stirring once, until softened and chips can be stirred smooth. Drizzle over cookies. Place on wax paper and let stand until set.

FLORIDA BREAD

Yield: 1 large loaf (2-pound loaf pan)

½ cup unsalted butter

¾ cup raw sugar

2 teaspoons fresh Florida orange zest

2 large eggs

1 cup white whole-wheat flour

¾ teaspoon baking powder

½ teaspoon baking soda

½ teaspoon sea salt

6 ounces yogurt, plain or flavored

¼ cup Florida orange juice

½ cup chopped plantains (or plantain chips if a crunchy bread is desired)

½ cup chopped sweet dried mangoes

DIRECTIONS:

1. Preheat oven to 350 degrees F.
2. Butter the 2-pound (9" × 5") loaf pan or line with parchment paper.
3. Cream the butter, raw sugar, and orange zest until light and fluffy in ceramic or stainless-steel bowl with a wire whip. Beat in eggs.
4. In a separate mixing bowl combine flour, baking powder, baking soda, and salt, and add to butter mixture, alternating with yogurt and orange juice. Mix with a wire whip or wooden spoon until well blended. Pour batter into prepared pan. Bake 40–45 minutes or until toothpick inserted in center of bread comes out clean.
5. Let stand 10 minutes before removing from pan. Allow to cool completely

Serving suggestion: serve with orange-blossom honey butter:

½ cup unsalted softened butter

1 teaspoon orange zest

¼ cup orange-blossom honey

1 teaspoon finely grated fresh ginger

DIRECTIONS:

1. Cream all ingredients in mixer until well blended and fluffy.

THINLY SLICED LEG OF LAMB
with Seasonal Florida Fruit
Yield: 6 servings

FOR THE LEG OF LAMB

4 tablespoons olive oil

1 tablespoon coriander seeds, crushed

1 tablespoon fennel seeds, crushed

1 teaspoon crushed red pepper flakes

coarse salt and freshly ground pepper

1½ pounds butterflied leg of American lamb

olive oil for grilling

8 key limes, quartered

FOR FIG-AND-CRAYFISH BUNDLES

3 cups fresh Florida orange juice

24 dried (or fresh) figs, whole

2 tablespoons sugar

24 (thinly sliced) roasted leg of lamb slices

24 bite-sized chunks Florida crayfish meat

24 chives

other fresh Florida winter fruit, such as mango, papaya, oranges, guava, and persimmons, cut to bite-sized pieces, as desired.

DIRECTIONS:

1. In a shallow dish, marinate lamb at room temperature for 30 minutes with first five ingredients (olive oil through freshly ground pepper). Turn lamb to coat.

2. Heat grill to medium low; lightly grease grates. Place lamb on grill. Cover and cook until meat thermometer in thickest part of lamb registers 130 degrees F for medium rare (6–8 minutes per side). Transfer lamb to a plate, covering loosely with aluminum foil. Let rest 5 minutes. Grill key lime wedges until cut sides are marked, about 1 minute per side.

3. Thinly slice lamb.

4. In a small saucepan, bring orange juice to boil about 5 minutes. Add figs and simmer, covered, until fig are tender. Remove figs and reserve. To the orange juice remaining in the pan, add sugar. Continue to simmer until reduced to about ¼ cup. Reserve.

5. Fold each lamb slice in half to make 4" × 4½" rectangles. Remove stems from figs. Cut a cross in the top of each fig. Place a piece of crayfish meat in the center of each cross, pressing slightly. Bring lamb up and around fig to make a bundle. Tie with a chive. Repeat for each remaining rectangle.

6. Arrange four pouches on each serving plate. Drizzle plate with orange-juice reduction. Garnish with fruit.

FLOUNDER STUFFED WITH GOAT CHEESE
Peanut Butter, Caramelized Spring Onions, and Thyme
Yield: 6 servings

1½ teaspoons olive oil, plus extra to coat the pan

1⅓ cups thinly sliced spring onions (about 1 pound)

½ cup smooth peanut butter, plus ¼ cup extra to brush fish fillets

¾ cup (3 ounces) crumbled goat cheese, plus ¼ cup extra to sprinkle on top of fillets

1 tablespoon chopped fresh flat-leaf parsley

1 tablespoon fat-free milk

1½ teaspoons chopped fresh thyme

6 (6-ounce) boneless, skinless flounder (or sole) fillets, cut thick to allow room for a pocket

½ cup dry white wine

1 cup fat-free, low-sodium vegetable broth

DIRECTIONS:

1. Heat oil in a large skillet over medium heat. Add onions and ½ cup peanut butter to pan; cook 12 minutes, stirring frequently. Cover, reduce heat, and cook 8 minutes more, stirring occasionally until spring onions are golden. Uncover and cook 5 minutes more or until onions are caramelized, stirring occasionally. Cool slightly.

2. Combine onion mixture, cheese, parsley, milk, and thyme in a small bowl, stirring with a fork.

3. Cut a horizontal slit through the thickest portion of each fish fillet to form a pocket; stuff 1½ tablespoons cheese mixture into each pocket. Brush fish fillets evenly with remaining ¼ cup peanut butter, and sprinkle with remaining ¼ cup goat cheese.

4. Return pan to medium-high heat. Coat pan with olive oil. Add fish fillets to pan and sauté 5 minutes. Cover, reduce heat, and cook 10 minutes longer, or until fish is done. Remove fillets from pan; let stand 10 minutes.

5. Add wine to pan and bring to a boil, scraping pan to loosen browned bits. Cook until reduced by half (about 2 minutes). Add broth and cook until reduced to ¼ cup (about 9 minutes). Serve with fish fillets in a side dish for dipping.

FLOURLESS CHOCOLATE CRAZE CAKE

Yield: 12 servings

12 ounces organic Green & Black's 70% cocoa dark chocolate, broken
   into small pieces
12 ounces Organic Valley European-style cultured butter
12 ounces granulated sugar
12 Organic Valley eggs, large, separated, plus 2 egg yolks

DIRECTIONS:

1. Lightly butter and flour two 9" springform pans.
2. Preheat oven to 350 degrees F.
3. Melt chocolate and butter in double boiler over simmering water. Remove from heat.
4. Beat yolks and whole eggs slightly. Add sugar, beating, until mixture doubles in volume.
5. Fold in chocolate mixture.
6. Beat egg whites just until they begin to stiffen and are still moist. Do not overbeat.
7. Fold egg whites into chocolate mixture.
8. Divide batter between pans. Place on baking sheet. Bake 20–25 minutes or until the cakes are firm to the touch at the edges and slightly jiggly in the center.
9. Remove from oven and cool 15 minutes on a rack at room temperature. Cakes will sink slightly in center as they cool. Invert cakes onto serving plates. Cool completely.

Suggestion: Serve with whipped cream and raspberries.

FOCACCIA AND PORCINI

Yield: 6 servings

Use any combination of porcini and other mushrooms you like. With red wine, chestnut honey, and vegetable broth, the sauce takes on distinct Italian Tuscan tones.

12 (3–4" square) focaccia rolls, sliced horizontally, centers scooped out
    to about a ½" thickness
4 cups vegetable broth
½ cup water
½ cup dried porcini mushrooms (about ½ ounce)
¾ cup dry red wine (chianti, if possible)
2 tablespoons chestnut honey (available in Italian markets)
2 tablespoons olive oil
2 cups chopped onion
2 (8-ounce) packages button or other mushrooms, coarsely chopped
8 ounces shiitake mushroom caps, coarsely chopped
½ teaspoon freshly ground black pepper
8 sage leaves
¼ teaspoon red pepper flakes
⅛ teaspoon salt
6 garlic cloves, minced
2 tablespoons water
2 teaspoons cornstarch
¼ cup finely chopped fresh Italian flat-leaf parsley

DIRECTIONS:

1. Bring broth and ½ cup water to a boil in medium saucepan, remove from heat, and stir in porcini. Let stand 30 minutes. Strain mixture through a sieve into a bowl; reserve broth mixture and porcini. Add red wine and honey. Set aside.
2. Heat 2 tablespoons oil in a large nonstick skillet over medium-high heat. Add onion and sauté 3 minutes. Add reserved porcini and sauté 1 minute. Add button and shiitake mushrooms; cook 4 minutes or

until mushrooms release moisture, stirring occasionally. Reduce heat to medium and stir in pepper, sage leaves, pepper flakes, ⅛ teaspoon salt, and garlic. Cook 1 minute, stirring frequently. Add ¾ cup broth mixture; reduce heat, and simmer 15 minutes, stirring occasionally.

3. Bring remaining broth mixture to a boil; cook until reduced to 1½ cups (about 12 minutes). Combine 2 tablespoons water and cornstarch, stirring with a whisk. Stir cornstarch mixture into broth mixture. Bring to a boil; cook 2 minutes or until sauce thickens.

4. Spoon ⅓ cup mushroom mixture in center of each focaccia roll and place each roll on a plate. Repeat procedure with remaining mushroom mixture and focaccia rolls, placing rolls on each of six plates. Top each serving with about ¼ cup sauce; sprinkle with 2 teaspoons parsley.

FRENCH ONION BURGER
with Red Onion Fritters
Yield: 6 burgers

FOR PROVENÇAL VEGETABLES
2 zucchini, quartered lengthwise

1 small eggplant (about 8 ounces) cut lengthwise into ¾"-thick slices

4 tablespoons olive oil

2 cups assorted cherry tomatoes, halved

2 teaspoons herbes de Provence (store-bought)

1 garlic clove, minced

FOR BURGERS
2 pounds ground beef chuck

1 tablespoon worcestershire sauce

1 teaspoon ground mustard

1 teaspoon garlic salt

1 teaspoon ground black pepper

2 (12-ounce) cans cheddar or original french-fried onions, crushed

FOR RED ONION FRITTERS
2 cups coarsely chopped red onions

½ cup grated parmigiano-reggiano

½ tablespoon chopped fresh oregano

½ teaspoon Kosher salt

¼ teaspoon freshly ground black pepper

1 beaten egg

½ cup flour

¼ cup olive oil

3 tablespoons butter, plus more for garnish

1 tablespoon chopped fresh flat-leaf parsley

YOU WILL ALSO NEED
6 brioche rolls, 6" diameter, toasted

½ cup spicy light mayonnaise, aioli-flavored (store-bought)

DIRECTIONS:

1. Place vegetables for provencal vegetables, tomatoes, herbes de Provence, and garlic in large bowl. Toss to blend. Set aside.

2. Brush grill with vegetable oil and grill vegetables until tender and lightly charred, turning occasionally, about 10 minutes. Remove from grill and cut into bite-sized chunks. Set aside.

3. Toss ground chuck lightly together with following 4 ingredients by hand. Shape into 6 equal patties, about ½" thick. To oil the grill rack, oil a folded paper towel, hold it with tongs, and brush it over the grill rack. Spray burgers with olive oil. Preheat grill to medium high. Grill burgers to desired doneness, about 4 minutes each side for medium rare. Dip burgers into crushed french-fried onions to completely cover.

4. For the red onion fritters, combine the onions, Parmesan-Reggiano, oregano, salt, pepper, and egg. Divide mixture into 6 equal patty-type cakes. Transfer cakes to a sheet pan and refrigerate for 10 minutes to allow to firm up.

5. Put flour on a plate and dredge cakes in flour. Heat oil and 3 tablespoons of the butter in a 10" skillet over medium-high heat on the grill. Working in two batches, fry cakes, turning once, until golden brown (about 4 minutes per side). Place cooked fritters on paper towel to absorb excess oil. Garnish each fritter with a thin slice of softened butter, and sprinkle with finely chopped flat-leaf parsley leaves.

6. To assemble the burgers, spread toasted brioche buns with spicy aioli-flavored mayonnaise. Place fritters on grilled brioche bun halves. Place grilled french onion burgers on fritters, topped with vegetables. Add top half of the brioche bun.

FRESH LEMON AVOCADO GRILLED
CHEESE SANDWICH

Yield: 6 servings

4 packs True Lemon

¼ cup water

3 large fresh hass avocados cut in half and sliced lengthwise*

12 slices brioche

12 (¼"-thick) slices vine-ripe tomato

12 ounces goat cheese

12 ounces mild white cheddar cheese, sliced to ¾ ounce per slice

3 ounces butter or extra-virgin olive oil

12 pickle wedges

6 servings chips (tortilla or potato or bagel, or fried Chinese noodles)

DIRECTIONS:

1. In a small bowl, stir 4 packs True Lemon into ¼ cup water. Set aside.

2. Peel pitted fresh avocados and cut into six halves. Slice avocados lengthwise and put into True Lemon water.

3. Spread 1 ounce goat cheese on each slice brioche. Place ½ of each sliced avocado on six slices brioche and top each of these with 1 slice of white cheddar cheese. Place 2 slices tomato on top of goat cheese on the six slices brioche without avocado, and top with a slice of white cheddar.

4. Coat a sauté pan or griddle with 1 tablespoon melted butter or extra-virgin olive oil. Toast bread until tops of slices are golden. Place topped grilled bread slices under broiler until cheese melts and the inside is hot (20–30 seconds). Place the two topped bread slices together and cut in half diagonally. Serve hot with two pickle wedges and chips or fried noodles.

* A large fresh hass avocado weighs about eight ounces when purchased.

FLORIDA BLUEBERRY TART

Yield: 8 servings

FOR FILLING

3 cups organic blueberries
1 cup sugar
⅛ teaspoon ground cinnamon

FOR CRUST

2 cups all-purpose flour
⅓ cup yellow cornmeal
½ cup sugar
1 teaspoon baking powder
½ teaspoon salt
12 tablespoons Organic Valley cold, pasture butter, cut into bits
grated zest of 1 lemon
1 Organic Valley egg, large
1 Organic Valley egg yolk, large
confectioner's sugar

DIRECTIONS:

1. In a heavy medium saucepan, combine the blueberries, sugar, and cinnamon. Cover and bring to a simmer, stirring occasionally, until the berries are burst and the mixture has thickened (about 20 minutes). Transfer to a bowl and let cool, then cover and chill.

2. In a large bowl, combine the flour, cornmeal, sugar, baking powder, and salt. With a fork, cut in the butter until the mixture resembles coarse crumbs. Stir in the lemon zest. Beat the egg and yolk together and stir lightly into the flour mixture until just mixed. The dough should remain crumbly.

3. Heat oven to 350 degrees F.

4. Scatter two-thirds of the crust mixture over the bottom of a 9" fluted tart pan with a removable bottom. Press the crumbs evenly over the bottom and sides of the pan. Spoon the blueberry mixture into the shell and smooth the top. On a floured surface, roll the remaining

dough into ½"-thick ropes and place 1" apart over top of filling. Press the ends against the pan.

5. Bake the tart 45 minutes or until golden brown. Remove the rim from the pan and let it cool. When ready to serve, sprinkle with confectioner's sugar.

FLORIDA STRAWBERRY SHORTCAKES

Yield: 1 dozen shortcakes

1 cup (2 sticks) Organic Valley organic cultured soft butter at room temperature
½ cup sugar
1½ teaspoons salt
4 cups sifted unbleached all-purpose flour
2 tablespoons baking powder
1½ cups Organic Valley organic whole milk at room temperature
2 cups Organic Valley heavy whipping cream

DIRECTIONS:

1. Preheat oven to 400 degrees F.
2. In a stainless-steel bowl with a wire whip cream the butter with the sugar and salt for 5 minutes.
3. Sift the flour and salt and baking powder and add to the creamed mixture.
4. Add the milk and mix until just combined.
5. Roll dough to 1" thickness. Cut with 3" round cookie cutter and place circles on a buttered cookie sheet pan. Lightly brush each with melted butter and sprinkle with granulated sugar.
6. Bake 10 minutes until golden brown. Slice each biscuit in half, and top with fresh strawberries and whipped cream.

FRESH OYSTERS AND ORANGE CANAPÉS

Yield: 12 canapés

12 Chesapeake Bay oysters on the half-shell
¾ pound boiled baby Yukon Gold potatoes
1 leek, cooked, whites only; plus 2 leeks, whites only, shoestring cut and
    fried
½ cup heavy cream
2½ tablespoons extra-virgin olive oil
2 cups water
3 teaspoons flaky sea salt
1 orange, zested and juiced; plus 1 orange, sliced paper-thin
1 tablespoon lemon juice
12 toasted focaccia canapés

DIRECTIONS:

1. Remove oysters from the shells and place in a bowl. Pour any juice
   that comes from the shells in with the oysters. Set the shells on a
   service tray.
2. Puree cooked baby potatoes and leeks. Season to taste and then
   slowly mix in cream and olive oil. Keep warm.
3. In a shallow saucepan, add 2 cups of water with 3 teaspoons sea
   salt and the juice from the orange and lemon juice, then bring to a
   simmer.
4. Quickly poach the oysters in boiling hot water (no longer than 30
   seconds) and place back in the shells. Allow to cool slightly.
5. Place 4 tablespoons potato/leek puree onto each oyster half and top
   with fried leeks and orange slices. Serve each oyster on a toasted
   focaccia canapé.

BABY RED-SKIN FRIES
with Crab and Florida Avocado Parfait
Yield: 8 servings

FOR CRAB AND AVOCADO PARFAIT
3 large, ripe Florida avocados, diced, plus 8 slices
1 pound crab meat from stone crab or Florida blue crab
½ cup sour cream
¼ cup coarsely chopped cilantro
3 tablespoons lime juice
2 tablespoons finely chopped shallots
2 tablespoons seeded and finely chopped jalapeños
¾ teaspoon salt, divided
¼ teaspoon ground black pepper
1 cup vine ripe Florida plum tomatoes diced for garnish

FOR FLORIDA BABY RED-SKIN FRIES
2 tablespoons butter
2 tablespoons roasted garlic oil or olive oil
½ red onion, thinly sliced
16 Florida skin-on baby red-skin potatoes, scrubbed and cut into ¼"
    slices
salt and black pepper to taste

FOR GARNISH
1 lime, sliced into 8 wedges
1 cup of the diced tomatoes

DIRECTIONS:
1. Pit, peel, and dice the avocados. In a bowl, combine diced avocados
    and all other parfait ingredients. Refrigerate until ready to use,
    covering tightly with a moist towel.
2. In a large skillet, heat the butter and oil. When the butter foams, add
    the onion. Stir until caramelized. Add the potatoes, and season all
    with salt and pepper. Stir, cover the skillet, and sauté for 10 minutes,

tossing often. Uncover and cook for 5–10 minutes, until nicely browned.

3. Serve on large platters. Each serving of two potatoes should be topped with ¾ cup of the parfait and garnished with 1 avocado slice, 1 lime wedge, and diced tomatoes.

FRUIT SALAD
with Fresh Figs and Honey Cream
Yield: 8 entrée servings

4 ounces fresh ricotta

3 ounces cream cheese

about 2 tablespoons milk, cream or crème fraîche

about 18 figs

1–2 teaspoons fresh mint, finely chopped

honey, as needed

½ sugar baby watermelon

½ cantaloupe, seeds removed and diced

2 kiwis, peeled and cut into ¼"-thick slices

½ pint fresh raspberries

½ pint fresh blackberries

½ pint fresh strawberries, sliced

1 cup seedless white grapes

1 cup diced fresh pineapple

1 Granny Smith apple, peeled, cored, diced, and tossed with 1
     tablespoon fresh lemon juice

½ cup fresh orange juice

honey-soy dressing, as needed

red lettuce leaf to line salad platters (optional)

½ cup fresh mint leaves

DIRECTIONS:

1. Beat the ricotta and cream cheese together with enough milk or cream to make the mixture soft and easy to work. Pass it through the fine screen of a food mill or sieve, then scrape it into a ball and refrigerate until ready to use.

2. Wipe the figs off with a damp towel and slice off the stems. Make two perpendicular cuts from the top down, stopping about ¾" from the base. Press each fig at the base, which opens the top like a flower. Slip a spoonful of the cheese mixture into each one. Drizzle with honey and sprinkle with mint leaves and set aside.

3. In a large bowl, combine watermelon, cantaloupe, kiwi, raspberries, blackberries, strawberries, grapes, pineapple, and apples. Drizzle with orange juice and honey-soy dressing and gently fold together. For a more elegant presentation, all melon can be cut into balls using a melon baller, and the rest of the fruit can be arranged on lettuce leaves on the platter. Garnish with honey, cream, fresh figs, and fresh mint leaves.

FRUITED COBB SALAD

Yield: 6 entree servings

½ head lettuce, torn into whole leaves
1 bunch watercress, torn into bite-sized pieces
½ head of romaine, torn into bite-sized pieces, about 2½ cups
1 small melon, preferably honeydew
2 oranges, sectioned
1 cup Roquefort cheese crumbs
2 cups (8 ounces) blue grapes
2 ripe mangoes, peeled, pitted, and sliced
2 cups roasted unsalted macadamia nuts
1 pint raspberries
1 small pineapple, sliced
2 cups shredded coconut
2 cups green goddess dressing
pesticide-free, nontoxic flowers, such as violas or violets
fresh parsley sprigs (optional)

DIRECTIONS:
1. Place lettuce leaf covering bottom of plate, slightly over the rim.
2. Fluff watercress and romaine greens on top of lettuce and shape in an oval.
3. Arrange the following ingredients (in this order) in bands across the platter: melon balls, orange sections, Roquefort cheese crumbs, blue grapes, mango slices, unsalted roasted macadamia nuts, raspberries, sliced fresh pineapple, shredded coconut.
4. Place green goddess dressing in small cups on the side and garnish with the flowers and herb sprigs.

GARLIC CHILI WINGS

Yield: 12 wings

3 ounces Taste of Thai garlic chili pepper sauce
1 ounces Taste of Thai sweet red chili sauce
1 ounce lemon sauce
2 ounces fresh mint, chopped
1 ounce lemongrass, thinly sliced
¾ cup sliced scallions, fine bias cut
23 fresh or frozen chicken wings

DIRECTIONS:

1. In a bowl combine all ingredients except wings to make a marinade. Fully immerse chicken wings and let marinate for 2 hours.
2. Remove wings from marinade; reserve marinade. Grill wings until golden brown with prominent marks on either side. Remove wings and place in a shallow baking dish.
3. Preheat oven to 375 degrees F. Cover wings with reserved marinade; bake until cooked through and internal temperature reaches 165 degrees F.
4. Serve hot.

GAUCHO STEAK
with Chimichurri and Red Chili Onion Rings
Yield: 4 Servings

FOR CHIMICHURRI
4 cloves garlic, peeled

2 fresh bay leaves

2 teaspoons dried oregano

1 shallot, finely chopped

1 jalapeño pepper

¼ cup Beringer Founder's Estate Cabernet Sauvignon

1 cup Italian parsley, finely chopped

½ cup extra-virgin olive oil

salt and freshly ground black pepper to taste

FOR STEAKS
4 room-temperature 1½"-thick beef rib steaks

salt and freshly ground black pepper to taste

FOR CHILI ONION RINGS
4 white onions cut into $\frac{1}{16}$"- to ⅛"-thick rings

3 cups milk

3 cups sifted all-purpose flour

½ cup chili powder

2 tablespoons + 2 teaspoons cornstarch

3 teaspoons salt

3 teaspoons ground cumin

2 teaspoons sugar

2 teaspoons hot paprika

vegetable oil for frying

DIRECTIONS:
1. To prepare the chimichurri, puree garlic, bay leaves, oregano, shallot, jalapeño, and Cabernet Sauvignon in a blender to a smooth paste. Transfer to a bowl and add parsley and oil. Stir, season to taste. Refrigerate until ready to serve.

2. For the steaks, prepare outdoor grill over medium-high heat. Season steaks with salt and pepper and grill as desired (about 7 minutes per side for medium rare). Drain chimichurri and spoon onto steaks. Serve steaks immediately with onion rings.

3. To prepare the onion rings, soak onions in milk for 1 hour. Drain. Mix all remaining ingredients except oil in a large bowl. Dredge onions in flour mixture, shake off excess flour. Heat oil in large heavy saucepan on outdoor grill, to 375 degrees. Add onions in batches and cook until golden brown, about 45 seconds. Transfer to paper towels, using slotted spoon. Drain well and serve immediately.

GIANT BREAKFAST
at the Berry Farmer's Market
Yield: 2 giant servings

Blending ricotta into the eggs gives this frittata a puffy lift. Goat cheese, gruyere cheese, and chard lend an emphatic flavor note.

2 tablespoons extra-virgin olive oil
1 small bunch red swiss chard leaves (no stems), shredded (about 1½ cups)
1 shallot, minced
6 large eggs
½ cup ricotta cheese
1 cup thickly sliced fresh California strawberries, plus 3 additional sliced strawberries for garnish
½ cup goat cheese—large crumbs or very thinly sliced
salt and pepper to taste
½ cup (2 ounces) shredded gruyere or emmentaler cheese
2 tablespoons minced fresh garlic chives

DIRECTIONS:
1. Preheat broiler. In a 10" ovenproof skillet over medium heat, heat 1 tablespoon of the oil, and sauté the chard and shallot until soft (about 1 minute).
2. In a medium bowl, beat the eggs just until blended. Mix in the ricotta, thickly sliced fresh strawberries, goat cheese, salt, and pepper. Mix in the chard mixture.
3. In the same skillet over medium heat, heat the remaining 1 tablespoon oil and pour in the egg mixture. Reduce the heat to low, and cook, lifting from underneath, until the eggs are set. Sprinkle with the shredded cheese, and place under the broiler to brown. Serve warm or at room temperature, garnished with thickly sliced strawberries and garlic chives.

GINGER SUGAR AND PINK GRAPEFRUIT CRISPS

Yield: 4 servings

2 small pink grapefruits, peeled, seeded, and sliced (about 12 ounces total)
2 tablespoons fresh pink grapefruit juice
4 teaspoons dried cranberries
4 teaspoons finely chopped crystallized ginger
½ teaspoon ground cinnamon
½ teaspoon vanilla
¼ cup rolled oats
2 tablespoons packed light brown sugar
4 teaspoons all-purpose flour
4 teaspoons sweet butter, melted
2 tablespoons sliced almonds
vanilla low-fat yogurt (optional)
4 tablespoons crystallized ginger, coarsely chopped (optional)

DIRECTIONS:
1. Preheat oven to 375 degrees F. In a small bowl, stir together sliced pink grapefruit, pink grapefruit juice, cranberries, 4 teaspoons finely chopped crystallized ginger, cinnamon, and vanilla. Spoon mixture into an ungreased 1-quart casserole.
2. In another small bowl, stir together oats, brown sugar, and flour. Stir in melted butter. Sprinkle oat mixture and almonds over grapefruit mixture in baking dish.
3. Bake for 15–20 minutes, or until grapefruit is tender and almonds are golden brown. Serve warm. If desired, top with yogurt and additional crystallized ginger.

GOLDEN GRILLED ITALIAN CHEESE
with Avocado and Crab
Yield: 4 servings

¼ cup extra-virgin olive oil

8 large basil leaves, sliced

3 cloves garlic, chopped

1 (9") square focaccia

a large hass avocado, peeled, pitted, and sliced

4 ounces lump blue crabmeat (canned or frozen and defrosted)

½ teaspoon balsamic vinegar

⅓ teaspoon lemon juice

2 teaspoons extra-virgin basil olive oil

2 thick slices teleme or taleggio cheese

DIRECTIONS:
1. Heat olive oil in a small saucepan with sliced basil leaves and garlic.
2. Set aside to infuse for 20 minutes. Strain and reserve oil.
3. Warm focaccia at 350 degrees F in oven. Slice avocado and top with crabmeat. Dress with balsamic vinegar, lemon juice, and basil oil.
4. Remove foccacia from the oven and split horizontally. Cover the bottom half of the roll with avocado and crab, then add thick slices of room-temperature teleme or taleggio. Add the top and place on the heated grill or into a panini press lightly sprayed with olive oil. Allow the cheese to melt into the avocado and crabmeat and bread for about 10 minutes. Cut into quarters and serve at once.

GOLDEN LEMON AND POTATO CAKES

Yield: 4 servings

2 pounds Yukon Gold potatoes
4 tablespoons Concord Foods lemon juice
2 ounces butter
2 leeks, chopped finely
1 onion, chopped finely
6 ounces grated cheddar
1 tablespoon chopped lemongrass
1 egg, beaten
2 tablespoons water
3 ounces fresh bread crumbs
vegetable oil to sauté cakes
½ tsp each sea salt and freshly ground pepper
fresh flat-leaf parsley springs for garnish

DIRECTIONS:
1. Boil potatoes until soft. Mash with Concord Foods lemon juice and butter.
2. Cook leeks and onion in leftover potato water until tender. Drain.
3. In large mixing bowl, combine leek/onion mixture with mashed lemon potatoes, cheese, and lemongrass.
4. Place the egg and water together in a bowl with salt and pepper and beat.
5. Shape potato-and-lemon mixture into twelve cakes. Brush the cakes with egg mixture, then coat in bread crumbs.
6. Heat oil in a large skillet and sauté the potato and lemon cakes in batches for 2–3 minutes each side or until golden brown. Garnish with flat-leaf parsley and serve hot or cold as snacks or as a main dish with a salad.

GOLDEN VEGAS HOLIDAY CELEBRATION TORTE

Yield: 6 servings

Crispy layers of chocolate meringue sandwiched with a dark ganache cream and scattered with golden fruits make an impressive "all win" holiday dinner party dessert. The meringue layers, cream, fruit, and caramel can all be prepared in advance and assembled when needed.

4 large egg whites

7 ounces caster sugar

4 ounces Ghirardelli or other premium 70% cocoa plain chocolate, chopped

1 pound mixed golden fruits (e.g., mango, apricot, golden berries)

FOR FILLING
8 fluid ounces heavy cream(40%)

10 ounces Ghirardelli premium 70% cocoa plain chocolate, chopped

FOR DECORATION
4 ounces caster sugar for caramel shapes

DIRECTIONS:
1. Heat oven to 225 degrees F. Line two baking sheets with baking parchment and draw 3" circles using a pastry circle cutter as template.
2. Whisk the egg whites until stiff peaks form. Whisk in the sugar a teaspoon at a time to begin with, and then add in a steady steam as the egg whites thicken. When all the sugar is added, fold in the chopped chocolate.
3. Spread the meringue over the drawn circles and bake for 2 hours, or until dry and crisp. Allow to cool in the turned-off oven, then carefully remove from the parchment. (If needed, lightly brush the underside of the parchment paper with warm water to allow the meringues to peel off easier, but make sure the meringues don't get wet.)

4. To prepare filling, place the cream and Ghirardelli chocolate in a bowl over a pan of hot water and leave until the chocolate has melted. Set aside until thick enough to spread, stirring occasionally.

5. To make caramel shapes, dissolve 4 ounces caster sugar in a heavy pan with 2 ounces water. When sugar has dissolved, boil rapidly until golden brown. Dip the base of the pan in cold water to prevent further cooking. Using a teaspoon, drizzle the caramel over a sheet of baking parchment in desired shapes. Leave to cool and set.

6. Sandwich meringues together in threes with the Ghirardelli chocolate filling and fruit. Decorate with caramel shapes just before serving.

NEAPOLITAN GORGONZOLA-FIG PIZZA
with Prosciutto and Roasted Hazelnuts
Yield: 12 servings (or 6 servings at 2 pizzas each)

6 Bays English muffins (12 halves)
2 tablespoons fresh rosemary, chopped
¾ cup and 2 tablespoons olive oil, divided
12 ounces mascarpone
½ cup toasted hazelnuts, finely crushed (or substitute hazelnuts with ¼
    cup hazelnut liqueur)
3 ounces thinly sliced prosciutto, diced
3 teaspoons minced mint
3 ounces (¾ cup) dried figs, thinly sliced
3 ounces (¾ cup) dried apricots, thinly sliced
6 ounces shredded mozzarella
6 ounces gorgonzola cheese, crumbled
3 ounces shallots, sliced

DIRECTIONS:
1. Preheat oven to 375 degrees F.
2. Marinate rosemary in ¾ cup olive oil for 10 minutes. When fragrant, place muffin halves on a sheet pan, brush rosemary olive oil over muffin halves, and lightly toast muffin halves in oven for 3–4 minutes.
3. Remove muffins from oven, and increase oven temperature to 450 degrees F.
4. In a medium bowl, combine mascarpone with finely crushed toasted hazelnuts (or hazelnut liqueur), diced prosciutto, and chopped mint leaves. Spread toasted muffin halves with mascarpone mixture within ¼" of edge.
5. Top each muffin half with ¼ ounce figs and apricots and ½ ounce mozzarella, gorgonzola, and sliced shallots. Bake 5–6 minutes, or until crust is crisp and golden brown. Drizzle with 2 tablespoons of the remaining olive oil.

GOURMET-SHRIMP-AND-EGGPLANT SALAD
with Spicy Fusilli, Almonds, Dates, and Mint
Yield: 4–6 servings

6 tablespoons extra-virgin olive oil, divided
1 eggplant, cut in ½"cubes
1 medium onion, chopped
1 medium red bell pepper, seeded and diced
1 medium zucchini, diced
1 tablespoon balsamic vinegar
1 tablespoon tomato paste
pinch each of sugar and red crushed pepper
salt and freshly ground pepper to taste
⅓ cup whole blanched almonds, lightly toasted and chopped
¼ cup chopped dates
1 tablespoon julienned fresh mint
½ cup extra-virgin olive oil
½ teaspoon crushed red pepper
8 ounces fusilli
1 pound (16 count) shrimp, peeled and deveined
mint leaves for garnish

DIRECTIONS:

1. Heat 2 tablespoons olive oil over high heat. Add eggplant and sauté for 7–8 minutes. Drain.
2. In same skillet sauté onion in 2 tablespoons olive oil over high heat. Add pepper and zucchini. Add vinegar to skillet and cook 1 minute. Return eggplant to skillet. Stir in tomato paste, sugar, crushed red pepper, and salt and pepper to taste. Set aside to cool.
3. In a small skillet, heat 1 tablespoon olive oil. Add almonds and dates. Sauté for about 5 minutes for the sugars to caramelize. Set aside to cool.
4. Place eggplant mixture in a salad bowl. Stir in half the almond mixture and julienned mint.

5. Heat ½ cup olive oil in a small saucepan; add red pepper. Set aside. Strain to remove red pepper when cool.
6. Cook fusilli al dente. Drain and cool.
7. Heat 1 tablespoon olive oil in a skillet. Add shrimp and sauté 3–4 minutes. Season with salt and pepper to taste. Serve over eggplant salad with almonds, dates, and mint, topping with fusilli. Garnish with remaining almond mixture and mint leaves. Serve at room temperature.

GRAND BEACH DESSERT PIZZA
with Candy Caramel Sauce
Yield: 2 each (10"–12") pizza

FOR THE DOUGH

2 (¼-ounce) envelopes dry yeast or 2 cakes(3–5 ounces) fresh yeast

1 teaspoon sugar

1 cup lukewarm water, divided

3 cups all-purpose flour

2 tablespoons yellow cornmeal

1½ teaspoons salt

2 tablespoons olive oil

FOR THE CANDY CARAMEL SAUCE

½ cup whipping cream

¾ cup Florida organic sugar

¼ cup melted butter

½ cup macadamia nuts, chopped

8 each Lindt Lindor truffles, sliced

FOR THE PIZZA

1 (10"–12") pizza crust (see recipe)

1 tablespoon soft butter

1½ cups shredded swiss cheese

1 (8 ounce) package soft cream cheese

1 large egg

1 tablespoon all-purpose flour

¼ cup Florida organic sugar

2 tablespoons vanilla extract

3 cups cored and diced (¼") Red Delicious apples

⅛ teaspoon nutmeg

⅛ teaspoon cinnamon

DIRECTIONS:

1. For the dough: Sprinkle dry yeast or crumble fresh yeast over ¼ cup water. Add sugar. Leave for 10 minutes. Combine flour, cornmeal,

and salt. Add remaining water and oil to yeast mixture. Form this dough into a ball. Let rise for 1 hour. Form this dough into two balls. Knead dough until smooth. Press with fingers or roll with rolling pin into two 14" × 16" oiled baking sheets. Let rise 30 minutes. Pierce dough with fork. Brush with olive oil.

2. To prepare the candy caramel sauce, combine cream, organic sugar, and butter in small saucepan over medium-low heat. Frequently stirring, bring the sauce to a boil until it thickens to a creamy consistency.

3. For the pizza: Preheat oven to 450 degrees F.

4. Brush pizza dough with soft butter. Sprinkle with shredded swiss cheese.

5. In a medium bowl, blend cream cheese with egg, flour, sugar, and vanilla. Spread over entire crust evenly.

6. In another medium bowl, toss apples with nutmeg, cinnamon, and remaining vanilla. Pour ⅔ cup candy caramel sauce over apples and toss well. Reserve remaining sauce. Spread caramel apples evenly over cream cheese.

7. Reduce oven heat to 425 degrees F. Leave pizza on pan and bake for 18 minutes. Remove from the oven and pan and top with chopped nuts and sliced Lindor truffles. Top with remaining caramel candy sauce.

8. Slice and enjoy.

GRAND SLAM NOIR MEATBALLS

Yield: 4 servings

3 pounds grand ground free-range beef chuck 90:10
¼ cup pinot noir
¼ cup heavy cream
1 cup italian-seasoned focaccia bread crumbs, lightly roasted
2 large eggs
¼ cup worcestershire sauce
1 small red onion, diced to ¼"
2 tablespoons finely chopped fresh rosemary
1 small red bell pepper, roasted, seeded, and diced
½ teaspoon red pepper flakes
12 ounces freshly grated Monterey Jack cheese
½ cup chocolate-covered almonds, finely chopped

FOR THE SAUCE
½ cup grape jelly
½ cup sweet chili sauce
2 tablespoons lemon juice, freshly squeezed
1 teaspoon grated lemon zest

DIRECTIONS:
1. Preheat oven to 350 degrees F.
2. Mix first nine ingredients in large bowl and roll into sixteen golf-ball-sized balls.
3. Place meatballs at least ½" apart on aluminum foil in a deep roasting pan.
4. In a bowl with a wooden spoon toss grated Monterey Jack cheese with red pepper flakes and chopped chocolate-covered almonds.
5. Sprinkle chocolate-almond-cheese mixture over the meatballs. Cover pan with aluminum foil and bake for 15 minutes. Then remove top aluminum-foil sheet and set oven temperature to 450 degrees F. With the oven door closed, watch closely and remove meatballs when cheese is melted and shows a light amber color.
6. Place all sauce ingredients in a small saucepan. Bring sauce ingredients to a rapid boil and serve over meatballs.

GRANOLA COCONUT-MILK MUESLI
AND SCRAMBLED EGGS

Yield: 6–8 servings

1 cup premade granola

1 cup coconut milk

1 halved vanilla bean

¾ cup fresh orange juice

¾ cup raisins

½ cup almonds

¾ cups pecan halves

½ cup toasted unsweetened shredded coconut

¼ cup sunflower seeds

3 tablespoons wheat germ

3 tablespoons wheat bran

2 tablespoons flaxseed

½ cup yogurt

¼ cup honey

15 pitted prunes, chopped

2 Granny Smith apples, cored and grated

2 kiwis, peeled and chopped

FOR SCRAMBLED EGGS

5 large eggs, or equivalent in egg whites

2 teaspoons Kosher salt

2 scallions, minced

DIRECTIONS:

1. Combine oats, coconut milk, and vanilla bean in a small bowl.

2. In another bowl, combine orange juice and raisins.

3. Cover both bowls with plastic wrap; refrigerate overnight to let oats and raisins soften.

4. Put pecans and almonds into a food processor and pulse to chop coarsely. Transfer nuts to a large bowl along with 6 tablespoons of

the shredded coconut, sunflower seeds, wheat germ, wheat bran, flaxseed, and salt.

5. Add oat mixture to orange juice and raisins, and add yogurt, honey, prunes, apples and kiwis until combined. Divide muesli between bowls and garnish with remaining coconut.

6. In a medium bowl, whisk the eggs, salt, and scallions. Drizzle a nonstick 10" skillet with olive oil and add egg mixture. Cook about 3 minutes, loosening the eggs with a spatula. Continue to scramble eggs until cooked. Serve with bowl of muesli.

FRESH CALIFORNIA GRAPES AND HUMMUS TOAST

Yield: 6 sandwiches

1 (14-ounce) can chickpeas
juice and grated rind of large fresh lemon
6 tablespoons tahini
2 tablespoons olive oil
2 garlic cloves, crushed
salt and pepper to taste
½ cup chopped fresh coriander
2 cups fresh California green or red grapes, chopped

FOR TOAST

2 ciabatta loaves, sliced into 12 ½-inch-thin slice and toasted lightly
3 garlic cloves, crushed
1 tablespoon chopped fresh cilantro
4 tablespoons extra-virgin olive oil

FOR GARNISH

several small bunches California grapes

DIRECTIONS:

1. Blend chickpeas and juice in a food processor. Add lemon juice and blend. Stir in the tahini and 1 tablespoon olive oil. Add the garlic. Season with salt and pepper to taste. Spoon into a serving dish and drizzle with remaining olive oil, chopped coriander, and grapes. Top with grated lemon rind. Chill until ready to use.
2. Grill sliced ciabatta in single layer. Mix crushed garlic, cilantro, and olive oil, and spread over toasted bread slices. Cook under hot grill for 2–3 minutes. Serve hot on a platter with California grape hummus, surrounded by small bunches of California grapes.

GREEK ISLAND LIGHT TILAPIA FILLETS

Yield: 4 servings

¼ cup crumbled basil-and-tomato feta cheese (1 ounce)*

2 tablespoons fat-free cream cheese (1 ounce)

4 boneless, skinless tilapia fillets (about 1¼ pounds total)

¼–½ teaspoon black pepper

dash salt

1 teaspoon olive oil or cooking oil

¼ cup vegetable broth

1 (10-ounce) package prewashed fresh spinach, trimmed (8 cups)

2 tablespoons walnut or pecan pieces, toasted

1 tablespoon lemon juice

4 lemons sliced or halved (optional)

DIRECTIONS:

1. In a small bowl, combine feta cheese and cream cheese; set aside. Using a sharp knife, cut a horizontal slit through the thickest portion of each tilapia fillet to form a pocket. Stuff pockets with the cheese mixture. If necessary, secure openings with wooden toothpicks. Sprinkle fish with pepper and salt.

2. In a large nonstick skillet, cook fish in hot oil over medium-high heat for about 12 minutes, or until tender and no longer pink, turning once (reduce heat to medium if fillets brown too quickly). Remove fish from skillet. Cover and keep warm.

3. Carefully add broth to skillet. Bring to boiling; add half of the spinach. Cover and cook about 3 minutes, or just until spinach is wilted. Remove spinach from skillet, reserving liquid in pan. Repeat with remaining spinach. Return all spinach to skillet. Stir in the nuts and lemon juice.

4. To serve, divide spinach mixture among four dinner plates. Top with tilapia fillets. If desired, garnish with lemon slices.

*If basil-and-tomato feta cheese is not available, stir 1 teaspoon finely diced and snipped fresh basil and 1 teaspoon diced snipped oil-packed dried tomatoes, drained, into ¼ cup plain feta cheese.

GREEK LENTIL SALAD

Yield: 8 servings

FOR DRESSING
3 cups extra-virgin olive oil
1½ cups red wine vinegar
¼ cup sugar

FOR PLATE GARNISH
8 hearts of romaine lettuce leaves
4 thinly sliced roasted peppers, seeded
1 cup cooked lentils
1 cup diced (¼") tomatoes with seeds
½ teaspoon plus 8 sprigs oregano

FOR SALAD
3 cups cooked lentils
3 cups diced tomatoes with seeds
4 seedless cucumbers, quartered lengthwise, then sliced
2 green peppers, deseeded and diced to ¼"
2 medium red onions, cut in half, thinly sliced
80 Kalamata olives, pitted
16 ounces feta cheese, crumbled
2½ teaspoons oregano, divided

DIRECTIONS:
1. To prepare the dressing, Drizzle oil into the vinegar, stirring constantly. Set aside. Stir again before using.
2. To prepare plates, place romaine just underneath the rims of the plates and top romaine in a Cobb-salad fashion with plate garnishes, drizzling with 2 tablespoons dressing.
3. To make the salad, mix lentils, diced tomatoes, cucumbers, peppers, red onions, Kalamata olives, crumbled feta cheese, and 2 teaspoons oregano. Add just enough dressing to coat the vegetables. Place equal amounts of salad in center of each plate, sprinkle with remaining oregano, and garnish with sprig of fresh oregano.

GREEN SAN FRANCISCO POTATOES
with Caramelized Sweet Onions and Oscar Mayer Hot Dogs
Yield: 8 servings

Add some green to your regular mashed potatoes with nutritious spinach! This is a great way to get some green stuff into kids' diets.

1 tablespoon light butter, softened
1 (10-ounce) bag Publix baby spinach leaves, triple washed and dried
2 cups water
1 clove minced garlic (optional)
2 pounds Yukon Gold potatoes, washed, peeled and chopped
½ cup shredded Cracker Barrel 2% fat cheese
¾ cup Greenwise Soy Milk, plain, warmed
1½ cups Kraft reduced-fat 2% shredded mild cheddar cheese
salt and pepper to taste
4 tablespoons extra-virgin olive oil
8 Oscar Mayer light hot dogs
12 ounces (1 large) sweet onion, peeled and thinly sliced

DIRECTIONS:
1. In a large skillet coated with 1 tablespoon light butter, cook spinach, covered, in water until it wilts but retains a fresh and green color. When cooked, place spinach in a colander, rinse well in cold water to cool, and squeeze out excess water by hand.
2. In a large pot, cook potatoes until tender (about 20 minutes). Drain well, return to pot, and mash well. Add Cracker Barrel cheese and soy milk gradually and stir until smooth. Add cheddar cheese and spinach, stirring until cheese melts. Season with salt and pepper. Keep hot.
3. In a 12" skillet over medium-high heat, heat olive oil until hot. Add hot dogs and cook, stirring, until browned (about 5 minutes). Transfer hot dogs to a plate and cook onion, stirring, in the same skillet until caramelized to a dark brown.
4. Divide mashed potatoes among eight plates, making a well in the middle of each pile for a hot dog. Add hot dogs and top with caramelized onions.

LAS PALMAS GRILLED AVOCADO AND BEEF TACOS

Yield: 8 servings

2 avocados from Mexico

2 tablespoons lime juice

1½ teaspoons McCormick Perfect Pinch Montreal steak seasoning,
  divided

1 pound flank steak

½ cup each shredded Sargento reduced-sodium mild cheddar cheese

*½ cup each shredded Sargento reduced-sodium shredded mozzarella
  cheese

½ cup olive oil

8 taco shells

DIRECTIONS:

1. Preheat broiler. Cut avocados lengthwise around pit; twist halves
    to separate. Strike pit with a knife blade and pull to remove. Place
    avocado halves in a small bowl. Sprinkle with lime juice and ½
    teaspoon McCormick Perfect Pinch Montreal seasoning; set aside.

2. Rub remaining Montreal seasoning over both sides of steak. Place
    steak on rack on a broiler pan and broil 2"–3" from heat source until
    cooked to desired doneness (about 5 minutes each side for medium).
    Remove to a cutting board, let rest for 5 minutes; cut diagonally into
    thin slices.

3. Place avocados on hot grill and cook until they start to show grill
    marks. Remove from grill. Slice avocado halves into approximately
    sixteen slices.

4. Place sliced steak in each taco shell, place about two avocado slices
    on top, and add shredded cheese.

5. Fold each taco, brush the outside with olive oil, and place the whole
    thing back on the grill but away from direct heat for a couple of
    minutes, or until the outside is crispy and the cheese is melted.

* Reduced-sodium shredded mozzarella may be replaced with sliced reduced-
sodium Colby Jack cheese.

GRILLED BLACKENED WILD SALMON
and Black Bean Fiesta
Yield: 4 servings

4 (8 ounces) boneless, skinless wild salmon fillets

FOR MARINADE
¼ cup each aged balsamic vinegar,* lemon juice, soy sauce
1 teaspoon sea salt
1 tablespoon brown sugar
1" piece fresh ginger, grated; or 1½ teaspoons ground ginger
2 tablespoons Cajun blackened seasoning, divided (or to taste)
½ cup extra-virgin olive oil or canola oil

FOR BLACK BEAN FIESTA
2 (15-ounce) cans Bush's Black Bean Fiesta Grillin' Beans

FOR GARNISH
long chives and scallions

DIRECTIONS:
1. To make the marinade, stir all ingredients (using only 1 of the 2 tablespoons Cajun blackened seasoning) together, making sure the salt and sugar are dissolved and all ingredients are well combined. Pour the marinade into a resealable plastic bag or large glass or ceramic bowl. Add salmon fillets to marinade.
2. Place bag or bowl in refrigerator for 1–2 hours, turning the salmon fillets occasionally.
3. Prepare an outdoor grill for medium to high heat, using wood chips if a smoky flavor is desired.
4. Drain excess marinade from salmon fillets, rub fillets with the remaining 1 tablespoon Cajun blackened seasoning and place toward center of hot grill for about 4–5 minutes. Sear fillets on both sides until opaque in color but still slightly firm.

5. Place Bush's Black Bean Fiesta Grillin' Beans together with the salmon fillets in an iron skillet or other grilling pan on outer edge of the hot grill. Stir occasionally until heated through.
6. Throw in scallions and chives at the last minute for color, and arrange fish on top or toward the side of Bush's Black Bean Fiesta Grillin' Beans.

*Aged balsamic vinegar (aged twelve years or longer) is a treat, but not an economical one. If you don't want to spring for a forty-dollar bottle, use regular balsamic. Alternatively, bring ½ cup regular balsamic vinegar to a boil over high heat in a small skillet. Cook until the vinegar begins to thicken and becomes syrupy (2–3 minutes).

GRILLED CITRUS KOBE BEEF BURGER
with Papaya Salsa
Yield: 6 burgers

The local flavors of Florida could hardly better be represented than in this Key West–inspired recipe.

32 ounces Kobe beef ground round
2 tablespoons finely chopped fresh oregano
2 tablespoons finely chopped fresh cilantro
2 ounces fresh garlic, chopped
4 tablespoons fresh orange juice
2 tablespoons fresh lime juice
2 tablespoons molasses
2 teaspoons Sutter Home pinot noir

DIRECTIONS:
1. On a chopping board with a sharp French knife combine the ground beef, oregano, cilantro, and garlic. Set aside.
2. In a bowl combine orange juice, lime juice, and pinot noir with a wire whip.
3. Add beef mixture to the liquid and shape into six equal-size burger patties.
4. Refrigerate to minimum temperature 40 degree F.
5. Brush patties with olive oil and grill on hot broiler to desired doneness for about 5 minutes for medium rare turning once.
6. Serve on toasted bun with Florida greens (1/2 hearts of romaine, 3 sprigs basil leaves, 1 cup sliced Belgian endive). Top with Papaya Salsa.
7. To prepare Papaya Salsa, one medium-size Florida papaya preferably red meat, ½ tsp cayenne, ½ tsp each sea salt and freshly ground pepper, and ½ cup extra-virgin olive oil, and ¼ cup sweet balsamic vinegar. In a bowl combine all ingredients and ladle over Florida greens.

ENGLISH ORANGE GROVE ENGLISH MUSTARD–SPICED CHICKEN

Yield: 4 servings

1 cup fresh orange juice
½ cup fresh key lime juice
2 tablespoons olive oil
3 teaspoons salt, divided
2 teaspoons freshly ground black pepper, divided
1 tablespoon finely chopped fresh tarragon
3 tablespoons Colman's English mustard, divided
2 teaspoons finely chopped fresh rosemary
2 garlic cloves, minced
1 whole chicken, about 3½ pounds, neck and giblets removed, butterflied
2–4 oranges
nonstick vegetable oil spray
2 foil-wrapped bricks

DIRECTIONS:

1. Whisk juices, olive oil, 1 teaspoon salt, 1 teaspoon pepper, tarragon, 1 tablespoon Colman's English mustard, rosemary, and garlic in a glass baking dish. Add chicken to marinate, turning occasionally to coat on each side. Allow to marinate overnight, refrigerated, or packed on crushed ice for 30 minutes.

2. Mix remaining salt, pepper, and Colman's English mustard in a separate bowl.

3. Spray grill rack with nonstick spray. Prepare barbecue grill for medium heat. Slice ½ orange into ¼"-thick slices. Remove chicken from marinade and pat dry. Loosen skin from breast and slide two orange slices between skin and breast. Loosen skin from thighs and slide two orange slices between skin and thighs. Rub English-mustard mixture over both sides of chicken. Place chicken, skin side down, on grill. Place foil-wrapped bricks on top of chicken. Cover and grill until skin is crispy and brown (about 15 minutes). Remove

bricks and turn chicken halves. Replace bricks and cook from other side. Cook, covered, until chicken is cooked through. Let chicken rest 10 minutes.

4. Meanwhile, place whole orange on grill and cook until lightly charred, turning often. Cut into wedges and serve with chicken.

GRILLED FRESH NEW ORLEANS VEGETABLE MUFFULETTA

Yield: 4 sandwiches

1 eggplant, sliced ½" thick
1 straight-necked yellow squash, sliced ½" thick at an angle
1 green or red bell pepper, quartered lengthwise
4 large white mushroom caps
1 red onion, sliced ¾" thick
½ cup Marzetti Roasted Garlic Italian Vinaigrette
½ cup store-bought pesto
1 cup store-bought giardiniera (pickled vegetable salad)
½ cup pimiento-stuffed green olives
1 (8"–9") round loaf crusty Italian bread
¼ pound deli-sliced provolone cheese

DIRECTIONS:

1. Preheat a grill or grill pan to medium high. Lightly brush the eggplant, yellow squash, bell pepper, and red onion with ½ cup Marzetti vinaigrette; season with salt and pepper. Cover and grill, turning once, until charred (about 6 minutes).

2. Using a food processor, pulse the giardiniera and olives into a coarse pesto.

3. Slice the top quarter off the bread and scoop out the insides. Spread half the pesto on the inside of the bread, layer with half the grilled vegetables, and then spoon the remaining pesto on top. Fill the bread with the remaining vegetables and top with the provolone. Spread the inside of the bread top with the vegetable relish and set into place. Press down firmly, and then cut into quarters (wedges).

GRILLED MANGO-LIME PORK CHOPS

Yield: 4 servings

2 (1-ounce) packages marjoram
4 garlic cloves, minced
1" ginger root, grated
1 shallot, chopped
½ serrano pepper, seeded and finely chopped
1 ripe mango, peeled, pit removed, and coarsely chopped
¼ cup fresh lime juice
½ cup fresh orange juice
¼ cup toasted sesame oil
¼ cup dark rum
½ teaspoon toasted cumin seeds, chopped
1 teaspoon chopped cloves
4 pounds bone-in pork loin chops
salt and freshly ground black pepper to taste
12 each fresh marjoram sprigs and 12 each lime wedges

DIRECTIONS:

1. Combine the first twelve ingredients in a blender or food processor and puree until smooth, stopping to scrape down the sides. Place the pork chops in a baking dish or zip-top plastic bag and pour the marinade over the pork chops, reserving 1 cup. Marinate for 2–4 hours, turning occasionally to coat.
2. Preheat grill to medium 1 hour before grilling time.
3. Remove meat from marinade. Pat the pork chops dry with paper towels. Lightly season the pork chops with salt and freshly ground black pepper on both sides. Place the pork chops on the grill and cook for 8–10 minutes on the first side. Turn and cook an additional 8–10 minutes, until internal temperature reaches 150–155 degrees F. Remove the pork chops from the grill and let stand for 5 minutes before serving. Garnish with fresh marjoram sprigs and lime wedges. Use the reserved 1 cup of marinade for dipping, if desired.

BANANAS IN A DARK RUM, LEMON, AND GINGER TAMARI SAUCE

Yield: 4 dessert servings

3 tablespoons butter

3 tablespoons brown sugar

4 tablespoons each lemon juice and orange juice

1 tablespoon tamari

½ teaspoon ground cinnamon

½" piece ginger root, grated

4 medium bananas, peeled and halved

4 tablespoons dark rum

DIRECTIONS:

1. Over medium heat in a 12" skillet, melt the butter and add the remaining ingredients, except the bananas and rum. Cook only until the sugar is dissolved, stirring occasionally. Raise the temperature to medium high, add the bananas, and cook them on both sides no longer than 10 minutes, basting them occasionally with the sauce. Sprinkle them with the rum. Use the remaining 1 cup of marinade as a dipping sauce.

FRESH OYSTERS WRAPPED IN ALARIA SEAWEED
and Spinach-Dipped Black Olive Tapenade
Yield: 12 servings

1½ cups Kalamata olives or Gaeta olives, pitted
3 tablespoons capers, drained
2 garlic cloves, minced
¼ cup minced fresh parsley
½ teaspoons sea salt
⅛ teaspoons freshly ground pepper
¼ cup extra-virgin olive oil
½ jar Tostitos spinach dip
12 medium Gulf Coast oysters
12 (1" × 5") strips from 1 frond of dried or rehydrated alaria seaweed

DIRECTIONS:

1. In a food processor, combine the olives, capers, garlic, parsley, salt, and pepper. Slowly add the oil and pulse, retaining some of the texture. Taste to adjust the seasoning. In a small bowl, fold the tapenade into ½ jar Tostitos spinach dip and refrigerate oyster topping until ready to serve.

2. Shuck oysters and transfer to a small bowl, reserving the shells. Scrub and rinse shells. Wrap 1 strip of seaweed around each oyster. Return each oyster to its shell. Put oysters in their shells on grill and cook, without turning, until just steaming (about 5 minutes).

3. Arrange oysters on a serving platter and top with large spoonful of spinach-dipped black olive tapenade.

GRILLED STEAK BALI

Yield: 4 servings

A simple marinade of pureed dried figs and store-bought balsamic vinaigrette adds intense flavor to steak. This recipe is adapted from Lori Welander's grand prize–winning recipe from the 2003 National Beef Cook-Off.

⅓ cup prepared balsamic vinaigrette
2 dried figs, stems trimmed, chopped
1 pound sirloin steak, 1" thick, trimmed
¼ teaspoon salt
freshly ground pepper to taste
⅓ cup herb-and-garlic creamy cheese spread (Make your own rich)

DIRECTIONS:

1. Place vinaigrette and figs in a blender or food processor; process until blended. Place in a large sealable plastic bag with steak, and turn to coat. Marinate in the refrigerator for at least 6 hours, up to 24 hours.
2. Preheat grill to medium.
3. Remove steak from marinade; discard marinade. Oil the grill rack (see tip below). Grill the steak for 4–6 minutes per side for medium rare, depending on thickness. Transfer to a clean cutting board. Season with salt and pepper, tent with foil, and let rest for 5 minutes.
4. Meanwhile, warm cheese in a small saucepan over medium-low heat, stirring often, until melted.
5. Carve steak into thin slices. Serve each portion with a dollop of the cheese sauce.

Tip: To oil a grill rack, oil a folded paper towel and use tongs to rub it over the rack. *Do not* use cooking spray on a hot grill.

KEY WEST GRILLED SUMMER SCALLOP
AND GORGONZOLA SKEWERS

Yield: 6 servings

2 pounds large scallops
¼ cup lemon juice
¼ cup extra-virgin olive oil
1 tablespoon rosemary
2 teaspoons dried oregano
3 cloves garlic, minced
1 teaspoon Kosher salt
½ teaspoon red pepper flakes
1 lemon, cut into wedges
½ cup crumbled gorgonzola cheese

DIRECTIONS:

1. Place scallops in a sealable plastic bag. Add lemon juice, olive oil, rosemary, oregano, garlic, salt, and pepper flakes. Seal bag and turn to coat. Marinate refrigerated for 30 minutes.
2. Discard marinade, then thread scallops onto skewers. Heat grill to medium and cook kabobs and lemon wedges, turning once, until scallops are just opaque and wedges are lightly browned (about 8 minutes). Sprinkle scallops with gorgonzola cheese.

GRILLED SWORDFISH
with Basil Spinach Aioli
Yield: 6 servings

The basil spinach aioli is a mayo-like emulsion made from raw egg yolks. For ease of preparation you can also replace the egg yolks with 1 cup of purchased mayo and whisk in the remaining ingredients.

FOR AIOLI
2 large egg yolks, preferably organic
2 tablespoons chopped fresh basil
2 garlic cloves, minced
1 anchovy fillet, minced
½ teaspoons red wine vinegar
½ teaspoons worcestershire sauce
1 cup olive oil
1 tablespoon warm water
1 tablespoon fresh lemon juice
¼ teaspoon cayenne pepper
½ jar Tostitos spinach dip

FOR SWORDFISH
olive oil for brushing
one 2½–3 pound boneless swordfish loin, about 1" thick

FOR GARNISH
12 ounces baby lettuce leaves
12 lemon slices
6 tablespoons tiny capers
12 rolled anchovy fillets

DIRECTIONS:
1. For the aioli, whisk egg yolks, basil, garlic, anchovies, vinegar, and worcestershire sauce in medium bowl. Whisk in 2 tablespoons oil a few drops at a time, then gradually add the rest. Add warm water,

lemon juice, and cayenne. Season with salt and pepper to taste. Blend sauce with ½ jar Tostitos spinach dip and refrigerate.

2. For the swordfish, prepare grill for high heat. Brush grill rack with oil. Brush Swordfish loin with oil. Sprinkle swordfish with salt and pepper. Grill Swordfish uncovered 5 minutes. Using 2 large spatulas, carefully turn fish over. Grill until fish just begins to flake in center, 4–5 minutes longer. Transfer swordfish to platter.

3. Arrange spinach-basil aioli in baby lettuce leaf cups around the fish. Garnish the fish with lemon slices, capers, and rolled anchovy fillets.

MARSEILLE SEA BASS SALAD NIÇOISE

Yield: 4 servings

Salad niçoise, a classic French salad, is typically made with tuna. Here I use sweet grilled tilapia (in season all year long) or striped bass. You may also skip the fish altogether for a vegetarian main-course salad using 1 pound summer squash or winter squash, cut into 1" slices. I call for serving it on a platter, but it's just as beautiful individually plated.

FOR VINAIGRETTE

1 medium clove garlic
¼ teaspoon salt
5 tablespoons extra-virgin olive oil
6 tablespoons fresh orange juice, plus more to taste
¼ cup white wine vinegar or red wine vinegar
1 tablespoon Dijon mustard

FOR SALAD

1½ pounds red potatoes, (5–6 medium), scrubbed and halved
1¼ pounds green beans, trimmed
juice of 1 large lemon
2 tablespoons extra-virgin olive oil
½ teaspoon salt, divided
1 pound tilapia, or striped bass

ALTERNATIVE INGREDIENTS FOR VEGETARIAN VERSION

1 pound 1"-sliced summer squash, zucchini, or yellow straight squash; or 1"-sliced winter squash (butternut or spaghetti squash)
¼ teaspoon coarsely ground pepper, plus more to taste
1 large head Boston lettuce
1½ cups grape tomatoes
3 hard-boiled eggs (see tip), peeled and cut into wedges
¼ cup sliced pitted black niçoise or Kalamata olives
¼ cup finely chopped fresh parsley

DIRECTIONS:

1. To prepare vinaigrette, peel garlic and smash with the side of a chef's knife. Using a fork, mash garlic with ¼ teaspoon salt in a small bowl to form a coarse paste. Whisk in olive oil. Add 6 tablespoons orange juice, vinegar, and mustard; whisk until well blended. Taste and whisk in up to 4 tablespoons more juice to mellow the flavor. Season with more salt if desired. Set aside at room temperature.

2. To prepare salad: Bring 1" of water to a boil in a large saucepan fitted with a steamer basket. Add potatoes; cook until tender (10–15 minutes). Remove to a cutting board. When cool enough to handle, slice and place in a shallow bowl. Drizzle with ⅓ cup vinaigrette; set aside.

3. Add beans to the steamer basket; cook until bright green and just tender (4–6 minutes). Rinse in a colander with cold water until cool. Drain well. Place in a medium bowl and toss with 2 tablespoons vinaigrette.

4. Combine lemon juice, olive oil, and ¼ teaspoon salt in a sturdy sealable plastic bag; shake until the salt dissolves. Add fish and marinate for up to 20 minutes while you ready the grill.

5. Preheat grill to medium high for 10 minutes, then reduce heat to medium. (For a charcoal grill, wait until the flames subside and only coals and some ash remain; flames will cause the oil on the fish to burn.)

6. Drain the fish and pat dry with paper towels. Season with the remaining ¼ teaspoon salt and ¼ teaspoon pepper. Oil the grill rack (see tip). Grill the fish, turning once, until browned and just cooked through (4–5 minutes per side for tilapia, 3–4 minutes per side for bass, 3–4 minutes for summer squash, 4–5 minutes for winter squash).

7. Arrange lettuce leaves on a large serving platter. Arrange the fish (whole or flaked into large chunks), potatoes, green beans, and tomatoes on top. Drizzle with the remaining vinaigrette. Garnish with eggs, olives, parsley, and pepper to taste.

Ingredient note: Wild-caught sea bass is sustainably fished and has a large, stable population, according to the Atlantic Coast Seafood Watch.

Kitchen tips: To hard boil eggs, place eggs in a single layer in a saucepan; cover with water. Bring to a simmer over medium-high heat. Reduce heat to low and cook at the barest simmer for 10 minutes. Remove from heat, pour out hot water, and cover with ice-cold water. Let stand until cool enough to handle before peeling.

To oil a grill rack, oil a folded paper towel and use tongs to rub it over the rack. *Do not* use cooking spray on a hot grill.

HAWAIIAN MACADAMIA NUT POUND CAKE

Yield: 1 (8" square) cake or 1 standard-sized loaf

1⅓ cups sifted unbleached all-purpose flour
1 teaspoon baking powder
1 cup unsalted butter, softened
½ cup powdered sugar
1 cup sweetened condensed milk
½ cup finely chopped fresh pineapple or pineapple puree
½ cup coarsely chopped macadamia nuts, lightly toasted
2 large eggs, whipped
1 teaspoon vanilla extract
½ teaspoon salt

DIRECTIONS:

1. Sieve the flour and baking powder until well combined. You can also whisk it well in a bowl until combined if you don't have a sieve.
2. Beat butter and sugar together with an electric mixer until soft and fluffy. Then add condensed milk, finely chopped pineapple, and toasted chopped macadamia nuts. Beating batter with electric mixer until well combined.
3. Whisk eggs in a bowl for 2 minutes and set aside.
4. Add flour to the butter-sugar-condensed-milk mixture and mix until just combined without beating too hard.
5. Add eggs, vanilla extract, and salt, and mix well again.
6. Transfer to a greased 8" cake pan, or 1-pound loaf pan, and bake in a preheated oven at 350 degrees F for 30 minutes, or until a toothpick inserted in center of cake comes out clean.

MIAMI BEACH HAZELNUT TURTLE CHEESECAKE

Yield: 16 servings

FOR CRUST
1½ cups hazelnut or shortbread cookies, crushed
3 tablespoons butter, melted

FOR FILLING
1 (8-ounce) package cream cheese
1 (8-ounce) package "lite" cream cheese or Neufchâtel
1 pound part skim ricotta cheese
½ cup sugar
1 (14-ounce) can Eagle Brand sweetened condensed milk, divided (see below)
4 large eggs
4 tablespoons butter, melted
3 tablespoons sifted unbleached all-purpose flour
3 tablespoons corn starch
2 teaspoons vanilla extract
1 cup sour cream

FOR TURTLE TOPPING
1 (5-ounce) bag caramels
4 tablespoons butter, melted
½ can (7 ounces) Eagle Brand sweetened condensed milk (see above)
½ cup mini milk-chocolate chips or white chips or caramel chips
1 cup coarsely chopped roasted hazelnuts*

DIRECTIONS:
1. To make the crust: Combine crushed cookies and butter and press into the bottom of a 10" springform baking pan. Bake at 350 degrees F in oven for 8–10 minutes. Remove from oven and proceed to make the filling.
2. To make the filling: In a mixer blend the cream cheeses and ricotta together until smooth. Gradually add the sugar and ½ can Eagle Brand sweetened condensed milk and beat until creamy and smooth.

331

Add the eggs, one at a time, beating well after each addition; then add the melted butter, flour, cornstarch, and vanilla extract. Beat until creamy and smooth. Gently fold in the sour cream until fully incorporated. Pour mixture into prepared baking pan crust and bake one hour at 325 degrees F. Turn off the oven and *do not* open the door. Allow the cake to cool in the oven for 2 hours. Remove the cake and cool on a rack. While the cake cools off, prepare the hazelnut turtle topping.

3. To make the topping: Melt caramel, butter, and Eagle Brand sweetened condensed milk in a heavy saucepan over medium-high heat, stirring until smooth. Let cool slightly. Spread the topping evenly over the top of the cheesecake. Top with mini chocolate or caramel chips and crushed roasted hazelnuts.

4. Chill the cake to serve. Remove sides of pan and divide into desired number of servings, dipping a sharp knife into hot water and wiping the blade after each cut.

*To roast hazelnuts, spread raw hazelnuts onto a baking sheet and roast in an oven at 395 degrees F, stirring occasionally, until the skins of the nuts crack and can be taken off easily. (Rub the nuts in a clean towel to make the skins come off.)

VEGETABLE SKEWERS
with Oregano Ginger Vinaigrette
Yield: 6 servings of 2 skewers

Nothing showcases the flavor of fresh-picked healthy, healing vegetables better than a great homemade marinade featuring lemon, fresh oregano, and ginger root with a quick sear on the grill.

FOR VINAIGRETTE
4 tablespoons sherry vinegar
4 tablespoons Dijon mustard
2 small shallots, minced (3 tablespoons)
2 tablespoons lemon juice
1 tablespoon grated lemon zest
½ tablespoon grated fresh ginger root
⅔ cup olive oil
2 tablespoons chopped fresh oregano

FOR VEGETABLE SKEWERS
6 small Yukon Gold potatoes, quartered
24 sugar snap peas
24 white or cremini mushrooms, stems removed
24 thin slivers of avocado
24 pieces of kale
24 brussels sprouts
1 red bell pepper, cut into 1" pieces
1 red onion, cut into 1" pieces
1 medium yellow squash, cut into 12 rounds
1 medium zucchini, cut into 12 rounds

DIRECTIONS:
1. To make oregano ginger vinaigrette: Whisk together vinegar, mustard, shallots, lemon juice, lemon zest, and ginger root in small bowl. Slowly whisk in olive oil until mixture thickens or emulsifies. Stir in oregano. Season with salt and pepper if desired. Set aside.

2. To make vegetable skewers: Cook potatoes for 3 minutes in large pot of boiling salted water. Add sugar snap peas and cook 1 minute more, or until sugar snap peas are tender-crisp. Drain vegetables and rinse under cold water. Drain once more and pat dry.

3. Wrap avocado slivers in kale leaves. Toss potatoes, sugar snap peas, mushrooms, kale-wrapped avocado, brussels sprouts, red bell pepper, red onion, yellow squash, and zucchini with ½ cup oregano ginger vinaigrette. (Reserve remaining oregano ginger vinaigrette for another use.) Cover, and refrigerate at least 1 hour, up to overnight.

4. Preheat grill to medium high heat. Thread vegetables onto twelve presoaked bamboo skewers, leaving ¼" space between each one to ensure even cooking.

5. Rub grate or vegetable grill topper with vegetable oil. Grill skewers 3–4 minutes per side, or until vegetables are slightly charred and soft. Season with salt and pepper, if desired, and drizzle with remaining ¼ cup oregano ginger vinaigrette.

HEARTY NEW ENGLAND WAFFLE BREAKFAST

Yield: 8 servings

1 pound sliced grilled back bacon—8 thick slices, 2 ounces each
2 cups all-purpose flour
2 tablespoons sugar
2 teaspoons baking powder
1 teaspoon salt
1½ cups milk
2 tablespoons unsalted butter, melted
2 large eggs at room temperature
1 cup Ocean Spray whole cranberry sauce
1 cup Heinz chili sauce

DIRECTIONS:

1. Grill bacon slices until heated thoroughly but not crispy, to avoid their being dried out.
2. Plug in an electric waffle iron to preheat.
3. Meanwhile, combine flour, sugar, baking powder, and salt in a large bowl; whisk together to blend.
4. Pour milk into a glass measuring cup and microwave for 1 minute at full power to heat slightly. Pour into medium bowl; whisk in melted butter and eggs. Add liquid ingredients to flour mixture, whisking just until blended.
5. Grease waffle iron with cooking spray. Spread about ⅓ cup batter over each iron (or appropriate amount according to manufacturer's directions). Close waffle iron and cook until done. Repeat with remaining batter. Spread waffles generously with equal amounts of chili sauce. Top with grilled back bacon and top with Ocean Spray cranberry sauce for a hearty New England waffle breakfast.

WOLFI'S ORIGINAL OATMEAL CRANBERRY STREUSEL PIE

Yield: 2 (9") pies (12–16 servings)

FOR DOUGH

1 package May Cookie Co. Hearty & Wholesome Oatmeal Cranberry
  Cookie Mix

FOR FILLING

approximately 5 pints (30 ounces) coarsely chopped fresh cranberries or
  2 bags frozen berries, no sugar added, not thawed (24 ounces)*
1 can (14 ounces) Eagle Brand sweetened condensed milk
1 egg, lightly beaten

FOR STREUSEL TOPPING

½ cup packed brown sugar
¼ cup all-purpose flour
¼ cup chopped pecans
½ teaspoon ground cinnamon
3 tablespoons cold butter

DIRECTIONS:

1. For the dough, follow package instructions.
2. When crumbly, gradually add water, tossing with a fork until a ball
   forms. Divide dough in half. Roll out each portion to fit a 9" pie pan;
   place in pie pans. Flute edges and set aside.
3. For filling, combine berries, sweetened condensed milk (I like Eagle
   Brand), and egg; pour into pastry shells.
4. For Streusel topping, Combine brown sugar, flour, pecans, and
   cinnamon in a small bowl. Cut in butter until crumbly. Sprinkle over
   filling. Cover edges of pastry loosely with foil.
5. Bake at 350 degrees F for 20–25 minutes or until a knife inserted
   near the center comes out clean. Cool on a wire rack for 2 hours.
   Refrigerate until serving.

HONEY AND PEPPER CHICKEN BURGER

Yield: 6 burgers

2 tablespoons minced garlic

2 teaspoons paprika

1 teaspoon chili powder

1 teaspoon salt

1 teaspoon ground cumin

1 teaspoon ground red pepper flakes (or to taste)

8 boneless skinless chicken thighs, coarsely ground

olive oil cooking spray

6 tablespoons orange-blossom honey

2 teaspoons cider vinegar

freshly ground red pepper to taste

6 (6") brioche rolls

2 roasted seedless Anaheim or poblano peppers, diced

1 cup shredded green cabbage

6 slices tomato

6 thin slices red onions

½ cup reduced-fat chili-spiced spicy mayonnaise (spiced to your taste)

⅓ cup chopped cilantro

DIRECTIONS:

1. Combine first six ingredients in a large bowl. Add chicken to bowl, toss. Form into six equal patties, about ½" thick.
2. To oil the grill rack, oil a folded paper towel, hold it with tongs, and rub it over the rack. (*Do not* use cooking spray on the hot grill.) Spray burgers with olive oil.
3. Preheat grill to medium high.
4. Combine honey and vinegar in a small bowl, stirring well.
5. Combine chili-spiced mayonnaise and chopped cilantro in a small bowl and set aside.
6. Grill the burgers on lightly oiled grill rack, turning once, until an instant-read thermometer inserted in the center reads 165 degrees F (about 6 minutes per side). Before turning the burgers, and again after

337

the burgers are turned over, brush ¼ cup honey-and-vinegar mixture onto chicken burgers.

7. Assemble the burgers on toasted brioche rolls with the chili mayonnaise, chopped roasted peppers, cabbage, tomato, and onion. Add freshly ground of red pepper to taste.

HOT GERMAN POTATO SALAD
for Parties and Barbecues
Yield: 6 side dish orders

4 pounds white or golden potatoes (best for peeling), preferably small

2 medium white onions, peeled and diced

16 ounces vegetable or meat broth, hot (preferably homemade)

6 tablespoons chopped fresh herbs (equal parts parsley, marjoram, and chives)

6 tablespoons vegetable oil

1 teaspoon German-style mustard, medium-hot

salt, white pepper, sweet Hungarian paprika, German-type liquid seasoning (e.g., Maggi or Knorr Aromat—available in specialty Kosher or German delis)

dash sugar

few splashes apple cider vinegar

FOR GARNISH

2 hard-boiled eggs, sliced

2 cups diced tomatoes

1 cup chopped chives

12 ounces crumbled crisp bacon or Black Forest ham crumbled (optional)

DIRECTIONS:

1. Wash potatoes and boil to al dente. Peel and slice thinly while still hot.

2. While potatoes are boiling, peel and dice onions. Dice tomatoes, eggs, and chives.

3. After potatoes are peeled and sliced, add the diced onions and, in a bowl, pour hot broth over potatoes and onions. Add the flavors and seasonings to taste, together with the mustard and vinegar. For mixing all salad ingredients, please use a wooden spoon. Cover the bowl tightly with a tight-fitting lid for 20 minutes, and place a towel over the lid to preserve all flavors and keep the potato salad hot.

4. Top with garnish ingredients before serving.

HOT INDIAN SPICED HONEY GARLIC WINGS

Yield: 4 Servings

2 pounds chicken wings (tips discarded)
3 teaspoons cayenne pepper (add more if you can stand it)
salt
black pepper
1 cup honey
½ cup melted butter*
½ cup freshly minced garlic
⅓ cup hot sauce (sriracha or Tabasco)

DIRECTIONS:

1. Preheat an outdoor grill for medium heat and lightly oil grate.
2. Wash wings well and pat dry with paper towel. Season with cayenne, salt, and pepper.
3. Cook the chicken wings on the preheated grill until cooked through and juices run clear (20–30 minutes, depending on the size of the wings). Brush the wings liberally, using ½ cup honey while they are cooking.
4. Melt the butter, pour into a large bowl, and mix in the remaining ½ cup of honey, minced garlic, and hot sauce.
5. Remove the wings from the grill and immediately toss them in the hot honey garlic butter sauce to coat. Serve the wings "wet" or return them to the grill for 1 minute per side to set the sauce.

I DREAM OF A WHITE CHRISTMAS CAKE

Yield: 10–12 servings

Combining traditional flavors with modern sensibilities, the creamed butter and sugar have been replaced with a simple meringue in this moist, luscious cake.

FOR THE CAKE
2 cups all-purpose flour
1½ teaspoons baking powder
1½ teaspoons baking soda
2 teaspoons ground cinnamon
½ teaspoon ground nutmeg
½ teaspoon salt
2 tablespoons butter
1 large egg white
1 large egg, separated
¼ teaspoon cream of tartar
1½ cups sugar, divided
1 cup mashed very ripe pears, peeled and cored (2 large)
3 tablespoons canola oil
1 teaspoon vanilla extract
½ cup buttermilk

FOR THE FROSTING
⅓ cup unsweetened coconut chips or flakes
12 ounces cream cheese
½ cup confectioner's sugar
½ teaspoon almond extract
½ teaspoon strained lemon juice
1 cup white marshmallows—the smallest you can find
powdered sugar, as needed

DIRECTIONS:
1. For the cake: Preheat oven to 350 degrees F.

2. Coat two 9" round cake pans with cooking spray. Dust lightly with flour, shaking out the excess (or use cooking spray with flour).

3. Whisk all-purpose flour, baking powder, baking soda, cinnamon, nutmeg, and salt in a large bowl.

4. Melt butter in a small saucepan over low heat. Cook, swirling, until it turns a nutty brown (1–3 minutes). Transfer to a bowl to cool.

5. Beat egg whites in a large bowl with an electric mixer on low speed until foamy. Add cream of tartar, increase speed to medium high, and beat until soft peaks form. Gradually add ½ cup sugar, beating until stiff but not dry (this can take up to 5 minutes).

6. Combine the melted butter, egg yolk, remaining 1 cup sugar, mashed pears, oil, and vanilla in a large bowl. With mixer on low speed, alternately add the dry ingredients and buttermilk; beat until just blended. Beat in a heaping spoonful of the whites. Using a whisk, fold in the remaining whites. Pour the batter into the prepared pans.

7. Bake the cake until a skewer inserted in the center comes out clean (30–40 minutes). Let cool in the pans on a wire rack for 10 minutes. Invert onto the racks and let cool completely.

8. For the frosting: Toast coconut in a pie pan at 350 degrees F until barely browned and fragrant (2–4 minutes).

9. Combine cream cheese, confectioner's sugar, almond extract, and lemon juice in a large bowl; beat with an electric mixer on medium speed until smooth and creamy. Fold the white marshmallows into the frosting.

10. Frost the cake, using a little less than half the frosting between layers and the rest on the top. Garnish with the toasted coconut and powdered sugar just before service

Tip: To make cake ahead of time, prepare through step 6. Wrap cake layers in plastic wrap, then foil, and refrigerate.

ITALIAN BASIL PESTO STEAK

Yield: 12 servings

1 (14-ounce) package ten-minute instant brown rice
12 (6-ounce) beef shoulder petite tender steaks
1–1½ cups prepared basil pesto
1½ cups mayonnaise
¼ cup creamy horseradish sauce
¼ cup pureed roasted garlic
2 teaspoons grated lemon zest
2 teaspoons lemon pepper seasoning
24 thin tomato slices
24 thin red onion slices
6 cups shredded fontina cheese
12 chopped basil leaves

DIRECTIONS:

1. Cook instant brown rice according to package directions. Set aside. Keep warm.
2. Brush steaks evenly on both sides with basil pesto, as needed; reserve in hotel pans.
3. Grill steaks over medium heat 10–12 minutes on each side, or until desired temperature is reached. Let stand 5 minutes. Cut into ½"-thick slices; keep warm.
4. Whisk mayonnaise, horseradish sauce, garlic puree, lemon zest, and lemon pepper to blend.
5. With large #16 ice cream scoop, place twelve portions cooked rice in buttered roasting pan. Spread each portion with 1 tablespoon garlic mayonnaise. Top each portion with 2 slices each tomato and onion, 6 ounces steak, 1 tablespoon pesto, and ½ cup cheese.
6. Cover roasting pan with aluminum foil; press down slightly with your hands and place underneath heated broiler or on flat-top griddle for 2–5 minutes, or until rice is golden brown and cheese melts.

7. Place each portion into freezer bag and freeze until ready to serve. Remove from freezer 30 minutes or up to 1 hour before reheating in oven preheated to 375 degrees F, uncovered in roasting pan. Remove from oven when thoroughly heated through. Sprinkle with chopped basil leaves.

ITALIAN HERBED PORK
with Sautéed Wild Porcini Mushrooms
Yield: 4 servings

1 teaspoon extra-virgin olive oil

olive oil cooking spray

3 cups sliced porcini mushrooms

1½ tablespoons steak seasoning of your choice (such as McCormick Grill Mates)

1 teaspoon dry thyme

4 (6-ounce) boneless center-cut loin pork chops (about ¾" thick)

1 cup fat-free no-sodium vegetable broth

2 teaspoons cornstarch

DIRECTIONS:

1. Heat olive oil in a large nonstick skillet coated with cooking spray over medium-high heat. Add sliced mushrooms and sauté 3 minutes or until tender.

2. Rub steak seasoning and thyme over pork. Add pork to pan; cook 3 minutes on each side or until done. Combine broth and cornstarch, stirring with a whisk. Add mushrooms and broth mixture to pan, bring to a boil, and transfer to slow cooker for 2½ hours, or until slightly thickened.

Serving suggestion: serve with polenta and grated Parmesan cheese.

ITALIAN STEAK CROSTINI

Yield: 30 appetizers

FOR CROSTINI

30 (⅜" thick) slices cut from a high-quality baguette (called *sfilatino*),
about 2–3" in diameter

8 tablespoons extra-virgin olive oil

4 garlic cloves, finely chopped

4 tablespoons chopped mint leaves

2 teaspoons dried Mediterranean oregano

4 tablespoons chopped basil leaves

salt and hot pepper flakes to taste

2¼ pounds Harris Ranch cooked tri-tip steak (12 [3-ounce] steaks, ⅜"
thick)

FOR STEAK RUB

2 ounces ground coriander

1 ounce paprika

1 tablespoon brown sugar

1 tablespoon Kosher salt

½ tablespoon garlic powder

½ tablespoon ground black pepper

½ tablespoon white ground pepper

FOR GOAT CHEESE SPREAD

1 pound goat cheese, softened

6 ounces Grey Poupon mustard

FOR SLAW

1½ cups shredded napa cabbage chiffonade

¼ cup shredded carrots

FOR SLAW TOPPING

½ cup balsamic vinegar

2 tablespoons sugar

¾ cup thinly sliced shallots

¾ cup chopped Italian parsley

½ cup chopped dill

1 tablespoon fennel seeds

DIRECTIONS:

1. Brush both sides of the crostini rounds with olive-oil mixture. Arrange on a baking sheet. Bake in 400-degree F oven until crisp and golden. Use bread hot or at room temperature.
2. Rub both sides of each steak with tri-tip steak rub to taste. Heat sauté pan on high heat.* Add steaks to heat, turning occasionally. Remove from pan; let stand 5 minutes. Thinly slice steak across the grain into 2" wide strips.
3. In a medium bowl, mix together with a wooden spoon goat cheese and Grey Poupon.
4. For each serving, spread 2 teaspoons goat cheese spread onto each toasted crostini slice, top with 1 ounce Harris cooked tri-tip steak and 1 tablespoon napa slaw.

FOR THE SLAW AND SLAW TOPPING:

1. Combine napa cabbage chiffonade and shredded carrots.
2. Combine all ingredients for the slaw dressing and pour over the cabbage chiffonade. Chill slightly before service and serve as a side dish with the crostini.

*You may not wish to heat the cooked Harris tri-tip steaks in a skillet before slicing, adding the beef at room temperature to the crostini.

"IT'S THE BERRIES" TACOS

Yield: 4 servings

FOR BERRY SALSA
1 tablespoon brown sugar

1½ teaspoons cornstarch

⅛ teaspoon each cinnamon and nutmeg

1 tablespoon butter

½ cup cran-raspberry juice

2 tablespoons red wine vinegar

½ cup seedless raspberry jam

YOU WILL ALSO NEED
¼ cup reduced-fat sour cream

1 teaspoon canola oil

1 medium onion, chopped

3 cloves garlic, minced

1 pound 93% ground lean turkey

2 large plum tomatoes, diced

1 (14-ounce) can kidney beans, rinsed

2 teaspoons cumin

2 teaspoons chili powder

¼ cup chopped fresh cilantro

8 cups shredded romaine lettuce

½ cup shredded sharp cheddar cheese

6 (8") corn or flour tortillas, warmed

DIRECTIONS:
1. For berry salsa: Heat skillet over medium heat, melt butter, add sifted mixture of brown sugar, cornstarch, cinnamon, and nutmeg and stir into melted butter. Add juice and vinegar. Cook, stirring until sauce thickens. Stir in jam and cook 1 minute.
2. For the tacos: Combine berry salsa and sour cream.
3. Heat oil in a large nonstick skillet over medium heat. Add onion and garlic and cook, stirring often, until softened (about 2 minutes). Add

348

turkey and cook, stirring often, until cooked through. Add tomatoes, beans, cumin, and chili powder. Cook, stirring, until tomatoes break down. Remove from heat and stir in cilantro and ¼ cup of the salsa mixture.

4. Add lettuce to the remaining salsa mixture in the bowl. Toss to coat. Divide lettuce between warmed tortillas. Top with the turkey mixture and sprinkle with cheese.

JAPANESE SKILLET-STEAMED HALIBUT STEAKS

Yield: 4 servings

4 each 4–6 ounces halibut fillets, skin removed
1 lemon, thinly sliced
1 orange, thinly sliced
2 whole star anise
2 garlic cloves, thinly sliced
1 cup freshly squeezed orange juice
1 teaspoon freshly squeezed lemon juice
2 tablespoons sake
½ cup San-J Japanese Steak Sauce
1 tablespoon San-J Sweet & Tangy sauce
8 fresh thyme sprigs, divided
4 tablespoons extra-virgin olive oil
sea salt and freshly ground black pepper to taste
1 cup melted butter

DIRECTIONS:

1. Place the halibut in a small baking dish, large enough to hold all the fish fillets. Place lemon and orange slices, star anise, garlic, orange juice, sake, San-J Japanese Steak Sauce, San-J Sweet & Tangy sauce, 4 sprigs of the fresh thyme, and 4 tablespoons extra-virgin olive oil on top, and season with salt and pepper to taste. Place all in a 12" sauté pan with 1 cup of water and steam on top of a stove over medium heat until cooked through. Add the butter and warm over low heat.

2. To serve, divide the vegetable bouquet among four serving plates and top each with 1 halibut fillet.

3. Reduce the cooking juices in a pan and spoon over halibut fillets. Adjust seasoning with salt and pepper.

4. Sauté the vegetables and remaining 4 sprigs thyme in 1 tablespoon olive oil in a heavy duty sauté pan over medium heat.

Serving suggestion: Serve with freshly blanched baby Yukon Gold potatoes, baby bok choy, and morel mushrooms.

JARLSBERG NAPOLEON JARDINIERE
with Fresh Herbs
Yield: 4 entrees

1 cup extra-virgin olive oil
½ teaspoons red chile flakes
6 sun-dried tomatoes, thinly sliced
6 cloves garlic, peeled and smashed
6 sprigs tarragon
1 lemon, ends trimmed, thinly sliced
1 large zucchini, cut diagonally into 1½"-long pieces
2 cups finely shredded Jarlsberg cheese, divided
1 pound baby Yukon Gold potatoes, thinly sliced
1 medium head broccoli, cut into florets, stalk cut into thin pieces
½ medium head cauliflower, cut into florets, stalk cut into thin pieces
Kosher salt and freshly ground black pepper to taste
2 tablespoons each finely chopped parsley and thyme

DIRECTIONS:
1. Put olive oil, chile flakes, sun-dried tomatoes, garlic, tarragon, and lemon slices in a 6-quart dutch oven. Place over medium-high heat and cook, stirring occasionally, until fragrant and the garlic and lemon slices are lightly browned (about 5 minutes).
2. Add the zucchini in a single layer and cook, without stirring, until lightly browned. Flip the zucchini and cook for 5 minutes
3. Add 1 cup Jarlsberg, potatoes, broccoli, and cauliflower to the pot and stir once or twice to coat in oil. Cook, covered, without stirring, until vegetables begin to brown and soften (about 15 minutes).
4. Stir vegetables gently, replace the lid, and reduce the heat to medium low; cook until the vegetables are very soft and tender (about 15 minutes more).
5. Remove vegetables from the heat. Season. Sprinkle with remaining cup Jarlsberg. Place underneath broiler until an amber color is achieved. Sprinkle with parsley and thyme.

JEWISH CHICKEN NOODLE SOUP
with Homemade Noodles
Yield: 4–6 servings

Chicken is to Jewish cooking what pork is to Chinese cuisine. But certainly the most popular, the most enduring, the most sustaining dish ever made from any chicken is the golden, glorious traditional Jewish chicken noodle soup. It takes but a little time and know-how to add the surprise of homemade noodles to the soup. Let it be known that gourmets the world over have declared Jewish chicken noodle soup the greatest of all soups.

FOR THE NOODLE DOUGH
2 cups all-purpose flour, plus additional flour for rolling out the dough
2 large eggs, beaten
½ teaspoon Kosher salt
1½ tablespoons cold water

FOR THE SOUP
1 large broiler chicken (3½ to 4 pounds) cut into 8 pieces
7–8 cups water—just enough water to cover chicken and vegetables
3 carrots, peeled but left whole
3 stalks celery with their leaves
1 large or 2 small leeks, without the dark green parts
½ yellow onion
½ bunch parsley with stems
½ bunch fresh dill with stems
½ bunch fresh marjoram with stems
¼ cup each basil leaves and oregano (for a Mediterranean taste)
3 cloves garlic, peeled but left whole
¼ cup sun-dried tomatoes

DIRECTIONS:
1. To make the noodles: Measure the flour into a large bowl. Make a well in the middle of the flour and pour in the beaten eggs, salt,

and water. Mix with a wooden spoon until the dough starts to hold together, then remove the dough to a well-floured board and knead until it feels smooth and satiny. Cover and let rest 30 minutes.

2. Roll out the dough to ⅛" thickness. Cut the dough into ½ inch squares or into string noodles spaghetti style.

3. Drop the noodles into a large pot of boiling water, lightly seasoned with salt and a touch of olive oil. However, be sure not to add more noodles than can float in a single layer. Bring water to a simmer and cook for 10–12 minutes. Remove noodles with a slotted spoon and serve with the chicken soup.

4. To make the chicken soup: Wash chicken pieces well. Place chicken in a 6-quart soup pot and add 8 cups water. Cut all washed vegetables into thick slices or julienne strips and add them to the pot. Wash fresh herbs and add to the pot, along with salt and pepper, tomatoes, and garlic. Add more water to cover chicken and vegetables. Bring to a boil and reduce heat to a simmer. Skim away any fat.

5. There are several ways to serve the soup. I like to serve everything together in a large bowl containing broth, chicken, and the noodles. (The soup greens can be served separately as a side dish with the chicken or used in latkes [pancakes]).

KEY LIME AND HIBISCUS BARBECUE SAUCE

Yield: 1/2 quart

1 cup honey
2 tablespoons peanut oil
4 chipotle peppers (canned, rinsed)
2 tablespoons balsamic vinegar
3 tablespoons grainy pommery mustard
4 tablespoons key lime juice
2 garlic cloves, minced
1 teaspoon ground cumin
1 teaspoon salt
1 teaspoon ground pepper
3 red bell peppers, seeded
3 hibiscus flowers

DIRECTIONS:
1. Heat oven to 450 degree F.
2. Roast and peel seeded bell peppers from a heated brown paper bag.
3. Roast hibiscus blossoms and puree with roasted peppers.
4. Heat peanut oil and add chipotle peppers, garlic, cumin, salt, and ground pepper. Strain oil and puree together with roasted bell peppers and hibiscus flowers. Add balsamic vinegar, mustard, and key lime juice and honey. Blend to mix thoroughly.

KEY WEST KEY LIME PIE
Award-Winning Florida Key Lime Pie
Yield: 3 (9" or 10") pies

FOR CRUST
6 ounces melted unsalted butter

16 ounces crushed coarse graham cracker crumbs

1 tablespoon ground cinnamon

7 ounces crushed coarse macadamia nuts

3 ounces granulated organic sugar

FOR FILLING
6 large egg yolks

48 ounces sweetened condensed milk

14 ounces unstrained pure key lime juice

FOR GARNISH
2 pints heavy whipping cream (40%)

2 tablespoons granulated organic sugar

2 ounces sliced toasted blanched and peeled almonds

1 whole key lime

DIRECTIONS:
1. In large bowl, mix and toss pie crust ingredients, making sure that all ingredients are thoroughly blended. Press crumb mixture evenly over bottom and sides of tin. Bake 5 minutes in preheated 350-degree F oven.

2. For the pie filling, beat egg yolks into lime juice and sweetened condensed milk. Bake for 10 minutes in a 350 degree F preheated oven.

3. In an electric mixer (or with a handheld blender) whip the heavy cream and sugar to soft peaks. Use a star-tube-fitted piping bag to place a star or rosette in the center of each of the slices. Top with one twisted, sugarcoated thin key lime slice, and sprinkle with sliced toasted almonds.

NEW ORLEANS BARBECUE SHRIMP LAGNIAPPE

with a Crust or Two of French Bread for Mopping

Yield: 2 servings

Whenever I am in New Orleans or I don't feel like cooking, this surely is my favorite meal from my hometown, New Orleans. Thinking deeply and affectionately of the this wonderful meal and wanting to celebrate my "hometown" is what prompted me to include this recipe.

2 pounds large shrimp, heads on
2 tablespoons Creole seafood seasoning (I like Chef Paul Prudhomme's best)
1 tablespoon olive oil
1 large head of garlic, cloves peeled and mashed
2 tablespoons fresh rosemary, chopped
4 ripe, fresh plum tomatoes, chopped
3 tablespoons worcestershire sauce
3 tablespoons Creole hot sauce or Tabasco, or to taste
2 large lemons, one with juice removed and reserved, quartered; one quartered for garnish
1 bottle dark beer (nonalcoholic if you prefer)
sea salt and freshly ground black pepper
8 tablespoons (1 stick) sweet butter, softened

DIRECTIONS:

1. Toss the shrimp with half the Creole seasoning. Preheat a large skillet over high heat. Put the oil in the pan and heat until the oil begins to smoke. Place the garlic and rosemary and tomatoes in the pan, and stir lightly till the garlic begins to brown. Add the shrimp and stir carefully. Add worcestershire sauce, hot sauce, lemon juice, and lemon quarters. Deglaze the pan with the beer, stirring to release any bits clinging to the bottom, and boil the mixture to reduce, while shaking the pan. Allow the shrimp to cook for 2–2½ minutes, and add the remaining seafood seasoning and salt and pepper. When the shrimp have finished cooking, the liquid should have a saucy

consistency. Reduce the heat to medium high and add the butter, a bit at a time, stirring until the sauce is thick. Adjust seasoning. Remove lemon pieces.

2. Serve with crusty French baguette bread (New Orleans baguettes if available), lots of paper napkins, and finger bowls. Garnish each serving with a lemon quarter.

Note: Don't overcook the shrimp. Leave the heads on, as that's where the flavor is. Have lots of crisp French baguettes on hand to mop up the sauce. Also, simply eat the shrimp with your hands to better peel them and soak them in the sauce.

LEAN ASIAN-STYLE PORK AND TOFU STIR-FRY
with Soba

Yield: 4 servings

FOR MARINADE

2 tablespoons light soy sauce

1 tablespoon fresh orange juice

1 tablespoon chopped garlic

2 teaspoons grated fresh ginger

1 teaspoon Asian sesame oil

1 teaspoon cornstarch

½ pound firm tofu, cut into thin strips

½ pound boneless pork loin, trimmed and cut into thin strips

FOR SAUCE

6 tablespoons low-sodium chicken broth

2 tablespoons rice wine vinegar

2 tablespoons light soy sauce

1 teaspoon sugar

2 teaspoons cornstarch

½ pound soba (buckwheat noodles) or whole-wheat spaghetti

2 teaspoons vegetable oil, divided

4 cups thinly sliced green cabbage

1 red bell pepper, thinly sliced

4 ounces shiitake mushrooms, stems removed and thinly sliced

1 cup fresh bean sprouts

¼ cup fresh cilantro leaves, for garnish

DIRECTIONS:

1. Combine soy sauce, orange juice, garlic, ginger, sesame oil, and cornstarch in a small bowl. Remove 2 tablespoons of mixture to another small bowl. Toss tofu in bowl with the 2 tablespoons marinade. Toss pork in the other bowl with the remaining marinade. Cover bowls and marinate refrigerated for 30 minutes.

2. Meanwhile, for the sauce, combine chicken broth, rice wine vinegar, soy sauce, sugar, and cornstarch in another small bowl.
3. Start to cook noodles according to package directions.
4. Heat 1 teaspoon of the vegetable oil in a 12" nonstick skillet over high heat. Add pork and cook, stirring, 1–2 minutes, or until dark brown; transfer to a small bowl.
5. Reduce heat to medium high. Add remaining 1 teaspoon vegetable oil to skillet. Add cabbage, bell pepper, and mushrooms; cook, stirring, 2–3 minutes or until lightly browned. Stir in sauce, pork, and tofu with marinade. Cook 2 minutes or until mixture is heated through and sauce thickens.
6. Drain noodles; divide among four serving plates. Top each serving with pork-tofu mixture and sprouts. Garnish with cilantro.

LENNY'S TITANIC SUB

Yield: 4 Subs

4 ounces Italian dressing
4 ounces mixed bell peppers, chopped
1 large pickled or fresh red onion, chopped
½ cup stuffed green olives
½ cup pitted black olives
about 1 tablespoon equal parts fresh basil and oregano leaves (or ½
    tablespoon dried) to taste
4 Italian sub rolls or 2 (15") loaves Italian baguette
8 ounces reduced-fat soft cream cheese
1 cup spinach leaves
8 tomato slices
4 hard-boiled eggs, sliced, or 2 cups egg salad
8 ounces sliced smoked turkey
16 ounces part-skim mozzarella slices
8 ounces sliced corned beef

DIRECTIONS:

1. In food processor, combine dressing, peppers, onion, olives, basil,
    and oregano. Pulse until finely chopped.
2. Cut rolls or bread in half lengthwise and remove bread from inside
    halves, leaving a 1" border attached to crust.
3. Spread cream cheese inside each half. Spread olive mixture over
    cream cheese. Layer in bottom half spinach leaves, tomato slices,
    egg slices or egg salad, smoked turkey, mozzarella, and sliced corned
    beef. Carefully close. Press together, and wrap tightly in plastic wrap.
4. Refrigerate several hours or overnight.
5. Cut each sandwich in half.

MEDITERRANEAN LENTIL LAMB BURGER

Yield: 8 servings

4 cups cooked lentils, pureed in a food processor or blender
½ cup crumbled feta cheese
¼ cup chopped pimiento-stuffed olives
¼ cup chopped pitted Kalamata olives
2 tablespoons Greek seasoning (such as McCormick)
½ teaspoons salt
1 pound lean ground lamb
cooking spray
8 crisp lettuce leaves
16 slices vine-ripe tomatoes
16 thin slices red onion
4 (6") pitas, cut in half

DIRECTIONS:
1. Prepare grill or broiler.
2. To prepare the burgers, combine lentils, cheese, and next five ingredients (lentils through ground lamb) in a large bowl. Divide mixture into eight equal portions, shaping each into a ½"-thick patty.
3. Place patties on a grill rack or broiler pan coated with cooking spray. Cook 4 minutes on each side or until done and lightly charred. Cut patties in half. Place 2 patty halves on a crisp lettuce leaf and top with 2 tomato slices and onion slices in each pita half.

LIGHT SLICED TURKEY CAESAR COBB SALAD

Yield: 4 entrée servings

10 turkey bacon slices
1 (10-ounce) package frozen corn, or 2 cups fresh cooked corn
6 cups romaine salad greens, torn
1 pound turkey breast, diced
6 scallions, chopped
3 medium diced tomatoes
1 cup shredded Parmesan cheese

DIRECTIONS:

1. In a large skillet, cook bacon; then drain, cool, and crumble. Prepare corn according to package directions; then rinse with cold water and drain. Toss romaine greens and ½ cup of Caesar salad dressing. Arrange romaine greens on a large plate or platter. Arrange turkey, bacon, and vegetables in sections on top of greens. Drizzle remaining Traditional Caesar Salad Dressing over salad. Sprinkle with Parmesan cheese.

PALM BEACH CHOCOLATE PRALINE CHEESECAKE
Yield: 1 (9") cake 12–16 slices

Palm Beach Post and Personal Letter from Lindt & Spruengli, Switzerland

"The grand prize winning recipe for the Lindt Fall Recipe Contest is the Palm Beach Chocolate Praline Cheesecake by Wolfgang Hanau. from West Palm Beach, Florida. Wolfgang created this cheesecake in honor of a dear friend and now it has become his signature dessert. Made with Lindt Excellence 70% Cocoa Nut Crunch and Lindt Grandeur Dark Hazelnut Chocolate bar, it is simply delicious! Congratulations Wolfgang!"

FOR THE CRUST
1 (3.5-ounce) bar Lindt Excellence 70% Cocoanut Crunch bar, ground or very finely chopped
1 cup chocolate graham cracker crumbs
4 tablespoons melted sweet butter

FOR THE FILLING
3 (8-ounce) packages cream cheese
1¼ cups dark brown sugar, firmly packed
1½ teaspoons vanilla extract
3 large eggs
1 cup (5.3 ounces) Lindt Grandeur dark hazelnut chocolate bar, finely chopped

FOR THE CHOCOLATE PRALINE SAUCE
¼ cup dark brown sugar, firmly packed
4 tablespoons sweet butter
½ cup Lindt chocolate-fudge sauce
1 cup (5.3 ounces) Lindt Grandeur dark hazelnut chocolate bar, chopped

DIRECTIONS:
1. Combine all ingredients for the crust with a wire whip in a stainless-steel bowl and press crumbs into the bottom of a 9" springform pan.

2. Combine the cream cheese with the brown sugar and vanilla. Add eggs, beating until smooth. Stir in Lindt finely chopped hazelnut chocolate bar.

3. Pour filling into crust and bake in an oven preheated to 300 degrees F for 90 minutes (until barely set). Cake will continue to set as it cools.

4. Cool on rack without removing mold. Cake may be prepared up to 48 hours in advance if covered and refrigerated.

5. For the chocolate praline sauce, heat brown sugar and butter, stirring until smooth. Whisk in Lindt chocolate-fudge sauce. Bring to a boil. While whisking, boil for 5 minutes until sugar just begins to caramelize. At this point, add chopped Lindt hazelnut chocolate bar. Cool to lukewarm.

6. Serve cake slices with ladle of sauce.

SVENSKA LINGONBERRY STARS
OF THE MIDNIGHT SUN

Yield: 36 cookies

These cookies from Sweden use all the unique flavors of countries of Scandinavia; lingonberries are blended with favorite spices used in all holiday breads in countries of the midnight sun.

1 cup butter
½ cup granulated sugar
¼ cup light brown sugar
2 tablespoons vanilla yogurt
1 egg
2½ cups unbleached all-purpose flour
¼ teaspoon ground star anise
¼ teaspoon ground nutmeg
1 teaspoon cinnamon
¼ teaspoon ground, roasted brown cardamom
¼ teaspoon salt
2 cups very finely chopped, peeled, and lightly toasted hazelnuts
2 lightly beaten egg whites
½ cup Swedish whole-fruit lingonberry marmalade
¼ cup powdered sugar

DIRECTIONS:

1. In a large mixing bowl, beat first four ingredients with an electric mixer on medium to high speed till creamy. Add whole egg; beat well. Beat in flour, anise, nutmeg, cinnamon, cardamom, and salt. Stir in nuts. Divide dough in half. Cover and chill for 3–4 hours.

2. On a floured surface, roll each half of dough ⅛" thick. Using a 3" star cookie cutter, cut out thirty-six stars from each half of the dough, rerolling scraps as needed. Place on lightly greased baking sheets. With a small star-shaped cutter, cut stars from centers of half of the stars. Brush all cookies with egg whites.

3. Bake cookies in a preheated oven at 355 degrees F for 8–10 minutes, or until golden brown. Cool on wire racks.

4. To assemble cookies, spread dull side of each whole star with ½ teaspoon lingonberry marmalade. Top each with a cut-out cookie, shiny-side up. Press cookies together gently. Dust with powdered sugar.

JARLSBERG CHEESE AND CHERRY BITES

Yield: 6 servings

cooking spray

1 tablespoon olive oil

¼ cup sliced scallions (white part only)

¼ cup diced fresh or canned cherries

1 cup baby spinach leaves, coarsely chopped

2 ounces shredded Jarlsberg cheese (about ½ cup)

¼ cup 2% reduced-fat milk

½ teaspoon Kosher salt

¼ teaspoon freshly ground black pepper

3 large eggs

DIRECTIONS:

1. Preheat oven to 350 degrees F.
2. Coat six muffin cups with cooking spray. Heat a medium nonstick skillet over medium-high heat. Add oil; swirl to coat. Add scallions and diced cherries; sauté 3 minutes or until almost tender. Add spinach; sauté 2 minutes or just until spinach begins to wilt, stirring constantly. Transfer spinach mixture to a small bowl; cool 3 minutes. Stir in Jarlsberg cheese.
3. Combine milk and remaining ingredients, stirring with a whisk until blended. Stir in cheese mixture. Divide mixture evenly among prepared muffin cups. Bake at 350 degrees F for 20 minutes or until puffed and set. (Quiches will deflate slightly as they cool.) Serve warm.

LOUISIANA BLUE CRAB AND
CRAB FENNEL RISOTTO

Yield: 4 servings

2 fennel bulbs with tops
1 cup sliced fresh mushrooms, such as shiitake, porcini, or button
½ teaspoon fennel seed, crushed
1 tablespoon olive oil
1 cup uncooked arborio or medium grain rice
3¼ cups water
1 teaspoon instant chicken bouillon granules
⅛ teaspoon pepper
1 cup cooked blue lump Louisiana crab meat; one 6-ounce can crab
    meat, drained, flaked, and cartilage removed; or one 6-ounce
    package frozen crab meat, thawed and drained
½ cup asparagus, cut into 1" pieces*
⅓ cup thinly sliced scallions

DIRECTIONS:

1. Trim fennel bulbs, reserving tops. Quarter bulbs lengthwise and
    slice. Measure 1 cup sliced fennel. Snip enough of the fennel tops to
    get 1 tablespoon; set aside.
2. In a large saucepan, cook the 1 cup fennel, mushrooms, and fennel
    seed in hot oil until tender. Stir in rice. Cook and stir over medium
    heat for 2 minutes.
3. Carefully stir in water, bouillon granules, and pepper. Bring to a boil;
    reduce heat. Cover and simmer for 20 minutes without lifting cover.
4. Remove saucepan from heat. Stir in crab meat, asparagus, and
    scallions. Let stand, covered, for 5 minutes. (The rice should be tender
    but slightly firm, and the mixture should be creamy. If necessary, stir
    in a little water to reach the desired consistency.)
5. Stir in the snipped fennel tops. If desired, garnish with additional
    fennel tops.

*Note: If using thick asparagus spears, halve spears lengthwise, cut into 1" pieces,
and cook in a small amount of boiling water until tender-crisp. Add to risotto.

DANIELLE'S SECRET LOUISIANA CRAYFISH SUPPER

Yield: 8 Servings

FOR FILLING

¼ cup sweet butter
2 cups sweet onions, finely diced
1 cup finely chopped red bell pepper
2 tablespoons minced garlic
1 pound Gulf crayfish tails with fat
⅓ cup scallions, sliced
½ tablespoon Tabasco green
½ teaspoon ground black pepper
1½ cups shredded mozzarella
1 cup shredded Monterey Jack cheese
½ cup shredded cheddar cheese
1 tablespoon melted butter for brushing.

FOR TOPPING

½ cup milk
1 (6-ounce) package Martha White Cotton Country corn bread mix, or
    1 (6-ounce) package Martha White buttermilk corn bread mix
2 tablespoons sweet butter, melted

DIRECTIONS:

1. For the filling, melt butter in a large 10" or 12" cast-iron skillet over medium-high heat. Add onions and cook for five minutes until translucent. Reduce heat to medium and add garlic and bell pepper until bell pepper is tender and garlic is light brown (about 7 minutes).

2. In a bowl, combine crayfish tails and scallions. Flavor with Tabasco and black pepper, and pour over vegetable mixture. Top with mixture of three cheeses.

3. Combine all topping ingredients in a medium bowl and stir until smooth. Pour evenly over cheese.

4. Bake 15–20 minutes or until golden brown.

5. Heat oven to 425 degrees F.

LOUISIANA GULF SHRIMP AND SWEET POTATO ENCHILADAS

Yield: 6 servings (2 enchiladas per serving)

14 ounces freshly cooked or canned Louisiana sweet potatoes

4 ounces cream cheese, in small pieces

4 whole scallions, finely sliced

½ teaspoon chili powder

¼ teaspoon ground cumin

¼ teaspoon ground coriander

¼ teaspoon oregano

12 large pink Louisiana Gulf shrimp, peeled and deveined, cooked tail-off, butterflied

¼ teaspoon salt

1 pinch cinnamon

1 pinch ground ginger

3 tablespoons vegetable oil

12 whole corn tortillas

12 ounces salsa

1 cup grated mild cheese

DIRECTIONS:

1. Preheat oven to 350 degrees F. In a medium bowl, mix Louisiana sweet potatoes, cream cheese, scallions, and spices until fairly smooth. Salt to taste. (I usually add another ¼ teaspoon or so.)

2. In a heavy skillet, heat the oil and dip tortillas briefly into hot oil to soften. Drain on paper towels. Tortillas can be steamed if you prefer. (I don't do anything with the tortillas at all. They roll just fine unless you get cheap, brittle tortillas.)

3. Spread about ¼ cup of squash filling in the middle of each tortilla. Top each with 2 Gulf shrimp. Roll up tortillas fairly tightly and place seam-side down in a 12" × 9" (approximate) baking dish.

4. Pour salsa over the enchiladas and sprinkle liberally with grated cheese.

5. Bake for 25–30 minutes, until heated through.

6. For a festive touch, toast chopped almonds or nuts and scatter on the top.

FRESH LOUISIANA OYSTERS WITH LEEK AND LOUISIANA SWEET POTATO WHIP

Yield: 12 canapés

FOR LEEK AND SWEET POTATO WHIP

1 cup cooked sweet mashed potatoes

2 ounces leeks, cooked

½ cup soy cream

2½ tablespoons grape-seed oil

1 tablespoon Tabasco Sweet & Spicy sauce

½ cup water from cooking potatoes

salt to taste

FOR OYSTERS

12 freshly caught Louisiana oysters on the half shell

2 cups water

1 lemon, zested and juiced

3 teaspoons flaky sea salt

DIRECTIONS:

1. Puree all the leek and potato whip ingredients except the cream and oil while still warm; season to taste and then slowly mix in the cream and oil.

2. Pour into an iSi whipping canister and set with two N_2O charges. Allow to cool in a chiller for 30 minutes; use as required.

3. Remove the oysters from the shells and place in a bowl. Pour any juice that comes from the shells in with the oysters. Set the shells on a service tray.

4. In a shallow saucepan, place water, salt, and the juice from the lemon, then bring to a simmer. Quickly poach the oysters (no longer than 30 seconds) and place back in the shells. Allow to cool slightly.

5. From the iSi whipping canister, gently express the leek and potato whip onto each oyster half and serve.

6. Garnish, if desired, with crispy fried leeks.

BIG AL'S LOUISIANA SWEET POTATO AND FENNEL SPOTTED SEA TROUT
on White Beans and Fries

Yield: 6 servings

Delicious warm white beans, sweet potatoes, and fennel are topped with succulent fennel-seed-crusted spotted sea trout for a double hit of flavor. For an extra-fresh look, set aside some additional chopped fennel fronds to use as a garnish.

5 teaspoons extra-virgin olive oil, divided

1 bulb fennel, halved, cored, and thinly sliced; plus 1 tablespoon chopped fennel fronds

1 large (16-ounce) Louisiana sweet potato, peeled, halved, and thinly sliced

2 (15-ounce) cans white beans, rinsed

2 medium bayou tomatoes, diced

⅓ cup white wine

1 tablespoon Dijon mustard

1 teaspoon freshly ground pepper, divided

1 tablespoon fennel seeds

1 tablespoon Tabasco Sweet & Spicy sauce

6 (8-ounce) Louisiana spotted sea trout fillets, skin removed

DIRECTIONS:

1. Heat 2 teaspoons oil in a large nonstick skillet over medium heat. Add sliced fennel and sweet potato. Cook, stirring occasionally, until lightly browned and fork-tender (about 6 minutes). Stir in beans, tomatoes, and wine. Cook, stirring occasionally, until the tomatoes begin to break down, about 3 minutes. Transfer to a bowl; stir in chopped fennel fronds, mustard, ¼ teaspoon pepper and Tabasco Sweet & Spicy sauce. Cover to keep warm.

2. Meanwhile, combine fennel seeds and the remaining ¾ teaspoon pepper in a small bowl; sprinkle evenly on both sides spotted sea trout fillets.

3. Wipe out the pan. Add the remaining 3 teaspoons oil to the pan and heat over high heat until shimmering but not smoking. Add the sea trout fillets, skin side up, and cook until golden brown (3–5 minutes). Turn the sea trout fillets over, cover, and remove from the heat. Let stand until the sea trout fillets finish cooking off the heat (3–5 minutes more). Transfer the sea trout fillets to a cutting board and flake with a fork. Serve fillets on top of the warm bean mixture.

NATIVE AMERICAN MAPLE SYRUP PECAN TART

Yield: 1 (4" × 14" or 9" round) tart

1¾ cups pecan halves

1¼ cups King Arthur all-purpose flour, leveled

¼ cup unsweetened cocoa powder

½ teaspoon Kosher salt, plus a pinch for the filling

½ cup (1 stick) unsalted butter, at room temperature

¼ cup pure organic 100% maple syrup

2 large egg yolks

½ pound semisweet chocolate, chopped

¾ cup heavy cream

DIRECTIONS:

1. Heat oven to 350 degrees F. Spread the pecans on a rimmed baking sheet and toast, tossing once, until fragrant, 6–8 minutes. Let cool, then roughly chop.

2. In a medium bowl, whisk together King Arthur flour, cocoa powder, and salt.

3. Using an electric mixer, beat the butter and maple syrup on medium high until creamy (2–3 minutes). Beat in the egg yolks. Reduce mixer speed to low, and gradually add the flour mixture; mix until combined but still crumbly.

4. Press the dough into the bottom and up the sides of a 4" × 14" rectangular (or 9" round) tart pan. Line with a large piece of parchment paper, leaving an overhang on all sides, and fill with dried beans or pie weights. Place the pan on a rimmed baking sheet and bake until the edges of the crust are dry (20–22 minutes). Remove the parchment and beans and bake until dry and set (10–12 minutes). Let cool completely.

5. Meanwhile, in a large bowl, combine the chocolate and pinch of salt. In a small saucepan, bring the cream to a bare simmer; pour over the chocolate and let stand 1 minute. Stir gently until the mixture

is smooth. Stir in 1½ cups of the pecans. Pour the mixture into the cooled tart shell and sprinkle with the remaining pecans. Refrigerate until set, at least 1 hour.

Tip: The tart can be made up to two days in advance and refrigerated, loosely covered. Bring to room temperature before serving.

MARVELOUS CANTON GINGER-SPICED MUFFINS

Yield: 12 muffins

FOR STREUSEL

2 tablespoons packed light brown sugar

4 teaspoons whole-wheat flour

½ teaspoon ground cinnamon

1 tablespoon butter, cut into small pieces

2 tablespoons finely chopped walnuts (optional)

2 tablespoons Domaine de Canton ginger liqueur

FOR MUFFINS

1 cup whole-wheat flour

1 cup all-purpose flour

1½ teaspoons baking powder

½ teaspoon baking soda

¼ teaspoon salt

1 tablespoon ground cinnamon

½ teaspoon ground nutmeg

1 large egg

⅓ cup packed light brown sugar

½ cup Domaine de Canton ginger liqueur

⅓ cup chopped candied ginger

⅓ cup apple cider

⅓ cup low-fat plain yogurt

¼ cup canola oil

DIRECTIONS:

1. Preheat oven to 400 degrees F. Coat twelve muffin cups with cooking spray or line with paper cups.

2. To prepare streusel, mix brown sugar, whole-wheat flour, and cinnamon in a small bowl. Cut in butter with a pastry blender or your fingers until the mixture resembles coarse crumbs. Stir in walnuts and Domaine de Canton ginger liqueur.

3. To prepare muffins, whisk whole-wheat flour, all-purpose flour, baking powder, baking soda, salt, cinnamon, and nutmeg in a large bowl.

4. In a medium bowl, whisk egg, brown sugar, and Domaine de Canton ginger liqueur in a until smooth. Add candied ginger, cider, yogurt, and oil. Make a well in the dry ingredients; add the wet ingredients and stir with a rubber spatula until just combined. Scoop the batter into the prepared muffin cups (they'll be quite full). Sprinkle with the streusel.

5. Bake the muffins until the tops are golden brown and spring back when touched lightly, (15–25 minutes). Let cool in the pan for 5 minutes. Loosen edges and turn muffins out onto a wire rack to cool slightly before serving.

MARYLAND OYSTER MIGNONETTES CROSTINI

Yield: 6 servings

FOR OYSTER MIGNONETTES

24 freshly shucked Maryland oysters (save the half shells if you wish to
   serve on the half shells)

2 cups brut prosecco or brut champagne

dash raspberry vinegar to taste

1 tablespoon crushed pink peppercorns

1 scallion, minced

Kosher salt to taste

12 teaspoons caviar (½–1 ounce), for garnish

FOR CROSTINI

24 thin slices toasted rye bread (2" × 2", crust removed)

4 ounces melted butter

DIRECTIONS:

1. Combine ingredients for the oyster mignonettes in a nonreactive
   medium-sized glass bowl and let sit for 30 minutes before serving
   oysters on top of crostini or on the half shell next to crostini.
2. Drizzle sliced rye bread with melted butter and lightly toast crostini
   before service. Place each shucked oyster directly onto a crostini or
   on a half shell next to a crostini.
3. Top each oyster with ½ teaspoon caviar.
4. Serve mignonettes on a presentation service platter.

NEAPOLITAN OYSTERS CAPELLINI PARMIGIANA

Yield: 4 servings

8 ounces premium capellini Italian pasta
1 tablespoon grape-seed oil
4 ounces minced pancetta
4 ounces minced scallions, green and white parts
1 tablespoon minced garlic
2 ripe Roma tomatoes, juiced and finely diced
¾ cup heavy cream
24 freshly shucked Maryland oysters

FOR GARNISH

4 ounces freshly shaved Parmigiana-Reggiano cheese
2 lemons, cut into wedges
2 plum tomatoes, cut into wedges
4 feathered scallions
½ cup chopped parsley

DIRECTIONS:

1. Cook the pasta according to package directions, adding a little of the oil.

2. As capellini cooks, in a medium saucepan render the pancetta with grape-seed oil on medium heat until crisp (about 10 minutes). Add scallions and cook 1 more minute, then add garlic and tomatoes and cook for another minute. Add heavy cream and bring to a rapid boil, then lower the heat and simmer for about 2 minutes. Since oysters will dilute the sauce, make sure it's thick before adding the oysters.

3. Turn heat up to high. When oysters start to curl at the edges, add pasta. Bring mixture to a simmer and add salt and pepper to taste. Garnish with shaved parmesan, and alternately with lemon and tomato wedges, topped with a sprig of feathered scallions and chopped parsley.

MATINEE PIZZA

Yield: 12 servings

12 Bays English muffin halves (6 Bays English muffins, sliced
    horizontally)
6 large Roma tomatoes, halved lengthwise
1 cup olive oil
1 tablespoon garlic, minced
1 tablespoon fresh basil, chopped
1 tablespoon fresh thyme, chopped
1 tablespoon chives, minced
1 tablespoon parsley, chopped
1 tablespoon fresh rosemary, chopped
⅛ teaspoon salt
⅛ teaspoon pepper
12 pancetta slices
12 large eggs
36 basil leaves
1 pound 8 ounces goat cheese

DIRECTIONS:

1. Heat oven to 275 degrees F. Blend olive oil, garlic, herbs, salt, and
    pepper. Place tomatoes, cut-side up, on parchment-lined sheet pan.
    Drizzle herbed oil over tomatoes. Roast 40 minutes; remove and
    keep warm.
2. Heat oven to 400 degrees F. Place pancetta slices on parchment-
    coated sheet pan. Cook until crisp; remove and keep warm.
3. Fry eggs over medium heat in nonstick pan until whites are set
    (completely coagulated and firm) and yolks begin to thicken (no
    longer runny, but not hard). Turn eggs over, if desired, for additional
    firmness of yolks. Keep warm.
4. For each muffin half, spread 1 ounce (2 tablespoons) goat cheese on
    cut sides of muffin. Place a roasted tomato slice on the muffin half
    bottom, then add a crispy pancetta slice and 3 basil leaves, and top
    with a cooked egg. Serve immediately.

MEATBALLS AND POTATO HASH

Yield: 4 servings

Hash isn't just for corned beef. It's also great made with Simek's meatballs. Simek's meatballs add flavor to the hash. Serve with a poached egg on top and a green salad.

2 small russet potatoes
3 teaspoons canola oil, divided
1 bag (1.5 pounds) Simek's meatballs, coarsely chopped
½ medium red bell pepper, diced
4 scallions, sliced
1½ teaspoons whole-grain mustard
⅛ teaspoon salt
⅛ teaspoon freshly ground pepper
4 lemon wedges
4 poached eggs

DIRECTIONS:

1. Poke several holes in potatoes and microwave on high until cooked through, 10–12 minutes. Cut the potatoes in half and set aside; coarsely chop when cool enough to handle.

2. Meanwhile, heat ½ teaspoon oil in a medium nonstick skillet over medium heat. Add meatballs and cook, stirring often, until just cooked (4–6 minutes). Transfer to a plate with a slotted spoon and discard any liquid in the pan. Add the remaining 1 teaspoon oil, bell pepper, and scallions, and cook, stirring, until the vegetables are soft (about 4 minutes).

3. Return the meatballs to the pan along with the chopped potatoes, mustard, salt, and pepper. Continue to cook, stirring gently, until combined and heated through (about 2 minutes more). Serve with lemon wedges and poached eggs.

SENEGALIA MEDITERRANEAN GRILLED CHICKEN
with Balsamic Vinegar
Yield: 4 servings

This is the perfection of the Mediterranean method of grilling chicken—a cross between grilling (hot, direct heat) and barbecuing.

1 (3-pound) chicken
salt and freshly ground black pepper to taste
Dijon mustard to taste
paprika to taste
¼ pound. butter, melted
⅓ cup balsamic vinegar
½ teaspoon crushed red pepper

DIRECTIONS:
1. Split chicken through the breast and flatten. Remove and reserve wings, then remove and discard tail. Wash chicken, dry with paper towels, and then season liberally with salt, pepper, mustard, and paprika.
2. Prepare grill for direct heat and preheat. Spray grill with vegetable oil. The grill will be ready about a half hour after lighting. Place chicken and wings on grill and cook, uncovered, for 5 minutes, then turn and baste with butter. Cook for 5 minutes more, then turn and baste again with butter. (Have lid handy. Cover grill when fire flares up, which it will.) Continue turning and basting chicken every 10–15 minutes until all butter is gone. Process will take about 50 minutes.
3. Meanwhile, heat vinegar and red pepper (for spicier chicken, add more pepper) in a saucepan over low heat. When finished with butter, begin basting with vinegar mixture, turning chicken every 5 minutes. Chicken may appear burned, but continue cooking another 25 minutes to cook off vinegar.

MEDITERRANEAN PANCAKES
with Maple Ricotta Red Beet and Fig Compote
Yield: 8 servings

FOR PANCAKES
1 cup flour
2 teaspoons baking powder
¼ teaspoon salt
1 tablespoon sugar
2 eggs
½ teaspoon vanilla extract
½ cup milk
16 ounces ricotta, divided
butter (for coating griddle)
½ cup maple syrup (served with ricotta as a side dish)

FOR BEET AND FIG COMPOTE
1 jar Aunt Nellie's sliced pickled beets, with juice
2 cups small–medium fresh figs, halved and sliced
½ cup sugar
1 teaspoon vanilla extract

DIRECTIONS:
1. To make pancakes, sift together flour and baking powder into a large bowl. Whisk flour, baking powder, and salt until well combined. Add sugar, eggs, vanilla, milk, and 1 cup ricotta, and whisk briefly (batter should be lumpy, so don't overstir). If the batter seems much too thick, add a splash of milk to thin it out.

2. Heat a griddle or skillet over medium-high heat and, once hot, coat with a little butter. Drop batter by ¼ cupfuls onto the hot griddle and cook until small holes begin to form on top. Using a spatula, flip the pancake and cook just a couple minutes more until golden. To keep other pancakes warm while making the rest, place pancakes on a baking sheet, cover with foil, and heat in a 175-degree oven.

3. To make compote, wash, dry, peel, and slice figs. Add to a saucepan together with Aunt Nellie's sliced pickled beets and their juice, sugar, and vanilla, and bring to a boil. Reduce heat and simmer until figs and beets become very soft, almost pureed. If necessary, add water. Take off the heat and allow to cool.
4. To serve, add large spoonful compote to each pancake, serving ricotta, drizzled with maple syrup on the side.
5. Serve pancakes with a spoonful of compote and the remaining ricotta cheese, drizzled along with maple syrup.

RIMINI WHOLE-WHEAT CHEESE MUFFINS

Yield: 12 muffins

2 tablespoons olive oil

⅔ cup finely chopped onions

⅔ cup finely chopped Kalamata olives

⅔ cup King Arthur white whole-wheat flour

2 teaspoons baking powder

1½ teaspoons fresh oregano, chopped

1 teaspoon honey

1 teaspoon chopped fresh garlic

⅓ cup low-fat milk

½ cup crumbled goat cheese, like feta

1 large egg, well beaten

2 tablespoons tomato paste

2 tablespoons chopped fresh peppers

DIRECTIONS:

1. Heat oil in a large skillet over medium heat. Add onions and olives. Cook, stirring often, until onions are tender. Transfer to a plate.

2. Preheat oven to 450 degrees F. Coat muffin tins with olive oil spray.

3. Whisk white whole-wheat flour, baking powder, oregano, honey, garlic, and salt in a bowl.

4. Stir milk, egg, tomato paste, and peppers into the onion mixture. In a well in the dry mixture, stir in the liquid mixture until just combined. Fill prepared muffin cups two-thirds full.

5. Bake muffins until lightly browned (about 15 minutes). Cool in the pans for 5 minutes before turning out onto a cooling rack. Serve warm with a light salad or guacamole.

A MEMORABLE BURGER

Yield: 6 burgers

30 ounces ground beef chuck
6 tablespoons purchased basil pesto
⅓ cup finely shredded Parmesan cheese
3 cloves garlic, minced
¼ teaspoon Kosher salt
6 (3") pieces ciabatta bread or ¾"-thick slices rustic Italian bread
3 tablespoons olive oil
6 slices fresh mozzarella cheese
6 cups fresh basil leaves or arugula or spinach leaves
12 small plum tomato slices
6 thin slices red onion rings
freshly ground black pepper

DIRECTIONS:
1. In a bowl, combine ground beef, half the pesto, parmesan, garlic, and salt. Shape into six ½" patties to fit the bread.
2. Halve the bread horizontally. Brush cut sides with olive oil; set aside.
3. Place patties on greased rack directly over medium coals. Grill, uncovered, 6–10 minutes for medium rare, turning once halfway through grilling. Top each patty with a mozzarella slice. Cover grill. Grill 2 minutes more or until cheese is melted. Add bread and grill for 2 minutes per side or until toasted. (For gas grill, preheat grill and reduce heat to medium. Place patties on grill rack over heat. Cover grill as above.)
4. Arrange greens on toasted bread. Top with grilled patties, tomato slices, and thin onion rings.
5. Stir any remaining olive oil into remaining pesto and drizzle over all. Sprinkle with ground pepper.

MEXICAN BREAKFAST TORTILLA
with Shrimp and Paprika

(Tortilla De Desayuno Con Camarones y Pimenton)
Yield: 4–8 servings

This classic Mexican dish can be served for breakfast, cut into cubes for tapas, or presented as a summer lunch with a bowl of gazpacho. A quick note: Add the potato mixture while it's hot enough to start cooking the eggs but not so hot as to soufflé them.

¾ cup peanut oil, vegetable oil, or olive oil
6 medium russet potatoes, peeled, quartered, and thinly sliced
1 medium yellow onion, peeled, halved, and thinly sliced
6 eggs blended with 1 teaspoon Mexican paprika and salt and pepper to taste
1 pound cooked peeled and deveined Gulf cocktail-sized shrimp (80–100 count)

DIRECTIONS:

1. Heat oil over medium-high heat in a 10" sauté pan. Add potatoes and onions and cook, lifting and turning, until potatoes are soft but not brown (about 20 minutes).
2. Beat eggs in a large bowl until pale yellow. Add Mexican paprika and salt and pepper to taste. Transfer sautéed potatoes and onions with a slotted spoon to beaten eggs. Reserve oil.
3. Heat 1 tablespoon reserved oil in the same pan over medium heat. Add egg-and-potato mixture. Add shrimp, spreading potatoes evenly in the pan. Cook uncovered until the bottom is lightly browned (about 3 minutes).
4. Gently shake pan so tortilla doesn't stick, then slide a spatula along edges and underneath tortilla. Place a large plate over pan and quickly turn plate and pan over so tortilla falls onto plate. Add 1 teaspoon reserved oil to pan, slide tortilla back in (uncooked side down), carefully tuck in sides with a fork, and continue cooking over medium heat until eggs are just set (about 3 minutes). Cut into wedges and serve at room temperature.

JOERGI'S MEXICAN FAMILY PORK FIESTA

Yield: 6 servings

3 pounds pork tenderloins, trimmed and silver skin removed
nonstick peanut oil cooking spray
16 ounces plantain chips, as needed (store-bought or homemade fried)
1 bunch cilantro
3 chopped tequila-marinated oranges
1 quart chilled Greek-style nonfat yogurt

FOR MOJO MARINADE
3 cups orange juice
3 teaspoons dried oregano
6 tablespoons minced fresh garlic
3 teaspoons ground cumin
3 teaspoons Kosher salt
1½ teaspoons ground black pepper
1½ teaspoons red chili flakes
1 tablespoon Mexican paprika
2 cups peanut oil

DIRECTIONS:
1. Place all mojo marinade ingredients in mixing bowl. Whisk to combine.
2. Combine pork tenderloins with mojo marinade and refrigerate for 6 hours minimum. Brush tenderloins with nonstick peanut oil, and grill each over medium-high grill for 15–17 minutes or until desired temperature is reached. If necessary, finish cooking in preheated oven.
3. Place fried plantain chips and yogurt on plate, slice one tenderloin into ¼"–½" slices, and shingle over beans. Place desired amount of plantain chips alongside pork and yogurt. Sprinkle with chopped cilantro and tequila-marinated chopped oranges.

STEFY AND SISTER'S SABROSO PAELLA MEXICANA

Yield: 6–8 servings

30 threads saffron, crushed (a scant ½ teaspoon)

¼ cup hot water

1 pound boneless, skinless chicken thighs cut into 2" pieces

10 large shrimp, peeled and deveined

sea salt and freshly ground black pepper to taste

½ cup extra-virgin olive oil

4 ounces dry-cured Mexican chorizo, cut into ¼"-thick coins

1 tablespoon smoked Mexican paprika

3 cloves garlic, minced

3 dried bay leaves

2 (10-ounce) cans Ro*Tel Mexican diced tomatoes with lime juice and cilantro

1 small onion, minced

7 cups chicken broth

2½ cups short-grain rice, preferably valencia or bomba

1 (9-ounce) box frozen artichoke hearts, thawed

8 ounces fresh or frozen peas

3 jars roasted red peppers, torn into ½"-thick strips

12 clams (or debearded mussels), cleaned

DIRECTIONS:

1. Put saffron and hot water in a small bowl; let rest for 15 minutes.
2. Season chicken and shrimp with salt and pepper. Heat oil in 16"–18" paella pan over medium-high heat. Add chicken, shrimp, and chorizo, and cook, turning occasionally, until browned (about 5 minutes). Transfer shrimp to plate, leaving meats in pan. Add paprika, garlic, bay leaves, diced tomatoes with lime juice and cilantro, and onions to pan and cook, stirring often, until onions soften (about 5 minutes). Add reserved saffron mixture and broth, season with salt, and bring to a boil over high heat.
3. Sprinkle in rice. Distribute evenly with a spoon. Add artichokes, peas, and peppers. Cook, without stirring, until rice has absorbed most

389

of the liquid (10–12 minutes). If your pan is larger than the burner, rotate it every 2 minutes so different parts are over the heat and the rice cooks evenly. Reduce heat to low, add reserved shrimp, and nestle in clams (or mussels), hinge side down. Cook without stirring until clams (or mussels) have opened and rice has absorbed liquid and is al dente (5–10 minutes more). Remove pan from heat, cover with aluminum foil, and let sit for 5 minutes before serving.

LIGHT CULINAIRE ASIAN TENDERLOIN
with Peanut Sauce
Yield: 4–5 servings

1 cup light coconut milk
½ cup smooth peanut butter, preferably a natural variety
¼ cup soy sauce
3 tablespoons fresh lime juice
3 tablespoons dark brown sugar
2 large cloves garlic, minced (2½ teaspoons)
2 teaspoons ground coriander
2 small pork tenderloins (about 2 pounds total)
vegetable oil for the grill

DIRECTIONS:

1. In a large bowl, whisk the coconut milk, peanut butter, soy sauce, lime juice, brown sugar, garlic, and coriander to make a smooth sauce.

2. Trim the pork of excess fat and silver skin. Butterfly the tenderloins by splitting each one lengthwise almost, but not quite, all the way through, so the halves remain attached.

3. Open each tenderloin like a book, cover with plastic wrap, and pound to an even ½" thickness with a meat mallet or the bottom of a small skillet. Put the pork tenderloins in the bowl with the marinade and turn to coat. Let marinate for 10–20 minutes (or up to several hours in the refrigerator).

4. While the pork marinates, heat a gas grill with all burners on high. Clean and oil the grate. Remove the tenderloins from the marinade, letting excess marinade drip back into the bowl. (Don't discard the marinade). Grill the tenderloins, covered, turning once, until just cooked through, 5–7 minutes total (cut into one to check). Transfer to a carving board and let rest for 5 minutes.

5. Meanwhile, pour the marinade into a small saucepan and add 2 tablespoons water. Bring to a boil, reduce the heat, and simmer for 3 minutes. Remove from the heat. If the sauce seems too thick, thin it with 1 or 2 teaspoons water. Slice the pork and serve with the sauce on the side.

Serving suggestions: Serve with steamed jasmine or short-grain rice and stir-fried spinach or snow peas. Also, you can exchange pork for boneless chicken or turkey breasts or thighs, using the same recipe otherwise.

UNCLE TOM'S MINNESOTA WILD RICE BARBECUE CHICKEN QUESADILLAS

Yield: 4 quesadillas

1 cup (4 ounces) cooked Gold'n Plump ground chicken
1 cup (8 ounces) Famous Dave's barbecue sauce, divided
1½ cups (8 ounces) cooked Minnesota wild rice
½ cup (2 ounces) shredded Sargento mozzarella cheese
½ cup (2 ounces) shredded Sargento cheddar cheese
2 scallions, thinly sliced
1 clove garlic, finely chopped
8 (8") flour tortillas
4 tablespoons butter, as needed (approximately 1 tablespoon per
    quesadilla)

DIRECTIONS:

1. Combine cooked chicken meat with ½ cup Famous Dave's barbecue sauce, mixing thoroughly; set aside until ready to use.

2. Next, combine cooked Minnesota wild rice with mozzarella cheese, cheddar cheese, scallions, and garlic in medium bowl; mix well. Spread about ½ cup wild-rice mixture onto each of 4 tortillas; sprinkle chicken meat evenly with barbecue sauce. Top with remaining tortillas.

3. Melt about 2 teaspoons butter in large skillet over medium-high heat. Add one quesadilla; cook for 2–3 minutes on each side, or until golden brown. Repeat with remaining butter and quesadillas. Cut each quesadilla into eight wedges. Serve with remaining barbecue sauce.

ALABAMA WEDDING COOKIES

Yield: 36 cookies

These delicate southern wedding cookies belong to a family of buttered confections similar to shortbread. They display a distinctive snowy coating of powdered sugar.

1½ cups (¾ pound) butter, softened
¾ pound powdered sugar, divided
1 egg yolk
1 teaspoon vanilla
1 cup finely ground pecans
3 cups all-purpose flour, unbleached

DIRECTIONS:

1. Beat butter until light and fluffy. Beat in 2 tablespoons of the sugar, egg yolk, vanilla, and pecans. Gradually add flour, beating to blend thoroughly. Pinch off pieces of dough the size of a pecan and roll between your palms into round balls. Place 1½" apart on ungreased baking sheets, flattening each ball lightly.
2. Bake in an oven preheated to 275 degrees F until very lightly browned (about 45 minutes). Let cool on baking sheets until lukewarm.
3. Sift half the powdered sugar onto a large sheet of paper. Roll each cookie lightly in sugar. With your fingers, pack more sugar all over cookies to a thickness of about ⅛". Place cookies on wire racks over wax paper, and dust generously with more sugar. Let cool completely and store in airtight containers, layered between sheets of wax paper.

MOROCCAN MOCHA CUPCAKES

Yield: 12 servings

2 eggs
½ cup brewed coffee, cold
½ cup canola oil
3 teaspoons cider vinegar
3 teaspoons vanilla extract
1½ cups all-purpose flour
1 cup sugar
⅓ cup Hershey's cocoa
1 teaspoon baking soda
½ teaspoon salt

FOR MOCHA FROSTING

3 tablespoons Hershey's milk chocolate baking chips
3 tablespoons Hershey's semisweet chocolate chips
⅓ cup butter, softened
2 cups confectioner's sugar
1–2 tablespoons brewed coffee
½ cup chocolate sprinkles

DIRECTIONS:

1. In a large bowl, beat the eggs, coffee, oil, vinegar, and vanilla until well blended. In a small bowl, combine the flour, sugar, cocoa, baking soda, and salt; gradually beat into coffee mixture until blended.

2. Fill paper-lined muffin cups three-fourths full. Bake at 350 degrees F for 20–25 minutes or until a toothpick inserted in the center of muffins comes out clean. Cool for 10 minutes before removing from pan to a wire rack to cool.

3. For frosting, melt chips and butter in a microwave; stir until smooth. Transfer to a large bowl. Gradually beat in confectioner's sugar and coffee until smooth. Pipe frosting onto cupcakes. Top with sprinkles; gently press down.

MOLTEN PRALINE CHOCOLATE-FILLED COOKIES

Yield: 60–75 tiny cookies

FOR FILLING

6 ounces Nestlé Tollhouse dark chocolate morsels

4 ounces (generous ¾ cup) blanched almonds

2 large eggs

1 teaspoon Nescafé Taster's Choice French roast 100% pure instant
    coffee granules

¼ teaspoon almond extract

½ cup granulated sugar

FOR CHOCOLATE PRALINE TOPPING

¼ cup dark brown sugar

4 tablespoons sweet butter

½ cup Eagle Brand or Nestlé Carnation sweetened condensed milk

1 cup chopped Butterfinger candy bar

FOR COOKIES

6 ounces (1½ sticks) unsalted butter, softened

¼ teaspoon sea salt

1 teaspoon vanilla extract

1½ cups granulated sugar

1½ cups sifted all-purpose flour

½ cup Nestlé Tollhouse baking cocoa

Note: You need 60–75 very small, shallow individual tartlet molds. They vary
in diameter about 1–2" and are ½" deep. (Disposable versions are available.)

DIRECTIONS:

1. To make the filling, grind together almonds and chocolate to a fine
    meal in a food processor.

2. In the small bowl of an electric mixer at high speed, whip the eggs for
    5 minutes until thick. On low speed mix in the coffee, almond extract,
    and sugar, and then gradually beat in the chocolate-almond mixture.
    Transfer mixture to a small bowl at room temperature. Set aside.

3. To make chocolate praline topping, heat brown sugar and butter, stirring until smooth. Whisk in condensed milk. Bring to a boil. While whisking, boil for 5 minutes until sugar barely begins to caramelize. Add chopped Butterfinger candy bar. Cool to lukewarm.

4. To make the cookies, preheat oven to 350 degrees F. Cream the butter in the bowl of an electric mixer and gradually add sea salt, vanilla, and sugar, and lastly the flour and cocoa. The mixture will be crumbly. Turn it out onto a board and squeeze it with your hands until it holds together. Break off about 2 tablespoons at a time, form the dough into a ball, and press dough into small tartlet molds. The dough should be level with the mold. Place molds on a cookie sheet and with a small spoon place some of the filling in each shell. Bake tartlets for 20 minutes, until pastry is barely colored. Remove from oven and top with praline topping.

MOROCCAN SEVEN-HERB COUSCOUS

Yield: 6 servings

2 tablespoons unsalted butter

2 tablespoons olive oil

2 large onions, quartered and cut into ½" slices

2 pinches saffron threads

1 pinch crushed red pepper

½ teaspoon ground turmeric

½ teaspoon ground cinnamon

1 teaspoon ground ginger

1 teaspoon coarsely ground black pepper

3 sprigs parsley and 3 sprigs cilantro, tied in a bundle with kitchen
    string

1 tablespoon shredded green spearmint

2 tablespoons shredded garlic greens

1 tablespoon shredded tarragon

1 teaspoon ground cumin

1 teaspoon ground fenugreek

½ teaspoon chopped rosemary

4 fresh or canned tomatoes, peeled, seeded, and quartered

1 quart vegetable stock

3 cups water

1 turnip, peeled and cut into 1" cubes

½ pound carrots, peeled, halved lengthwise, and cut into 2" sticks

¾ pound butternut squash, peeled, seeded, and cut into 1½" chunks

1 medium-sized zucchini, quartered lengthwise and cut into 2" sticks

1 cup raisins

1 (14-ounce) can chickpeas, rinsed and drained

2 tablespoons granulated sugar

salt and freshly ground black pepper to taste

3 cups quick cooking couscous

½ cup blanched slivered almonds, toasted

6 sprigs mint for garnish

DIRECTIONS:

1. Heat butter and olive oil in stockpot over medium heat. Add onions and cook for 15 minutes. Stir in saffron, crushed red pepper, turmeric, cinnamon, ginger, and black pepper. Sauté 5 minutes. Add herbs, tomatoes, stock, and water. Bring to a boil, reduce heat to low, and cook for 10 minutes.

2. Add turnip, carrots, and squash. Bring to a boil and cook for 10 minutes. Add zucchini, raisins, chickpeas, and sugar. Cook 10 minutes more, or until vegetables are tender. Add salt and pepper.

3. Cook couscous according to package directions. Mound couscous on large serving platter and make a well in center. Use a slotted spoon to transfer vegetables to well. Ladle stock over entire dish. Sprinkle with toasted almonds. Serve immediately with fresh mint sprigs.

MOUTHWATERING BANH MI
THAI STEAK SANDWICH
with Peanut Dipping Sauce
Yield: 2–4 servings

FOR PEANUT DIPPING SAUCE
½ cup and 2 tablespoons Mezetta white balsamic vinegar
½ cup cane sugar
1 tablespoon minced ginger
4 fresh mint sprigs
¼ teaspoon Mezetta habanero hot sauce
½ cup peanuts, toasted, coarsely crushed

FOR SANDWICH
1 long (15") loaf crusty French baguette
½ head crisp iceberg lettuce, leaves separated
1 medium-sized cucumber, peeled, seeded, and sliced thinly
1 cup Mezetta Chicago-style mild jardinières
1 cup Mezetta sun-dried tomatoes in olive oil, julienned

FOR DRESSING
¼ cup freshly squeezed lemon juice
½ cup Mezetta extra-virgin olive oil
1 teaspoon Mezetta crushed garlic
2½–3 teaspoons cane sugar
¼ teaspoon Mezetta habanero hot sauce

FOR STEAK AND STEAK TOPPING
1 (16-ounce) flank steak, grilled medium rare, sliced thin
vegetable oil spray for the grill
2 cups Mezetta roasted red pepper strips with caramelized onions
2 each Mezetta habanero peppers, sliced thin
2 teaspoons mint sprigs, chopped
2 teaspoons cilantro, chopped

DIRECTIONS:

1. For the peanut dipping sauce, combine all ingredients except peanuts in a medium saucepan. Bring to a simmer and cook for 1 minute. Remove from heat and strain. Add peanuts and reserve, refrigerated.

2. For the thai steak sandwich, slice the baguette in half lengthwise and remove ½" of the soft inside, leaving ½" of the crusty border. Add the next four ingredients in this order: lettuce, cucumbers, jardinières, and sun-dried tomatoes. For the dressing, combine in a blender all five dressing ingredients until smooth and thoroughly combined. Drizzle salad greens and vegetables with dressing.

3. For the steak and steak topping, heat the grill or grill pan to medium high and coat lightly with vegetable oil. Grill the steak to desired order. Set aside and slice thinly. Add to the sandwich. Combine the pepper strips, peppers, mint, and cilantro and serve on top of the sliced steak. Carefully close the sandwich with the top half baguette. Press together and cut loaf into two or four slices (based on the number of sandwiches desired).

4. Serve with peanut dipping sauce as a side.

NAPA LAVENDER BACON GREEN GRAPE JUICE JUS VERTS SALAD

Yield: Entrée salad serviings

FOR VINAIGRETTE

16 ounces Sugardale bacon, diced and crisped, divided, and fat reserved
¼ cup chopped celery
½ cup honey
½ cup Napa Valley verjus
½ cup sliced shallots
½ cup seedless blonde raisins
¼ cup roasted garlic
1¼ tablespoons Jus Verts (Green Grape Juice from Napa Valley)
½ tablespoon Dijon mustard
¼ cup extra-virgin California olive oil
Kosher salt and freshly ground black pepper to taste

FOR SALAD

1 pound fresh mozzarella, halved crosswise and thinly sliced
4 vine-ripened Napa Valley tomatoes, julienned
1 tablespoon fresh lavender leaves
1 medium sweet onion, sliced paper-thin and separated into rings

DIRECTIONS:

1. Make the vinaigrette: In a large food processor, process 8 ounces bacon, celery, honey, verjus, shallots, raisins, garlic, lemon juice, and mustard until smooth. With the processor running, slowly add oil and the reserved bacon fat; season with salt and pepper.

2. Make the salad: Combine mozzarella, tomatoes, and lavender leaves. Season with salt and pepper, and drizzle with vinaigrette. Garnish with remaining 8 ounces bacon and thinly sliced sweet onion rings. Add a few sprigs lavender to the top of the salad.

NAPA VALLEY SMOKED DRUNKEN BEEF TENDERLOIN

Yield: 12 servings as main dish or 24 servings as appetizer

6 pounds beef tenderloin
6 strips bacon

FOR THE MARINADE
12 ounces Dickey's basting sauce
1 cup California red wine
1 cup apple cider
½ cup brown sugar
1 medium onion, chopped
2 cloves garlic, minced
1 teaspoon dry mustard

FOR THE SAUCE
1 quart Dickey's barbecue sauce
½ bottle California red wine
½ bottle port wine
1 medium onion, chopped fine
6 garlic cloves, chopped
2 bay leaves
2 dashes Dickey's hot sauce
1 tablespoon butter
2 tablespoons strawberry jam

FOR GRILLING
3 chunks hickory, oak, maple, or apple wood, each about 2" in diameter, or one small plank. Soak wood overnight in water.

FOR GARNISH
1 each red and yellow sweet bell peppers sliced into ½"-wide strips
4 sprigs fresh rosemary or thyme chopped
4 teaspoons smoked Hungarian paprika

DIRECTIONS:

1. Trim any fat from the tenderloin. Place in a nonreactive container. Combine marinade ingredients in stainless-steel bowl well and pour over meat. Cover and marinate overnight, refrigerated.

2. For the sauce: prepare one day in advance by combining all ingredients except butter and jam. Simmer on stovetop until reduced to 2 cups. Strain. Continue to simmer, adding butter and jam. Reduce to ¾ cup or until sauce has consistency of maple syrup. Cover and refrigerate until needed.

3. Remove meat from marinade, let warm to room temperature. Preheat grill or smoker. Wrap soaked wood chips in aluminum foil; pierce to allow smoke to escape. For gas grill, turn off one burner and place wood on other burner. Close lid and wait for it to smoke.

4. Place thermometer in tenderloin and oven thermometer on grill. When grill smokes, add bacon strips on meat and place on grill above unlit burner. Close lid. Adjust heat for the inside of the grill to be 225 degrees F. Don't open the lid to peek. After 1 hour, turn the meat around, close lid, and cook until inside meat temperature is 140 degrees F (about 30–45 minutes longer). Remove meat and let rest.

5. In the meantime, grill pepper strips.

6. Reheat sauce.

7. To assemble, cut tenderloin into 1" cubes. Place a strip red and yellow pepper on each cube, then a piece of bacon. Secure with toothpicks. Garnish with rosemary and thyme, and sprinkle with paprika and serve.

NEW ORLEANS SOUP
with Spring Vegetables and Crayfish
Yield: 6 generous servings

Like a bouquet of fresh vegetables, this light but soothing soup is just the thing on a cool spring evening on the Mississippi riverbank. It is important to cut the green vegetables into small pieces so they cook quickly while retaining their bright color. Finally, add boiled and Cajun-seasoned whole crayfish in their shells, which gives the soup that native New Orleans river flavor.

1 tablespoon extra-virgin olive oil
2 medium leeks, trimmed, washed, and finely chopped (1½ cups)
2 cloves garlic, minced
½ pound new potatoes, scrubbed and diced (about 1⅔ cups)
2 cups reduced-sodium chicken broth or vegetable broth
1 pound fresh asparagus, trimmed and cut into ½" pieces (1½–2 cups)
⅔ cup snow peas or sugar snap peas, stemmed and cut into ½" dice
3 tablespoons chopped fresh chives, divided
2 tablespoons chopped fresh flat-leaf parsley
1 tablespoon chopped fresh dill
2 teaspoons chopped fresh chervil* or flat-leaf parsley, plus sprigs for
 garnish
2 cups 1% milk
1 tablespoon lemon juice
½ pound boiled crayfish, seasoned with Cajun seasoning to taste
12 cups French-bread cubes or New Orleans French baguette cubes
 fried in butter or olive oil

DIRECTIONS:
1. Heat oil in a large saucepan over medium-low heat. Add leeks and cook, stirring often, until softened but not browned(about 5 minutes). Add garlic and cook, stirring, for 1 minute.

2. Add potatoes and broth; bring to a simmer over medium-high heat. Cover and reduce heat to medium low. Simmer, stirring occasionally, until the potatoes are tender (10–15 minutes).
3. Increase heat to medium high and stir in asparagus and peas; simmer, covered, stirring two or three times, until just tender (3–4 minutes). Remove from heat; stir in 1 tablespoon chives, parsley, dill, and chopped chervil (or parsley). Transfer the soup to a blender and blend until smooth. (Use caution when pureeing hot liquids.)
4. Return the soup to the pan. Add milk and bring to just below a simmer, stirring, over medium heat. Stir in lemon juice. Ladle into soup bowls. Serve with Cajun-seasoned crayfish, a sprinkling of the remaining chopped chives, and a sprig of chervil (or parsley). On the side, in a bowl, serve French-bread cubes fried in butter, and/or whole New Orleans French baguettes.

*Chervil has a mild flavor between that of parsley and anise. It doesn't dry well, so it is best used fresh.

NEW ORLEANS MARDI GRAS
STRAWBERRY AND PRALINE TOAST

Yield: 8 servings

4 large eggs or 8 egg whites

8 ounces crushed fresh strawberries

¼ cup soy milk

1 tablespoon each maple syrup, sour cream, and sugar

8 slices whole-wheat bread

4 tablespoons butter

½ cup powdered sugar

1 cup chopped pecans

½ cup unsweetened coconut

2 cups sliced or crushed fresh strawberries, to be used as topping

DIRECTIONS:

1. In a blender, whirl the eggs (or egg whites), strawberries, soy milk, syrup, sour cream, and sugar until smooth.

2. Trim bread slices and place in a large shallow dish. Pour egg mixture over bread and turn bread to coat from other side.

3. While the bread soaks, preheated oven to 375 degrees F. Place on a baking sheet lined with aluminum foil a mixture of powdered sugar, chopped pecans, and coconut for the pralines. Place sheet in oven and stir from time to time until sugar begins to caramelize, about 15 minutes, stirring often. When crunchy, remove from oven and crumble pralines for the topping with a rolling pin or bottle.

4. Melt 1 tablespoon of butter in a nonstick frying pan or skillet over medium heat. Place 2 slices bread in pan and cook until browned on both sides. Repeat with remaining slices of bread. Before serving, top with sliced or crushed fresh strawberries and top with crumbled New Orleans pralines.

MY SECRET OKTOBERFEST POTATO SALAD

Yield: about 8 servings

Note: The secret to this potato salad recipe is the hot chicken broth, powerfully infused into sliced hot potatoes, giving this potato salad a flavor no other potato salad can match. Also, the unique blend of the multiple natural ingredients only intensifies and complements the warm potato salad.

3 pounds fingerling or other small golden potatoes, scrubbed, unpeeled
1 cup boiling hot chicken broth

SMALL BOWL 1
⅓ cup each chopped parsley, cilantro, and marjoram
½ cup finely diced red onions
⅓ cup diced (¼") vine-ripened tomatoes

SMALL BOWL 2
½ cup diced, cored, but unpeeled tart apples (e.g., Granny Smith)
½ cup chopped bread-and-butter pickles
1 tablespoon finely chopped garlic
2 hard-boiled eggs, sliced

SMALL BOWL 3
¼ cup apple cider vinegar
¾ cup vegetable (canola) oil
2 tablespoons sugar
1 teaspoon Cajun seasoning (to taste)
½ teaspoon each sea salt and white ground pepper
2 tablespoons Vegenaise or top-brand olive oil mayonnaise (available in natural foods markets)
2 teaspoons Dijon mustard

DIRECTIONS:
1. Place the potatoes in a medium saucepan and add enough water, with 1 teaspoon salt, to cover by 2". Bring to a boil over high heat

and cook until the potatoes are done, about 15 minutes. Drain, cool slightly until you can handle the potatoes, and slice the potatoes into a large bowl. Immediately drench the sliced potatoes with piping-hot chicken broth. Cover with a clean kitchen towel and let rest for 10–15 minutes or until most of the broth is absorbed by the potatoes.

2. Add the prepared ingredients from each of the three small bowls to the potatoes, and gently toss to combine.

ORGANIC BABY LETTUCE
with Fresh Figs, Prosciutto, and Pistachios
in Honey-Balsamic Vinaigrette

Yield: 4 servings

Sweet fresh figs, crunchy bites of Olivia's organic greens, prosciutto, and honey-balsamic vinaigrette sing a song of summer when accompanied by a chilled glass of lightly sweet cider or a light dry or fruity red wine.

FOR VINAIGRETTE

2 teaspoons organic honey

1 teaspoon Dijon mustard

2 tablespoons aged balsamic vinegar

½ cup extra-virgin olive oil (I prefer olive oil from Sardinia for its earthy, green flavors)

¼ teaspoon light sea salt

orchid blossoms to garnish

FOR SALAD

⅔ pound Olivia's Organics Crunch Bunch baby greens

1 small head radicchio

8 fresh ripe figs

12 paper-thin slices prosciutto di Parma

4 tablespoons toasted pine nuts

DIRECTIONS:

1. To make the vinaigrette, combine all vinaigrette ingredients in a blender and blend till smooth.
2. Refrigerate and dry greens and radicchio leaves. Tear larger leaves into bite-sized pieces.
3. Rinse figs under cold water and pat dry. Cut figs inn half, removing tough stems.
4. Toss greens with enough vinaigrette to just coat the leaves. Toss pine nuts with a little vinaigrette to make them shiny. Reserve remaining vinaigrette.

5. Place salad greens mixed with radicchio on four chilled plates. Arrange 3 slices of prosciutto in center of each plate to form a circular pattern. Stand 4 fig halves in center of prosciutto to form yet another circle (with stem ends up and cut sides out).

6. Spoon pine nuts over figs. Drizzle reserved dressing over figs and prosciutto. Place a small flower blossom (I prefer orchid blossoms) on top of figs.

ON AND OFF AGAIN OLIVE AND BLACK FIG SPREAD

Yield: 1 quart

1 pound Sugardale Bacon strips roasted to a crisp and crumbled
1 cup (about 5 ounces) finely chopped dried black mission figs
¾ cup (about 5 ounces) pitted dry-cured black olives
½ cup extra-virgin olive oil
¼ cup salt-packed capers, rinsed and drained
1 tablespoon fresh lemon juice
6 oil-packed anchovies, drained
3 cloves garlic, finely chopped
freshly ground black pepper to taste

DIRECTIONS:

1. Combine all ingredients in a food processor and pulse until evenly chopped and combined. Transfer to a bowl, cover with plastic wrap, and store in the refrigerator for up to 1 week.

PACIFIC ORANGE AND MACADAMIA NUT CHEESECAKE

Yield: 1 (9") cheesecake, 10 servings

FOR THE CRUST
¼ cup unsalted macadamia nuts, coarsely crushed pieces
¼ cup granulated sugar
¼ teaspoon coarse sea salt
1¼ cups graham cracker crumbs or cookie crumbs (your choice)
5 tablespoons melted butter
5 tablespoons coarse orange marmalade, no sugar added, best quality

FOR THE FILLING
2 pounds Philadelphia cream cheese, at room temperature
1⅓ cups granulated sugar
½ teaspoon coarse sea salt
2 tablespoons vanilla paste, or seeds from 2 whole vanilla beans
5 large eggs at room temperature
⅔ cup sour cream
1 tablespoon coarse orange marmalade
grated zest of 1 medium-sized orange
½ cup unsalted macadamia nuts, coarsely crushed pieces

FOR THE FROSTING
½ cup unsalted butter, softened
1 tablespoon orange marmalade
1½ teaspoons orange zest
2½ cups powdered sugar
2 tablespoons orange juice concentrate

FOR THE TOPPING
frosting (see above)
10 cleaned orange sections with no white pith
¼ cup crushed macadamia nuts
1 tablespoon grated orange zest

DIRECTIONS:

1. Preheat oven to 300 degrees F. Bring water to a boil for a water bath. Butter the bottom and the sides of a 9" × 2" cake pan and set aside.

2. To make the crust, pulse the macadamia nuts in a food processor with sugar and salt until coarsely ground. Transfer to a large bowl; add the crumbs (graham cracker or cookie) and butter, and mix to combine. Press the crumb mixture over the bottom of the buttered pan and spread orange marmalade across the crust. Set aside.

3. To make the filling, beat the cream cheese, sugar, salt, and vanilla paste or seeds in the bowl of a standing mixer fitted with a paddle attachment on medium high speed, scraping down the bowl several times, until the mixture is completely smooth (about 5 minutes).

4. Turn the mixer to low and beat in the eggs one at a time until blended, scraping down the sides after each addition. Beat in the sour cream, orange marmalade, and macadamia nut pieces until blended.

5. Place the cake pan in a roasting pan. Pour the cream cheese mixture into the cake pan all the way to the top. Place the roasting pan in the oven and pour in the boiling water to come about ½" up the sides of the cake pan. Bake until the filling is set but still jiggles slightly in the center (about 1 hour 20 minutes). Remove from the water bath and let cool to room temperature. Chill for 4 hours in refrigerator.

6. To make the frosting, beat the first three frosting ingredients at low speed with an electric mixer until creamy. Gradually add sugar, beating until combined. Gradually add orange juice concentrate, beating at medium speed 30 seconds or until frosting is spreadable. Beat at medium high for 30 seconds or until fluffy.

7. To finish, heat the bottom of the pan about 5 minutes over an electric element or on an electric stove element to loosen the crust, and invert onto a larger round plate. Remove pan from the cake. Brush the sides and top of the cake with frosting. Gently press coarsely ground macadamia nuts all around the sides of the cake. Place 1 cleaned orange section on each of ten slices. In center, sprinkle top with 1 tablespoon each grated orange zest and 1 tablespoon coarsely chopped macadamia nuts. Dust with powdered sugar if desired.

ORANGE THYME-TINGED CORN SAUTÉ

Yield: 5-7 portions

Fresh corn on the cob is wonderful, but fresh corn off the cob is a real treat too. Your reward for spending a few pleasant minutes cutting kernels off the cob is a sweet and flavorful corn sauté brightened with diced red peppers, thyme, and a lift of orange—a subtle, delicious vegetable side dish that goes splendidly with crab cakes.

5–7 ears fresh corn, husked
1 tablespoon extra-virgin olive oil
2 scallions, thinly sliced
1 small red bell pepper, seeded and diced
1 small stalk celery, finely chopped
2 tablespoons water
1 tablespoon butter
1 teaspoon fresh lemon thyme, or thyme leaves
½ teaspoon freshly grated orange zest
¼ teaspoon salt

DIRECTIONS:

1. Remove as much silk as possible from the corn and then, using a sharp chef's knife, cut the kernels off the cob. You want to end up with 3–3½ cups corn. You may not need all the corn if the ears are large. Set aside.

2. Heat oil in a large nonstick skillet or sauté pan over medium-low heat. Stir in scallions, bell pepper and celery. Cover and cook, stirring occasionally, until the vegetables are softened but not browned (about 5 minutes).

3. Add the reserved corn and water to the pan. Cover and cook, stirring often, until the corn is tender (4–5 minutes). Add butter and stir until it has melted. Stir in the thyme, orange zest, and salt. Remove the pan from the heat, cover, and let sit for several minutes before serving.

ORANGE GROVE FARMER'S GLAZED FLANK STEAK

Yield: 4–6 servings

1 cup prepared teriyaki marinade
½ cup chopped onions
⅓ cup orange-blossom honey
⅓ cup fresh orange juice
1 tablespoon dark sesame oil
1 large clove garlic, crushed and peeled
pepper to taste
1 (2-pound) flank steak
12 orange slices, 2 large oranges
12 tarragon sprigs
24 ounces Bush's Steakhouse Recipe Grillin' Beans

DIRECTIONS:

1. In a medium, shallow dish, combine teriyaki marinade, onions, honey, orange juice, sesame oil, garlic, and pepper; whisk until blended. Remove and reserve ¾ cup marinade for basting.

2. With a sharp knife, lightly score both sides of flank steak in a crisscross pattern. Place steak in marinade in dish, turning to coat. Cover with plastic wrap and marinate in refrigerator for 30–60 minutes, turning twice.

3. Remove steak from marinade; discard marinade. Place steak on grid over medium ash-covered coals. Grill, uncovered, for 15–20 minutes for medium rare, basting occasionally with reserved marinade and turning once.

4. Place remaining marinade in small saucepan; place on grid of grill and bring to a boil. Meanwhile, remove steak from grill, keeping hot, and place Bush's Steakhouse Recipe Grillin' Beans in a skillet on outer perimeter of grill to heat, stirring occasionally until heated thoroughly.

5. To serve, carve steak diagonally across the grain into thin slices; arrange on a platter. Spoon hot marinade over steak as desired. Garnish with orange slices and tarragon sprigs and serve with Bush's Steakhouse Recipe Grillin' Beans.

EL VIGO ORANGE JUICE–GLAZED RED PAPAYAS
with Serrano Spanish Ham

Yield: 40 appetizers

1 perfectly ripe red papaya, peeled, seeded, and sliced into wedges
½ cup extra-virgin olive oil
½ cup fresh Florida orange juice
½ cup key lime juice
20 slices smoked Spanish serrano ham, thinly sliced
40 fresh basil leaves

DIRECTIONS:

1. Peel and half the papaya and remove the seeds with a large Parisian scoop. Cut the two papaya halves into 4 wedge quarters, and each wedge into 5 for 40 small wedge-shaped sections. Toss in olive oil and the two citrus juices, allowing to macerate for 15 minutes while the charbroiler preheats.
2. Meanwhile, cut the serrano ham lengthwise into ½" strips.
3. Drain the marinade from the papaya, reserving the liquid, and grill the papayas until nice grill marks appear on each side.
4. When cooled, wrap each grilled papaya wedge with a thin slice of serrano ham and a basil leaf, and then put on a skewer. 8 papaya pieces per skewer.
5. Drizzle the skewered serrano ham papaya with reserved marinade and quickly place on the grill prior to serving.
6. The skewers may be cooled at this point and served at room temperature if a grill is not available at the serving place.

ORECCHIETTE WITH CANNELLINI BEANS
Broccoli Rabe and Parmesan Cheese
Yield: 4 servings

1 pound broccoli rabe

½ cup olive oil, divided

1 medium onion, minced

1 (15-ounce) can Italian-style tomato marinara sauce

9 ounces tomato paste

1 (15-ounce) can cannellini beans, drained and rinsed

1 pound orecchiette pasta

¼ teaspoon red pepper flakes

4 garlic cloves, finely chopped

1 fluid ounce chicken stock or water

½ bunch chopped parsley

2 tablespoons chopped basil

2 tablespoons chopped oregano

1 tablespoon minced chives

1 cup grated parmesan

DIRECTIONS:

1. Clean the broccoli rabe by cutting off 1" from the bottom of each stem. Blanch the broccoli rabe in boiling salted water until 90% cooked (about 4 minutes). Remove and shock in ice water. Set aside.

2. In a large sauté pan, heat ¼ cup of the oil over medium heat. Add onions and garlic and cook until tender (about 4 minutes). Add the marinara sauce, tomato paste, and cannellini beans, stirring with a wooden spoon in the pan. Let the mixture cook until well combined and bubbling hot. Add Italian-style sauce and cook about 5 minutes more. Remove from the pan and reserve.

3. Meanwhile, bring a large pot of salted water to a boil and cook the pasta until al dente (about 6 minutes). Remove from the water and drain.

4. While the pasta is cooking, heat a large sauté pan over medium heat with the remaining ¼ cup oil. Add the garlic, red pepper flakes, stock

(or water), and reserved cannellini bean–tomato mixture. Cook for 1 minute, stirring to combine. Add half of the chopped herbs and broccoli rabe. Add the cooked pasta and ½ cup of the parmesan; toss to mix. Garnish with the remaining parmesan, sprinkle with remaining chopped herbs, and serve immediately.

TUSCAN OREGANATO SHRIMP
PANINI FOR COMPANY

Yield: 4 servings

10 ounces angel hair pasta, cooked al dente

FOR FOCACCIA
1 (10") loaf focaccia bread, split lengthwise and halved
¼ cup extra-virgin olive oil
2 tablespoons dried or fresh oregano
2 tablespoons minced garlic
8 sprigs fresh oregano

FOR SHRIMP
2 cups sliced zucchini
½ cup thinly sliced red onions
2 garlic cloves, minced
1 teaspoon dried or 1 tablespoon chopped fresh oregano
1 tablespoon extra-virgin olive oil
32 ounces raw, peeled, and deveined large shrimp, 20–26 count
juice of ½ lemon
¼ teaspoon sea salt
⅛ teaspoon freshly ground black pepper
2 ripe plum tomatoes, diced
1½ cups shredded part-skim provolone
¼ cup grated Parmigiano
½ bunch fresh Italian parsley, chopped

DIRECTIONS:
1. In a 2-quart saucepan, boil the pasta al dente. Drain and keep hot.
2. Brush split focaccia halves with olive oil and minced garlic, and generously sprinkle with oregano.
3. In a 12" nonstick skillet coated with olive oil, sauté zucchini, onion, garlic, and oregano for 5 minutes or until onions are tender. Sprinkle shrimp with salt and pepper and lemon juice; place over zucchini

mixture. Add diced tomatoes, reduce heat, cover, and simmer for 10 minutes or until shrimp turn pink. Sprinkle with mixture of Parmesan and provolone cheeses. Cover and simmer until cheese is melted (2–3 minutes).

4. Preheat oven to 425 degrees F. Bake oreganato focaccia bread halves until crispy on the outside and golden brown.

5. To serve, plate oreganato shrimp over the pasta and serve the panini toast on the side with crisp hearts of romaine with light vinaigrette.

OREGON'S FAMOUS HAZELNUT APPLE COFFEE CAKE ROULADEN

Yield: 12 slices

FOR CAKE
1 cup lukewarm milk
1½ sticks (6 ounces) softened unsalted butter melted and cooled
2 packages dry yeast
¼ teaspoons sugar
4 ⅓ cups sifted unbleached flour
1 tablespoon grated lemon peel
5 tablespoons light brown sugar
2 egg yolks at room temperature
2 whole eggs at room temperature
1 teaspoon salt

FOR FILLING
¼ cup milk
1 cup sugar
10 ounces ground, toasted hazelnuts
1 grated peel of 1 lemon
1½ cups sliced apples
½ teaspoons cinnamon
2 ounces butter, softened

DIRECTIONS:
1. Dissolve yeast in milk and add ¼ teaspoon sugar. In a large, dry, and warm bowl, mix yeast mixture with ⅓ cup flour, stirring. Let rise for ½ hour in a warm place. Add lemon peel, light brown sugar, egg yolks, whole eggs, salt, and cooled liquid butter. Stir in remaining flour and beat until smooth. Cover and let rise until dough doubles in size (about 1 hour).
2. Spread dough onto a half-sized baking sheet pan and dot with a fork several times. Preheat oven to 350 degrees F.

3. Meanwhile, prepare hazelnut apple filling. Bring milk, sugar, lemon peel, and nuts to a boil. Let boil for 5 minutes and cool down; add sliced apples, cinnamon, and butter. Set ½ cup filling aside to top the cake roll.

4. Spread filling over the dough in same thickness. Roll dough from one long end of the sheet pan to opposite end.

5. With a brush evenly spread 1/2 cup of the reserved filling over the rolled dough and place in preheated oven for ½ hour or until lightly browned. Allow to cool and slice evenly into 12 servings.

ORGANIC MAC AND CHEESE
with Creamy Spinach Sauce
Yield: 4 servings

FOR ORGANIC MAC AND CHEESE
2 pints organic cream
1 pound organic American cheese
¼ cup shredded organic Colby cheese
¼ cup shredded organic Monterey Jack cheese
1 pound dry whole-wheat elbow macaroni
4 tablespoons chopped parsley

FOR SPINACH SAUCE
2 tablespoons plus 1 teaspoon olive oil, divided
1 medium onions, chopped
2 cloves garlic, minced
1 package 8 ounces organic baby spinach leaves
1 cup fresh parsley
juice of ½ lemon
1 cup low-fat cottage cheese
freshly ground black pepper

DIRECTIONS:
1. To prepare mac and cheese, reduce cream by one-third. Whisk in cheeses over low heat until smooth. Cook pasta according to manufacturer's directions and drain. Incorporate pasta into melted cheeses. Sprinkle with chopped parsley.
2. To prepare spinach sauce, add garlic and onion to 1 teaspoon olive oil. Cook over medium heat until softened. Add spinach, cover, and let cook 3–4 minutes, occasionally stirring. In a blender, place parsley, lemon juice, and cottage cheese, and process until well blended. Drizzle with remaining olive oil and process until creamy. Scrape mixture into a saucepan with cooked spinach and onions, and stir until well combined. Serve over cooked organic mac and cheese.

ORGANIC PARSLEY-GARLIC SPAGHETTI
with a Crimini Mushroom Basil Sauce
Yield: 4 servings

4 tablespoons extra-virgin olive oil

3 cloves garlic, minced

8 ounces shiitake mushrooms, stemmed and sliced (2 cups)

2 teaspoons freshly grated lemon zest

2 tablespoons lemon juice,

¼ teaspoon salt, or to taste

freshly ground pepper to taste

14 ounces Eden whole-grain parsley-garlic spaghetti

½ cups freshly grated Parmesan cheese (1 ounce)

½ cups chopped fresh basil, divided

DIRECTIONS:
1. Bring a large pot of lightly salted water to a boil for cooking pasta.
2. Heat oil in large nonstick skillet over low heat. Add garlic and cook, stirring, until fragrant but not browned, about 1 minute. Add mushrooms and increase heat to medium high; cook, stirring occasionally, until tender and lightly browned (4–5 minutes). Stir in lemon zest, lemon juice, salt, and pepper. Remove from heat.
3. Meanwhile, cook pasta, stirring occasionally, until just tender (9–11 minutes, or according to package directions). Drain, reserving ½ cup cooking liquid.
4. Add the pasta, the reserved cooking liquid, parmesan, and ¼ cup basil to the mushrooms in the skillet; toss to coat well. Serve immediately, garnished with remaining basil.

ORIENTAL RAINBOW SPRING SALAD
Tossed with a Rich Poppy Seed Dressing
Yield: 4–6 servings

2 ounces mung bean noodles

3 cups shredded napa cabbage

1 cup torn arugula

1 red beet, julienned

½ cup julienned green squash

1 scallion, sliced

½ cup each julienned red, green, and orange bell peppers

2 tablespoons cilantro

2 tablespoons chopped green mint leaves

½ cup (or as much as you like) Brianna's Rich Poppy Seed Dressing

FOR GARNISH
¼ cup toasted poppy seeds

6 sprigs fresh mint

DIRECTIONS:
1. Soak the noodles in warm water and cover for 10 minutes or until pliable. Drain, then cook noodles in boiling water for just a few minutes, until they expand and look glassy. Drain and rinse with cold water. Drain again. Cut into 1"–2" lengths.
2. Place noodles in a large bowl along with the rest of salad ingredients. Toss Brianna's Rich Poppy Seed Dressing into the salad until ingredients are well coated.
3. Garnish with sprinkles of lightly toasted poppy seeds and sprigs of fresh mint.

OMAR'S PARK LANE CHOCOLATE TORTE

Yield: 12 servings

FOR CAKE

2 cups all-purpose flour (about 9 ounces)

1 cup granulated sugar

1 cup packed dark brown sugar

¾ cup unsweetened Dutch-processed cocoa

1½ teaspoons baking soda

1½ teaspoons baking powder

½ teaspoon salt

1 cup reduced-fat sour cream

3 tablespoons olive oil

1 cup brewed espresso coffee

2 teaspoons vanilla extract

⅓ cup bittersweet chocolate morsels

cooking spray

FOR ESPRESSO CREAM

¼ cup boiling water

1 tablespoon fine-ground espresso coffee

2 cups heavy whipping cream

1 cup powdered sugar

⅓ cup light chocolate ganache

12 bittersweet chocolate truffles

DIRECTIONS:

1. Preheat oven to 350 degrees.
2. To prepare cake, lightly spoon flour into dry measuring cups; level with a knife. Combine flour and next six ingredients (through salt) in a large bowl. Add sour cream and oil; beat with a mixer at low speed until well blended. Slowly add brewed espresso and vanilla; beat with a mixer at low speed for 1 minute or until well blended. Stir in chocolate; pour batter into a 13" × 9" baking pan coated with cooking spray. Bake at 350 degrees F for 30 minutes or until a wooden

427

toothpick inserted in center comes out clean. Cool completely in pan on a wire rack.

3. To prepare espresso cream, combine water and espresso grounds in a large bowl; stir until grounds dissolve. Allow to cool before adding to heavy cream. Beat with a mixer at low speed to form soft peaks. Fold in powdered sugar.

4. Spread espresso cream over top of torte; drizzle with chocolate ganache. Chill until ready to serve.

5. Decorate each slice with 1 bittersweet chocolate truffle.

OVEN-FRIED KEY WEST OCEAN SEA STRIPS

Yield: 5 servings (3 strips per serving)

2 tablespoons butter

juice of 1 lime

2 teaspoons Dijon mustard

dash hot sauce

½ cup finely crushed Crunchmaster original multigrain crackers

1 cup finely crushed Crunchmaster multiseed crackers

⅓ cup grated Parmesan cheese

1½ teaspoon Old Bay seasoning

⅛ teaspoon freshly ground black pepper

2 pounds grouper (or other whitefish) fillet strips (about 2½" × ½")

DIRECTIONS:

1. Melt butter in a 15" × 10" jelly-roll pan in an oven heated to 425 degrees F. Add lime juice, Dijon mustard, and hot sauce to taste.
2. Place crushed Crunchmaster crackers and next three ingredients in a large zip-top plastic bag; shake well to combine. Arrange fish strips in melted-butter mixture in hot baking dish.
3. Bake at 425 degrees F in a preheated oven for 30 minutes or until sea strips are done. Serve immediately.

OVEN-ROASTED FRESH TURKEY BREAST
with Maple Syrup
Yield: 6–8 servings

You can dress up this dish by adding a few dried cranberries or plums if you like. Soak cranberries or plums in the sherry for 10 minutes and then drain them, reserving the sherry. Add the sherry as directed, and add the fruit to the sauce along with the broth.

2 boneless skin-on turkey breast halves (about 2 pounds each)
Kosher salt and freshly ground black pepper to taste
¼ cup dry sherry
¼ cup sherry vinegar
½ cup homemade or low-salt canned chicken broth
1 cup maple syrup
2 teaspoons lightly chopped fresh marjoram
4 tablespoons unsalted butter

DIRECTIONS:
1. Heat the oven to 425 degrees F. Rinse the turkey breasts and pat dry. Trim any silver skin from the meat side of the breasts. Scrape the tendon out of the tender, if it's still attached, and pat the tender back into place. Trim the edges of the skin so there's about ¼" overhang.* With a sharp chef's knife or boning knife, score the skin in a ½" crosshatch pattern. Try to cut only through the skin and not into the meat. Season the breasts on both sides with salt and pepper.
2. Heat one large (or two if needed) ovenproof sauté pan or skillet (don't use nonstick) over medium-high heat for 1 minute. Put the turkey in the pans, skin side down, and let it sear. As fat collects in the pan, spoon it off once or twice. When the skin turns medium brown, after about 6 minutes, reduce the heat to medium. Continue to cook until much of the fat is rendered from the turkey and the skin looks crisp and deep golden brown (another 2–4 minutes).
3. Flip the breasts to lie skin side up. Spoon off any remaining fat, and put the pan in the hot oven at 425 degrees F. Reduce heat to 395 degrees.

Roast until the turkey is cooked to your liking: 20–30 minutes for medium rare and 30–40 minutes for medium well. To check for doneness, cut into a breast or use an instant-read thermometer; cook to 135 degrees F for medium rare, 155 degrees F for medium well.

4. Transfer the turkey to a plate or platter and tent with foil to keep warm. Combine pan juices in one pan if two pans were used in the oven. Place pan on medium high heat on the stove and pour in the sherry and sherry vinegar. Immediately scrape the pan with a wooden spoon to release any cooked-on bits. Boil until the liquid has reduced to about ⅓ cup (about 3 minutes). Add the broth, maple syrup, marjoram, and ¼ teaspoon salt. Boil until the liquid is reduced by about half (about 6 minutes). Reduce the heat to low and blend the butter into the sauce by consistently stirring or swirling the pan. Slice the turkey thinly on an angle, arrange it on heated plates, and spoon the sauce over or around it. Serve right away.

*For convenience you may ask the butcher in your market to trim the turkey breasts according to the above guidelines.

PALM BEACH LINZER TORTE
with Dark Chocolate Dobosh Glaze

Yield: 1 (11" or 12") torte

FOR CRUST

2 cups sifted all-purpose flour

1 cup Scharffenberger unsweetened natural cocoa powder, sifted

2 teaspoons sifted cinnamon

½ teaspoon powdered cloves

¼ teaspoon salt

10 ounces (1¼ cups) butter, cut up

1⅔ cups sugar

1 pound (4½ cups) walnuts, finely ground

1 egg plus 1 egg yolk

rind of 1 large Meyer lemon (or 2 small), finely grated

FOR FILLING

¼ cup fine dry bread crumbs

24 ounces (2 cups) seedless lingonberry or raspberry jam

FOR ALMOND TOPPING

1 egg yolk

1 teaspoon water

1 cup slivered almonds

FOR CHOCOLATE FILLING AND GLAZE

8 ounces Scharffenberger 70% cacao bittersweet chocolate, chopped

½ pound (1 cup) sweet butter

1 teaspoon vanilla extract

3 egg yolks

2 tablespoons confectioner's sugar

DIRECTIONS:

1. To make the crust, put flour, cocoa powder, cinnamon, cloves, and salt in a large mixing bowl. Cut in butter until mixture resembles coarse crumbs. Stir in the sugar and walnuts. Mix egg and yolk slightly and

add along with lemon rind. Work the dough with your hands a bit and then turn it out into a large bowl and blend until it firmly holds together. Form it into a slightly flattened ball.

2. Adjust rack one-third of the way up from bottom of oven. Preheat oven to 400 degrees. Butter an 11"–12" shallow pan, preferably with a removable bottom. The bottom must be lined with buttered paper or the crust will stick to the pan. Also butter the pan to hold the paper in place. Divide the dough in half, and press one half evenly and firmly over the bottom of the pan. Press into place with your fingers, about 1¼" to 1½" up on the sides. Bake the shell for about 15 minutes, or until barely colored.

3. While the shell is baking, roll the remaining dough between two large pieces of wax paper to about ¼" to ¾" thickness. Leave both pieces of paper on the dough and slip a cookie sheet underneath. Place in freezer for 15 minutes.

4. Meanwhile, remove baked shell from the oven. Reduce temperature to 350 degrees and raise the rack to ⅓ of the way down from top of oven

5. For the filling, sprinkle bread crumbs evenly over bottom of crust. Stir the jam until soft, and spread into shell. Remove the dough from the freezer and from cookie sheet. Place on a large board. Remove top piece of paper and cut the dough through bottom of paper into 11"–12" round pan, removing paper. Place dough round on top of jam-filled bottom of torte. Press the outer edge with your fingertips to the prebaked shell.

6. For almond topping, first make egg glaze by mixing yolk and water. Brush over pastry and sprinkle with slivered almonds. Bake for 1 hour or so, until almonds are browned. Remove from oven and cool inverted on rack. When removing torte from pan, if the sides stick, release them carefully with a sharp small knife. The sides should be crisp. Remove torte from pan and invert again, and remove clear wrap or foil.

7. For the dark chocolate dobosh filling and glaze, melt the chocolate in the top of a small double boiler over hot water on moderate heat. Remove and stir until smooth. Set aside to cool.

8. In the small bowl of an electric mixer, cream the butter. Add vanilla and egg yolks and beat well. Add sugar and cooled chocolate. Beat until thoroughly mixed, scraping the bowl occasionally.

9. Place four strips of wax paper around the outer edges of a large (12" plus) cake plate. Place torte on the plate and, with a narrow spatula, spread with a thin layer of chocolate filling. Spread the remaining chocolate smoothly around the sides first and then over the top.

10. Remove the wax paper strips by pulling out by a narrow end. Refrigerate torte for several hours to set the glaze. Store in refrigerator and serve cold.

———————

Is it a chocolate Linzer torte or a Linzer dobosh torte? The question is not meant to be a puzzle but to show a creative conversion of a traditional chocolate torte (dobosh) to a wonderful new creation, combining traditional Scharffen Berger chocolate with the tasty addition of what made the Linzer torte famous. This is a famous Viennese pastry with the addition of the flavor of the world's finest chocolate, worthy of the extravagant surroundings and cuisines of Palm Beach.

PALM BEACH CLUB PIZZA

Yield: 2 (10"–12") pizza

FOR THE DOUGH

2 (¼-ounce) envelopes dry yeast; or 2 (3–5-ounce) cakes fresh yeast
1 teaspoon sugar
1 cup lukewarm water, divided
3 cups all-purpose flour
2 tablespoons yellow cornmeal
1½ teaspoons salt
2 tablespoons olive oil

FOR THE SAUCE

2 tablespoons butter
¾ cup chopped scallions
½ cup chopped green peppers
¾ cup chopped mushrooms
3 cups diced (¼") tomatoes
½ cup sour cream
4 tablespoons sugar
¾ tablespoons salt

FOR THE TOPPINGS

1 tablespoon olive oil
6 slices thick-cut lean bacon, cooked and crumbled
2 cups rotisserie-cooked chicken breast, sliced thin
¼ cup sliced scallions
1 cup diced (¼") Roma tomatoes
½ teaspoon celery salt
¾ cup sour cream tomato sauce (from recipe)
¼ cup mayonnaise
1½ cups shredded swiss cheese
1 medium avocado, sliced lengthwise

DIRECTIONS:

1. To make dough, sprinkle dry yeast (or crumble fresh yeast) and sugar over ¼ cup water. Leave for 10 minutes. Combine flour, cornmeal, and salt. Add remaining water and oil to yeast mixture. Form this dough into a ball. Let rise for 1 hour. Form this dough into two balls. Knead dough until smooth. Press with fingers or roll with rolling pin into two oiled 14" × 16" baking sheets. Let rise 30 minutes. Pierce dough with fork. Brush with olive oil.

2. For sauce, heat butter in heavy skillet. Add onions, peppers, and mushrooms, and cook for 10 minutes, until lightly browned. Add tomatoes and juice, sour cream, sugar, and salt and simmer for 1 hour or until thickened.

3. To assemble and cook pizza, preheat oven to 450 degrees F. Brush pizza crust with olive oil. In large bowl combine bacon, sliced chicken, onions, tomatoes, and celery salt. Fold in sour cream sauce and mayonnaise. Spread mixture over entire crust. Top with cheese. Bake 12 minutes. Remove from pan in the oven. Arrange avocado slices in pinwheel fashion on top.

PALM BEACH WILD BURGERS

Yield: 6 burgers

24 ounces ground sirloin
8 ounces yellowfin tuna, ground
¼ cup Sutter Home Zinfandel
12 scallions, minced
3 tablespoons sesame seeds
6 ounces teriyaki sauce, divided
6 tablespoons grated ginger
¼ cup fine fresh Italian bread crumbs
vegetable oil for brushing the grill
6 tomato slices
6 ounces sesame oil, divided
3 teaspoons sriracha chili sauce (may be substituted with your favorite
    hot chili sauce)
3 ounces raisin juice concentrate
3 ounces red onion, minced
9 garlic cloves, minced
3 jalapeños, seeded and minced
3 teaspoons lemon zest
3 teaspoons shredded carrot
3 teaspoons minced cilantro
3 teaspoons five-spice powder
3 tablespoons lemon juice
3 ounces rice wine vinegar
3 cups mixed greens
6 ciabatta rolls, halved

DIRECTIONS:

1. In a grill with cover, prepare a medium-hot fire for direct-heat cooking.
2. In a medium-sized bowl, combine sirloin, yellowfin tuna, Zinfandel, scallions, sesame seeds, 3 ounces teriyaki sauce, ginger, and fresh bread crumbs. Form into six patties. Reserve, refrigerated.

3. Marinate tomato slices in 3 ounces sesame oil, sriracha hot sauce, and raisin juice concentrate. Caramelize in a sauté pan on the grill. Set aside.
4. Combine red onion, garlic, jalapeño, lemon zest, apples, cilantro, five-spice powder, lemon juice, remaining teriyaki sauce, rice wine vinegar, and remaining sesame oil. Toss with mixed greens.
5. Brush the grill with vegetable oil. Place the patties on the grill and cook, turning once, until done to your preference (5–6 minutes each side for medium rare). During the last few minutes of cooking, mark ciabatta on grill.
6. Put burgers on buns with caramelized tomato and salad and serve.

PALM BEACH BRIE, MANGO, AND ROASTED ALMOND NAPOLEON

Yield: 16 servings

1 (15–16-ounce) Brie wheel
6 tablespoons softened cream cheese
6 ounces Breakstone's sour cream
1 tablespoon freshly squeezed key lime juice
6 ounces thinly sliced Scottish smoked salmon
⅓ cup almond granola
⅔ cup toasted chopped almonds, divided
1 cup sliced fresh or dried mango, divided
1 tablespoon chopped fresh fine herbs (equal parts dill, chives, tarragon, and Italian parsley), divided
⅓ cup apricot jam, stirred and heated until liquid
⅓ cup toasted chopped almonds
4 key limes, sliced

DIRECTIONS:

1. Refrigerate Brie until firm and slice horizontally into two halves.
2. Combine softened cream cheese, sour cream, and lime juice and spread evenly over cut side of bottom half of brie. Add thin layer of smoked salmon. Sprinkle with granola and ⅓ cup chopped almonds.
3. Top granola and toasted almonds with ⅔ cup of thinly sliced fresh or dried mango and ½ tablespoons fresh herbs. Top with remaining half of brie. Add ⅓ cup mango to heated apricot jam and spread over top half of brie. Sprinkle with remaining herbs and almonds.
4. For each serving cut a small wedge, about 1 ounce, and serve with a selection of crackers and sliced key limes.

PALM BEACH'S FAVORITE CLASSIC PRALINE AND PEANUT BUTTER CHEESECAKE

Yield: 10 servings

FOR THE CRUST
1 cup roasted peanuts, ground

2 cups graham crackers, coarsely crushed

4 ounces Jif creamy peanut butter, melted

1 teaspoon grated fresh orange peel

FOR THE FILLING
8 ounces Jif creamy peanut butter

½ ounce orange liqueur (e.g., Grand Marnier, Cointreau, etc.) or orange
  juice concentrate

1 pound light cream cheese

1¼ cups dark brown sugar

1½ teaspoons vanilla

3 large eggs

1 cup roasted peanuts, finely chopped

FOR THE PRALINE SAUCE
¼ cup dark brown sugar

4 tablespoons Simply Jif peanut butter

½ cup heavy cream

½ ounce orange liqueur

½ cup roasted peanuts, chopped

20 roasted peanut halves

DIRECTIONS:
1. To make the crust, combine the roasted ground peanuts, crushed graham crackers, and melted Jif peanut butter in a nonreactive bowl. Press into the bottom and 1" up the sides of a 9" springform pan.
2. For the filling, preheat oven to 300 degrees F.
3. Cream Jif peanut butter with orange liqueur (or juice concentrate), cream cheese, sugar, and vanilla. Add eggs gradually, beating until

smooth. Stir in peanuts. Pour filling into crust and bake for 1½ hours, until barely set. Cool in pan on rack. (Note: filling may be prepared 48 hours in advance if covered and refrigerated.)

4. For the sauce, heat sugar and Simply Jif peanut butter over medium-high heat, stirring until smooth. Whisk in cream and orange flavor (liqueur or concentrate) until sugar barely begins to caramelize. Add peanuts. Cool to lukewarm. Slice cheesecake, top with praline sauce, and garnish with peanut halves.

GRILLED SWORDFISH CUBAN STYLE
Pescado ala Parilla La Cubano

Yield: 4 servings

FOR FRESH TOMATO SALSA

1 cup chopped red and yellow tomatoes

¼ cup chopped tomatillo

¼ cup chopped avocado

2 tablespoons snipped fresh cilantro

1 medium fresh jalapeño, seeded and finely chopped

1 clove garlic, minced

½ tablespoon each fresh lime and lemon juice

¼ teaspoon salt

¼ teaspoon freshly ground black pepper

FOR SWORDFISH

2 pounds fresh or frozen swordfish steaks cut 1" thick

2 large cloves garlic, halved

4 cups 7UP

2 tablespoons each freshly squeezed lime and lemon juice

½ teaspoon salt

1 teaspoon ground cumin

¼ teaspoon freshly ground pepper

¼ cup pure Spanish olive oil, plus olive oil to season the grill

DIRECTIONS:

1. In a medium bowl combine all salsa ingredients. Serve immediately or cover and chill for up to 4 hours.

2. Thaw the fish, if frozen. Rinse fish, pat dry with paper towels. Cut fish into four serving-size pieces. Rub fish on both sides with cut sides of garlic. Place fish in a shallow glass dish and drizzle with 7UP and lemon and lime juice. Cover and marinate, refrigerated, for 30 minutes, turning once. Drain fish. In a small bowl combine salt, cumin, black pepper, and olive oil. Brush both sides of the fish with this seasoned olive-oil mixture.

3. Brush a cold grill with olive oil. Grill fish on rack of uncovered grill directly over medium-hot heat for 8–12 minutes or until fish flakes easily when tested with a fork, turning once halfway through grilling. Serve swordfish with fresh tomato salsa.

CRISPY PHYLLO NAPOLEONS

with American Maytag Blue Cheese and Washington State Apples

Yield: 8 servings

FOR COMPOTE

4½ cups diced apple compote (using water to cover, ½ cup sugar, 2 [1"] cinnamon sticks); or 4½ cups apple pie filling

FOR PHYLLO NAPOLEONS

3 large sheets frozen phyllo dough, thawed
2 tablespoons butter, melted
6 tablespoons powdered sugar, divided
¼ cup ground hazelnuts, divided
cooking spray

YOU WILL ALSO NEED

6 ounces Maytag blue cheese, crumbled
½ cup fat-free caramel sundae syrup or maple syrup

DIRECTIONS:

1. To prepare compote, combine apples, water, sugar, and cinnamon in a large saucepan; bring to a boil. Reduce heat; simmer, uncovered, 35 minutes or until liquid almost evaporates. Cool completely. Discard cinnamon sticks and vanilla bean.

2. To prepare phyllo Napoleons, preheat oven to 350 degrees F. Line a large baking sheet with parchment paper. Place 1 phyllo sheet on parchment paper and lightly brush with butter. Sprinkle with 2 tablespoons powdered sugar and 4 teaspoons hazelnuts. Repeat layers twice.

3. Using a sharp knife or pizza cutter, cut the phyllo into 24 (3" × 2½") rectangles. Cover phyllo with parchment paper. Coat bottom of another baking sheet with cooking spray; place, coated side down, on top of phyllo.

4. Bake at 350 degrees for 12 minutes or until golden. Carefully remove top baking sheet and parchment paper; cool phyllo rectangles on bottom baking sheet on a wire rack.
5. Place 1 phyllo rectangle on each of eight dessert plates. Top each rectangle with 1½ tablespoons compote (or pie filling) and about 1 tablespoon crumbled blue cheese. Repeat layers with remaining phyllo rectangles, compote, and cheese, ending with phyllo rectangles. Drizzle each serving with 1 tablespoon caramel syrup (or maple syrup). Serve immediately.

Tip: Use a pizza cutter to slice through the sheets of phyllo dough without ripping and tearing.

PICANTE SLICED PORK
with Cheddar and Goat Cheese
Yield: 6 servings

4 garlic cloves

2 teaspoons salt

1 teaspoon ground black pepper

1 teaspoon ground allspice

1 teaspoon ground cardamom

½ teaspoon ground nutmeg

1 cup plain yogurt

2 ounces lemon juice

2 pounds boneless pork collar butt, thinly sliced

24 mint leaves, chopped, divided into thirds.

8 ounces crumbled goat cheese

8 ounces shredded mild or sharp cheddar cheese

DIRECTIONS:

1. In large bowl, combine garlic, salt, pepper, allspice, cardamom, and nutmeg. Stir in yogurt and lemon juice. Add pork; coat well and marinate for 1 hour.

2. Meanwhile chop mint leaves, setting ⅔ of the chopped leaves aside for garnish.

3. On grill, cook marinated pork 5–8 minutes, turning as needed, until it reaches an internal temperature of 138 degrees F. Let rest briefly. Sprinkle evenly with half of the remaining chopped mint leaves.

4. Top grilled pork slices with crumbled goat cheese and shredded cheddar.

5. Place pork slices underneath broiler just long enough to melt the cheese. Sprinkle with remaining mint leaves and wrap in freezer bag to freeze until ready to serve.

6. Remove from freezer 30 minutes to 1 hour before reheating at 375 degrees F in preheated oven in uncovered roasting pan. Remove from

oven when heated through. Sprinkle with remaining chopped mint leaves before serving on large platter or on individual dinner plates.

Serving suggestions: Great with risotto rice; short-cut pasta, such as penne; or garlic mashed potatoes.

PIEDMONT WHITE TRUFFLE BURGERS
Al Gremolata with Frisée Greens and Pancetta

Yield: 6 burgers

FOR GREMOLATA FONTINA

1 lemon
¾ cup finely chopped parsley
3 garlic cloves, finely chopped
6 ounces shredded fontina

FOR FRISÉE GREENS AND PANCETTA

8 ounces (½ regular head) frisée leaves, torn into bite-sized pieces
2 ounces pancetta, cooked to a crisp and coarsely chopped
2 tablespoons fine extra-virgin olive oil
1 tablespoon champagne vinegar
2 tablespoons Sutter Home chardonnay
freshly ground pepper and fine sea salt to taste
6 ounces grated Grana Padano, as a topping or garnish

FOR BURGERS

2 pounds ground beef chuck
2 tablespoons plus ¼ cup extra-virgin olive oil, divided
2 tablespoons white truffle paste
2 tablespoons fresh lemon juice
1 tablespoon chopped fresh sage leaves
¼ cup Sutter Home Cabernet Sauvignon
½ cup coarsely ground Grissini breadsticks
2 teaspoons fine sea salt
1 teaspoon finely ground pepper
vegetable oil for brushing the grill rack, as needed
6 rosemary focaccia rolls

DIRECTIONS:

1. Light a charcoal grill with cover, or ignite a gas grill and set to medium high.

2. To make the gremolata, remove lemon peel in long strips from lemon, using a vegetable peeler. Mince lemon peel. Transfer to a small bowl. Mix in parsley, garlic, and fontina. Gremolata may be made 1 day in advance.

3. To prepare frisée greens and pancetta, wash and dry frisée leaves and tear into bite-sized pieces. Cook pancetta to a crisp, chop coarsely, and add to frisée. In a small bowl, whisk olive oil, champagne vinegar, and chardonnay; season to taste. Toss with greens and pancetta mixture. Keep refrigerated.

4. For the white truffle burgers, gently mix the ground beef in a large bowl with olive oil, white truffle paste, lemon juice, chopped sage leaves, wine, and coarsely ground Grissini breadsticks. Season to taste. Shape the meat into six equal-sized patties, slightly larger than the size of the rolls. Cover and refrigerate until ready to grill. Brush the grill with vegetable oil. Grill burgers over medium-hot fire for about 4 minutes each side, turning once. Top burgers with equal amounts of gremolata fontina and cook 4 minutes longer, or until cheese mixture begins to melt. Meanwhile, brush roll halves on top side with olive oil and place on grill rack to toast until golden brown.

5. To assemble the open-faced burgers, top all twelve roll halves with frisée green mixture; sprinkle greens with grated Grana Padano. Place the six burger patties on bottom halves of rolls and serve immediately.

REDLANDS POTATO AND AVOCADO PIZETTA
with Farm-Made Lake Okeechobee Goat Cheese
Yield: 8 Pizettas

16 ounces pizza dough

3 tablespoons olive oil

4 cloves roasted garlic cloves, pureed

8 ounces Lake Okeechobee farm-made goat cheese, crumbled

1 cup diced avocados, ¼" dice

4 tablespoons extra-virgin olive oil

salt and pepper to taste

FOR POTATOES

2 tablespoons butter

2 tablespoons roasted garlic oil or olive oil

8 Redland, Florida, baby red-skin potatoes, scrubbed and sliced into ¼"
   slices, peel on

salt and pepper to taste

DIRECTIONS:

1. Preheat oven to 475 degrees F. Partition dough into 2-ounce portions.
   Roll to ¼" thickness. Arrange circles on heavy baking sheet. Brush
   dough with extra-virgin olive oil. Spread with roasted garlic puree
   and salt to taste. Prepare goat cheese and avocados and set aside.

2. In the meantime, prepare the potatoes. In a large skillet, heat the
   butter and oil. When the butter foams, add the potatoes. Season
   with salt and pepper. Stir, cover the skillet, and cook for 10 minutes,
   tossing often. Uncover the skillet and fry until nicely browned and
   crisp. Place on paper towels to drain.

3. Spread potatoes in one layer on pizettas, covering the garlic puree.
   Sprinkle pizettas with avocados and goat cheese crumbs.

4. Bake pizettas until golden brown, about 10 minutes. Arrange pizettas
   on a platter and serve.

POACHED GULF OYSTERS
with Savory Plum Mango Salsa
Yield: 12 servings

12 Gulf (or Maryland, or Pacific) oysters
2 cups water
1 teaspoon flaky sea salt
1 lemon, zested and juiced

FOR SALSA
2¼ cups fresh California red-fleshed plums, diced
2¼ cups fresh mango, diced
¼ cup red onion, diced
4–5 plum tomatoes, seeded, peeled, and diced
4 fresh lemons, juiced
¼ cup extra-virgin olive oil
1 cup chopped fresh basil, plus 12 small basil sprigs for garnish
salt and freshly ground pepper (optional)

DIRECTIONS:
1. Remove the oysters from the shell and place in a bowl. Pour any juice that comes from the shells in with the oysters. Set shells on a service tray.
2. In a shallow saucepan, place 2 cups of water with 1 teaspoon salt and the juice from the lemon. Bring to a simmer.
3. Quickly poach the oysters (no longer than 30 seconds) and place back in the shells. Allow to cool slightly.
4. Mix all salsa ingredients. Let sit to mingle flavors. Place on chilled appetizer dish. Add 1 oyster to each dish and garnish with a sprig of basil.

POLLOCK FROM THE OVEN
with Almonds and Herbs
Yield: 4 servings

4 (8–12-ounce) Buena Ventura salted Alaskan pollock fillets

2 cups milk

2 cloves garlic, chopped

1½ cups blanched almonds

6 tablespoons olive oil, divided

1 cup finely chopped onions

1 teaspoon finely chopped garlic

1 tablespoon finely chopped fresh parsley

1½ cups fish stock or fresh or canned chicken or vegetable broth,
   divided

1 large onion, peeled and sliced paper-thin

1 medium bay leaf, sliced

½ teaspoon crumbled dry thyme

¼ cup strained fresh lime juice

1 teaspoon sea salt, divided

freshly ground black pepper to taste

DIRECTIONS:

1. Soak the salted fish in water for three days, changing the water every 12 hours. Add milk and garlic to the fish and leave in the refrigerator an added day. Remove from the refrigerator, drain, the water and rinse. Set aside until ready to use.

2. Preheat oven to 350 degrees F, and toast the almonds for 10 minutes. Remove almonds from oven and raise the heat to 400 degrees F. In an electric blender, grind the almonds very finely.

3. In a heavy 12" skillet, heat 2 tablespoons olive oil over moderate heat. Add almonds, onions, garlic, and parsley, stirring frequently. Cook 5 minutes, until onions are translucent. Add ½ cup fish stock and ½ teaspoon sea salt, stirring well. Remove the pan from the heat.

4. Pour remaining olive oil into a shallow open baking pan that is large enough to hold the fish. Spread oil evenly over bottom of pan. Spread

sliced onions in the dish and scatter sliced bay leaf and thyme over all. Place the fish on top. Sprinkle with the lime juice, a little salt (if any), and pepper to taste.

5. With a small spatula, spread the onion-and-almond mixture evenly over the fish. Pour on the remaining cup of stock. Bake uncovered in the middle of the oven at 400 degrees F for 30–40 minutes, or until fish is firm when pressed lightly with a finger. Serve at once from the baking dish.

POMEGRANATE BREAKFAST OR BRUNCH WAFFLES
with Pomegranate Chocolate Sauce and Crumbled Bacon

Yield: 8 medium waffles

FOR CHOCOLATE SAUCE

1½ cups half-and-half cream or whole milk

½ cup semisweet chocolate-fudge sauce or syrup

6 egg yolks

½ cup Stiebs pomegranate juice

¼ cup Stiebs freeze-dried pomegranate powder

FOR WAFFLES AND BACON

½ pound sliced bacon

2 cups unbleached all-purpose flour

2 tablespoons sugar

2 teaspoons baking powder

1 teaspoon sea salt

2 tablespoons unsalted butter, melted

1 cup whole milk

½ cup Stiebs pomegranate concentrate

2 large eggs, at room temperature

DIRECTIONS:

1. Combine half-and-half or milk with chocolate-fudge sauce or syrup. Constantly stirring, bring to a boil. Remove from heat.
2. Combine pomegranate juice and powder and blend to combine.
3. Lightly whip the yolks. Add the pomegranate juice–powder mixture to the whipped egg yolks.
4. Slowly add the hot chocolate cream or whole milk to the pomegranate-egg mixture. Stir to combine, and return to the saucepan. Bring slowly to a simmer, constantly stirring with a wooden spoon until the sauce coats the back of a spoon. To avoid curdling, never allow the sauce to come to a boil
5. Cook bacon to a crisp, drain, and coarsely crumble.
6. Preheat an electric waffle iron.

7. Combine flour, sugar, baking powder, and salt in a large bowl. Whisk together to blend.

8. Pour milk and pomegranate concentrate into a glass measuring cup and microwave for 1 minute at full power. Pour into medium-size bowl, and whisk in melted butter and eggs. Add liquid ingredients to flour mixture, whisking just until blended. Grease waffle iron with cooking spray. Spread ⅓ cup batter over each iron and sprinkle with 8 ounces of crumbled bacon on top. Close waffle iron and cook until done. Repeat with remaining batter and bacon. Serve with warm pomegranate chocolate sauce.

POMEGRANATE CHOCOLATE PUDDING

Yield: 8 servings

1/3 cup sugar

1/3 cup Dutch-process cocoa powder

2 tablespoons cornstarch

1/8 teaspoon salt

1¾ cup whole milk

¼ cup heavy cream

4 ounces bittersweet chocolate, finely chopped

8 ounces pomegranate seeds with arils

1 teaspoon vanilla

1 tablespoon dark rum

DIRECTIONS:

1. Whisk sugar, cocoa, cornstarch, and salt in a 2-quart saucepan. Slowly add milk and cream, whisking constantly; bring to a simmer over medium heat. Cook while whisking until thickened and beginning to bubble at edges (12–15 minutes). Add chocolate and pomegranate seeds and stir until well combined (about 30 seconds). Remove from heat; stir in vanilla and rum.

2. Divide between eight 4-ounce ramekins, cover with plastic wrap, and chill until set (about 1½ hours).

POMEGRANATE ICE CREAM SODA COCKTAIL

Yield: 4 (12–16 ounce) highball cocktails

3 cups (24 ounces) pure pomegranate juice
1 cup (8 ounces) soda water or sparkling mineral water
½ cup (4 ounces) agave nectar
⅛ teaspoon champagne yeast
4 scoops (#12 or #16) low-fat vanilla ice cream

DIRECTIONS:

1. Bring pomegranate juice, sparkling water, and agave nectar to a simmer in a 4-quart saucepan over medium-low heat, and cook, stirring occasionally, until lightly reduced, about 20 minutes. Stir in yeast and drape a large kitchen towel over saucepan; let cool for 24 hours.

2. Using a funnel, pour soda cocktail into a sterilized 1-quart plastic soda bottle and allow to refrigerate until icy cold. Open bottle and pour over 1 scoop ice cream in a 6- to 8-ounce martini cocktail glass just before serving.

POMEGRANATE NUT GRANOLA BARS

Yield: 12 servings

4 cups rolled oats
1 cup raw sliced almonds
1 cup sweetened shredded coconut
1 cup fruit-and-nut granola mix
1 cup pomegranate seeds
½ cup coconut oil
½ cup light brown sugar
½ cup almond butter
½ cup maple syrup
1 teaspoon vanilla extract
½ teaspoon salt
1½ teaspoons cinnamon
½ teaspoon nutmeg

DIRECTIONS:

1. Preheat oven to 350 degrees F with a rack in the middle position. Line an oiled 13" × 9" pan with parchment and set aside. Mix oats, almonds, coconut, granola mix, and pomegranate seeds in a large mixing bowl.

2. Combine coconut oil, brown sugar, almond butter, and maple syrup in a small saucepan over medium-low heat and stir until dissolved (3–4 minutes). Stir in vanilla, salt, cinnamon, and nutmeg and pour over oat mixture, tossing well to combine.

3. Press the granola mixture evenly into a prepared pan by pressing against a sheet of wax paper or plastic wrap on surface. Remove paper or plastic wrap and bake 20–25 minutes, until lightly golden and fragrant. Remove from oven and allow granola bars to cool completely before cutting into twelve bars. Wrap bars in wax or parchment paper and store in an airtight container for up to three weeks.

PORTOBELLO AND PROSCIUTTO PIZZA
with Raspberry
Yield: 2 (12") pizza

FOR THE DOUGH
2 (¼-ounce) envelopes dry yeast or 2 (3–5-ounce) cakes fresh yeast
1 teaspoon sugar
1 cup lukewarm water, divided
3 cups all-purpose flour
2 tablespoons yellow cornmeal
1½ teaspoons salt
2 tablespoons olive oil

FOR THE SAUCE
1½ tablespoons extra-virgin olive oil
¾ cup finely diced shallots
½ cup crushed fresh raspberries
¾ cup finely diced baby portobello mushrooms, stems and caps
½ cup diced tomatoes (¼" dice)
2 tablespoons organic sugar
¾ teaspoon sea salt
½ cup Sebastian Zinfandel

FOR THE TOPPINGS
½ cup sugar-free seedless raspberry jam
2 ounces gorgonzola dolce
2 ounces fontina cheese, shredded
2 garlic cloves, finely diced
sea salt and freshly ground black pepper to taste
2 teaspoons freshly chopped oregano
10 ounces baby portobello mushrooms, whole or halves
1 ounces Parmigiana-Reggiano, shaved
2 ounces prosciutto, thinly sliced and cut into squares
1 scallion, slivered into long ribbons

DIRECTIONS:

1. To make dough, sprinkle dry yeast (or crumble fresh yeast) and sugar over ¼ cup water. Leave for 10 minutes. Combine flour, cornmeal, and salt. Add remaining water and oil to yeast mixture. Form this dough into a ball. Let rise for 1 hour. Form this dough into two balls. Knead dough until smooth. Press with fingers or roll with rolling pin into two oiled 14" × 16" baking sheets. Let rise 30 minutes. Pierce dough with fork. Brush with olive oil.

2. For the sauce, heat the olive oil in a heavy skillet. Add shallots, raspberries, and mushrooms, and cook for 5 minutes, until lightly browned.

3. Add diced tomatoes, sugar, and salt and simmer over low heat until thickened (about 30 minutes). Add Zinfandel and reduce lightly for 10 minutes, then remove the sauce from the heat.

4. To top and cook pizza: Preheat oven to 450 degrees F. Brush pizza crust with 2 tablespoons olive oil. Evenly spread raspberry jam onto the pizza. Cover with gorgonzola and fontina.

5. In a large iron skillet over medium heat, add the remaining olive oil. Add shallots and cook until softened (about 8 minutes).

6. Add the garlic and oregano, and cook until fragrant (about 2 minutes). Add portobello mushrooms and cook until the liquid is evaporated and mushrooms become tender (about 10 minutes). Add salt and pepper to taste.

7. Fold in the Zinfandel sauce and spread the whole mushroom mixture with sauce over the entire crust. Sprinkle with parmesan.

8. Reduce the oven heat to 425 degrees F and bake the pizza on the prepared, lightly oiled baking pan for 15 minutes.

9. Remove from the oven and allow to cool for a short while. Top pizza with prosciutto and slivered scallions. Cut into six to ten wedges, and serve immediately.

PORTUGUESE SEAFOOD WOK
with Lemon, Saffron, and Spices
Yield: 8 servings

2 pounds Baca Rico salted pollock or scrod

2 cups milk

2 garlic cloves

12 shrimp, peeled and deveined

½ pound scallops

12 mussels in shells

12 small clams in shells

3 tablespoons olive oil

1 bay leaf

1½ cups sliced carrots

2 cups sliced white onions

2 cups chopped celery

1 fennel bulb, sliced

3 jalapeño peppers

¼ cup sliced shallots

3 tablespoons roasted garlic

2 pinches saffron

2 tablespoons butter

2 tablespoons chopped fresh thyme

2 tablespoons dried mint

1 cup sherry

½ cup lemon juice

2 quarts fish stock or clam juice

salt and pepper to taste

¼ cup chopped parsley

DIRECTIONS:

1. Soak the salted fish in water for three days and refrigerate, changing the water every day. Add milk and garlic to the salted fish and leave refrigerated one added day. Remove from refrigerator, drain the

water, and rinse. Cut into big pieces and sprinkle the pieces with flour. Set aside until ready to use.

2. Heat oil in a large open pan or wok. Add bay leaf, vegetables, jalapeños, shallots, garlic, and saffron. Sauté until onions are translucent. Stir in butter, thyme, and mint. Add sherry and lemon juice to deglaze the pan. Add fish stock and bring to a boil. Poach fish, shrimp, and scallops for 8 minutes. Do not bring stock to a boil. Add mussels and clams.

3. When shells open (6–8 minutes), add salt and pepper to taste. Garnish with parsley.

PORTABELLA VIVANTI* RISOTTO
with Lightly Toasted Hazelnuts and Basil Truffle Oil
Yield: 6 servings

1 quart vegetable broth
4 tablespoons Tuscan basil truffle oil**
½ cup finely chopped scallions
1 pound thinly sliced fresh baby portabella mushrooms
1¼ cups arborio rice
½ cup pinot grigio dry Italian white wine
1 cup shaved Parmesan cheese, divided
1 cup toasted and peeled hazelnuts, chopped
½ cup thinly sliced basil leaves

DIRECTIONS:

1. Heat the broth in a 2-quart saucepan over high heat, just to simmer. Reduce heat to low.
2. Heat basil truffle oil in 4-quart sauce pot over medium-high heat and cook scallions and sliced portabella mushrooms until onions are tender, stirring occasionally (about 2 minutes). Stir in rice and cook for 3 minutes, stirring occasionally. Stir in wine and cook 1 minute.
3. Pour in just enough broth to cover rice. Bring to a boil over high heat, stirring frequently, until liquid is absorbed.
4. Continue adding broth, 1 cup at a time, stirring frequently until broth is absorbed and rice is creamy and just tender (about 25 minutes). Add in ½ cup Parmesan cheese and hazelnuts until heated through. Season, if desired, with salt and freshly ground black pepper. Top with remaining ½ cup shaved Parmesan cheese and garnish of thinly sliced fresh basil leaves.

*"Vivanti" was the name of our Florence host family, who cooked for us at one of their family dinner gatherings.

**For 4 tablespoons Tuscan basil truffle oil: marinate 1 tablespoon finely chopped basil leaves in 4 tablespoons truffle oil, allow to marinate for 1 hour, and strain the oil before using it.

BAHAMAS POTATO CONCH FRITTER

Yield: 36 fritters

3 large baking or russet potatoes
5 eggs, lightly beaten
1 onion, finely chopped
1 teaspoon ground allspice
1 teaspoon Kosher salt
1 pound conch meat, finely chopped
1 green bell pepper, finely minced
½ scotch bonnet pepper, seeded and minced (about 1 tablespoon)
¼ cup parsley, chopped
1 cup vegetable oil

DIRECTIONS:

1. In a food processor fitted with a grating disk, grate the potatoes. Transfer the mixture to a colander. With your hands, squeeze the mixture to remove excess water.

2. In a large bowl, combine the potatoes with the following eight ingredients (everything except the oil), and mix well.

3. In a heavy 12" skillet, heat the oil over medium high until it sizzles. Add heaping tablespoons of the batter into the pan. Flatten the mounds with the back of a spoon. Fry to a golden brown, turning once. If needed, add more oil to the pan. Dry on paper towels. Serve with lime wedges on the side.

PRALINE CHICKEN ROULADEN

Yield: 4 servings

2 teaspoons olive oil
1 cup sliced mushrooms
¼ cup dry white wine or sherry
¼ teaspoon nutmeg, or to taste
8 ounces cream cheese, softened
1 teaspoon dried thyme
1 teaspoon garlic salt
1 teaspoon dried oregano.
4 boneless, skinless chicken breasts
¼ cup Dixie Crystals free-flowing brown sugar
¼ cup chopped pecans
¼ cup Dijon mustard
⅓ cup chopped parsley

DIRECTIONS:

1. Preheat oven to 350 degrees F. In a small skillet, add the oil. Sauté mushrooms with wine and nutmeg until the wine has evaporated and the mushrooms are softened. Set aside to cool.

2. In a bowl combine cream cheese, thyme, garlic salt, and oregano. Add mushrooms and stir to combine.

3. Pound out each chicken breast until flat. Spread with equal parts of the filling. Roll the chicken and place seam-side down in a baking pan. Bake for 15 minutes.

4. Mix brown sugar, pecans, mustard, and parsley and spread on top of the chicken. Bake an additional 15 minutes, or until cooked through.

PRALINE-SPECKLED WISCONSIN ROUND WHITE POTATOES
with Crabmeat Butter Sauce

Yield: 6 side dishes

2 shallots, minced
6 ounces dry white wine
juice of 1 fresh lime
1 tablespoon heavy cream
6 ounces cold butter
½ mango, sliced
1 tablespoon grated lime zest
6 round white Wisconsin potatoes, medium–large
2 tablespoons Creole seasoning
2 tablespoons vegetable oil
3 ounces lump crabmeat (picked through for shells)
6 ounces Louisiana pecan pralines, coarsely crushed

DIRECTIONS:

1. Place shallots and wine in a pot. Gently reduce to 1 ounce. Add lime juice and heavy cream, and reduce until lightly thickened. Add 2–4 tablespoons butter at a time, fully incorporating each addition by swirling the pot very often. Do not let the sauce boil. Move the pot on and off the heat to maintain a very warm temperature. Strain the sauce into another pot. Add the mango. Using a stick blender, puree the sauce until smooth. Warm the sauce, stir in the lime zest, and keep warm until ready to use.

2. Wash, peel and pat the potatoes dry. Allow potatoes to come to room temperature. Slice potatoes into ¼"–½" slices. Season with Creole seasoning to taste. Sauté potatoes in oil over high heat, turning only once and keeping the seasoning a light brown, not black.

3. Place 2 ounces of the sauce on each of six plates. Place the sliced potatoes on the sauce, split evenly among the plates. Warm 1 ounce of the sauce and the crab meat in a skillet, and place a small amount of crab meat on top of each potato stack. Just before service, sprinkle with crushed pralines.

PULLED PORK WITH LIMONCELLO
on Toasted Foccacia Rolls
Yield: 8 servings

1 (2½–3 pound) pork sirloin roast

½ teaspoon sea salt

½ teaspoon red pepper flakes

1 tablespoon olive oil

2 medium onions, cut into wedges

4 cups limoncello (lemon-flavored beverage from Italy), divided, plus
   more to taste

6 cloves garlic, minced

1 cup marinara sauce

several dashes hot sauce (optional)

8 (4"–6") focaccia rolls, lightly brushed with olive oil and toasted.

8 lettuce leaves

16 ripe tomatoes, sliced

DIRECTIONS:

1. Trim fat from meat if necessary. Cut roast to fit into 3½- to 5-quart crockery cooker. Sprinkle meat with the salt and pepper flakes. In a large skillet, brown roast on all sides in hot oil. Drain off fat. Transfer meat to cooker. Add onions, 1 cup limoncello, and garlic.

2. Cover and cook on low heat for 8–10 hours, or on high heat for 4–5 hours.

3. Meanwhile, in a medium saucepan combine 3 cups limoncello and the marinara sauce. Bring to boiling; reduce heat. Boil gently, uncovered, stirring occasionally, for about 30 mutes, until mixture is reduced to 2 cups. Add limoncello if needed and hot pepper sauce if desired.

4. Transfer roast to a cutting board or serving platter. Using a slotted spoon, remove onions from cooking sauces and place on serving platter. Discard juices. Using two forks, pull meat apart into shreds. To serve, line each focaccia roll with 1 lettuce leaf and 2 tomato slices. Add meat and onions. Spoon on sauce.

PUMPKIN-GLAZED PORK CHOPS
with Fresh Pumpkin Sauce
Yield: 4 servings

4 thick pork chops (approximately 6 ounces each)

½ cup pumpkin puree

½ cup maple sugar

½ cup sauterne or other lightly sweet white wine

½ teaspoon sea salt

pinch ground allspice

3 whole cloves

1 (1") cinnamon stick

1 tablespoon pumpkin seed oil or olive oil

1 cup finely diced fresh pumpkin flesh

2 tablespoons fresh strips of orange zest

DIRECTIONS:

1. In a medium bowl, whisk together the pumpkin puree and sauterne. Add the salt, allspice, cinnamon stick, and cloves. Marinate the pork chops in this from about 3–4 hours up to overnight.

2. Heat the oil in a large skillet over medium-high heat. Lift the pork chops from the marinade and sear in the hot oil until they are browned (2–3 minutes each side). Pour in half the marinade and bring to a boil. Reduce the heat to low and simmer, covered, turning frequently, until the pork chops are cooked through (6–8 minutes). Remove the pork chops from the sauce and keep warm.

3. Reduce the sauce to a sticky glaze, adding finely diced pumpkin and orange zest. Stir well. Plate pork chops and spoon sauce on the side or over the top. Serve immediately.

QUICK 'N' EASY CHICKEN ASPARAGUS PASTA DINNER

Yield: 4 servings

Lemon zest ties all the flavors together in this light and creamy pasta. To make it a meal, serve with a salad of sliced fresh mozzarella and cherry tomatoes tossed with a little fresh basil, balsamic vinegar, and olive oil.

8 ounces whole-wheat penne pasta
1 bunch asparagus, trimmed and cut into ¾" pieces
1½ cups cream of chicken, canned*
4 teaspoons whole-grain mustard
1 teaspoon dried tarragon leaves
1 teaspoon freshly grated lemon zest
2 teaspoons lemon juice
½ cup grated Parmesan cheese, divided

DIRECTIONS:

1. Bring a large pot of water to a boil. Add pasta and cook for 3 minutes less than the package directions. Add asparagus, and continue cooking until the pasta and asparagus are just tender (3 minutes more). Drain and return to the pot.
2. Meanwhile, whisk cream of chicken soup and mustard in a medium saucepan. Bring to a simmer, stirring constantly, and cook until thickened (1–2 minutes). Stir in tarragon, lemon zest, and juice.
3. Stir the sauce into the pasta-asparagus mixture. Cook over medium-high heat, stirring, until the sauce is thick and creamy and coats the pasta (1–2 minutes). Stir in ¼ cup parmesan. Divide the pasta among four bowls and top with the remaining ¼ cup Parmesan.

*If you have leftover rotisserie-cooked chicken, chop into dice and add to the canned cream of chicken.

TOASTED QUINOA SALAD
with Oysters and Snow Peas
Yield: 8 appetizer or 4 main-dish servings

This oyster-studded quinoa salad gets an exciting texture from crunchy snow peas, red bell pepper, and scallions. Feel free to use the oysters fried.

32 fresh Maryland oysters in the shell, shucked and cut into ½" pieces
4 teaspoons reduced-sodium tamari or soy sauce, divided
4 tablespoons plus 2 teaspoons canola oil or extra-virgin olive oil, divided
1½ cups quinoa, rinsed well and drain
2 teaspoons grated or minced garlic
3 cups water
1 teaspoon salt
1 cup trimmed and diagonally sliced snow peas (½" thick)
⅓ cup rice vinegar
1 teaspoon toasted sesame oil
1 cup thinly sliced scallions
⅓ cup finely diced red bell pepper
¼ cup finely chopped fresh cilantro, for garnish

DIRECTIONS:
1. Toss oysters with 2 teaspoons tamari (or soy sauce) in a medium bowl. Set aside.
2. Place a large, high-sided skillet with a tight-fitting lid over medium heat. Add 1 tablespoon canola oil (or olive oil) and quinoa. Cook, stirring constantly, until the quinoa begins to color (6–8 minutes). Add garlic and cook, stirring, until fragrant (about 1 minute more). Add water and salt and bring to a boil. Stir once, cover, and cook over medium heat until the water is absorbed. (Do not stir.) Remove from the heat and let stand, covered, for 5 minutes. Stir in snow peas. Cover and let stand for 5 minutes more.

3. Meanwhile, whisk 3 tablespoons canola or olive oil, the remaining 2 teaspoons tamari, vinegar, and sesame oil in a large bowl. Add the quinoa, snow peas, scallions, and bell pepper; toss to combine.

4. Remove the oysters from the marinade and pat dry. Heat a large skillet over medium-high heat until hot enough to evaporate a drop of water upon contact. Add the remaining 2 teaspoons canola oil and cook the oysters, turning once, until golden and just firm (about 2 minutes total). Gently stir the oysters into the quinoa salad. Serve garnished with cilantro, if desired.

RASPBERRY CHAMBORD BAKED ALASKA TORTE

Yield: 4 servings

1 pint high-quality vanilla ice cream (so there is little air and few ice
    crystals)
1 pint high-quality raspberry ice cream
2 (10-ounce) packages frozen raspberries in syrup, defrosted
1 all-butter pound cake, or any unfrosted cake of your choice
raspberry jam
Chambord liqueur
8 egg whites
½ teaspoon cream of tartar
1 cup sugar

DIRECTIONS:

1. One day before serving, soften vanilla ice cream by placing into a
   freezer at 32-36 degree F so it is pliable enough to incorporate other
   ingredients. Mix about 12 tablespoons vanilla ice cream with about 4
   tablespoons drained raspberries. Fill a 1-quart soufflé dish one-third
   full with this mixture. Freeze for about 3 hours.

2. Soften raspberry ice cream and pack into the dish to two-thirds below
   level. Return to freezer for another 3 hours.

3. Repeat steps 1 and 2 with the two ice creams, filling soufflé dish
   to top.

4. Cover with plastic and return to freezer until ready to use. Refrigerate
   remaining raspberries to use when assembling the dessert.

5. About 1 hour before serving, slice the cake horizontally in half and
   spread raspberry jam on bottom half, topping with second slice.
   Sprinkle each slice generously with Chambord. Cover with plastic
   and set aside.

6. About 30 minutes before serving, beat egg whites and cream of tartar
   on high speed until frothy. Gradually beat in sugar until meringue is
   stiff and glossy.

7. Remove ice cream soufflé mold from freezer. Preheat oven to 500
   degrees F. Unmold ice cream and center on cake base. Drain the

reserved raspberries, add 4–6 tablespoons Chambord, and spoon over and around ice cream soufflé mold. With a rubber spatula, liberally cover the dish with meringue, sealing the meringue to the edge of the dish. Make certain there are no bare spots where ice cream shows through. Swirl the meringue in a pretty pattern. With the back of the spoon, make a depression in the meringue crown.

8. Place Alaska on a cookie sheet and bake on center rack for 3–5 minutes or until meringue is nicely browned but not leathery. Remove from oven and fill depression with Chambord, which will drizzle down. Serve immediately.

RECADO PORK ROAST FROM SPAIN

Yield: 6 servings

3 pounds, one-half Boston butt roast
banana leaves to wrap the pork (optional)
2 cups pitted green Spanish olives
6 thin slices serrano ham (about 3 ounces)
6 ounces shredded manchego cheese
1 tablespoon paprika
6 tablespoons Spanish olive oil
1 cup dry white wine
2 cups diced piquillo peppers

DIRECTIONS:

1. If you are using banana leaves, roll them up, fold them in half, and steam them for 5–10 minutes to make them pliable. When the leaves have cooled, place them shiny-side up on a work surface. Place the pork on the leaves, wrap into a tight bundle, and tie with cotton string.
2. In a small saucepan, combine olives with 1 quart water, bring to a boil, and boil for 5 minutes.
3. Rub pork roast with olive oil and paprika. Top with serrano ham and manchego cheese. Wrap with banana leaves and place in slow cooker. Add white wine and peppers. Cook in slow cooker for 4 hours.
4. To serve, divide olive-and-piquillo-pepper mixture evenly among six serving plates. Top each serving with sliced pork roast, serrano ham, and manchego.

Serving suggestion: If desired, serve with rice and sprinkle with chopped parsley.

WARM SALMON SALAD
with Crispy Potatoes Ala Oasis
Yield: 4 servings

In a kind of updated homage to Swiss rösti, this light salad combines things I love: a bed of crispy potatoes, some delicious fish, flavorful greens, and a perk-you-up dressing.

2 tablespoons extra-virgin olive oil, divided
2 small yellow-fleshed potatoes, such as Yukon Gold, scrubbed, boiled, and cut into ⅛" slices
½ teaspoon salt, divided
1 medium shallot, thinly sliced
2 teaspoons rice vinegar
¼ cup buttermilk
2 (7-ounce) cans boneless, skinless salmon, drained
4 cups arugula

DIRECTIONS:
1. Heat 1 tablespoon oil in a large nonstick skillet over medium-high heat. Add potatoes and cook, turning once, until brown and crispy (5–6 minutes per side). Transfer to a plate and season with ¼ teaspoon salt. Cover with foil to keep warm.
2. Combine the remaining 1 tablespoon oil, ¼ teaspoon salt, shallot, and vinegar in a small saucepan. Bring to a boil over medium heat. Remove from the heat and whisk in buttermilk.
3. Place salmon in a medium bowl and toss with the warm dressing. Divide arugula among four plates, and top with the potatoes and salmon.

ADRIATIC SEA RED COASTAL SHRIMP

Yield: 12 servings

8 tomatoes, chopped
2 garlic cloves, chopped
3 tablespoons capers
¼ cup green olives, sliced
3 tablespoons currants, plumped
1 medium ripe banana, diced to ¼"
olive oil, as needed
3 (12-ounce) packages Contessa Ragin' Cajun Shrimp
¾ cup scallions, sliced
herbed new baby Yukon Gold potatoes, as needed
seasoned black beans, as needed

DIRECTIONS:

1. In a saucepan over medium heat, combine tomatoes, garlic, capers, olives, raisins, and bananas. Simmer approximately 20 minutes, until sauce reaches desired consistency. Reserve and keep warm

2. Brush a 12" skillet with oil and heat over a medium-high flame. Season shrimp. Sauté shrimp until opaque (done), turning once (about 5–7 minutes).

3. Plate shrimp, cover with red sauce, and garnish with scallions. Surround with herbed potatoes and black beans.

JUTTA'S RED CURRANT MERINGUE PIE

Yield: 10 servings

1½ cups sifted, unbleached all-purpose flour
1 teaspoon baking powder
½ cup unsalted soft butter
½ cup sugar
2 egg yolks
1½ teaspoons grated lemon peel

FOR MERINGUE
2 egg whites
½ cup sugar
2 teaspoons cornstarch
2½ cups red currants*

DIRECTIONS:
1. Make the dough in a mixing bowl, sifting together flour and baking powder. Mix in soft butter, sugar, yolks, and lemon zest until mixture holds together. Refrigerate the dough for 30 minutes to 1 hour to make it firm enough to be rolled with a rolling pin.
2. Preheat oven to 325 degrees F. Roll out the dough and put into 10" springform pan.
3. Bake in preheated oven for 25 minutes or until golden brown.
4. To make the filling, whip egg whites until stiff, gradually adding sugar and cornstarch. Beat for 5 minutes. Fold currants into meringue mixture and pour into the prebaked pie crust.
5. Bake for 10 minutes or until the meringue is lightly browned.

*If red currants are not available, try raw raspberries, blackberries, blueberries, or cranberries.

PEASANT-STYLE RED WINE–BRAISED CHICKEN
with Orechiette
Yield: 6 servings

6 large chicken thighs, skinned and boned

sea salt and freshly ground black pepper to taste

2 tablespoons olive oil

½ pound fresh porcini or shiitake mushrooms, sliced

1 cup sliced yellow onion

3 tablespoons slivered garlic

½ cup diced carrots

½ cup thinly sliced celery

2 cups Santa Margarita Chianti red wine

2 cups seeded and diced red tomatoes

1 teaspoon each chopped fresh thyme and marjoram

4 cups fat-free and low-sodium chicken broth

1 tablespoon balsamic vinegar

⅓ cup each chopped fresh flat-leaf parsley and basil leaves

½ pound orecchiette pasta

6 ounces fresh basil leaves

6 ounces freshly shaved Asiago or Parmesan cheese

DIRECTIONS:

1. Season the chicken with salt and pepper. In a large, heavy-bottomed saucepan, heat the oil and quickly brown the chicken. Remove and set aside. Add mushrooms, onions, garlic, carrots, and celery, and sauté until lightly browned.

2. Return the chicken to the pan and add wine, tomatoes, thyme, marjoram, and broth, and bring to a simmer. Cover and simmer until chicken is tender (about 25 minutes). Remove chicken and cut the meat into bite-sized pieces; set aside.

3. Strain the pan liquids, reserve the vegetables, and return liquid to the pan. Bring to a boil and cook over high heat for 5 minutes to thicken it

lightly. Adjust the seasoning with salt, pepper, and balsamic vinegar. Add chicken and vegetables to heat. Stir in parsley.

4. Cook the orecchiette pasta to al dente. Serve the pasta, surrounded by the chicken and sauce. Garnish with fresh basil leaves and shaved cheese.

SPICY BROWN RICE BOWL
with Grilled Shrimp
Yield: 4–6 servings

1 cup American whole-grain brown rice
½ cup plus 1 tablespoon extra-virgin olive oil, divided
½ teaspoon crushed red pepper
16 medium shrimp, peeled and deveined
8 yellow beefsteak tomatoes, peeled, seeded, and chopped
1 cup chopped fresh parsley
3 tablespoons julienned fresh basil leaves
¼ cup toasted pine nuts
salt and freshly ground black pepper to taste

DIRECTIONS:

1. Bring 2¼ cups water to a boil, and cook whole-grain brown rice for 40–45 minutes, until al dente, to get about 3–4 cup cooked rice. Drain and cool.

2. Heat ½ cup olive oil in a small saucepan; add red pepper. Set aside until cool. Strain to remove red pepper.

3. Heat 1 tablespoon olive oil in a skillet. Add shrimp and sauté 3–4 minutes until cooked through but still tender. (Shrimp may be cooked on a charcoal grill.) In a large bowl, combine all ingredients and toss. Season with salt and pepper to taste. Serve at room temperature.

ASPARAGUS AND BLUE CRAB RISOTTO

Yield: 4 servings

20 thin stalks asparagus
2 tablespoons extra-virgin olive oil
2 shallots, minced
1½ cups American arborio rice
½ cup dry white wine
4 cups chicken broth
20 thin stalks asparagus
1 cup grated Parmesan-Reggiano cheese
2 tablespoons chopped flat-leaf parsley
2 tablespoons chopped fresh scallions
1 teaspoon chopped thyme
salt and freshly ground pepper to taste
16 ounces lump blue crabmeat, canned, at room temperature
½ cup shaved Parmesan-Reggiano cheese

DIRECTIONS:

1. Cook asparagus in a large pot of boiling water until crisp and tender (1–2 minutes). Drain. Cut asparagus into ½" pieces, leaving tips whole. Set aside.

2. In a large, heavy saucepan, heat olive oil over medium heat. Add shallots and cook 2 minutes. Add rice and cook 3 minutes, stirring often. Add wine. Cook, stirring, until wine is almost completely absorbed. Add chicken broth ½ cup at a time. Simmer, stirring constantly, until each addition is almost completely absorbed. After 2 cups of broth have been added, add asparagus. Continue until all broth is added. Cook until rice is firm but cooked through and mixture is creamy.

3. Stir in grated Parmesan cheese and herbs. Season with salt and pepper to taste. Serve immediately in a large bowl, stirring in 16 ounces canned lump blue crabmeat. Sprinkle with shaved Parmesan-Reggiano.

ROADSIDE FRIED OYSTER TOSTADA

Yield: 4 servings

FOR OYSTERS
16 Maryland oysters
2 cups seasoned breading (fish fry)
oil for frying

FOR HABANERO CREAM SAUCE
2 habanero peppers, seeds removed, chopped extremely fine
1 teaspoon lemon juice
2 tablespoons clear blue agave juice
2 tablespoons heavy cream
4 tablespoons liquid heavy cream

FOR TOSTADAS
4 tostadas
4 ounces lemon juice
4 cups finely cut cilantro
8 ounces ponzu
1 cups guacamole
1 cup spring mix greens
4 ounces fresh cream
1 teaspoon sesame seeds
4 tablespoons radish, cut into strips

DIRECTIONS:
1. Place the oysters in a large colander and allow them to drain for 15 minutes.
2. Place breading in a large mixing bowl.
3. Pour oil ½" deep in a large heavy frying pan and heat over medium high heat to 375 degrees F.
4. Dredge oysters in breading, coating well. Shake off excess flour and carefully lower each oyster into hot oil. Fry 2–3 minutes, until golden and crispy. Remove onto paper towels to drain.

5. For habanero cream sauce, place habaneros in a small bowl. Sprinkle with lemon juice, clear blue agave juice, and heavy cream. Stir all together.
6. To assemble tostadas, toss fried oysters with lemon juice, cilantro, and ponzu. Cover a side of the tostadas in guacamole. Cover tostadas with prepared oyster mix. Add spring mix greens and strips of radish on top. Add habanero cream sauce on top, and sprinkle with a pinch of sesame seeds.

ROASTED PHEASANT

Yield: 4 servings

Tip: Coarse salt acts as an abrasive, making garlic easier to chop finely. Tangerine juice adds a bright, exotic flavor to roasting vegetables.

1 clove of garlic
1 tablespoon coarse salt
juice of 2 tangerines
1½ teaspoons finely grated tangerine peel
1 tangerine, halved
2 tablespoons olive oil
1 teaspoon dried tarragon
freshly ground black pepper to taste
2 carrots, halved lengthwise and cut into 2" lengths
½ pound white new potatoes, scrubbed and quartered
4 large ripe plum tomatoes, halved lengthwise and seeded
1 pheasant, about 2½ pounds
2 sprigs fresh tarragon, or flat-leaf parsley
½ tart apple, cored and cut into pieces
2 shallots, peeled and halved
3–4 sprigs fresh sage, plus extra for garnish
3 slices turkey bacon
⅛ cup defatted chicken broth

DIRECTIONS:
1. Preheat oven to 350 degrees F. Mince the garlic with the salt; place in a bowl. Add the tangerine juice and peel, 1 tablespoon olive oil, dried tarragon, and pepper. Set aside.
2. Blanch the carrots and potatoes for 7–8 minutes in boiling water. Drain and place in a bowl with the tomatoes. Reserve.
3. Carefully loosen breast skin of the pheasant; place a sprig of tarragon underneath each side of the breast. Replace the skin neatly. Squeeze the halved tangerine into the cavity, then sprinkle with salt and

pepper. Place the apple pieces, shallots, and sage in the cavity; tie legs together with kitchen string.

4. Place reserved vegetables in a small roasting pan. Toss with garlic-tangerine mixture. Place the pheasant, breast side up, on top of the vegetables. Brush pheasant with the remaining tablespoon of oil. Lay bacon slices over the breast. Pour broth in the bottom of the pan.

5. Roast in the center of the oven for 1 hour, basting two or three times. Remove bacon and continue to roast until the breast is brown and the pheasant is cooked through (about 20–30 minutes longer). Test for doneness with the tip of a knife in the thickest part of the thigh. The juices should run clear. Let pheasant rest 10 minutes before carving.

6. Carve the pheasant, remove to a serving platter, and surround with the vegetables. Spoon some of the juices over top. Serve extra juices alongside. Garnish with fresh sage.

ROASTED PORTOBELLO CAPS
Yield: 6 servings

Think of a jumbo stuffed mushroom without all the high-fat ingredients but with all the flavor. Serve alongside grilled meat or seafood.

6 large portobello mushrooms, stems removed
¼ teaspoon salt, divided
freshly ground pepper to taste
⅓ cup Heinz chili sauce
⅓ cup Ocean Spray cranberry sauce
¼ cup plain dry bread or rice crumbs
2 tablespoons grated Parmesan cheese
1 tablespoon minced fresh parsley
1 tablespoon extra-virgin olive oil

DIRECTIONS:
1. Preheat oven to 450 degrees F. Coat a rimmed baking sheet or roasting pan with cooking spray.
2. Place mushroom caps gill side up on the prepared pan. Sprinkle with ⅛ teaspoon salt and pepper. Roast until tender (about 20 minutes).
3. Meanwhile, combine bread crumbs, parmesan, parsley, oil, the remaining ⅛ teaspoon salt, and pepper in a small bowl.
4. Remove the mushrooms from the oven and top each cap with equal amounts of cranberry and chili sauce, spreading evenly. Return to the oven and roast until the sauces are bubbling hot (about 5 minutes).
5. Top mushrooms with bread-crumb mixture, spreading evenly. Return to the oven again. Roast until bread crumbs are browned (about 5 more minutes).

SALMON AND LEMONGRASS SAUSAGE PATTIES

Yield: 8 servings

1 (30-ounce) boneless, skinless Columbia River salmon fillet, cut into
    1" cubes
10 ounces pork back fat, cut into 1" cubes
1 tablespoon fine sea salt
2 teaspoons freshly ground black pepper
2 tablespoons pure maple syrup
2 teaspoons fish sauce
1 tablespoon minced shallot
1 tablespoon minced lemongrass
1½ teaspoons peeled, grated, and then chopped fresh ginger
1½ teaspoons minced garlic

DIRECTIONS:

1. Place the salmon and fat in a nonreactive bowl or container. In a
    separate bowl, combine the salt, pepper, sugar, fish sauce, shallot,
    lemongrass, ginger, and garlic, and mix well. Mix the spices evenly
    with the meat; cover, and refrigerate overnight.

2. Refrigerate the parts of your grinder until ready to use. Fit the grinder
    with the smallest plate and grind the meat once. Mix the ground meat
    well by hand for 2 minutes. Cook a small sample of the mixture in a
    roasting pan, and adjust the seasonings if necessary.

3. For patties, divide the ground meat into eight equal portions and
    carefully flatten each portion into a ¾"-thick patty. Start roasting on
    a nonstick pan at 400 degree F. After 10 minutes reduce to 350 degree
    F until done. Crumble and enjoy.

4. Serve leftover patties over freshly baked waffles for breakfast or
    brunch, topped with pure maple syrup.

SARDINIAN MUSIC PIZZA
with Rosemarie and Parmigianino
Yield: 2 servings

While visiting Sardinia I was served this very simple and flavorful snack.

4 halves of Bays English muffins
4 tablespoons fruity olive oil for brushing muffin halves
4 teaspoons fresh rosemary chopped
1 tablespoon coarse sea salt
4 ounces grated Parmigiano

DIRECTIONS:
1. Preheat oven to 425 degrees F. Break Bays English muffins into rough quarters. Moisten 1 quarter at a time in a pan of warm water until its edges soften (about 5 seconds). Transfer softened muffin quarters to a sheet pan in a single layer, and set aside until pliable (about 1 minute).
2. Brush bread with some olive oil and then sprinkle with a generous pinch of rosemary and salt. Then drizzle with more oil and sprinkle with more rosemary and salt. Bake until edges are crisp and centers are still a bit chewy (10–12 minutes).
3. After baking muffin quarters for 10 minutes, sprinkle with a generous amount of grated Parmesan cheese.

SCRAPE-THE-BOWL POTATO SALAD

Yield: 6 generous side dishes

2 poblano peppers cut in half and stripped of inside strings

2 pounds new or fingerling potatoes

1 teaspoon sea salt

1 large red or white onion (if you use white, use less, as the red has a
more mellow flavor)

⅓ cup olive or canola oil

3 tablespoons rice or champagne vinegar

1 tablespoon chopped fresh oregano or 1 teaspoon dried crushed
oregano leaves

½ teaspoon ground black pepper (or use about 20 grinds from a pepper
mill)

1 hefty handful of cilantro leaves grabbed off the top of the bunch,
rinsed, dried, and chopped

1 can packed white tuna in water; or 1 (8-ounce) chicken breast,
poached and shredded; or 8 ounces crispy bacon crumbs, baked to
crackling from a hot oven and cooled

DIRECTIONS:

1. Roast the poblano peppers on a grill or over the open flame of a gas
   stove until the skin is blackened and blistered. Alternatively, roast the
   peppers in an oven at 450 degrees F until blackened. Place roasted
   peppers into a brown paper bag and allow to sweat for 1 hour. This
   makes it easier to peel the peppers later.

2. Peel and dice potatoes. You may wish not to peel the potatoes, if they
   are cleaned and scrubbed; the taste is just as good or better, and it's
   healthier. You may boil or microwave the potatoes, tossed with sea
   salt and a little olive oil. If in microwave, microwave on high for 5
   minutes or until tender. If boiling, boil potatoes until tender for about
   15 minutes and drain.

3. Chop your onion(s) into thin slivers about ¼" thick. Peel cooled
   poblano, removing the black skin carefully. Remove seeds and veins.

Then cut peppers into thin slivers. Don't mix onions and peppers together yet.

4. Heat the oil in a large skillet over medium-high heat. Add your onions until the pieces have gotten a little brown and crunchy. Turn off the flame, and add the poblano strips, vinegar, oregano, and pepper. Mix together until thoroughly combined. Pour mixture over warm potatoes.

5. When the salad has cooled to room temperature, add your cilantro and tuna, chicken breast, or crispy bacon crumbles. Toss and serve.

SEARED SCALLOPS WITH BIGELOW PORT SAUCE

Yield: 6 servings

Pan-searing and grilling scallops are the two most popular ways of cooking and eating this tender fruit of the ocean. Here they are combined with a flavorful sauce created from the tropical gardens of the Orient.

¼ cup concentrated Bigelow tea (same flavor as in Port wine sauce) (1 quart water and 13 Bigelow tea bags)
1 tablespoon balsamic vinegar
2 tablespoons soy sauce
⅛ teaspoon freshly ground black pepper
2 teaspoons extra-virgin olive oil
1 teaspoon lime juice
1½ pounds sea scallops

FOR PORT CONCENTRATE SAUCE
2 cups port wine
½ cup concentrated Bigelow tea (your choice of flavor) (1 quart water and 13 Bigelow tea bags)
1 tablespoon butter

DIRECTIONS:
1. Warm a nonreactive saucepan over medium heat. Combine the ¼ cup Bigelow tea concentrate (your choice of flavor), balsamic vinegar, soy sauce, and black pepper. Stir the ingredients well, bring to a boil, and cook until desired thickness is reached. Remove from the heat and set aside.
2. Rinse the scallops and pat dry. Heat oil in a skillet over medium-high heat. Lightly season the scallops with salt and pepper and add them to the pan once the oil is heated. Sear the scallops for 2 minutes on each side, until cooked through and golden brown.
3. Make port concentrate sauce: Add the butter and wine to a saucepan over medium-high heat, and reduce liquid by half to roughly 1 cup.

Add sauce which was set aside from paragraph 1 and allow to heat through.

4. Place the scallops on individual plates. Whisk the lime juice into the warm Bigelow tea port concentrate sauce and stir a few times. Drizzle the sauce over the scallops and serve.

SICILIAN HARVEST PASTA ANGELICA

Yield: 4 servings

FOR SHRIMP

1 pound. fresh tiny shrimp, cleaned and deveined, 300 count

1 pint light cream

1 cup dry white wine

½ cup all-purpose flour

½ cup grated Parmesan cheese

¼ teaspoon cayenne pepper

salt and ground pepper to taste

approximately 1 quart Zoye soybean oil to fry shrimp

FOR SAUCE

6–8 whole garlic cloves, crushed

6 tablespoons Zoye soybean oil

1 tomato, diced

1 shallot, diced

1 cup white wine

1 pint light cream

¼ cup fresh basil, julienned, plus 12 fresh leaves for garnish

¼ cup fresh Italian parsley, chopped

salt and pepper to taste

FOR PASTA

1 pound Sicilian golden durum wheat spaghettini pasta

1 tablespoon Zoye soybean oil

DIRECTIONS:

1. Place shrimp in a large bowl. Add cream and wine; mix thoroughly. In a separate bowl, mix Parmesan cheese, flour, cayenne pepper, and salt and pepper. Coat the soaked shrimp with the dry mixture. Over medium-high heat, pour 1" of Zoye soybean oil in a large saucepan to coat the bottom of the pan. Fry the shrimp in the oil until golden brown (about 2 minutes per side). Add more oil between batches if necessary. Drain shrimp on paper towel and set aside.

493

2. To make the sauce, add the garlic to the 6 tablespoons Zoye soy oil and sauté until it just begins to turn golden (2–3 minutes). Turn heat to medium low. Add the shallot, tomato, cream, and wine, and bring to a boil. Turn the heat to low and let the wine reduce for about 10–15 minutes. Add basil and parsley, and season to taste.

3. In a separate pot, cook spaghettini pasta in lightly salted water until al dente and 1 tablespoon Zoye soybean oil (5 quarts water for 1 pound pasta). Drain. Add fried shrimp to tomato / white wine sauce, and serve over hot pasta. Garnish with basil leaves.

SICILIAN MUFFULETTA PICNIC TORTA
with Radicchio Ham, Provolone, and Herbs
Yield: 12 servings

This stunning sandwich pie is loaded with flavor. It is a special dish that's easier to make than it looks. You can assemble it a day ahead of time and then bake it the morning of the picnic. To prevent a soggy crust, be sure to dry the peppers and spinach by blotting with paper towels.

8 ounces fat-free Italian dressing
8 ounces green bell pepper, cored, seeded, and coarsely chopped
8 ounces red onion, peeled and coarsely chopped
6 ounces stuffed green olives
6 ounces pitted ripe olives
4 garlic cloves, peeled and chopped
2 tablespoons dried basil leaves, or ¼ cup fresh basil leaves
2 teaspoons dried oregano, or 1 tablespoon fresh oregano leaves
2 (10"–12") round Italian country bread loaves
12 ounces reduced-fat cream cheese, softened
16 ounces (2 large heads) fresh radicchio leaves, julienned
24 tomato slices
24 eggs, hard-boiled, peeled, and sliced
1 pound turkey ham slices
1 pound part-skim mozzarella slices
1 pound provolone cheese slices
1 pound turkey breast slices
1 jar (8 ounces) roasted red peppers, rinsed, drained, and patted dry

DIRECTIONS:
1. In a food processor fitted with a metal blade, combine dressing, green pepper, onion, olives, garlic, basil, and oregano. Pulse ingredients until finely chopped, similar to pesto.
2. Cut bread horizontally into two for two torta layers. Remove bread from inside halves, leaving 1" border attached to crust. Spread 3 tablespoons cream cheese inside each bread half. Spread ½ cup

olive mixture over cream cheese. Layer 1½ cups radicchio leaves, 4 tomato slices, 10 ounces egg slices, 4 ounces turkey ham, 4 ounces mozzarella, 4 ounces provolone, and 4 ounces turkey breast. Top with roasted red peppers and more radicchio.

3. Carefully close torta. Press together and wrap tightly in plastic wrap. Refrigerate several hours or overnight. To serve, cut each torta into six slices.

4. Roll out smaller piece of dough a little bigger than pan, then cut to size of pan. Transfer circle to a plate, discarding scraps. Chill shell and circle until ready to use.

SLOW-COOKED GRANOLA BIRCHER MUESLI

Yield: 8 servings

Here's an easy way to serve a crowd a hearty breakfast before facing the elements for a day of winter sports. You can assemble it in the slow cooker in the evening and wake up to a bowl of hot, nourishing oatmeal with a creamy consistency. No need for constant stirring either. Use steel-cut oats; the old-fashioned kind get too soft during slow cooking.

8 cups soy milk
2 cups steel-cut oats
⅓ cup dried cranberries
⅓ cup dried apricots, chopped
⅓ cup freeze-dried diced apples
⅔ cup fresh or frozen raspberries
¼ teaspoon salt, or to taste
2 cups Greek-style yogurt, plain or with fruit
½ cup or more freshly squeezed orange juice

DIRECTIONS:

1. Combine soy milk, oats, dried cranberries, dried apricots, dried apples, raspberries, and salt in a 5- or 6-quart slow cooker. Turn the heat to low. Put the lid on and cook until the oats are tender and the porridge is creamy (7–8 hours). To serve, top with Greek-style yogurt and a generous dash of freshly squeezed orange juice.

SMORGASBORD FRITTATA FEAST

Yield: 4 servings

1 tablespoon olive oil, divided
½ cup vertically sliced red onion
¼ cup thinly sliced scallions
1 tablespoon minced fresh marjoram
½ teaspoon freshly ground black pepper, divided
cooking spray
2 cups preshredded raw potatoes (such as Simply Potatoes brand)
8 large eggs
2 tablespoons heavy cream
3 ounces smoked salmon, sliced thinly
8 sardines
4 anchovy fillets
8 thin slices air-cured ham (e.g., prosciutto, serrano, Black Forest)
2½ ounces sour cream with chives
4 tablespoons lingonberries (use lingonberry marmalade containing
    whole lingonberries)
1 tablespoon black or red American caviar
4 sliced red radishes, held together at the green stem and leaf
½ cup sliced tart apples (e.g., Granny Smith)

DIRECTIONS:

1. Heat 1½ teaspoons olive oil in an 8" cast-iron or other heavy skillet over medium heat Add onion and sauté 5 minutes or until tender. Remove from heat. Stir in scallions, marjoram, and ¼ teaspoon pepper. Remove onion mixture from the skillet and set aside.

2. Preheat broiler.

3. Coat skillet with cooking spray. Combine the potatoes and remaining 1½ teaspoons olive oil and ¼ teaspoon pepper. Press potato mixture into the bottom of skillet. Broil for 15 minutes, or until potatoes are crispy and golden brown.

4. Reduce oven temperature to 375 degrees F.

5. Spread the onion mixture over the potatoes.

6. In a bowl, combine eggs and heavy cream and whip mixture slightly. Pour egg mixture over the top and bake at 375 degrees F for 30 minutes, or until puffy and lightly browned.
7. Place on hot, large oval platter.
8. Spread next nine ingredients smorgasbord-style on top of frittata.

NEW GERMAN APPLE PANCAKES

Yield: 4 servings

2 thinly sliced Granny Smith or other tart apples

1 (29-ounce) jar apple butter (replacing 2 apples in Mama's original
recipe)

4 tablespoons unsalted butter

⅔ cup plus 2 tablespoons sugar, divided

2 tablespoons cinnamon

6 large whole eggs

2 large egg yolks

⅔ cup sifted unbleached all-purpose flour

½ teaspoons salt

⅔ cup light cream or half-and-half

DIRECTIONS:

1. Preheat oven to 400 degrees F.
2. In a heavy, ovenproof 1" skillet, cook apple slices in butter over moderate heat, turning once, for 2 minutes. Remove the skillet from the heat. Stir in apple butter.
3. In a small bowl, combine ⅔ cup sugar and cinnamon, and sprinkle over the apple mixture.
4. In a bowl, whisk together the whole eggs and the yolk.
5. In another bowl, whisk together the flour, the remaining 2 tablespoons sugar, and the salt. Add the cream, whisking, and whisk in the egg mixture.
6. Pour the batter over the apple mixture.
7. Bake the pancake in the skillet in the middle of the oven for 12–15 minutes, or until it is puffed and golden. Invert it on a heated platter.

SPICY CAJUN FRIED PEKIN DUCK
with Covington, Louisiana, Tomato Dip
Yield: 4 servings

FOR TOMATO DIP

3 tomatoes, diced (I like heirloom Covington, Louisiana, tomatoes best)

½ onion, diced

¼ cup tomato paste

2 tablespoons extra-virgin olive oil

1 teaspoon granulated sugar

1 tablespoon dry oregano

3 garlic cloves, minced

1 thin red chili pepper

1 tablespoon chopped cilantro

salt and pepper and Cajun vegetable spice (Paul Prudhomme or any of
your choice) to taste

FOR DUCK

1 teaspoon finely chopped garlic

1 teaspoon fine sea salt

1 teaspoon each ground cardamom, finely grated fresh ginger, ground
nutmeg, and freshly ground pepper

4 (12-ounce) Maple Leaf Farms pekin duck leg and leg quarters
combinations, cut in 2 parts each and skinned

2 tablespoons vegetable oil

1 hot green chili pepper, seeded and chopped

½ cup roasted pine nuts or cashews, chopped

¼ cup water

2 medium carrots cut into 2" sticks

2 medium celery sticks, peeled and cut into 2" sticks

½ cup fresh green peas, cooked tender-crisp

2 cups each cauliflower and broccoli florets, cooked tender-crisp

2 hard-boiled eggs, sliced

1 cucumber, sliced

2 firm red tomatoes, sliced

4 cilantro sprigs

DIRECTIONS:

1. For the tomato dip, blend all ingredients except the cilantro, salt, pepper, and Cajun spice in a blender for a few seconds until the ingredients are coarsely chopped, Mix in cilantro, salt and pepper, and Cajun spice before serving.

2. Place garlic on a hard, flat surface and sprinkle with salt. Crush to a smooth paste.

3. In a small bowl, place garlic-salt mixture, cardamom, ginger, nutmeg, and pepper. Rub spice mixture over duck, and marinate, refrigerated, for at least 30 minutes.

4. Place oil in large frying pan and heat to medium high. Add duck and cook, turning, for about 15 minutes, or until brown from all sides. Add chili pepper and pine nuts or cashews. Cook 1 minute. Add water, cover, reduce heat to low, and simmer about 10 minutes, or until fork can be inserted easily into the duck meat.

5. Remove duck from frying pan and place on serving dish.

6. Add vegetables to frying pan and toss to coat in remaining gravy. Arrange vegetables on dish with duck. Garnish with egg, cucumber, and tomato slices, and cilantro sprigs.

SPICY GRILLED TOFU MUFFINS

Yield: 8 servings

2 (16-ounce) packages water-packed firm tofu, drained
4 Bays multigrain English muffins, lightly toasted with a light brushing
    of peanut oil
1 cup fresh lime juice
1 cup honey
½ cup lemongrass, peeled and thinly sliced
4 tablespoons low-sodium soy sauce
½ teaspoon freshly ground black pepper
4 garlic cloves, peeled and minced
1½ teaspoons chili paste with garlic
2 tablespoons peanut oil
8 baby iceberg leaves
1 cup cilantro leaves
4 tablespoons dry-roasted peanuts
1 cup small mint leaves
1 cup fresh basil leaves
1 large carrot, julienned

DIRECTIONS:

1. Cut 2 tofu blocks into eight equal slices.
2. Place tofu slices between several heavy-duty paper towels. Place a cutting board on top, and let the paper towels draw the moisture away for 20–30 minutes. (The tofu is ready when a slice is easily bendable without tearing.) Place tofu in a single layer on a cookie sheet.
3. Combine lime juice, honey, lemongrass, soy sauce, pepper, garlic, and chili paste in a small saucepan, and bring to a boil. Cook for 1 minute, stirring well to dissolve honey.
4. Pour mixture evenly over the tofu, cover with plastic wrap, and let rest for 1 hour.
5. Prepare your barbecue grill or oven broiler.
6. Remove tofu from the marinade and coat lightly with peanut oil, reserving the marinade.

7. Place tofu on hot grill or 6"–8" underneath broiler. Cook until each side is golden brown (about 3 minutes per side).

8. Place a baby iceberg lettuce leaf on each of the 8 toasted muffin halves, and place one slice grilled tofu on each baby iceberg leaf. Sprinkle with cilantro, peanuts, mint, basil, and julienned carrot. Serve with the reserved marinade.

SPICY ASIAN BURGER
on a Toasted Brioche Roll
Yield: 4 burgers

FOR PICKLED ONIONS
½ red onion, sliced into thin rings
1 teaspoon Kosher salt
2 tablespoons water
juice of ½ lime

FOR SPICY BARBECUE SAUCE
4 cups premade barbecue sauce (I suggest Annie Chun's Korean
   Barbeque sauce) or Annie Chun's gochujang sauce

FOR BURGERS
24 ounces ground meat (80% beef/veal and 20% pork)
1 scallion, minced
2 cloves garlic, minced
1 tablespoon minced cilantro
1 teaspoon minced ginger
1–2 tablespoons Annie Chan's gochujang sauce
1 teaspoon sesame oil
1 teaspoon hoisin sauce
¼ teaspoon ground white pepper
4 brioche rolls (or other slightly sweet rolls)
8 slices gruyere cheese
8 slices tomato
4 ounces mizuna greens

DIRECTIONS:
1. For pickled onions, combine all pickled onion ingredients in a bowl at room temperature for 30 minutes.
2. To make spicy barbecue sauce, combine equal amounts of the two sauces in a bowl and stir to mix well.
3. Preheat grill or grill pan to medium high. Spray with vegetable oil to avoid sticking.

4. Mix first nine ingredients; do not overmix, as this will toughen the burgers.

5. Shape into four patties slightly larger than the roll's diameter. Cook to desired doneness (for medium rare, about 3–4 minutes on each side, turning once). Baste the top of both sides of the burger at 2-minute intervals with the spicy barbecue sauce. Add 2 slices gruyere cheese to melt just before removing patties from the grill.

6. To assemble, lightly toast brioche rolls on the perimeters of the grill. For each burger, add 1 ounce greens, 2 tomato slices, and a burger patty. Distribute pickled onions evenly among burgers, and add the tops of the rolls.

SPICY STIR-FRIED PORK
with Brown Rice
Yield: 6 servings

You'll purchase more pork than needed for this dish, but it's a better buy in bulk. Freeze the rest to use later. Use sriracha, a Thai-style hot sauce made with sun-ripened chiles to add bright flavor and heat to this dish. Spend a bit more and you can add a bell pepper to this stir-fry; slice it thinly and add to the pan with the broccoli.

1½ cups uncooked brown rice
2 tablespoons low-sodium soy sauce
2 teaspoons sriracha hot sauce, or Tabasco
1 teaspoon cornstarch
1 garlic clove, thinly sliced
2 tablespoons canola oil
1 pound broccoli crowns, cut into florets
1 (1") piece ginger root, peeled and minced
12 ounces boneless pork loin chops, trimmed and cut into ½" strips
1 bunch scallions, cut into 1" pieces

DIRECTIONS:
1. Cook rice according to package directions or place rice in 3 cups boiling water and 1 teaspoon salt cover pot with lid and cook for 15–20 minutes to al dente or desired doneness, strain and keep warm.
2. While the rice cooks, combine soy sauce, hot sauce, cornstarch, and garlic in a medium bowl, stirring with a whisk.
3. Heat a wok or large skillet over high heat. Add oil. Add broccoli and ginger; stir-fry 3 minutes, or until broccoli is tender-crisp. Transfer broccoli mixture to a large bowl; keep warm.
4. Add pork to wok; stir-fry 3 minutes. Add soy-sauce mixture; cook 2 minutes, or until pork is done. Add broccoli mixture and onions; stir-fry 30 seconds or until hot. Serve over rice.

ITALIAN SPINACH RAVIOLI TORTA

Yield: 8 servings

1½ jars (26 ounces) marinara sauce (your choice)
1 (13") Schwann's prepared crust, thawed
3 (13-ounce) packages frozen ravioli (your choice)
1 (10-ounce) package frozen chopped spinach, thawed and
   squeezed dry
8 ounces grated mozzarella
½ cup grated parmesan

DIRECTIONS:
1. Preheat oven to 350 degrees F.
2. Spread a thin layer of sauce on the prepared, thawed crust and arrange ravioli in a single layer, then add half the spinach, half the marinara, and half the mozzarella.
3. Repeat layers. Top with Parmesan cheese.
4. Cover pan with foil. Bake for 35 minutes. Uncover and bake for 15 minutes more, or until cheese is melted and pasta is cooked. Let stand for 5 minutes.

Note: For a nice browned top, place under the broiler for 2 minutes.

Serving suggestion: Serve with a crisp Italian green salad.

SPRING SALAD PIZZA

Yield: 8 servings

1 (11-ounce) can refrigerated thin-crust pizza dough
cooking spray
¼ cup (1 ounce) crumbled blue cheese, divided
1 tablespoon extra-virgin olive oil
1 tablespoon white wine vinegar
½ teaspoon ground black pepper, divided
½ teaspoon Dijon mustard
8 tablespoons chopped red onion
2 cups lightly packed mixed baby greens
½ cup diced peeled avocado
2 slices apple wood–smoked bacon
8 ounces boneless, skinless chicken breast cutlets
½ cup quartered cherry tomatoes
1 cup snipped green English spring peas, quarter-sized

DIRECTIONS:
1. Preheat oven to 425 degrees F.
2. Unroll dough on a baking sheet coated with cooking spray; pat dough into a 14" × 12" rectangle. Lightly coat dough with cooking spray. Bake at 425 degrees for 8 minutes, or until golden. Remove from oven; sprinkle evenly with 2 tablespoons cheese. Set aside.
3. Combine oil, vinegar, mustard, and ¼ teaspoon pepper in a large bowl; stir with a whisk.
4. Cook bacon in a large nonstick skillet over medium heat until crisp. Remove bacon from pan; crumble bacon into oil mixture. Wipe pan clean with paper towels. Heat pan over medium-high heat. Coat pan with cooking spray. Sprinkle chicken with remaining ¼ teaspoon pepper. Add chicken to pan; cook 4 minutes on each side, or until done. Remove chicken from pan and chop into ½" pieces.
5. Add chicken, tomatoes, and onion to oil mixture; toss gently to combine. Add greens; toss gently. Top crust evenly with chicken mixture, avocado, and remaining 2 tablespoons cheese. Cut into eight pieces.

SPRING SHOWER SALAD

Yield: 4 servings

1 tablespoon Rodelle herbes de Provence seasoning
1 tablespoon extra-virgin olive oil
2 tablespoons aged balsamic vinegar*
4 cups baby arugula, or torn arugula leaves
2 cups sliced strawberries (about 10 ounces)
1 cup paper-thin shaved Parmesan-Reggiano
½ cup chopped walnuts

DIRECTIONS:

1. In the bowl of a mixer, whip together herbes de Provence, extra-virgin olive oil, and balsamic vinegar. Refrigerate for ½ hour to blend flavors.

2. Toast walnuts in a small, dry skillet over medium-low heat, stirring frequently, until lightly browned and aromatic (3–5 minutes). Transfer to a salad bowl; let cool for 5 minutes.

3. Add arugula, strawberries, and Parmesan to the light herbes de Provence salad dressing.

4. Sprinkle toasted walnuts over salad. Serve at once.

*Aged balsamic vinegar (aged twelve years or longer) is a treat, but not an economical one. If you don't want to spring for a forty-dollar bottle, use regular balsamic. Alternatively, bring ½ cup regular balsamic vinegar to a boil over high heat in a small skillet. Cook until the vinegar begins to thicken and becomes syrupy (2–3 minutes).

SPRING VEGETABLE NAPOLEON
with White Spring Asparagus, Fresh Porcini Mushrooms, and Blue Cheese Cream
Yield: 4 servings

25 asparagus stalks

2 ounces extra-virgin olive oil

1 pound fresh porcini mushrooms, small mince

2 shallots, minced

1 cup white wine

3 fresh thyme sprigs, leaves only

40 flat spinach leaves, large

½ cup cream

1 cup soft blue cheese

1 tablespoon honey

salt and freshly ground black pepper to taste

1 puff pastry sheet, large, rolled thin

½ cup Parmesan cheese, grated

2 eggs, beaten into egg wash

DIRECTIONS:

1. Remove 2" off bottom of each asparagus stalk and peel halfway up each stalk. Bring a large pot of salted water to a boil and prepare an ice bath. Blanch asparagus for 1 minute, then shock in ice bath. Remove and reserve.

2. Heat a large sauté pan over high heat. When pan is hot, add olive oil and toss in mushrooms. Sauté until most of the natural moisture is evaporated, then add shallots and white wine. Cook until pan is almost dry. Remove from pan and set aside to cool.

3. Bring a large pot of salted water to a rolling boil. Blanch spinach for 10 seconds and then shock in ice bath. Lay spinach on paper towels on a few large trays to dry.

4. Bring cream to a simmer in a small pot, and add blue cheese and honey. Reduce by half; reserve to cool. Adjust seasoning with salt and pepper.

5. Take a large piece (8" × 12") of plastic wrap and lay it on the counter. Carefully start to lay spinach, one piece at a time, overlapping just a little. When spinach rectangle is about 6" × 8", spread a layer of mushrooms over spinach to form a 5" × 7" shape on top of spinach.

6. Season asparagus with salt and pepper and add to one end of spinach. Gently start to roll asparagus with the spinach and mushrooms, using plastic wrap as a guide. Make a tight little package and let set for about 10 minutes.

7. Cut puff pastry into four rectangular pieces measuring 4" × 6" and eight 4" rounds.

8. Sprinkle Parmesan cheese on one side of puff pastry rectangle, place asparagus rolls on rectangular pieces of puff pastry, and start to roll until asparagus is covered by puff pastry. Seal all ends with circular pieces of puff pastry and brush with egg wash. Set aside.

9. Preheat a convection oven to 375 degrees F. Place Napoleon on a nonstick baking sheet. Bake Napoleon until the puff pastry is nice and crispy (about 15 minutes).

CRANBERRY RUBY-RED MAGIC STARS

Yield: 36 cookies

1 cup unsalted butter

½ cup granulated sugar

¼ cup packed light brown sugar

2 tablespoons vanilla yogurt

1 large egg

2½ cups all-purpose flour

1 tablespoon ground cinnamon

¼–½ teaspoon ground cardamom

¼ teaspoon salt

2 cups finely chopped shelled, roasted hazelnuts

2 lightly beaten egg whites

¾ cup Ocean Spray whole cranberry sauce

¼ cup Ocean Spray Craisins, finely chopped

¼ cup powdered sugar

DIRECTIONS:

1. In a large mixing bowl, beat butter with first four ingredients using an electric mixer on medium to high speed for 30 seconds or till creamy. Beat in whole egg; beat well. Beat in flour, cinnamon, cardamom, and salt. Stir in nuts. Divide dough in half. Cover and chill for 2 hours.

2. On a floured surface, roll each half of dough ¼" thick. Using a 3" star cookie cutter, cut out 36 stars from each half of the dough, rerolling scraps as needed. Place on lightly greased cookie sheets. With a small star-shaped cookie cutter, cut stars from centers of *half* of the stars. Brush all cookies with egg white.

3. Bake cookies in oven preheated to 375 degrees F for 8–10 minutes, or until lightly browned. Cool on wire racks.

4. In a bowl, combine cranberry sauce and Craisins, stirring to mix well. Spread dull side of each whole star cookie with 1 teaspoon of the cranberry mixture. Top each with a cut-out cookie, shiny-side up. Press cookies together gently. Sift powdered sugar lightly on top.

STIR-FRIED CAJUN TURKEY

Yield: 4 servings

1 pound turkey breast or tenderloin strips, raw
2 tablespoons Cajun seasoning (purchased)
1 teaspoon vegetable or olive oil
1 red bell pepper, seeded and diced
1 tart green apple, cored and diced
½ cup pecan pieces

DIRECTIONS:
1. Season turkey strips with 2 tablespoons Cajun seasoning.
2. In a bowl, toss pepper, apple, and pecans with the remaining seasoning.
3. Heat oil in a large nonstick skillet over medium-high heat. Stir-fry turkey strips without crowding. Remove and keep warm. Add the pepper-apple mixture. Cook and stir 2 minutes. Remove turkey to skillet and stir to mix well.
4. To freeze stir-fried turkey, allow to cool for 10–20 minutes before placing the dinners into a freezer bag for freezing.
5. To defrost, remove the frozen dinners from freezer and allow to thaw for 30 minutes in freezer bag under running cold water, making sure the freezer bag remains closed and sealed. Place turkey dinners into 10"–12" nonstick skillet over medium-high heat, stirring occasionally until completely heated through.

Serving suggestion: Serve with rice and tossed green salad.

MAMA SALZBURG STREUSEL KAFFEE KUCHEN

Yield: 8 servings

While certainly not quick, this is an excellent, light-textured, and flavorful morning treat. It is truly a comfort food, with fragrant cinnamon and the lovely taste of butter and maple syrup.

FOR THE STREUSEL

3⅜ ounces (¾ cup) King Arthur all-purpose flour, plus more for the pan
½ cup packed light brown sugar
½ teaspoon ground cinnamon
⅛ teaspoon table salt
2¼ ounces (4½ tablespoons) unsalted butter, melted; more if needed

FOR THE CAKE

½ cup sour cream, at room temperature
1 teaspoon pure vanilla extract
2 drops pure almond extract
4 ounces (½ cup) very soft unsalted butter, plus more for the pan
¾ cup Burton's maple syrup
1 large egg yolk, at room temperature
1 large egg, at room temperature
¼ plus ⅛ teaspoons table salt
5¼ ounces (1⅓ cups) King Arthur cake flour
1 teaspoon baking powder
⅛ teaspoon baking soda

DIRECTIONS:

1. To make the streusel, stir the flour, brown sugar, cinnamon, and salt together in a small bowl. Drizzle the melted butter over the dry ingredients, and stir until well combined. The streusel should feel clumpy, not sandy. If it seems dry, add more melted butter.

2. For the cake, position a rack in the center of the oven and heat the oven to 350 degrees F. Lightly butter the bottom and sides of an 8" square metal cake pan. Line the bottom of the pan with parchment,

and butter the parchment. Dust the pan with flour, tapping out any excess.

3. In a small bowl, whisk the sour cream, vanilla, and almond extract.

4. In a large bowl, cream the butter, Burton's maple syrup, and egg yolk with a wooden spoon until blended, about 20 seconds. Using a whisk, whisk in the whole egg and salt, and continue to whisk until the batter is smooth (about 30 seconds). Whisk in the sour cream mixture. Sift the cake flour, baking powder, and baking soda directly onto the batter. Whisk until the mixture is smooth and free of lumps.

5. Spread the batter evenly in the pan. Sprinkle the streusel over the batter, squeezing it with your fingertips to form small clumps. Bake until puffed and golden and a skewer inserted in the center of the cake comes out with only moist crumbs clinging to it (45 minutes). Set the pan on a rack to cool for 15 minutes.

6. Run a knife between the cake and the sides of the pan. Invert the cake onto the rack and remove the parchment. Invert again onto a serving plate, so the streusel is on top. Let cool at least 10 minutes before serving. This cake is best served warm.

STREUSEL PUMPKIN PIE

Yield: 2 pies 12 servings

Basic pumpkin pie is good, but we think this dressed-up version is even better. Plenty of pecans add a nutty crunch to the pastry and the streusel topping. It's a perfect dessert for Thanksgiving or any time you want to end a dinner with something special.

Special Recipe by Chef Wolfgang's Mama

2 cups all-purpose flour
¼ cup finely chopped pecans
1 teaspoon salt
⅔ cup plus 1 tablespoon shortening
4–5 tablespoons water

FOR FILLING
1 (30-ounce) can pumpkin pie filling
1 (14-ounce) can sweetened condensed milk
1 egg, lightly beaten

FOR STREUSEL TOPPING
½ cup packed brown sugar
¼ cup all-purpose flour
¼ cup chopped pecans
½ teaspoon ground cinnamon
3 tablespoons cold butter

DIRECTIONS:
1. In a bowl, combine flour, pecans, and salt; cut in the shortening until crumbly. Gradually add water, tossing with a fork until a ball forms. Divide dough in half. Roll out each portion to fit a 9" pie plate; place pastry in pie plates. Flute edges and set aside.
2. Combine pie mix, milk, and egg; pour into pastry shells.

3. For topping, combine brown sugar, flour, pecans, and cinnamon in a small bowl; cut in butter until crumbly. Sprinkle over filling. Cover edges of pastry loosely with foil.
4. Bake at 375 degrees for 40–45 minutes or until a knife inserted near the center comes out clean. Cool on a wire rack for 2 hours. Refrigerate until serving.

GEORGIA MOUNTAIN PECAN AND GOAT CHEESE STUFFING
with Vidalia Sweet Onions

Yield: 8 servings

2 tablespoons extra-virgin olive or peanut oil, plus more for baking dish

2 large sweet Vidalia onions, diced small

3 celery stalks, diced medium (about 3 cups)

coarse salt and ground dark pepper to taste

10 ounces wild mountain-grown champignon mushrooms

2 tablespoons fresh sage leaves, finely chopped

1 loaf crusty white bread, cut into ¾" pieces, left uncovered overnight or toasted

½ cup dry white wine

1 cup toasted pecan pieces

3 cups crumbled Georgia native mountain goat cheese

1½ cups low-sodium chicken or turkey broth

2 large eggs, lightly beaten

DIRECTIONS:

1. In a large skillet, heat 1 tablespoon olive or peanut oil over medium-high heat. Add onions and celery. Season with salt and pepper. Cook, stirring occasionally until vegetables are soft (about 5 minutes). Transfer vegetables to a large bowl.

2. Add 1 tablespoon oil, mushrooms, and sage to the skillet and adjust seasoning again. Stir often until mushrooms are browned (about 5 minutes). Add wine and cook, scraping up any browned bits with a wooden spoon, until wine is almost evaporated. Transfer to bowl with vegetables. Add pecans, bread, and crumbled goat cheese. Add enough broth to moisten. Season with salt and pepper, and toss to combine.

3. Add eggs to bread mixture and toss well to combine. Spoon finished stuffing into a lightly buttered or oiled 2-quart baking dish. Can be store refrigerated for 1–2 days.

4. Preheat oven to 400 degrees F. Place stuffing on rack in upper third of oven. Bake, uncovered, until golden brown on top (about 30 minutes) and add to your favorite roasted bird.

SWEET ISLAMORADA COCONUT COOKIE BAR

Yield: 20 cookie bars

The mystery of Islamorada is well known to those who have been there once and want to come back again and again and again. The mystery in the coconut cookie bars is the sweet taste of Eagle Brand sweetened condensed milk, without which they would be just ordinary coconut bars.

3 cups (16 ounces) chocolate graham cracker crumbs
16 ounces unsalted butter
1 can Eagle Brand sweetened condensed milk
3 cups semisweet mini chocolate chips
2 cups vanilla chips
2 cups (8 ounces) coconut flakes

DIRECTIONS:

1. Preheat oven to 350 degrees F.
2. Place graham cracker crumbs in a bowl and set aside.
3. Place the butter in a medium saucepan over low heat. Cook for 4 minutes, or just until the butter has completely melted. Immediately pour the butter into the cracker crumbs and stir to combine.
4. Press graham-cracker-crumb mixture into the bottom of a 17¼" × 11½" × 1" baking pan, making sure that the crumbs are evenly mixed.
5. Pour condensed milk over the crumb-mixture crust, making the layer even.
6. Top with chocolate and then vanilla chips, and finally with coconut flakes.
7. Place in the preheated oven for 10–15 minutes or until chocolate and vanilla chips are melted and coconut is lightly browned.
8. Allow to cool, and cut into 2" square bars. Store in airtight cookie jar or eat while still warm with a glass of cool milk.

SWEET POTATO–STUFFED FLATBREADS

Yield: 6 servings

This mild side dish comes from early Louisiana natives. While tortilla-like Indian flatbread roti is the traditional accompaniment, whole-wheat tortillas or pitas are great for sopping up the liquid. Serve with lime wedges and rice.

1¼ teaspoons salt
2 teaspoons ground cumin
1½ teaspoons ground turmeric
1 teaspoon ground ginger
¼ teaspoon ground allspice
¼ teaspoon crushed red pepper
1 tablespoon canola oil
1½ cups chopped onion
4 garlic cloves, minced
7 cups 1"-cubed peeled Louisiana sweet potatoes (about 1½ pounds)
1 cup chopped red bell pepper
2 cups water
½ cup light coconut milk
½ cup chopped fresh cilantro
12 tortilla-like Indian flatbreads, or whole-wheat tortillas or pitas

DIRECTIONS:

1. Combine first six ingredients; set aside.
2. Heat oil in a large dutch oven over medium heat. Add onion; cook 3 minutes or until tender, stirring frequently. Add garlic; cook 15 seconds, stirring constantly. Add spice mixture; cook 30 seconds, stirring constantly. Add potatoes and bell pepper, stirring to coat with spice mixture; cook 1 minute, stirring constantly.
3. Stir in water and coconut milk, scraping pan to loosen browned bits. Bring to a boil. Cover, reduce heat, and simmer 25 minutes or until potatoes are tender.
4. Sprinkle with cilantro. Serve with lime wedges and whole-wheat flatbreads, tortillas, or pitas and rice to sop up the liquid.

SWEET SOUTHERN BAKED POTATOES
with Hickory Smoked Bacon, Ham, Pecans, and Raisins
Yield: 4–8 servings (1–2 baked potato halves per person)

¼ cup butter

¼ cup olive oil

1 medium yellow onion, finely chopped

1 clove garlic, minced

¼ pound Bryan sweet hickory bacon, finely diced, blanched

¼ pound Bryan Centerpiece hickory-smoked boneless ham, finely diced

salt and pepper to taste

1 teaspoon Cajun seasoning

¼ cup pecan pieces

⅓ cup dried raisins or currants, soaked until tender

¼ cup dry bread crumbs

1 tablespoon fresh thyme, chopped

1 tablespoon fresh rosemary, chopped

1 teaspoon fresh lime zest, grated fine

4 sweet baking potatoes, 1 pound each

8 slices Bryan sweet hickory bacon

chicken stock, as needed

cream sherry, as needed

DIRECTIONS:

1. Melt the butter and olive oil in large sauté pan to a pecan-brown color. Add diced onions, garlic, diced bacon, and ham. Season with salt and pepper and Cajun seasoning to taste. Add pecan pieces and raisins/currants. Stir in enough bread crumbs to bind mixture. Add herbs and lime zest. Set aside.

2. Preheat oven to 375 degrees F.

3. Wash and scrub potatoes. Place in a pan and top each potato with 2 slices Bryan sweet hickory bacon. Bake for 45 minutes or until fork-tender. Cut each potato horizontally in half and scoop out the inside. Mash inside with a fork and mix with the filling from the sauté pan.

4. Place the 8 slices baked bacon from the potatoes in bottom of a large pan and splash with chicken broth and sherry. Add the filled potato halves to the bacon and bake for 10–12 minutes or until crunchy and brown on top.

SWISS ALPINE OATMEAL AND APPLE MUESLI

Yield: 8 servings

Here is an easy way to serve a crowd a healthy, hearty Switzerland breakfast before facing the elements for a day of winter sports. You can assemble it in the slow cooker in the evening and wake up to a bowl of hot, nourishing oatmeal with a creamy consistency. No need for constant stirring either. Use steel-cut oats; the old-fashioned kind get too soft during slow cooking.

8 cups soy milk (or water)
2 cups plain or apple no-fat yogurt
2 cups steel-cut oats
⅔ cup dried chopped Michigan apples
⅓ cup golden raisins
1 cup chopped fresh Michigan Red Delicious apples, peeled and cored
½ cup chopped blanched almonds or other nuts (hazelnuts are the
    preferred nuts in Switzerland), skin removed
¼ teaspoon salt

DIRECTIONS:
1. Blend soy milk (or water) with the yogurt. Combine in a large bowl with the oats and all other ingredients, and ladle into a 5- or 6-quart slow cooker. Turn heat to low. Put the lid on and cook until the oats are tender and the muesli is creamy (7–8 hours).

WILD-CAUGHT ALASKAN SPOT PRAWNS
with Warm Tacos and Crumbled Goat Cheese
Yield: 6 servings

1½ pounds peeled Alaska spot prawns (16–20 per pound), tails on

2 cups red-wine-vinegar-and-olive-oil salad dressing, divided (store-bought or homemade)

6 (8") corn tortillas

1 tablespoon honey

1 tablespoon coarse mustard

4 cups mixed greens (a combination of iceberg lettuce, red leaf lettuce, and chicory)

2 cups flowering purple kale*

1½ cups sweet corn kernels

1½ cups onion, sliced paper-thin

1½ cups crumbled goat cheese

DIRECTIONS:

1. Place prawns in a bowl with 1 cup salad dressing. Mix to coat. Cover and refrigerate for 45 minutes. Dispose of the marinade. Thread prawns onto metal or soaked wooden skewers, running the skewers though each prawn once near the tail and once near the head so it looks like the letter C. Lay skewers on a well-oiled barbecue grill over hot coals or high heat on a gas grill. Cook, turning once, just until prawns are opaque throughout (about 3–5 minutes total). Push prawns off skewers and place on a platter, keeping them warm.

2. Warm tortillas, one at a time, in a large cast-iron (or similar heavy) skillet over medium heat until soft and pliable. Wrap tortillas in a clean towel to keep them warm as you go.

3. In a medium bowl, combine warm grilled prawns with remaining 1 cup salad dressing, honey, and mustard. Set aside.

4. Place remaining ingredients in a large bowl, tossing to combine. Add prawns along with salad dressing.

5. Place each warmed taco on a separate large platter, and fill the tacos evenly with the mixture of prawns, greens, and crumbled goat cheese.

*2 cups shredded red cabbage may be substituted.

TAMPA BAY GULF SHRIMP AND EGG-FRIED RICE BURRITO WRAPS

Yield: 4 servings

6 (10") low-fat flour tortillas (warmed)
1 bunch washed and dried arugula, leaves only
2 cups leftover cooked brown and white rice, combined
2 tablespoons olive oil
2 lightly whipped eggs
1 tablespoon soy sauce
½ pound 20-25 count small shrimp, raw, cleaned, peeled, and patted
    dry (or frozen and defrosted)
2 cups minced fresh vegetables (available at your produce market or
    supermarket, or make your own combination of scallions, celery,
    tomatoes, carrots, and corn)

DIRECTIONS:

1. Spread the rice in a single layer on rimmed cookie sheets and let come to room temperature before using.
2. Put the olive oil in a medium nonstick saucepan, and place over medium-high heat. Add lightly whipped eggs with soy sauce, and scramble stirring with a wooden spoon until set before adding the rice and shrimp and vegetables, stirring for an additional 3 minutes over high heat to combine.
3. Spread warmed tortillas in a single layer, and top generously with arugula leaves.
4. Top with egg-fried rice and shrimp, and close the tortilla wraps.

MUSHROOM RISOTTO

Yield: 4 servings

4 ounces fresh fall crimini mushrooms or other fresh mushrooms, finely
    chopped
2 tablespoons virgin olive oil
1 Tender Choice Peppercorn Medley pork loin fillet, sliced and coarsely
    diced (½" dice)
1 clove garlic, minced
½ cup minced onion
1 cup Arborio rice
1 cup dry white wine
3 cups vegetable broth
⅓ cup grated Parmesan cheese
4 ounces unsalted butter
¼ cup flat-leaf parsley, finely chopped
Kosher salt and freshly ground black pepper to taste
1 tablespoon fresh lemon juice

DIRECTIONS:

1. Finely chop the mushrooms and set aside.
2. Heat olive oil in a saucepan over low heat. Add the diced pork loin
   and cook for 3–4 minutes, stirring constantly. Add mushrooms and
   cook for another 2–3 minutes. Add the rice, and stir 2–3 minutes.
   Add the wine, and raise the heat to high. Stir and allow the wine to
   reduce until almost dry. Add the vegetable broth, half at a time, until
   most of the liquid is absorbed and the rice is slightly chewy. Stir in
   the Parmesan and butter and parsley. Season with salt and pepper to
   taste and finish by stirring in the lemon juice. Garnish with freshly
   chopped flat-leaf parsley.

TENDER CHOICE OLD VINE BARBECUE BABY BACKS

Yield: 6 servings

2 racks Tender Choice baby back pork ribs (5–6 pounds)

FOR BARBECUE SAUCE
2 cups finely chopped seedless black grapes
1 cup earthy Cabernet Sauvignon or hearty Zinfandel
⅓ cup packed brown sugar
1 large clove garlic, finely chopped
2 tablespoons Chinese hot mustard powder
1 tablespoon worcestershire sauce
1 tablespoon orange zest
1 tablespoon chopped ancho chiles
1 tablespoon paprika
1 tablespoon ground chili pepper
1½ teaspoons sea salt
1 teaspoon ground cumin
1 tablespoon chopped fresh thyme
¼ teaspoon ground black pepper
⅛ teaspoon five-spice powder

DIRECTIONS:
1. Bring meat to room temperature (usually takes 25–30 minutes).
2. Place ribs bone-up on flat surface. Slide a butter knife under the membrane, one rib at a time, then pull the end with a pair of pliers; the membrane will pull right off.
3. Prepare gas or charcoal grill to medium heat for indirect heating.
4. To make the sauce, combine black grapes, red wine, and brown sugar in a bowl, and allow to sit for 30 minutes. Puree, together with remaining ingredients, in food processor.
5. Grill ribs over indirect heat for 3 hours, lid closed, turning every 30 minutes. While ribs are grilling, brush with old vine barbecue sauce.

During last 15 minutes of cooking, baste ribs again and turn ribs two or three more times. Remove ribs from grill and allow to rest about 5 minutes. Sprinkle cilantro on top before serving.

Tip: To add extra moisture, place cake pan filled with water over direct heat on grill.

TENDER CHOICE PORK CHOPS
with Fall Flavors
Yield: 4 servings

4 Tender Choice bone-in pork chops (1¼" thick)
1 tablespoon vegetable oil
2 tablespoons butter
salt and pepper to taste
1 cup sifted flour for dredging
1 large butternut squash, skin removed, seeded, diced to ¼"
1 large yellow onion, thinly sliced
4 cloves garlic, minced
1 (10.75-ounce) can cream of mushroom soup
1 packet onion gravy mix
2 cups vegetable broth
1 teaspoon dried leaf thyme
4 tablespoons parsley, chopped

DIRECTIONS:
1. Heat oil and butter in a large skillet over medium-high heat. Season pork chops with salt and pepper, and dredge in flour. Fry pork chops in oil until browned.
2. While chops are browning, add the sliced squash and onions to the slow cooker. Place browned pork chops over squash and onions, and top with remaining ingredients.
3. Cook on the low setting of your slow cooker for 3–4 hours.
4. Garnish with chopped parsley and serve.

THAI FRIED RICE, CHICKEN, AND SHRIMP BOWL

Yield: 6 servings

Chicken, shrimp, and fried rice are combined in this traditional version of the classic Thai one-dish meal, made intense and spicy with authentic Asian soy sauce.

1½ cups long-grain white rice (10 ounces)
¾ cup water
1¾ cups reduced-sodium chicken broth (14 fluid ounces)
1 cup ketchup
1 quart plus 3 tablespoons vegetable oil
2 cups Chinese rice noodles
2 cups thinly sliced shallots (¾ pound)
2 large garlic cloves, finely chopped
1 pound boneless, skinless chicken breast, cut into ¾" pieces
1 pound medium shrimp in shell (31–35 count), peeled and deveined
2–3 (2½") fresh hot red chiles, such as Thai or serrano, minced,
    including seeds
1¼ teaspoons salt
2 tablespoons low-sodium soy sauce
1 tablespoon Asian fish sauce
4 scallions, thinly sliced
12 English cucumber slices
12 wedges hard-boiled egg

DIRECTIONS:

1. Rinse rice in a large sieve and drain well. Bring rice, water, and 1½ cups chicken broth to a full rolling boil in a 4-quart heavy saucepan. Cover pan, then reduce heat to very low and cook until liquid is absorbed and rice is tender (about 15 minutes). Remove pan from heat and let rice stand, covered, 5 minutes. Gently fluff with a fork, then transfer to a large shallow bowl or a large shallow baking pan and cool to room temperature, about 30 minutes. Chill rice, covered.

2. Heat 1 quart of oil in a 4-quart pot over high heat until thermometer registers 375 degrees F. Gently drop 2 cups rice noodles into oil, then fry until they float to the surface, curl up, and expand (about 20 seconds). Turn rice noodles over and fry until pale golden (about 10 seconds), then transfer with a slotted spoon to paper towels to drain. Fry remaining rice noodles in 3 batches in same manner, transferring to paper towels to drain, then cool and break into pieces.

3. Break up rice into individual grains with your fingers.

4. Heat remaining 3 tablespoons oil in wok over high heat until hot but not smoking, then add shallots and stir-fry 1 minute. Add garlic and stir-fry 30 seconds. Add chicken and stir-fry until outside is no longer pink (about 2 minutes). Add shrimp, chiles, and salt, and stir-fry until shrimp are just cooked through (2–3 minutes). Add remaining ¼ cup broth with ketchup and rice, and stir-fry until rice is heated through (about 2 minutes). Remove wok from heat and stir in fish sauce and scallions until combined well. Top with fried noodles. Garnish with sliced cucumbers and wedges of hard-boiled egg.

THAI PEANUT AND TERIYAKI FLANK STEAK

Yield: 4 servings

FOR MARINADE:
1 cup San-J Thai peanut
1 cup San-J Teriyaki sauce
1 cup dry sherry
1 tablespoon maple syrup
½ cup tomato paste

YOU WILL ALSO NEED
2 pounds flank steak
1 pound scallions, sliced thin
salt and pepper to taste

DIRECTIONS:
1. Combine all ingredients for marinade in a small pan.
2. Flatten flank steak with a mallet, and spread with scallions, salt, and pepper. Roll up and marinate, refrigerated, for at least 2 hours, up to overnight.
3. Remove flank steak from pan, reserve marinade for basting, and slice flank steak into 16 pinwheels. Skewer and grill steaks at high heat, basting with marinade and turning every two minutes or until charcoal grilled.

THE 1934 RED PEPPER AND ORANGE-BLOSSOM HONEY BURGER

Yield: 6 servings

2 tablespoons minced garlic

2 teaspoons paprika

1 teaspoon chili powder

1 teaspoon sea salt

1 teaspoon ground cumin

1 teaspoon ground red pepper corns

2 pounds ground beef sirloin, coarsely ground

½ cup olive oil

6 tablespoons orange-blossom honey

2 ground cloves

2 teaspoons white balsamic vinegar

1 tablespoon plus ¼ teaspoon freshly ground red peppercorns, divided

½ cup reduced-fat chili-spiced mayonnaise (spiced to your taste)

2 roasted seedless Anaheim peppers, chopped

1 cup shredded green-and-red-cabbage mix

6 (6" diameter) brioche rolls

6 center-cut slices ripe tomato

6 thin slices red onion

⅓ cup chopped cilantro

⅓ cup sliced arugula

6 thinly sliced circles red bell pepper

DIRECTIONS:

1. Combine first six ingredients in a large bowl. Add ground beef to the bowl and toss lightly by hand. Shape into six equal patties, about ½" thick.

2. To oil the grill rack, oil a folded paper towel, hold it with tongs, and rub it over the rack. (Do not use cooking spray on the hot grill). Spray burgers with olive oil.

3. Preheat grill to medium high.

4. Mix and combine orange-blossom honey, ground cloves, vinegar, and 1 tablespoon ground red peppercorns in a small bowl, stirring well.

5. In a separate bowl, combine chili-spiced mayonnaise, chopped roasted peppers, and cabbage.

6. Grill the burgers on lightly oiled grill rack until an instant-read thermometer inserted in the center reads 165 degrees F (about 6 minutes per side, turning once). Before turning the burgers, and again after the burgers have been turned, brush ¼ cup honey mixture onto burgers.

7. Assemble the burgers on toasted brioche rolls spreading evenly between the burgers the chili-mayonnaise mixture. Top the burger with 1 slice tomato, 1 slice red onion, cilantro, arugula, red pepper rings, and ¼ teaspoon ground red peppercorns.

CHEF WOLFGANG HANAU'S ORIGINAL MEATBALLS

Yield: 8 servings (2 meatballs per serving)

8 ounces extra-lean ground beef

⅔ cup (1 ounce) chopped sun-dried tomatoes

1½ teaspoons Italian herb seasoning

1 teaspoon garlic powder

1 teaspoon Dijon mustard

sea salt and freshly ground black pepper to taste

1 teaspoon olive oil

½ cup thinly sliced red onions

½ cup thinly sliced carrots

2 ribs celery, thinly sliced

8 plum tomatoes, sliced and chopped

1 cup tomato juice

4 cups chicken broth

½ cup acini, orzo, or other cut small pasta

1 (10-ounce) package frozen chopped spinach, thawed, drained, and
squeezed dry

½ cup cooked garbanzo beans, drained

1/2 cup chopped fresh cilantro

2 cups grated Romano cheese

DIRECTIONS:

1. Combine ground beef with finely chopped sun-dried tomatoes. Add the next four ingredients and shape mixture into 16 meatballs. Heat olive oil in 12" nonstick skillet and brown meatballs over medium-high heat; remove from skillet.

2. In same skillet, sauté onions, carrots, and celery for 5 minutes, stirring occasionally.

3. Transfer vegetables and meatballs to a 4-quart soup pot. Add plum tomatoes, tomato juice, and chicken broth. Bring to a boil. Add pasta and continue to boil gently for 10 minutes, stirring frequently add more chicken broth as needed to make a tomato sauce. Add spinach and garbanzo beans; boil for 5 minutes. Garnish with freshly chopped cilantro and grated Romano cheese.

THE NEW YORK DELMONICO STEAK
on a Mirror of Clear Beringer Merlot Wine Sauce with Grilled Fresh Corn on the Cob and Delmonico Potatoes

Yield: 4 Servings

Regardless of the cut of the Delmonico steak, if you ordered one in the late nineteenth century, you would get a large and flavorful cut of meat. The recipe for the Delmonico steak was very simple and delicious. The steak was lightly seasoned with salt, basted with melted butter, and grilled over a live fire. You would typically find it served up with a thin, clear Cabernet wine gravy and a good helping of grilled fresh corn and potatoes. Basically this was the perfect restaurant steak.

FOR THE DELMONICO STEAK
¼ cup butter, softened
1 tablespoon finely chopped shallots
2 teaspoons snipped fresh basil or cilantro
1½ teaspoons fresh lemon juice
½ teaspoon sea salt
½ teaspoon ground white pepper
1 tablespoon olive oil
4 (20-ounce) boneless rib-eye steaks

FOR THE SAUCE
¼ pound shallots, peeled
¼ pound bacon
¼ pound butter
1 cup veal or vegetable stock
1 cup port wine
1 cup Beringer Estate Merlot
1 teaspoon sea salt
¼ teaspoon white pepper
½ ounce sugar

FOR THE CORN ON THE COB AND DELMONICO POTATOES

1 pound small baby Yukon Gold potatoes, scrubbed

4 ears corn with husks attached

6 tablespoons butter, softened

2 tablespoons minced fresh parsley

1 garlic clove, minced

DIRECTIONS:

1. To prepare the steaks, place the butter in a small bowl, and blend together the butter, shallots, snipped basil (or cilantro), lemon juice, salt, and pepper. Stir in oil until a paste forms. Spread mixture over both sides of steaks.

2. Grill steaks on the rack of an uncovered grill over medium coals until desired doneness (14–18 minutes for medium at 160 degrees F).

3. For the wine sauce: In a sauté pan, sauté the shallots and bacon in butter. Add the port wine and red wine. Add the veal or vegetable stock, and reduce. Make a "mirror" of the sugar and some Beringer Estate Merlot. Make an emulsion with the butter in the strained sauce. Add the "mirror" for a shiny and nicely colored sauce. Season to taste.

4. For the corn and potatoes: Cook potatoes in boiling water to cover until almost tender (10–15 minutes). Drain and rinse. Set aside to slightly cool.

5. In a small bowl, mix butter with parsley and garlic.

6. Peel husk away from corn, leaving it attached to the base; remove corn silk. Brush potatoes and each ear of corn with a small amount of butter-herb mixture, and arrange on hot grill grate. (Position so the husk handles are not above the flames.) Grill corn and potatoes 6–8 minutes, turning occasionally and basting with remaining butter mixture until corn and potatoes are tender and browned. Sprinkle with salt and pepper.

7. To serve, plate steaks on red wine sauce alongside grilled corn and Delmonico potatoes.

ORGANIC AMERICAN THREE-CHEESE BISCUITS

Yield: 12 servings

½ cup grated Organic Creamery Parmesan cheese, divided

½ cup plus 1 tablespoon grated Organic Creamery mild or sharp cheddar cheese, divided

½ cup plus 1 tablespoon crumbled Organic Creamery goat cheese, divided

½ cup organic unbleached flour

½ cup organic unbleached whole-wheat flour

2 teaspoons baking powder

1 teaspoon baking soda

½ teaspoon sea salt

1 clove garlic, minced

½ cup fresh oregano leaves, finely chopped; or ¼ cup crushed dried oregano leaves

1 stick (4 ounces) unsalted organic or other unsalted butter (use organic if available)

¾ cup organic whole or reduced-fat milk, or soy milk

¼ cup paprika

DIRECTIONS:

1. In a small bowl, blend ¼ cup grated Parmesan cheese with 1 tablespoon cheddar cheese. Set aside.

2. In another bowl, blend other ¼ cup grated Parmesan cheese with 1 tablespoon goat cheese, and set aside.

3. In a large bowl, sift together the flour, baking powder, baking soda, and sea salt. Stir in the remaining two cheeses (cheddar and goat cheese).

4. With a pastry blender, cut in the butter, garlic, and oregano. Stir in the milk, and fold together until just incorporated. Do not overmix.

5. Using a tablespoon, drop biscuits onto a parchment-lined cookie sheet. Sprinkle half of the biscuits with the Parmesan-cheddar mixture and half with the Parmesan-goat-cheese mixture. Dust all biscuits lightly with paprika.

6. Bake at 375 degrees F for 12–15 minutes or until golden brown. Serve hot from the oven.

TIRAMISU PEACHES
with Roasted Hazelnut Chocolate and Espresso-Dipped Mascarpone Cream

Yield: 12 Servings

½ cup hazelnuts

1 quart water

1 cup sugar

1 cinnamon stick

6 large, ripe peaches, peeled

1 cup heavy cream

½ cup light corn syrup

½ cup mascarpone

½ cup Breakstone's sour cream

12 soft ladyfinger cookies

½ cup freshly brewed espresso coffee (or espresso liqueur)

2 ounces gianduia chocolate (premium milk chocolate with hazelnuts)

½ cup unsweetened baking cocoa powder

DIRECTIONS:

1. Preheat oven to 375 degrees F. Toast hazelnuts on a sheet pan, stirring frequently, until skin is cracked. To remove the peels, rub hazelnuts in a kitchen towel. Coarsely chop hazelnuts and set aside.

2. In a 2-quart saucepan, combine water with sugar and cinnamon stick, and bring to a boil. Drop in the peaches, and continue to boil until the skin cracks or can be easily lifted off with a slotted spoon. Immediately transfer the peaches with a slotted spoon to a large gallon-sized bucket filled with ice and water. Peel the fruit, cut in half, and remove the pit.

3. Whip heavy cream to soft peaks, and fold in the corn syrup. Blend mascarpone and sour cream, and fold whipped heavy cream into mascarpone-sour cream mixture to blend.

4. Dip ladyfinger cookies into espresso or espresso liqueur. Melt gianduia chocolate in a 1-quart stainless-steel bowl in double boiler over simmering water, stirring until melted and smooth. Place 1

ladyfinger cookie in the bottom of each of twelve glass dessert dishes or champagne glasses. Place in center 1 peach half. Top the peach center with mascarpone cream. Sprinkle with hazelnuts, dust with cocoa powder, and drizzle with melted gianduia chocolate.

INDEX

RECIPE INDEX

C

F

G

S